A Field of Divine Wonders

The Kenneth Scott Latourette Prize
in Religion and Modern History

The Conference on Faith and History, an organization of more than 600 scholars devoted to exploring the relationship of faith to historical study, sponsors a series of historical monographs which assess religion's role in modern culture. These books are the prizewinners of an annual manuscript competition conducted by the Conference.

With this series, we honor the memory of a founding member of the Conference on Faith and History, Kenneth Scott Latourette (1884–1968). Latourette was Sterling Professor of Missions and Oriental History at Yale University and the author of more than a score of books on Asian history and on the history of Christianity. Recognized as a foremost authority on the history of Christianity, of its development in non-Western cultures, and of the history of East Asia, Professor Latourette served as President of the American Historical Association, the Association of Asian Studies, and the American Society of Church History. His deep interest in the study of modern religious and cultural history, his gracious example as a Christian historian, and his outstanding scholarly accomplishments make him our obvious choice for naming this prize.

Religious and cultural history, as Professor Latourette demonstrated throughout his work, is much broader than church history. Indeed, the unifying theme for this competition is the historical study of religion's interplay with other elements of modern culture. The period of history since 1500 has brought a complex of social and cultural developments that provide the common reference point for this series. Religion provides another, for this series will focus on the profoundly human propensity to ground one's identity and life's meaning in a transcendent purpose or force. A historical approach is a fitting way to explore the interaction of religion and modern culture since it allows scholars to address the element so characteristic of modernity, namely, change.

It is the Conference on Faith and History's hope that these books will stimulate further scholarly interest in a field which has already produced path-breaking work, and that they will provide exciting and worthwhile insights for anyone interested in the complex dynamics of religion and modern culture.

David W. Kling

A Field

of

Divine Wonders

The New Divinity and Village Revivals
in
Northwestern Connecticut
1792–1822

The Pennsylvania State University Press
University Park, Pennsylvania

Library of Congress Cataloging-in-Publication Data

Kling, David William, 1950–
    A Field of divine wonders : the new divinity and village revivals
in northwestern Connecticut, 1792–1822 / David W. Kling.

        p.   cm.
    Includes bibliographical references and index.
    ISBN 0-271-00906-3 (alk. paper)
    1. Revivals—Connecticut—History.   2. Connecticut—Church
history.   I. Title.
BV3774.C8K56   1993
269'.24'09746109033—dc20   92-31831
                                                                 CIP

Published by The Pennsylvania State University Press,
Barbara Building, Suite C, University Park, PA 16802-1003

It is the policy of The Pennsylvania State University Press to use acid-free paper for the
first printing of all clothbound books. Publications on uncoated stock satisfy the minimum
requirements of American National Standard for Information Sciences—Permanence of
Paper for Printed Library Materials, ANSI Z39.48–1984.

To Barbara

Be still, and know that I am God.
—Psalms 46:10

A work is not to be judged of by any effects on the bodies of men;
such as tears, trembling, groans, loud outcries, agonies of body, or
the failing of bodily strength.
—Jonathan Edwards
The Distinguishing Marks of a Work of the Spirit of God (1741)

God's ministers, a flaming fire,
  Are passing through the land,
Their voice is, "hear, repent, and fear,
  King Jesus is at hand."

Come sinners, all, hear now God's call,
  And pray with one accord!
Saints, raise your songs, with joyful tongues,
  To hail th' approaching Lord.
—"Rejoicing in a Revival of Religion"
Hartford Selection of Hymns (1799)

There is a melancholy interest thrown over the places which have
been distinguished as the residence of our ablest divines. Most of
them are rural villages, . . . where but few relics remain of the
greatness that has left them. Formerly they were the seats of the
oracles.
—Edwards A. Park
"Miscellaneous Reflections of a Visitor" (1842)

CONTENTS

FIGURES AND TABLES

ABBREVIATIONS

AAS   American Antiquarian Society, Worcester, Massachusetts
BL   Beinecke Rare Book and Manuscript Library, Yale University,
            New Haven, Connecticut
BPL   Boston Public Library
CEM   *Connecticut Evangelical Magazine*
CEMRI   *Connecticut Evangelical Magazine and Religious Intelligencer*
CHS   Connecticut Historical Society, Hartford, Connecticut
CLB   Congregational Library, Boston, Massachusetts
CLH   Congregational Library, Hartford, Connecticut
CSL   Connecticut State Library, Hartford, Connecticut
FVL   Farmington Village Library, Farmington, Connecticut
HC, SBC   Historical Commission, Southern Baptist Convention, Nashville,
            Tennessee
HSP   Historical Society of Pennsylvania, Philadelphia, Pennsylvania
SML   Sterling Memorial Library, Yale University, New Haven,
            Connecticut
WC   Williams College Library, Williamstown, Massachusetts
WJE   *Works of Jonathan Edwards* (Yale University editions)
YDL   Yale Divinity School Library, Yale University, New Haven,
            Connecticut

PREFACE

In a formal sense, this book had its inception in a course on "The American Religious Canon" Martin Marty taught in the fall of 1977. Typical of Marty (and perhaps this is why he is associated with a *divinity* school), no sooner had he spoken the word than it appeared—in articles, then in a book (*Pilgrims in Their Own Land*, 1984). For my part, I was satisfied to complete a paper on the Second Great Awakening in New England. From Marty's course, and subsequently in Jerald Brauer's seminar on American revivalism, I laid the basis for a doctoral thesis submitted to the Divinity School of the University of Chicago in 1985.

In a less formal sense, this book began long before that first course at the University of Chicago. Growing up as a "P.K." (preacher's kid) in a pietistic, evangelical home, I was immersed in a subculture that uplifted the conversion experience, and revivalism as a means to produce it. I recall the day when, as a youngster of seven or eight, at a children's home Bible study conducted by our neighbor, I "accepted Jesus into my heart." That day of conversion, my parents assured me, would forever change my life—just as it had done for my father, who, as a result of his own conversion some twenty years before, felt called out of the "lukewarm," mainline church of his youth and into the evangelical ministry. I also remember those special week-long services in our church, when an evangelist or an itinerant revivalist came to shake people out of their spiritual lassitude. The week presented a special opportunity for the "twice-born" to renew their fervor and dedication to the faith, as well as to invite non-Christian "once-born" friends in hopes that the speaker's zeal would move them to find the Savior. In addition, I attended our denominational summer camp, the spiritual highlight of my adolescence (or the highlight of my spiritual adolescence?), from fifth grade through high school. The camp's themes varied from year to year, as did the mix of campers, but one event remained constant: every evening—in the auditorium during the week and around the campfire on Friday night—an invitation was proffered by the week's camp pastor "to accept Jesus as your personal Savior."

I offer these autobiographical snippets to the reader as a way of saying that this book represents the fruits of historical-critical research on a subject similar to my own experience—an experience typical of children of the post–World War II generation of northern white Evangelicals. I am something of a participant in, as well as an observer of, the particular phenomenon I describe. I say "something" because I am a participant and observer *secondhand*. I write not of that which I have personally experienced but of that which a select group of people experienced nearly two hundred years ago. But I do write out of a tradition related to the subject at hand in that both are Protestant and evangelical. Both demand some kind of a conversion experience as a line of demarcation between the old self and the new self, and as a primary criterion for church membership. Both appeal to a plenary-inspired scripture as the basis of authority. Both are preoccupied with "living the Christian life" in a secular, fallen world. And yet each of these traditions is located in its own setting and time, each distinct from the other.

The conversion of my youth differed considerably from the conversions I relate in this study. For me, there was no arduous, painful striving after conversion, no knowledge of or references to the "means of grace," no standard or lengthy "morphology of conversion," no highly doctrinal explication of the faith. My conversion was much simpler. I needed only to be convinced that I was sinful and could not save myself, and that only God in Christ, who died for my sins, could save me. Once I recognized my condition and then appropriated Christ's provision by faith in a personal way ("Jesus did this for *me*," or as the popular chorus for children goes, "Jesus loves me, this I know"), I then became "a new creature" in Christ. This simple message of sin and salvation has been at the heart of the American revivalist tradition from Charles Grandison Finney in the mid-1820s to Billy Graham in the early 1990s. When considering my own conversion, I am certain that the cognitive distance from Finney in the 1820s to the present day is shorter than that from Finney to the revivals in northwestern Connecticut in 1800.

Nevertheless, certain expressions, certain ways of understanding conversion, and certain sociological factors present during the initial years of the

Second Great Awakening persist to this day. For example, from my own experience I think of my father, who annually observes the day of his conversion (his "second" birthday or the day of his "rebirth") with a time of devotion and prayer. So too did converts of the Second Great Awakening reflect on their biological birthdays. And just as New Year's Eve was set aside as a special time for reflection and spiritual resolutions in the life of our church (after watching "Christian" movies, we "prayed in" the new year), so in journals, diaries, and religious periodicals, many early nineteenth-century pious Christians reflected on the previous year and often appended resolutions for the next.

A more significant connection between my life experience and one of the themes of this book concerns the role of women. I recall the neighbor who "led me to the Lord." She was female, as were nearly all of my Sunday school teachers, who Sunday after Sunday related episodes in the Bible—from the Patriarchs to Paul—often utilizing the visual aid of a flannel graph board. Not that men had absconded from their spiritual responsibilities. There were the men of the church who led the weeknight Christian boys club, but for all their well-meaning attempts to provide spiritual guidance, they were not as skilled in communicating or as comfortable in describing the gospel plan as were the women. The perfunctory remarks at the end of each week's meeting were more of an afterthought than a well-planned homily. Early on, it was clear that our male leaders felt more at home in joining the boys in a softball game or in playing "capture the flag" than in struggling through a devotional.

Not until the twilight of my father's ministerial career during my years in college did it strike me that women, despite their absence from positions of leadership, formed the spiritual backbone of the church. I should not have been surprised. While my father provided the daily evening devotionals and applied the necessary doses of discipline to his five children, my mother provided the daily spiritual nurture and comfort. She was, after all, the one who was always at home. And so it was that in my father's rural Iowa church, women were more actively involved than men and had, by all accounts, a spiritual fervor and depth that was missing in their husbands. Were the men, I wondered, too involved in or too exhausted from farm chores to give their attention to the life of the church? Did they socialize primarily outside the church, while their wives found the church the hub of social activity? Could it be that these women were more active in the church as a way to compensate for their relative isolation on the farm?

These questions, which were relevant to my own situation, I asked also of my historical research, leading to a kind of inner dialogue between past and present. Thus arose the question of gender: Why in early nineteenth-century rural New England villages were women more likely to convert than men and to take such an active role in the church and in the spiritual nurture of their children? Were they predisposed toward religion in ways that men were not? These and other related questions, as applied to another era, I attempt to answer in what follows.

Other themes and issues from my own background converge in my attempt to understand the dynamics of the Second Great Awakening. The "generation gap," of which so much was made in the 1960s and 1970s and which sparked an interest in generational studies, informs my discussion of "the brotherhood of ministers." And consider the matter of church divisiveness, a plague as old as the Christian church. For a decade, my father was one of our denomination's district superintendents. His responsibilities included assisting in planting new churches, but also intervening in churches where seeds of discord were sown. On several occasions during my high school years, I eavesdropped on my parents' conversations—really monologues—in which my father described the latest power struggle or scandal in a particular church. Doctrinal divisiveness was seldom an issue; more often, people's feelings had been hurt, or the pastor had used indiscretion, or he was perceived to be ineffective by disgruntled parishioners. As I will show, similar issues rent Farmington First Church in the late eighteenth century.

In many respects, then, this book about history is also an attempt to come to terms with my own history—to understand it critically, to gain some distance from it, to appreciate it, to converse with it. But as should also be apparent, this reconciliation is not my main purpose. My primary purpose is to show how the complex phenomenon of religious revival occurred, how it was conveyed, and how it was appropriated. And that is a story far more interesting than my own.

ACKNOWLEDGMENTS

Over the years I have incurred many debts to many people. I now acknowledge and cheerfully repay them with gratitude. Some debts are intellectual, others are emotional. In many cases, as the subjects of this study recognized, the two cannot be separated. Nearly all of my mentors and colleagues along the way have combined intellectual rigor with human sensitivity—even humor. I have not always heeded their advice, but I have always learned from them. Twenty-five years ago, Douglas W. Frank, then at Trinity College (Illinois), first piqued my interest in history by asking questions. He remains the best teacher I have ever had. During my graduate years, Alfred F. Young of Northern Illinois University provided a model for research and meticulous scholarship and indirectly guided me to the present study. Martin E. Marty and Jerald C. Brauer of the University of Chicago sagely advised and criticized this work in its dissertation stage. Marty, Mark Noll of Wheaton College, and Harry Stout of Yale deserve special thanks for their comments and encouragement at various stages in the revision process. Allen Guelzo, John Corrigan, and two anonymous readers offered extensive commentary about the content and structure of the book in several of its various drafts. Finally, Peter Potter of Penn State Press expressed enthusiasm about this project from the beginning and provided astute commentary about the book's structure.

I would also like to express my gratitude to a number of colleagues, past and present, at the University of Miami. As only he could do, James L. Ash, Jr., came to my rescue in 1986. For his wit, high expectations, and generosity, I will always be thankful. Several colleagues in the Department of Religious Studies deserve thanks, especially Daniel Pals, who read nearly every chapter, marked nearly every page, and greatly improved my prose. In light of my administrative responsibilities, Deborah Triol Perry, vice provost and dean of enrollments, allowed me the uncommon luxury of undisturbed quiet. She also provided funds for a weekend research foray at a critical juncture in the revision process. Suzanne Klekotka graciously went beyond the call of her administrative duties to offer computer assistance to an interloper. I also thank Scott Marshall, my student assistant, who made more trips to the library stacks and filled out more interlibrary-loan request cards than he cares to remember.

The directors and staffs at the following institutions generously offered assistance in my research: the Connecticut State Library; the Connecticut Historical Society; the Congregational Library (Connecticut Conference of the United Church of Christ), Hartford; Sterling Memorial Library, Yale; Beinecke Rare Book and Manuscript Library, Yale; the Farmington Village Library, Farmington, Connecticut; the Congregational Library, Boston; Boston Public Library; the Williams College Library; the Historical Society of Pennsylvania; and the University of Miami.

Finally, my wife, Barbara, has encouraged me, has prodded me, and has borne this work with me. Moreover, she has reminded me, in word and deed, that the world of the awakened is not merely a historical construct but a present reality.

INTRODUCTION

"ONE FIELD OF DIVINE WONDERS"

The Contours of the Revival

In a letter to William B. Sprague in 1832, Edward Dorr Griffin surveyed the tumultuous events he had witnessed in his lifetime. Nearing the end of an illustrious career as pastor, revivalist, and college president, Griffin confidently proclaimed the year 1792 as the *annus mirabilis*. In that year, he wrote, there "commenced three series of events of sufficient importance to constitute a new era." First, "the blood began to flow in Europe," inaugurated by the French Revolution; second, the modern missionary movement was launched in Kettering, England; third, there "began the unbroken series of revivals" in New England.[1]

The first two events cited by Griffin bear an intimate relation to the third. As the French Revolution plunged into its radical stage, American clergy interpreted it as the culminating debacle of a nation long mired in political corruption, monarchical tyranny, and heretical Catholicism. If the infant American republic hoped to escape the fate of France—namely, God's judgment and wrath—then ministers had to sound the alarm and turn back the incursions of infidelity by promoting religious renewal. They did so, inaugurating a "second" Great Awakening. At the same time—and indicative

---

1. Edward Dorr Griffin, "A Letter to the Rev. Dr. William Sprague," in William Buell Sprague, *Lectures on Revivals of Religion*, 2d ed. (New York, 1833), 359.

of the transatlantic ties of American Evangelicalism to Britain—some of the more selfless and adventuresome converts of the Awakening followed the English example of extending the gospel overseas by committing to missionary work.[2] The French Revolution, the Second Great Awakening, and the launching of America's modern missionary movement thus came to influence each other in a dynamic way.

This book focuses on the last event in Griffin's triad—the religious revivals in New England, and more particularly the Congregational revivals in the northwest region of Connecticut encompassing Hartford and Litchfield counties. In assigning 1792 as the point of departure for what is commonly labeled the Second Great Awakening,[3] Griffin disclosed his own role as an important figure in the Awakening. Indeed, revivals occurred in that year, for Griffin cited the spiritual quickening of eighty souls in the Rev. Alvan Hyde's congregation in Lee, Berkshire County, Massachusetts. But something more personal was at stake, something more important to Griffin's sense of a historical watershed. In 1792 a Griffin-led revival in his hometown of East Haddam, Connecticut, resulted in the conversion of several members of his family. The scattered sprinklings of 1792, however, were far removed from the torrential outpouring of revival in the late 1790s, when the revival spread from house to house, church to church, and village to village. Young and old, parents and children, males and females, farmers and merchants, rich and

2. On the transatlantic connection during the colonial period, see Michael J. Crawford, *Seasons of Grace: Colonial New England's Revival Tradition in Its British Context* (New York, 1991); for the early national and antebellum periods, see Richard Carwardine, *Transatlantic Revivalism: Popular Evangelicalism in Britain and America, 1790–1865* (Westport, Conn., 1978).

3. To refer to the reemergence of religiosity in the late eighteenth century as the Second Great Awakening assumes a continuity with the first Great Awakening. The Great Awakening was so titled because presumably the scope of the revival was both "great and general." Supporters of the Awakening found the appellation appealing, for it carried the weight of a unified and widespread outpouring of the Spirit. Jon Butler, however, has questioned the accuracy of the title. In "Enthusiasm Described and Decried: The Great Awakening as Interpretive Fiction," *Journal of American History* 69 (September 1982): 305–25, he contends that the Great Awakening obscures regional and denominational variations in the revival, and that it distorts the extent of political unification between the colonies. "In religion," he writes, "it is a deus ex machina that falsely homogenizes the heterogeneous; in politics it falsely unites the colonies in slick preparation for the Revolution" (322). Butler's criticism applies even more forcefully to the Second Great Awakening, for more heterogeneity was exhibited in the nationwide revivals from 1780 to 1835 than in the first Awakening. Nevertheless, scholars have been more inclined to isolate the various manifestations of revival in the Second Great Awakening than in the first: for example, the southern revivals, the New England revivals, the Finney revivals, etc. Still, there have been attempts to view the Second Great Awakening as a "nationalizing force," much as the Great Awakening has been viewed as a unifying event in the colonies. For examples, see Perry Miller, "From the Covenant to the Revival," in *The Shaping of American Religion*, ed. James W. Smith and A. Leland Jamison (Princeton, N.J., 1961), 322–68, and Donald G. Mathews, "The Second Great Awakening as an Organizing Process, 1780–1830: An Hypothesis," *American Quarterly* 21 (Spring 1969): 23–43.

poor—all types of people were caught up in the ground swell. By the turn of the century, Hartford and Litchfield counties were awash in revival. A "great" or quantifiable awakening was in the making. It was then, recalled Griffin, that "in 1799, I could stand at my doorstep in New Hartford, Litchfield county, and number fifty or sixty congregations laid down in one field of divine wonders."[4]

This study examines the making of revival in Connecticut. It illumines the origins and nature of a field "white unto harvest" by providing a detailed portrait of the Awakening's leaders and auditors. The revivals were led mostly by pastors from a few specific designations. These pastors referred to themselves simply as Calvinists or "Consistent Calvinists." Opponents gave them a variety of sobriquets, all intended to disparage and to imply a departure from the traditional tenets of Calvinism: "New Divinity," "Hopkin-tonians," or "Hopkinsians"—the last two referring to those who embraced the theological system of Samuel Hopkins. The term New Divinity (or New Divinity men), first invoked in the 1760s, has stuck, and is used along with "Edwardseans"—that is, the followers of the teachings of Jonathan Edwards—to describe the primary subjects of this study.

Geographically, I have chosen to focus on Litchfield and Hartford counties. To be sure, revivals in Berkshire County, Massachusetts, in the Hudson River valley in New York, and in parts of Vermont and New Hampshire—in general, those places where the New Divinity theology had taken hold—resembled the shape of revival in northwestern Connecticut. However, I have singled out the initial area of intense, prolonged, and widespread revival. Here the Awakening could be appropriately called a village revival, for most of the renewed churches were located in rural towns, each with dispersed populations ranging from one thousand to twenty-five hundred inhabitants. That the Awakening was not strictly confined to these hamlets attests to the potence of the revival, as well as to the revival-minded New Divinity clergy in the more populated Hartford area.

Chronologically, this work covers a generation (ca. 1790–1820) of New Divinity revivals, although special attention is given to the formative decade of the Awakening, 1798 to 1808. By the 1820s, revivals bearing the imprint of the New Divinity had run their course. Revivals by no means faded away—for revivalism had become the main recruiting device of the churches—but throughout the 1820s several developments coalesced to weaken New Divinity influence. First, within the Calvinist Congregational orbit, the New Divinity theology competed with and was eventually subdued by the New Haven Theology, a softer brand of Calvinism.[5] Second, Asahel

---

4. Griffin, "Letter to Sprague," in Sprague, Lectures, 360.

5. On the principal architect of the New Haven Theology, see Sidney E. Mead, Nathaniel William Taylor, 1786–1858: A Connecticut Liberal (Chicago, 1942).

Nettleton, the immensely successful itinerating revivalist who toured Connecticut from 1812 to 1822 with the blessing of his New Divinity cohorts, withdrew from the circuit due to ill health and dedicated the remainder of his life to defending the New Divinity scheme against Taylorism, Beecherism, and Finneyism.[6] Third, the "conference meeting" gave way to the "protracted meeting" made popular by Charles Grandison Finney. Finney's "new measures" supplanted the New Divinity "old measures" in conducting revivals. Fourth, by the 1820s, similar "new measures" introduced by aggressive Arminian Methodists and Calvinist Baptists in Connecticut challenged the hegemony of Congregationalists. Finally, the axis of revivalism in the North shifted from rural areas to urban centers such as Boston, New York, and Rochester. Together these changes signaled a new era of what William McLoughlin has called "modern revivalism."[7]

Because the term revivalism conjures up all kinds of images, it may be helpful at the outset to clarify briefly the nature of New Divinity revivals. Apart from stressing the necessity of a renewed heart, New Divinity revivals—as shaped and described by their clerical advocates—scarcely resembled the spiritual convulsions of the Second Great Awakening in other denominations and regions of the country. The difference was one of means, not ends. All Protestants involved in the three main geographical theaters of the national revival—the Cumberland Valley, western New York, and New England—shared the same goal: to revive the backslidden or save the lost. In that sense they were evangelical; that is, they all uplifted the centrality of conversion and a personal appropriation of faith. But the means employed, the efforts expended to awaken the slumbering, diverged markedly. Ultimately, such efforts were rooted in theology, in how preachers and their auditors apprehended the divine-human transaction.

What set New Divinity revivals apart from others—less so from revivals within kindred Reformed groups (say, Presbyterians) and more so from revivals within the Arminian tradition (say, Methodists)—was their preoccupation with doctrine. From the New Divinity perspective, right doctrine validated the new birth, not vice versa. Indeed, one of the beguiling issues raised during the Great Awakening of the 1740s and subsequently analyzed in Edwards's major writings was the inextricable relation of belief to regeneration. Depending upon one's beliefs and attitudes, conversion could be either genuine or spurious. That one "got there" could not be separated from "getting there." The means to conversion were just as important as conversion itself. Thus, from the New Divinity perspective, potential

6. On Nettleton's qualms with these isms, see Bennet Tyler, *Memoir of the Life and Character of Rev. Asahel Nettleton, D.D.*, 2d ed. (Hartford, Conn., 1845).

7. See William G. McLoughlin, *Modern Revivalism: Charles Grandison Finney to Billy Graham* (New York, 1959).

converts needed to grasp correct theology before manifesting true religious affections. As humanly as possible, they needed to understand *how* God saved before they truly could be saved. In this scheme, the drama of salvation was played out as much in the understanding as in the emotions. Put another way, words or language ordered the nature of the conversion experience in profound ways. Illustrative of this relation between thought and reality is the figurative language drawn from Scripture and used to narrate the work of the Spirit. New Divinity ministers appealed repeatedly to the "still small voice" (1 Kings 19:12) to describe the work of the Spirit rather than to the "rushing, mighty wind" (Acts 2:2) of Pentecost.[8] The New Divinity psychic counterpart—if it can even be called that—to the physical shaking, rolling, dancing, jerking, and barking of frontier revivals was stillness, silent weeping, and melancholy. Not one homogeneous revival, then, but several distinct modes and expressions of revival characterized the nationwide Second Great Awakening.

Past interpreters have generally employed a "history from above" approach to the Awakening by stressing the role of clerical elites and the institutional nature of the revival. A half century ago Charles Keller emphasized primarily the voluntary societies (Bible, education, reform, and humanitarian) that sprang from the enthusiasm generated by the revival, whereas a more recent interpreter focused on the leaders of the revival as Congregational members of the Connecticut Missionary Society and editors of the *Connecticut Evangelical Magazine*.[9] Although these approaches have informed my work, and although a full account of the Second Great Awakening cannot be told without including these institutional components, many questions remain unanswered—in part because they have remained unasked. How, for instance, was the revival transmitted? Who were its preachers, and what was their message? Who were its auditors, and why and how did they respond? What indeed was the shape of the revival? Finally, in what sense did these village revivals relate to a nationwide awakening, as well as to broader changes in American society?

In attempting to answer these questions, several dominant themes emerge. The first involves the nature of leadership in revivals. It has been characteristic to view the itinerant charismatic revivalist as the personification of revivalism. George Whitefield, James Davenport, James McGready, Charles Grandison Finney, Dwight L. Moody, Billy Sunday, and Billy Graham presumably embody all that is in American revivalism. Similarly, Lyman Beecher and Timothy Dwight are often cited as the key figures in uplifting

---

8. All quotations from the Bible are from the King James Version.

9. Charles R. Keller, *The Second Great Awakening in Connecticut* (New Haven, Conn., 1942), esp. chaps. 5, 6; Richard D. Shiels, "The Connecticut Clergy in the Second Great Awakening" (Ph.D. diss., Boston University, 1976).

the sagging spiritual fortunes of Connecticut Congregationalists and inaugurating the Second Great Awakening.[10] To be sure, these men were crucial actors in the broader institutional outworking of the revival, but neither can be credited with a leading role in the early phase of the Awakening. The flames of revival swept over northwestern Connecticut several years before President Dwight revived an "infidel" Yale College in 1802; and Beecher did not arrive on the Connecticut scene until 1810, after leaving his Presbyterian charge on Long Island to accept the Congregationalists' call to Litchfield.

This is not to say that great revivalists were unknown in Connecticut during the formative years of the revival. But if we were to choose a foremost figure, a far better candidate then either Dwight or Beecher would be the unheralded preacher, Edward Dorr Griffin. His contemporaries acknowledged as much, but Griffin's success as a revivalist has escaped the scrutiny of historians. Why this is so is answered in part by Griffin's short-lived presence in Connecticut. Although born and educated in Connecticut, Griffin left New Hartford as early as 1801, at the age of thirty-one, never to return to his home state in a professional capacity.

While Griffin is an important figure in the Awakening—and thus he assumes a prominent role in parts of my narrative—his success was linked to the support of a network of New Divinity ministers in northwestern Connecticut. Here were concentrated colleagues who, since the days of Edwards, increased in numbers to the point that, by 1800, they dominated the form and structure of religious life in Hartford and Litchfield counties. Within this group, a younger generation of clergy (post-1790 Yale graduates) supplied the impetus for revival as they altered the thrust of Edwardsean preaching from a preoccupation with elucidating dogma to a broader emphasis on both evangelical and apologetic preaching.

In addition, the New Divinity men allied for prayer, mutual encouragement, and regular pulpit exchanges. They often traveled in groups, either to assist in an ongoing revival or to promote a new one. "Conference meetings" were instituted by both the clergy and pious laypersons for spiritual

10. For example, on Beecher, see William G. McLoughlin, *New England Dissent: Baptists and the Separation of Church and State, 1670–1830* (Cambridge, Mass., 1971), 2:984; on Dwight, see Stephen E. Berk, *Calvinism versus Democracy: Timothy Dwight and the Origins of American Evangelical Orthodoxy* (Hamden, Conn., 1974), 123. Shiels, in "Connecticut Clergy," corrects this interpretation; however, his primary concern is with the institutional, not the grass-roots, leaders of the Awakening. Admittedly, there is an overlap of leadership, but my concern is with the way the clergy functioned in their churches to lead revival. Sydney E. Ahlstrom adds a similar corrective to the "great men" theory regarding the origins of the Second Great Awakening in New England, in *A Religious History of the American People* (New Haven, Conn., 1972), 416. These correctives notwithstanding, William R. Sutton identifies Dwight as the initiator of the New England phase of the Second Great Awakening, in "Benevolent Calvinism and the Moral Government of God: The Influence of Nathaniel W. Taylor in Revivalism in the Second Great Awakening," *Religion and American Culture: A Journal of Interpretation* 2 (Winter 1992): 24, 26.

improvement. In these meetings one can see most clearly the inner dynamic of the revival, as potential converts, together with old and new Christians, met to hear the gospel proclaimed and taught, to testify to God's work of redemption, and to express their emotions and inner thoughts through hymns and prayers.

Clerical supporters of the Awakening have often been pictured as reactionaries. Threatened by a growing infidelity, the loss of status, and general social instability, the clergy (so the argument goes) introduced revival in order to defeat godlessness, regain clerical status, and ensure the Standing Order's privileged place in Connecticut.[11] The merit of this argument lies in its rudimentary psychological principle: those who are anxious seek ways to resolve their anxiety. Anxiety resolution has a way of motivating individuals beyond their normal activities. And collective anxiety produces a social strain that results in mass movements such as the Second Great Awakening.[12] To be sure, the New Divinity men and inhabitants of New England had much to be

---

11. Theories of clerical reaction can be broken down into two types: responses either to external threats or to internal threats. The great external fear was of the French Revolution, "a volcano," in the words of Robert Baird, that "threatened to sweep the United States into its fiery stream" (*Religion in the United States of America* [1844; reprint, New York, 1969], 102). The theme of the French menace has persisted from Baird to Richard Purcell's work in the early part of the present century through Charles Keller's monograph in the 1940s to Shiels's dissertation. See Richard J. Purcell, *Connecticut in Transition, 1775–1818* (Washington, D.C., 1918); Keller, *Second Great Awakening*; and Shiels, "Connecticut Clergy."

Other scholars have shifted their attention from external threats to indigenous social unrest as a reasonable explanation for the revival. They stress the psychological, or spiritual, void created by the shifting locus of authority unleashed by such post–American Revolutionary developments as democracy, individualism, and acquisitiveness. See Miller, "From the Covenant to the Revival," 353–54; Bernard Weisberger, *They Gathered at the River: The Story of the Great Revivalists and Their Impact upon Religion in America* (Boston, 1958), 52; Richard D. Birdsall, "The Second Great Awakening and the New England Social Order," *Church History* 39 (September 1970): 355; David W. Lewis, "The Reformer as Conservative: Protestant Counter-subversives in the Early Republic," in *The Development of American Culture*, ed. Stanley Coben and Lorman Ratner (Englewood Cliffs, N.J., 1970), 75; McLoughlin, *New England Dissent*, 2:1021; Joseph A. Conforti, *Samuel Hopkins and the New Divinity Movement: Calvinism, the Congregational Ministry, and Reform in New England between the Great Awakenings* (Grand Rapids, Mich., 1981), 184; and esp. Mathews, "Second Great Awakening," 27.

Still others have refined this theme by pointing to discordant relations between the clergy and their congregations. Political wranglings (Federalists versus Democratic-Republicans); disputes over church membership, piety, and doctrine (pure church versus Half-Way Covenant principles, the New Divinity versus moderate Calvinism); and a changing conception of the ministry (from the life-tenured parson to a mobile, professional clergy) are cited as crises that triggered the outbreak of revival. See John A. Andrew III, *Rebuilding the Christian Commonwealth: New England Congregationalists and Foreign Missions, 1800–1830* (Lexington, Ky., 1976), chap. 2; Donald M. Scott, *From Office to Profession: The New England Ministry, 1750–1850* (Philadelphia, 1978), chaps. 1, 2.

12. I am following Neil Smelser's definition of social strain: "an impairment of the relations among and consequently inadequate functioning of the components of action" (*Theory of Collective Behavior* [New York, 1963], 47). See also William G. McLoughlin, *Revivals, Awakenings, and Reform: An Essay on Religion and Social Change in America, 1607–1977* (Chicago, 1978), who applies a particular kind of social-strain model to America's religious past, borrowing A.F.C. Wallace's concept of "revitalization movements" (9–23).

anxious about, and hundreds resolved their anxiety through the traditional channels of religious commitment.

But one must go further. Knowledge of God's purposes in history offered hope for renewal. Faith in God more than fear of men motivated New Divinity adherents.[13] For them, revival was more than a means to personal ends or social control. If intention, expression, and action are reliable indicators, then the clergy more often sought the greater glory of God than their own. The vertical dimension of life—pleasing God rather than men, fulfilling the hope that was in them—consumed their lives. While the New Divinity clergy lived in a fallen world and could not escape the limitations of their culture, they nevertheless construed spiritual realities as ultimate reality. The nature and destiny of human existence lay beyond whatever meaning mere humans gave it. Considerations aside from one's relationship with God were secondary, for all of life was endowed with religious meaning. Hence, while the Second Great Awakening in Connecticut influenced many aspects of American life, those who participated in the revivals were most concerned with the immediate question of the eternal destiny of the converted. All that took place on this earth was peripheral and only important insofar as it reflected the divine will.

This kind of religious thinking and piety drew from a long and durable New England tradition. Recent studies on the nature and intensity of spiritual life in early America focus on what Philip Greven labels "the persistence of piety."[14] Contending that the oft-repeated spiritual declension theme was a rhetorical device used to reinvigorate the people rather than a true indicator of the state of religion, scholars such as Greven stress the episodic yet sustained nature of the piety of Puritans and their progeny. Another study by Gerald Moran is particularly illuminating, for by statistical analysis he documents the uneven though persistent upswing in church membership throughout Connecticut in the seventeenth and eighteenth centuries.[15] Despite periods of decline in church membership, succeeding periods of gain offset the declines. Measured over several generations, church membership increased at a steady rate. Hence, the New England conversion experience, introduced in the 1630s as a prerequisite for church membership, stubbornly remained the yardstick of true piety well into the nineteenth century. The means to bring about conversion were altered, but the goal remained the

13. For a similar estimation of clerical motivation in the South, see John B. Boles, *The Great Revival, 1787–1805: The Origins of the Southern Evangelical Mind* (Lexington, Ky., 1972), 27. For a contrary conclusion about the New England clergy ("they acted more out of fear than hope"), see Joseph W. Phillips, *Jedidiah Morse and New England Congregationalism* (New Brunswick, N.J., 1983), 105.

14. Philip Greven, *The Protestant Temperament: Patterns of Child-Rearing, Religious Experience, and the Self in Early America* (1977; reprint, New York, 1979), 6–7.

15. Gerald Francis Moran, "The Puritan Saint: Religious Experience, Church Membership, and Piety in Connecticut, 1636–1776" (Ph.D. diss., Rutgers University, 1974).

same. The conversion experience continued to measure the distance between heaven and hell.

Although the clergy were the primary leaders in promoting and perpetuating revival, their efforts reveal only part of the story. The lay roots of the revival constitute an important second theme. Accounts of the revival written by local ministers and published in the widely read *Connecticut Evangelical Magazine* often emphasize the popular roots of the Awakening. In a number of instances laypeople met together for prayer and encouragement without the presence of their pastor. On other occasions, solicitous youth of a parish approached their pastor and requested a conference meeting. Nor was it uncommon for church members to visit a neighboring town in the throes of revival, become caught up in its fervor, and return home to ignite a spiritual fire in their own parish. At times, they petitioned their minister to convene a conference meeting; in other instances, they called and led their own. Here the typical role of the clergy was minimized, if not reversed, as ministers became spectators to an event outside their direct control.

Preaching, promoting, praying—these the clergy did with an energy exceeded only by Baptist and Methodist itinerants. Yet the true measure of their success lay not in the proclamation of the gospel alone, but in the numbers responding to their pleadings for a remade heart. Herein lies a third theme: those converted in the Awakening. Only recently have historians begun to do the necessary empirical spadework to discover what kinds of people responded to clerical pleas for conversion.[16] No matter how much the clergy sought to induce revival, the true measure of their success depended upon the receptiveness of their audience. Richard Birdsall captured the reciprocal nature of the revival when he noted that "the intricate and delicately balanced religious situation in New England was engulfed by the insistent religious needs of the people. The clergy responded and the Second Great Awakening was underway."[17] Ministers might perceive and articulate

16. For examples of recent works utilizing statistical studies of church membership in the Second Great Awakening, see Martha Tomhave Blauvelt, "Society, Religion, and Revivalism: The Second Great Awakening in New Jersey, 1780–1830" (Ph.D. diss., Princeton University, 1974), chap. 1; Paul Johnson, *A Shopkeeper's Millennium: Society and Revivals in Rochester, New York, 1815–1837* (New York, 1978); Richard D. Shiels, "The Feminization of American Congregationalism, 1730–1835," *American Quarterly* 33 (Spring 1981): 46–62; idem, "The Scope of the Second Great Awakening: Andover, Massachusetts, as a Case Study," *Journal of the Early Republic* 5 (Summer 1985): 223–46; Mary P. Ryan, *Cradle of the Middle Class: The Family in Oneida County, New York, 1790–1865* (New York, 1981), 75–83; and Terry D. Bilhartz, *Urban Religion and the Second Great Awakening: Church and Society in Early National Baltimore* (Madison, N.J., 1986).

17. Birdsall, "Second Great Awakening," 352. Richard Bushman, writing about Jonathan Edwards and the Great Awakening, makes the same point: The people "followed Edwards, or others like him, because they were ready. . . . Something common to all, some prevailing strain on their institutions, some pressure in the culture prepared people for the new life he urged upon them. They listened because the truth of his experience was also the truth of theirs" ("Jonathan Edwards as Great Man:

the spiritual needs of their people as best they could, but ultimately, they triggered a response in the laity beyond their control. And they admitted this fact. What they did not always notice was that besides God and themselves there might have been other players on the scene—the people who heard them.

Viewing the Awakening from the perspective of gender, females were more receptive to the revivalists' message than males. Increasingly throughout the antebellum period in New England, American Protestantism assumed a feminine cast both in its theological orientation and in the sheer number of church members. Those females converted during the Second Great Awakening in Connecticut were the harbingers of this transformation. Why the appeal to females? Why this transformation? During the colonial period, females outnumbered males in church membership, yet in the early republic the disparity became even more pronounced. The years of the Connecticut revival coincided with significant economic, social, political, and theological transformations. At times subtly, at others blatantly, these transformations recast gender roles. The growing differentiation of the marketplace economy, the male-dominated political sphere, and the New Divinity sensual vocabulary of conversion—all conspired to attract a greater proportion of females than males to the faith. Ironically, the very men who sought to build a male-dominated "righteous empire" in America unwittingly laid the basis for the feminist movement in New England.[18] Denied access to the normal channels of power for men, females found in revivals their own personal identity, a sense of solidarity, and a sphere of influence.

The nature of the revivalists' message—their theology—forms the fourth theme of this study. That message owed a profound debt to Jonathan Edwards, the "founder" of the New Divinity. Edwards gathered disciples who lived and studied with him; he was dismissed by his own parishioners and exiled; he died an untimely death; he was revered in life and exalted in death; he left writings—philosophical, theological, historical, and devotional—that his followers pored over, expanded upon, and systematized. Above all, Edwards's views on the will and the nature of revival constituted the New Divinity identity.

Regardless of any debt to Edwards, the New Divinity was subjected to its own changing theological climate. The first quarter of the nineteenth century was a crucial time theologically for New England Congregationalists. One of the clearest signs of theological change was the way in which New Divinity

---

Identity, Conversion, and Leadership in the Great Awakening," in *Religion in American History*, ed. John Mulder and John Wilson [Englewood Cliffs, N.J., 1978], 121). See also Patricia J. Tracy, *Jonathan Edwards, Pastor: Religion and Society in Eighteenth-Century Northampton* (New York, 1979), 4.

18. The term is from Martin E. Marty, *Righteous Empire: The Protestant Experience in America* (New York, 1970).

pastors viewed God's role in the historical process at the beginning and at the end of our period. In 1798, prior to the outbreak of the Awakening and amid perceived spiritual laxity and infidelity, New Divinity men consoled themselves that man's ways were not God's ways, that God had purposes beyond the reason of mere mortals for permitting the continued spiritual decline. In the 1820s, however, after waves of revivals, friends of the New Divinity abandoned the inscrutable God motif. God seemed closer, less distant, more benevolent, more amenable to human schemes than thought previously. As Calvinists, the New Divinity men continued to emphasize the chasm separating mortals from the Divine, but with God now obviously blessing their efforts, they concluded that they and God were somehow engaged in an active partnership. The "God chained" of Puritan covenant theology (as Perry Miller called it), though unfettered briefly by Jonathan Edwards's insistence on the absolute sovereignty of God, returned in a different guise.[19] Common sense dictated, particularly in an age of great human confidence and exertion, that God could and would reward the efforts of his people. This confident reading of history, supported by results (i.e., conversions), was part of a larger debate over such theological issues as the nature of humanity, the means of grace, the nature of God, and views of the millennium. Eventually the balance tipped toward an optimistic view of human capabilities and human partnership with God in carrying out the divine will.

A final underlying theme of this work is the broad and profound transformation of American society in the early republic. Viewed against the general backdrop of American society, the revivals in northwestern Connecticut represent the emergence within the New England Congregational community of the right of Americans to determine their own destiny.[20] The postrevolutionary democratic surge in America that affected economic opportunity and the structure of political authority also profoundly altered the religious life of the nation. Eschewing all religious authority, various primitivist and restorationist groups uplifted individual conscience as the sole arbiter in matters religious, forging a religion of the people and by the people.[21] To be sure, the mental universe of Connecticut New Divinity men was far removed from the popular Methodists, Disciples, Shakers, Univer-

---

19. Perry Miller, *Errand into the Wilderness* (1956; reprint, New York, 1964), 63.

20. See Robert H. Wiebe, *The Opening of American Society: From the Adoption of the Constitution to the Eve of Disunion* (New York, 1984), chap. 8.

21. See Nathan O. Hatch, "The Christian Movement and the Demand for a Theology of the People," *Journal of American History* 67 (December 1980): 545–67; idem, "Evangelicalism as a Democratic Movement," in *Evangelicalism and Modern America*, ed. George Marsden (Grand Rapids, Mich., 1984), 71–82; Stephen A. Marini, *Radical Sects of Revolutionary New England* (Cambridge, Mass., 1982); Randolph A. Roth, *The Democratic Dilemma: Religion, Reform, and the Social Order in the Connecticut River Valley of Vermont, 1791–1850* (New York, 1987); and Jon Butler, *Awash in a Sea of Faith: Christianizing the American People* (Cambridge, Mass., 1990).

salists, or the Free-Will Baptists. Nevertheless, during the first decades of the nineteenth century, the Connecticut Congregational clergy was transformed from a self-regulating, settled office into an audience-oriented, mobile profession.

Some historians have chosen to downplay the revivals in northwestern Connecticut, because of the relative emotional restraint of these village awakenings and also because Congregationalists were the eventual "losers" to the more aggressive Baptists, Methodists, and Presbyterians on the national front. They have looked instead either to the frenzied frontier revivals as the dominant image of the Awakening or to the remarkable success of nonelites in capturing the loyalty of the populace.[22] To slight the Awakening in northwestern Connecticut, however, by consigning it to a secondary status, not only minimizes the rich regional variation of a national awakening, but also ignores the subsequent impact of Connecticut's Awakening on America's modern missionary movement and age of reform. Indeed, a significant impetus for the "benevolent empire" originated in Connecticut. Revivalist clergy exerted a crucial influence in western New York, introducing the Great Revival in that region, while other clergy and converts from the Awakening fanned out into the sparsely settled northern areas of New England and the Ohio River valley. Moreover, the American Board of Commissioners for Foreign Missions held its first meeting in revival-soaked Farmington in 1810 and could trace much of its inspiration to the awakened from that town. Finally, the revival spirit in northwestern Connecticut was transmuted into a reform impulse that made the state, according to one historian, "probably the most active reform center in the country" during the first quarter of the nineteenth century.[23]

22. In *The Democratization of American Christianity* (New Haven, Conn., 1989), Nathan O. Hatch concludes, "The adjustment of staid churches was only a secondary theme in the awakening's story" (226). A generation before, Perry Miller downplayed the New England Awakening, characterizing it as a "local phenomenon, which by itself would not have captivated the imagination of the expanding country." Rather, the dominant image came from the West, from Cane Ridge, where a "religious revolution" transpired (*The Life of the Mind in America: From the Revolution to the Civil War* [New York, 1965], 6). Paul K. Conkin concurs with Miller, contending that the Cane Ridge sacrament "arguably remains the most important religious gathering in all of American history, both for what it symbolized and for the effects that flowed from it" (*Cane Ridge: America's Pentecost* [Madison, Wis., 1990], 3). The views of Hatch, Miller, and Conkin reflect a long trend in American historiography. In *A History of American Christianity* (New York, 1897), Leonard W. Bacon's scanty treatment of New England and his extended accounts of the wild excesses in the West and South (which enliven an otherwise ponderous text) reflect the direction American historiography would take in the next two generations. Whether he realized it or not, Bacon gave implicit credence to Frederick Jackson Turner's frontier thesis. The Turnerian frame of mind stressed the ever-moving frontier as the environment within which the uniqueness of the American character developed. Hence, the true character of revivals and their driving force in American life were found in the camp meetings on the raw western frontier, not in the spired churches of decorous New England.

23. Keller, *Second Great Awakening*, 136; see also Whitney R. Cross, *The Burned-Over District: The Social*

This study of New Divinity revivals in Connecticut, then, presents an episode in the history of America's Second Great Awakening. This period of nationwide revival, from about 1790 to 1835, is probably the most lively, energetic, and pulsating time in American religious history. On the one hand, the rash of revivals in Connecticut must be seen as part of a national and transatlantic explosion of spiritual energies probably not witnessed since the Protestant Reformation. On the other hand, the New Divinity revivals displayed features that were clearly peculiar to their own time and space. Thus, to understand this regional revival is to understand its internal history. To that end, this work aims to be both narrower and broader than other works on the subject. It looks specifically at northwestern Connecticut. Unlike other studies that focus chiefly on leaders or institutions or theology or converts, this study seeks to integrate all of these profiles into a three-dimensional portrait. In the early chapters I look at New Divinity leaders of the revival: their professional circumstance (Chapter 1), their social agenda and institutions (Chapter 2), their theology (Chapter 3), their preaching, and then, narrowing to exemplars, two of the most illustrious of its preachers, Edward Dorr Griffin and Asahel Nettleton (Chapter 4). I then look at the Awakening's leaders and the receptivity of their message within a single congregation, Farmington First Church (Chapter 5). Shifting from leaders and local circumstances to those who were led, I turn to the ordinary people

---

and Intellectual History of Enthusiastic Religion in Western New York, 1800–1850 (1950; reprint, New York, 1965), 19–21. Keller's and Cross's nineteenth-century forebears failed to perceive the connection between revivals and the voluntary reform movement. For Robert Baird and Philip Schaff, both of whom wrote for European audiences in midcentury, revivals characterized American life, but not nearly so much as the unique voluntary nature of American Protestantism. Missionary organizations, tract and reform societies, benevolent associations—all of these grew out of the voluntary principle. Baird and Schaff neglected to mention that what energized this voluntary principle, what made it work so well, was derived from the revivalist impulse. See Baird, Religion in the United States, 452, 456, and Schaff, America: A Sketch of Its Political, Social, and Religious Character (1854; reprint, Cambridge, Mass., 1961), 98, and elsewhere. Following Baird and Schaff later in the century, Leonard Bacon gave short shrift to the connection between the Second Great Awakening and the organizational movements that followed in its wake (History of American Christianity, 244–45).

Since the 1940s, historians have stressed that the early nineteenth-century New England voluntary societies sprang primarily from the enthusiasm generated by the revivals. In addition to Keller, Second Great Awakening (chaps. 5, 6), see Ahlstrom, Religious History, 442. For broader developments, see Oliver W. Elsbree, The Rise of the Missionary Spirit in America, 1790–1815 (Williamsport, Pa., 1928); Charles I. Foster, An Errand of Mercy: The Evangelical United Front, 1790–1837 (Chapel Hill, N.C., 1960); Clifford S. Griffin, Their Brothers' Keepers: Moral Stewardship in the United States, 1800–1865 (New Brunswick, N.J., 1960); Andrew, Rebuilding the Christian Commonwealth; Shiels, "Connecticut Clergy"; and Scott's perceptive study, From Office to Profession. Attention given to the broad influence of revivals has increased in proportion to the historical distance from the original events. In the words of Robert T. Handy, "Revivalistic Protestantism deeply influenced the mind and heart of the nation" (A History of the Churches in the United States and Canada [New York, 1976], 163). See also Jerald C. Brauer, Protestantism in America: A Narrative History, rev. ed. (Philadelphia, 1965), 116; and William G. McLoughlin, ed., The American Evangelicals, 1800–1900 (New York, 1968), 1.

of the Awakening: their background, their response to revival, and their spiritual life (Chapters 6 and 7). By providing a close analysis of the clerical and popular roots of the revival within a limited framework, I hope to demonstrate how people articulated their faith, how they acted out their religious convictions, how they shaped the revival and were shaped by their historical context, how they endowed their world with meaning, and how at times they rose above that context to articulate a message as old as Christianity itself.

Before proceeding, several matters of usage require clarification. First, this book is about a religious *awakening* that took place in Connecticut. Throughout the narrative I use the terms *revival* and *awakening* interchangeably, though in a fairly specific sense. When Charles Keller wrote about the Second Great Awakening he included not only the waves of mass conversions at local churches (he tracked seven waves from 1797 to 1826) but the united, parachurch efforts of evangelical Protestants to transform society through missionary, moral, educational, and charitable organizations. Although renewed evangelical fervor, missionary outreach, and social reform were integrally related (for example, a number of pastors whose churches experienced revival were intimately involved in missionary outreach), I have chosen to focus on the origin and meaning of those initial "waves of mass conversion."

More recently, scholars have used the terms *revival* and *awakening* to refer to two different but related phenomena. William McLoughlin, for example, distinguishes between "Protestant rituals" (revivals) and "periods of cultural revitalization" (awakenings).[24] In Protestant revivals (and, as Jay Dolan has shown, in Catholic as well),[25] evangelists preach the gospel to an audience who, captivated by the message, experience salvation, conversion, regeneration, or the new birth. In awakenings, a whole people or culture experience a "rebirth"—not necessarily in the traditional Protestant sense (though this may be an aspect of the awakening)—but in the general sense of a reorientation of values, of meaning, of perspective. Within the categories McLoughlin employs, I am writing about revivals that represent one aspect of a "second great awakening," one part of a profound ideological transformation of American society rooted in a general crisis over belief and values.

Second, this book is about a religious awakening that took place in *Connecticut*. As I have already noted, my focus is on the religious revivals among Congregationalists in northwestern Connecticut. Of course, Congregationalists were not the only players in this region, but if any region of the country was marked by religious homogeneity at the beginning of the nineteenth century, it was the area of Litchfield and Hartford counties. As

---

24. McLoughlin, *Revivals, Awakenings, and Reform*, xiii.
25. Jay P. Dolan, *Catholic Revivalism: The American Experience, 1830–1900* (Notre Dame, Ind., 1978).

Nathan Hatch has so clearly demonstrated, all of that soon changed.[26] In 1800, Methodists, Baptists, and, to a lesser extent, Episcopalians were firmly established in the southern and eastern portions of the state. Not until the second and third decades of the nineteenth century did Baptist and Methodist itinerants aggressively invade New Divinity territory—the last stronghold of Congregational power—and compete successfully for the souls and loyalty of the people.[27] All of which is to say that in 1800, religious pluralism existed in Connecticut, albeit in a selective, regionally limited way. I mention the presence of these other religious groups so as not to distort the picture when referring to "Connecticut" revivals. Because I find the repeated use of "northwestern" or "Litchfield and Hartford counties" or "New Divinity revivals" cumbersome, I sometimes revert to "Connecticut." As I make clear in the conclusion, there was much more to the Second Great Awakening in Connecticut than Congregational revivals in Litchfield and Hartford counties—just as there was much more to the Second Great Awakening in America than revivals in Connecticut.

In its broadest sense, this study describes and analyzes how one group in one area grappled with the multiple meanings of freedom in postrevolutionary America—freedom of political choice, freedom of the will, freedom of religion, freedom of the marketplace. Individuals, however, not groups, live and breathe, act and think, and, in this case, made sense of their world in explicitly religious ways. Thus, I have tried to give attention to the details of individual experiences as much as to the more abstract generalizations about collective thought and behavior.

26. Hatch, *Democratization of American Christianity.*
27. See Keller, *Second Great Awakening*, chap. 8.

1

"THE UNITED BROTHERHOOD OF MINISTERS"

The Awakeners

On 10 March 1798, Thomas Robbins penned the following words in his diary: "Mr. Hallock came here from Simsbury to preach. Some awakening up the country."[1] This terse entry opens a window to the world of the Connecticut clergy on the eve of the Second Great Awakening. "Mr. Hallock" was the Rev. Jeremiah Hallock, pastor of the Canton Center parish in West Simsbury. On 10 March Hallock repeated a familiar routine: he rose at dawn, saddled his horse, and rode eleven miles southwest to Torringford, where he preached the Sabbath day sermon for his longtime friend and colleague, the Rev. Samuel Mills, Sr. Such an "exchange" with another minister was typical of the New England ministry, for since early colonial times this practice had occurred frequently. Robbins's notation "Hallock came here" prompts one to ask what Robbins himself was doing in Torringford. The circumstances surrounding his presence were no less ordinary than Hallock's exchange. Because Robbins had set his sights on the ministry, he was doing what most New England clerical aspirants did to prepare for the ministry, previous to the introduction of formal seminaries in the United States. Robbins was getting a pastoral and theological education with a seasoned professional, that is, an

1. Thomas Robbins, *The Diary of Thomas Robbins, D.D., 1796–1854*, ed. Increase N. Tarbox (Boston, 1886), 1:52.

experienced minister. The son of the Rev. Ammi Robbins of Norfolk, Thomas graduated from both Williams and Yale colleges in 1796—a rather unusual feat in its day. He then followed a typical course for those pursuing ministerial careers. For several years he taught in village schools during the winter months and used the remainder of the year to concentrate on theological studies under local ministers. Robbins studied initially under the Rev. Ephraim Judson of Sheffield, Massachusetts, and then in the summer and fall of 1797 with the acerbic Stephen West, an intransigent New Divinity man and successor to Jonathan Edwards, in Stockbridge, Massachusetts. Now, while teaching at Torringford, Robbins continued to pursue pastoral and theological training under Mills.[2]

And what of Robbins's second sentence in his 10 March entry? In hindsight, his mild reference to "some awakening up the country" anticipated the flood of revivals that covered northwestern Connecticut seven months later. During his visit, Hallock undoubtedly told of the quickened spiritual interest among his people in West Simsbury. Had Robbins's subsequent diary entries remained silent on the matter of "awakening," his fairly innocuous comment might easily be glossed over as an anomaly. But more was to follow. June 3: "Great attention to religion here" (Norfolk). September 23 (after returning to study with Dr. West): "There seems to be some hopeful religious attention at Torringford." November 15: "I came to West Simsbury, and tarried at Mr. Hallock's." And then the tidal wave. Robbins's usage shifts from his earlier tentative entries ("some," "attention to," and "hopeful") to the simple declarative: "A great awakening there." The dam had burst. January 30, 1799: "Awakening very great and remarkable in Hartford." February 4: "Good news of awakenings in Litchfield County." April 17: "The awakening at Hartford still continues." By now, the "greatness" of the awakening called to mind the previous Great Awakening. April 20: "Awakenings are very great. . . . I believe there was never a greater work of God in this land; perhaps not so universal as in 1741 and '42, but where it is, more powerful and more evidently the work of God only. . . . It is in about half of the towns of this county [Litchfield], and perhaps nearly as great a part of the county of Hartford."[3] In the span of six months, northwestern Connecticut was soaked in revival. By the end of 1800, over seventeen hundred saints were added to the church membership rolls.[4]

There is no telling exactly when and where the Second Great Awakening in Connecticut began, but traces left by Robbins, references in Hallock's memoir, and clerical reports of the revival in the *Connecticut Evangelical Magazine* all point to its beginning at the West Simsbury meetinghouse of

---

2. On Robbins's background, see *Diary of Robbins* 1:iii–vii.
3. *Diary of Robbins* 1:57, 65, 68–69, 74, 75, 80.
4. See Chapter 6.

Jeremiah Hallock on the second Sunday of October 1798. Hallock, of course, had no inkling that the revival in his parish would mark the beginning of a series of divine showers in Hartford and Litchfield counties. An unassuming, uneducated pastor, he appeared an unlikely revivalist. Only after his conversion at age twenty-one did he consider furthering the meager education of his adolescent years. Too old, too ill-equipped, he dismissed the possibility of attending Yale College—the traditional training ground for Connecticut's learned ministry.[5]

Yet in other more significant ways Hallock resembled the clerical leaders of Connecticut's New Divinity Awakening. All revivalist clergy knew first-hand, had heard stories of, or had read about the previous Great Awakening when Gilbert Tennent invaded New Haven with George Whitefield and trumpeted about "the danger of an unconverted ministry." Tennent's manifesto excoriated unregenerate ministers whom he likened to "caterpillars" who "labor to devour every green thing."[6] If left to themselves, these consuming worms would suck the spiritual juices out of America's churches. But Hallock was no caterpillar, for he had experienced the new birth, the raison d'être of revivals. After all, a minister could not preach, "Ye must be born again," without being reborn himself. Nathan Perkins, a colleague of Hallock's in nearby West Hartford, put the issue to a simple question: "How can one whose eyes were never opened lead the blind?"[7] Defined simply, the new birth was the religious turning point of regeneration where God, by a supernatural act of saving grace, transformed the wicked bias of the heart and set the sinner's affections on divine things. Like many of his ministerial cohorts, Hallock's profound conversion experience occurred in his early twenties, that critical period when a previous "calling" to the ministry now approached the actual assumption of the ministerial task.

But the experience of regeneration alone did not a minister make, particularly within New England congregationalism. Baptists, Quakers, Methodists, and other "odious sects" might flaunt an uneducated leadership, but the congregational way of New England demanded, according to the "Heads of Agreement" (1691), that ministers "be endued with *competent Learning*."[8] With this mandate, Yale College was founded in 1702. And yet Jeremiah Hallock was a minister of the gospel without formal training at Yale or any other college. What theological education he did have was acquired from other

---

5. See Appendix 1, "Jeremiah Hallock" and Cyrus Yale, *The Godly Pastor: Life of the Rev. Jeremiah Hallock, of Canton, Conn.* (New York, [1854]).

6. Gilbert Tennent, "The Danger of an Unconverted Ministry," in *The Great Awakening: Documents Illustrating the Crisis and Its Consequences*, ed. Alan Heimert and Perry Miller (Indianapolis, Ind., 1967), 72.

7. Nathan Perkins, "A Sermon, preached at the Installation of the Rev. Mr. Solomon Wolcott . . . May 24th, 1786" (Hartford, Conn., [1786]), 8.

8. Williston Walker, ed., *The Creeds and Platforms of Congregationalism* (1893; reprint, Philadelphia, 1969), 458.

New Divinity ministers in their "schools of the prophets." These schools, be they "parish parlors" or "log colleges," functioned as New Divinity finishing schools. Nearly all New Divinity men, Yale-educated or not, studied with a leading New Divinity pastor/theologian. Hallock, then, compensated for his lack of a college education by apprenticing himself to five different "prophets."

Clerical aspirants such as Hallock lived in the home or on the estate of their teacher. Under a minister's tutelage and watchful eye, these young men studied Greek, learned New Divinity theology, and observed their teacher perform the roles of preacher, pastor, husband, and father. In the years between the Great Awakening and the opening of Yale Divinity School in 1822, these informal seminaries flourished among devotees of the New Divinity, and they provided the environment for a well-defined, cohesive movement.[9] Their existence enabled the New Divinity leaders to mold a cadre of dedicated ministers, as well as to secure a stronghold in the sparsely settled areas of northwestern Connecticut.

Not every New Divinity minister fostered a revival during the Second Great Awakening, but nearly every revival that did occur took place within the parish of a New Divinity pastor. Samuel Hopkins, a patriarch of the New Divinity movement, calculated that the number of New Divinity clergy grew from a handful in 1756 to nearly fifty in 1773 and by 1797 topped the one hundred mark.[10] By Ezra Stiles's reckoning in 1792, over one-third of the Connecticut Congregational pulpits ("58 or 60 out of 168") were filled with New Divinity men.[11] The suspicious President Stiles noted the grandiose plans of the New Divinity men to wrest control of Yale from the Old Calvinists, "as they say they are already half the Ministers and have all the Candidates" for the ministry.[12]

Edward Dorr Griffin was one such New Divinity candidate. Converted and then catechized in New Divinity dogma, Griffin soon emerged as the preacher par excellence of revival. A rising star among a young generation of gifted New Divinity men, Griffin became a commanding figure in New England evangelical life during the first third of the nineteenth century. Unlike Hallock, but more typical of the Connecticut clergy, Griffin attended

9. Joseph A. Conforti, *Samuel Hopkins and the New Divinity Movement: Calvinism, the Congregational Ministry, and Reform in New England between the Great Awakenings* (Grand Rapids, Mich., 1981), 35.

10. Samuel Hopkins, *Sketches of the Life of the Late Rev. Samuel Hopkins, D.D.*, ed. Stephen West (Hartford, Conn., 1805), 102–3; see also Ezra Stiles, *The Literary Diary of Ezra Stiles*, ed. Franklin B. Dexter (New York, 1901), 1:363.

11. Stiles, *Diary* 3:463–64.

12. Ibid. 3:464. Stiles was particularly suspicious (and jealous) of Timothy Dwight and the "New Divinity Connexion" in their attempt (which eventually failed) to create an alternative to Yale in Vermont, and then in their later attempt to gain control of Yale College. Dwight indeed became Yale's president in 1795, but by this time his New Divinity theological convictions were suspect. On the Vermont scheme, see *Diary* 2:438, 449–50, 529; on Yale, see *Diary* 3:203, 317, 451.

Yale. Converted at age twenty-one, he prepared for the ministry under Jonathan Edwards, Jr., of New Haven. Following a stint as "stated supply," or interim pastor, in Middlesex County in 1792, Griffin took Hartford and Litchfield counties by storm, where under his powerful preaching revivals rocked Farmington in 1793 and New Hartford in 1798.

Who were those like Hallock and Griffin who championed revival? Why were they concentrated in northwestern Connecticut? And what precisely was their contribution to the Second Great Awakening? A social portrait of these New Divinity pastors reveals a close-knit, homogeneous group whose background, education, theological convictions, and aspirations enabled them to work effectively together to promote revival. At the same time, something of a generation gap existed among this group, the significance of which had profound implications for the future of the ministerial profession as well as for the revivalist tradition in New England. A brief excursus into colonial Puritanism and the Great Awakening will shed light on the origins of the New Divinity movement.

The Puritan Legacy and the Great Awakening

When the Great Awakening swept across Connecticut, its duration was short-lived. Following an outbreak of religious excitement in the Connecticut River valley in 1734–35, the revival erupted in the fall of 1740, crested during the remainder of 1740 and throughout 1741, and then ebbed in 1742–43. Though lasting only a few years, the results and ramifications of the Awakening shaped religious life for the remainder of the eighteenth century. Spawned by the itinerant preaching of George Whitefield, Gilbert Tennent, Eleazar Wheelock, and James Davenport, as well as by the "settled" preaching of ministers and laymen of Connecticut, the Great Awakening was the response of a people whose ways had become increasingly secular.[13] Convicted of their material, acquisitive ways, of strife against their neighbor, and, above all, of their religious indifference and hardness of heart, hundreds of colonists turned to the religion of their forefathers as a way of assuaging personal guilt, rectifying torn social relationships, and living at peace with their Creator.

The unleashed Spirit knew no bounds. Although the Awakening brought spiritual healing to many, it ravaged the public order of the colonies. Traditional forms of authority, characterized by deference and hierarchical

13. Richard Bushman, *From Puritan to Yankee: Character and Social Order in Connecticut, 1690–1765* (New York, 1970), 188; see also Edwin S. Gaustad, *The Great Awakening in New England* (New York, 1957).

relationships, were undercut by the inner convicting work of the Spirit. In particular, the ministerial ranks severely divided. Initially, clerical differences were not so much centered on theology as upon style, taste, and decorum, for on the eve of the Great Awakening, a broad consensus regarding the basic tenets of New England Puritan theology still existed. Based upon the doctrines of John Calvin and modified by federal or covenantal concepts, Puritan theology emphasized the utter dependence of humans upon the judgment and grace of a sovereign God. Sinful, vile, helpless, and deserving the condemnations of hell, the human race was inherently alienated from God. However, known only to the counsel of a wise, righteous, holy, and loving God, some individuals were predestined to salvation. Those saints "effectually called" contributed nothing of their own merit, but solely by God's grace, Christ's righteousness was imputed to them. Once made righteous, they could fulfill the purposes for which they were created by living a holy life and serving God in all ways.

By a "voluntary condescension," God entered into covenantal relationships with his elect. While these covenants assumed several forms, the saving covenant of grace between the individual and God sustained all other covenants. According to the Old Testament pattern, which the Puritans adopted as a blueprint for their holy commonwealth, covenants extended to families, churches, and governments. Whereas the covenant of grace affected one's eternal destiny, the other covenants were necessary to guide temporal human relationships and ensure obedience to God on this earth. Thus, in its civil form, covenant theology included the total society, both saints and sinners.

To join in a covenantal relationship with a local church (i.e., to become a church member) required a testimony to God's work of grace in an individual's life. Although it was not necessary to point to the exact place and time of conversion (though many could), applicants for church membership were required to give a detailed account of their new hope in Christ. At the same time, since God's original covenant with Abraham extended to his "seed," so too, according to Puritan theology, the covenant included physical descendants. Families, not individuals, constituted churches; and children, by virtue of their parents' covenant, partook in a number of privileges of church membership.[14] Baptism marked the entrance into this covenant, though the covenant was not fully secured until children (usually as young adults) gave a satisfactory account of their conversion experience. Living in a godly family and attending the preaching of the Word prepared one for salvation but by no means assured it.

Changes in Puritan church polity did not alter the necessity of conversion.

14. Edmund S. Morgan, *The Puritan Family: Religion and Domestic Relations in Seventeenth-Century New England* (New York, 1966), 6–12.

The Half-Way Covenant (1662) permitted the unregenerate married children of regenerate parents to present their infant children for baptism (and thereby "own" the covenant), and yet the terms of salvation remained unaltered. The architects of this plan anticipated that these children of the regenerate would at some point testify to God's gracious work in their lives. Similarly, when Solomon Stoddard of Northampton opened participation in the Lord's Supper to the unconverted in the 1680s, intending the sacrament as a converting ordinance, his goal was evangelistic. Hence, up to the Great Awakening, the lineaments of New England Puritan theology remained firm. Among a few, a greater emphasis was placed on intrinsic human ability and worth, but this so-called Arminian thinking was restricted to the wealthy elite along the eastern seaboard, most notably in Boston. Not until after the Awakening did this theology take hold and seriously threaten the Calvinist consensus.[15]

Old Lights and New Lights

The Great Awakening unleashed a debate not over the desirability of conversion—after all, a primary purpose of the ministry was evangelical—but rather over the means to and the meaning of conversion. In the throes of this controversy, the authoritative basis of the New England social order was transformed. Religious authorities (i.e., the Congregational clerical elite) were at the center of this debate and initially divided into two camps. On one side stood the antirevivalists, often designated Old Lights. Through legal channels and appeals to their authority as God-ordained ministers, Old Lights sought to eliminate itinerating preachers, curb the emotional excesses attending the revival, and retain the ecclesiastical status quo. New Light advocates of the revival often questioned the ability of the Old Lights to lead men and women to conversion. Many New Lights echoed Tennent's sentiments about unconverted Old Light clergy being unfit ministers of the gospel.[16]

With their Old Light antagonists, the New Lights agreed that the doctrines of Calvinism had not changed. But they insisted, in the words of Jonathan Edwards, that "our people do not so much need to have their heads stored, as to have their hearts touched; and they stand in greatest need of that sort of preaching, that has the greatest tendency to do this."[17] New England society was reborn through simple, aggressive New Light preaching directed at the

15. See Conrad Wright, The Beginnings of Unitarianism in America (Boston, 1955), for the erosion of Calvinism and the rise of liberal, or "Arminian," theology.

16. See Gaustad, Great Awakening in New England.

17. Jonathan Edwards, The Works of President Edwards (New York, 1844), 3:336.

wills—"the hearts"—of the people. Such New Light preaching, however, was refracted in many different directions. Ironically, the Connecticut New Light group, intending to reunite a grasping, factious society through the call to repentance, splintered within, belying the simple twofold division between pro- and antirevivalists. New Light Separatists, many of whom eventually embraced principles of the Baptists, demanded withdrawal from those churches where the wheat mixed with the tares, the regenerate with the unregenerate. The strongholds of those supporting pure church principles were Windham and New London counties in the east. Here the Awakening reached its highest peak of intensity as one ecclesiastical body after another split from within.[18] Advocates of New Divinity views gained a foothold on the other side of the state in northwestern Connecticut, particularly in the backwoods region of Litchfield County. With Jonathan Edwards as their spiritual and theological mentor, these men neither separated from existing churches nor supported the emotional excesses and anarchic individualism of the Separates. Finally, less numerous and less vocal than either the Separates or the New Divinity, a group of New Light moderates such as President Thomas Clap and Professor Naphtali Daggett of Yale formed the third grouping of New Lights.[19]

A Movement Takes Shape

As is evident from Thomas Robbins's diary entries, the Great Awakening became the touchstone for measuring the spiritual vitality of New England. In the half century following the colonial upheaval, sporadic tremors of revival activity shook the New England Congregational landscape.[20] Few forgot, nor would the revival-minded New Divinity clergy allow their parishioners to forget, the divine outpourings of the 1740s. Those favoring revival—the reviving of the heartfelt piety of their Puritan forefathers—were persuaded that a remade heart was God's way of building up the Church.

18. See Clarence C. Goen, *Revivalism and Separatism in New England: Strict Congregationalists and Separate Baptists in the Great Awakening* (New Haven, Conn., 1962).

19. On Clap, see Louis Leonard Tucker, *Puritan Protagonist: President Thomas Clap of Yale College* (Chapel Hill, N.C., 1962); Bushman, *Puritan to Yankee*, 241–42. Tucker details Clap's *volte-face* from Old Light to New Light in Chapter 9. On Daggett, see Franklin B. Dexter, ed., *Biographical Sketches of the Graduates of Yale College with Annals of the College History* (New York, 1885–1912), 2:153–57, esp. 156.

20. In *The Great Awakening and Other Revivals in the Religious Life of Connecticut* (New Haven, Conn., 1934), Mary Hewitt Mitchell plotted approximately twenty-five revivals from 1760 to 1790. Cf. Luther Hart, "A View of the Religious Declension in New England, and of its Causes, during the latter half of the Eighteenth Century," *Quarterly Christian Spectator*, 3d ser., 5 (June 1833), who cites fifteen revivals in all of New England between the Great Awakening and Second Great Awakening (208).

Memories of the Awakening provided spiritual sustenance in times of declension, and, paradoxically, an impetus to recapture the spontaneity of "experimental" religion.

During the last half of the eighteenth century, the New Divinity men labored to promote and to defend the revival. Their strenuous efforts in the latter far outweighed their success in the former, but with notable exceptions. Historians both past and present have claimed that these men were theological obscurantists, content to spin metaphysical cobwebs in their intellectual defense of the faith, while neglecting or unable to touch the hearts of their parishioners.[21] To a degree, this criticism is valid, but it does not do justice either to Joseph Bellamy in Connecticut or to a handful of other New Divinity pastors in New England who lit fires of revival in their parishes before the conflagrations of 1798–99.[22] Bellamy's detractors knew him as the "Sovereign Lord" and "Pope" of Litchfield County for his ecclesiastical machinations in turning Litchfield into a New Divinity citadel, but he was also a successful revivalist in his Bethlehem parish.[23]

To dismiss the first and second generations of New Divinity men (i.e., the students of Edwards and their students, ca. 1740–90) as arcane theologizers who ignored heartfelt revivalist religion is to portray them as betrayers of the very man they revered and followed. This dismissal also fails to recognize the continuity between the older New Divinity teachers and their students—the third generation—who sparked the Second Great Awakening. Both Bellamy and Samuel Hopkins, two of Edwards's first disciples, trained many of the pastors who either led local revivals at the turn of the century or educated others directly involved in the Awakening.[24]

In addition to their avid support of heartfelt, experiential faith, the New Divinity men resolutely defended what they often called Consistent Calvinism. They believed that Old Lights had suffered a failure of nerve and that by default they alone were entrusted with the task of beating back the advance

---

21. See especially Joseph Haroutunian, *Piety versus Moralism: The Passing of the New England Theology* (1932; reprint, New York, 1970); Sidney E. Mead, *Nathaniel William Taylor, 1786–1858: A Connecticut Liberal* (Chicago, 1942); and Edmund S. Morgan, "The American Revolution Considered as an Intellectual Movement," in *Paths of American Thought*, ed. Arthur M. Schlesinger, Jr., and Morton White (Boston, 1963), 20. For a more recent reiteration of these views, see Barbara M. Solomon's introduction to Timothy Dwight, *Travels in New England and New York*, ed. Barbara M. Solomon (Cambridge, Mass., 1969), 1:xv; Cedric B. Cowing, *The Great Awakening and the American Revolution: Colonial Thought in the Eighteenth Century* (Chicago, 1971), 197–98; and Stephen E. Berk, *Calvinism versus Democracy: Timothy Dwight and the Origins of American Evangelical Orthodoxy* (Hamden, Conn., 1974), 62.

22. See Allen C. Guelzo, *Edwards on the Will: A Century of American Theological Debate* (Middletown, Conn., 1989), 92.

23. John Devotion to Ezra Stiles, 4 December 1766, in Ezra Stiles, *Extracts from the Itineraries and Other Miscellanies of Ezra Stiles . . . With a Selection from His Correspondence*, ed. Franklin B. Dexter (New Haven, Conn., 1916), 460; Stiles, *Diary* 3:464.

24. Conforti, *Samuel Hopkins*, 36, 178.

of Arminianism. As Samuel Hopkins viewed it, Old Light moderate Calvinism (later called Old Calvinism) was little more than a veiled moderate Arminianism.[25] In short, New Divinity adherents purposed to retain the spiritual vitality unleashed by the Great Awakening within the structures of Edwardsean thought. They envisioned themselves as the guardians of evangelical Calvinism, the self-appointed heirs of Jonathan Edwards.

Just as Edwards accepted exile to the remote Indian mission in Stockbridge, Massachusetts, his students followed and accepted similar positions in the hamlets and sparsely settled regions of Berkshire (Massachusetts) and Litchfield counties.[26] Once established in these areas, New Divinity men fanned out north into Vermont and New Hampshire, west into the Ohio River valley, and back east into those counties torn earlier by the controversy over the Awakening. Their strength grew so that by the end of the eighteenth century and into the first decades of the nineteenth, the New Divinity dominated theological discourse in New England. The Rev. William Bentley, the proto-Unitarian from Salem, Massachusetts, whose distaste for the New Divinity was matched only by his venomous anti-Federalist politics, recorded the progress this group had made by 1813: "This System of Divinity is the basis of the popular theology of New England."[27]

The appeal of the New Divinity to New England's best minds was a constant mystery to Old Calvinist Ezra Stiles. As an opponent of the Great Awakening, Stiles could only conclude that the "multitudes were seriously, soberly and solemnly out of their wits."[28] He failed to perceive that most people were unlike himself, for he was balanced in judgment, polite in manners, and above all guided by the light of reason.[29] He found the rigors of New Divinity theology extreme; he was more interested in observing the silkworms spinning thread in his garden than in spinning theological truths in his own mind.[30]

However enigmatic to Stiles, there were good reasons for the success of the New Divinity movement. It, like sixteenth-century Calvinism, bred a band of heroes—and, as I will show in a later chapter, a bevy of martyrs. First, as a theological system, the New Divinity offered more than an Old Calvinist rehashing of the Reformed doctrines embodied in the Westminster Confes-

25. Ibid., 4.

26. On New Divinity hegemony in Berkshire County, see Richard D. Birdsall, *Berkshire County: A Cultural History* (New Haven, Conn., 1959), 33–66.

27. William Bentley, *The Diary of William Bentley, D.D., Pastor of the East Church, Salem, Massachusetts* (1905–14; reprint, Gloucester, Mass., 1963), 4:302.

28. Quoted in Gaustad, *Great Awakening in New England*, 103.

29. Edmund S. Morgan, *The Gentle Puritan: A Life of Ezra Stiles, 1727–1795* (New Haven, Conn., 1962), 176; Richard D. Birdsall, "Ezra Stiles versus the New Divinity Men," *American Quarterly* 17 (Summer 1965): 257.

30. Stiles, *Diary* 1:295; Morgan, *Gentle Puritan*, 22.

sion. It was indeed a "new divinity" that tested, challenged, and attracted New England's best minds. And once smitten by the New Divinity theology, its proponents demonstrated unswerving devotion to the cause, as attested by Stiles, who recorded hearing Gile Cowles, a junior at Yale College, "preach a New Divy Sermon with great confidence."[31] Second, the theological rigors of the New Divinity were equaled by a spiritual fervor that demanded nothing less than perfection.[32] The New Divinity spiritual and ethical life appealed not to the fainthearted but to the ascetically inclined, to those willing to embrace the New Divinity ethic of "disinterested benevolence." In revising this aesthetic concept of Edwards's into an ascetic one, Samuel Hopkins reasoned that all acts of love should exhibit a desire for the greater glory of God, not for any personal glory or benefit. The committed Christian sacrifices self-interest for the greater interest of God's kingdom. Indeed, one reason for the New Divinity movement's concentration in the backwoods regions of New England was its appeal to abstemious, missionary-minded clerics. Finally, the New Divinity attracted a considerable following because of the dedication of New Divinity men to theological instruction. Maintaining "schools of the prophets" in their homes, the New Divinity leaders, by precept and example, taught a generation of ministers come of age by the Second Great Awakening.

A Social Portrait

Recent historians have constructed a collective biography of the first two generations of New Divinity men, those whose careers ended or who were in their twilight by 1790,[33] but the third generation—those who assumed leadership of the Second Great Awakening in Connecticut—has not been fully investigated. Taken together, the three generations were similar in social upbringing and educational training, but in other ways, particularly in the concept of the ministry, the third differed significantly from the first two.

The collective portrait that emerges for the New Divinity clergy from 1740 to 1820 reveals a homogeneous, well-defined social group. In the eyes of many opponents they were an inferior social class, ill-bred, ill-mannered, uncouth, and contentious. William Bentley dubbed them "Farmer Metaphysicians" who "create contentions wherever they come." In his eyes, "the

31. Stiles, *Diary* 3:458.
32. Guelzo, *Edwards on the Will*, 113–17.
33. See biographical appendixes in Wright, *Beginnings of Unitarianism*, 288–91, and in Conforti, *Samuel Hopkins*, 227–32.

unsocial character of this sect" made them "odious."[34] To the sophisticated Stiles, the New Divinity men lacked the graces necessary to maintain peace and order within their congregations.[35] Joseph Bellamy, leader and educator of New Divinity men from his rural parish in Bethlehem, confirmed the estimations of Stiles and Bentley. In 1754 his candidacy at the First Presbyterian Church in New York City was rejected by a vocal minority because, he felt, "I am not polite enough for them! I may possibly do to be minister out in the woods, but am not fit for a city."[36] As Alan Heimert has observed, Bellamy's remark reflected more about his evangelical style of preaching than about his rough and ready country-bumpkin image. The real issue separating the Bellamy of rural Bethlehem from the pulpit in urbane New York was one of rhetorical taste, for by the mid–eighteenth century, the Old Light–New Light split played itself out not only theologically but socially and rhetorically.[37] An affectionate preaching style, suited more for the frontier, set New Divinity men apart from the decorous preaching style of Old Lights in urban, cultured areas. For this reason, New Divinity ministers preferred the backcountry areas to the more heavily populated coastal regions. To a large extent, their apparent lack of gentility and manners originated in a style of preaching whose aim was to convict and arouse, not to console and impress. And by concentrating in rural Massachusetts and Connecticut, the New Divinity men reinforced their image as "Farmer Metaphysicians" and gave fuel to those who labeled their provincial theology "Berkshire" or "Litchfield" divinity.

A recent investigation into the social origins of the first two generations of New Divinity men (ca. 1740–90) concludes that "the vast majority . . . were from modest or obscure social backgrounds."[38] These clerics represented a self-conscious social group. Nearly all of them graduated from Yale, and a high proportion came from "middling" farming or artisan families. When this analysis is extended to the twenty-six Connecticut clergymen whose congregations experienced revival from 1798 to 1808, a very similar portrait emerges (see Appendix 1). While biographical data gaps exist for determining the status of some of the clergymen's fathers, such omissions suggest that their fathers were undistinguished in both occupational and community standing. Nearly one-half (twelve) of the ministers had fathers of unknown socioeconomic backgrounds. Four clergymen had fathers of respectable standing; for example, the father of Ebenezer Porter was a town magistrate in Cornwall, Connecticut, and a member

---

34. Bentley, *Diary* 1:275, 196–97; 2:139; see also 1:161.

35. Stiles, *Diary* 3:343, 358–59, 384–85.

36. Quoted in Mary L. Gambrell, *Ministerial Training in Eighteenth Century New England* (New York, 1937), 106.

37. Alan E. Heimert, *Religion and the American Mind, from the Great Awakening to the Revolution* (Cambridge, Mass., 1966), 209; see also Conforti, *Samuel Hopkins*, 10.

38. Conforti, *Samuel Hopkins*, 10.

of the state legislature; the occupations of the other three pastors' fathers have been identified as "wealthy farmer," "substantial farmer," and "extensive landholder" of "respectable status." Only two of the New Divinity pastors' fathers were considered "farmers." Thus, the remaining twenty ministers (77 percent) whose congregations experienced revival came from families of obscure and, at best, modest backgrounds.

Placing the New Divinity group within the larger social structure of Connecticut sheds further light on the status of this subgroup. In his study of colonial Connecticut, Jackson Turner Main determined that throughout the eighteenth century, 42 percent of the clergy lacked family connections—the highest percentage among groups within the class of Connecticut's leaders (i.e., teachers, doctors, lawyers, ministers), yet quite low vis-à-vis the New Divinity subgroup.[39] A comparison of the social origins of the third-generation New Divinity cohort to the eighteenth-century colonial Connecticut clergy aggregate reveals that the New Divinity group reflects a disproportionately lower background status by 35 percent. In this respect, the third-generation New Divinity anticipated the pious, poor, and rural students—in Nathaniel Hawthorne's words, the "great unpolished bumpkins, who had grown up farmer boys"—of the early nineteenth-century provincial colleges such as Williams, Bowdoin, and Amherst.[40]

Significantly, a lack of family connections did not obviate social mobility. Nearly all of the New Divinity men's fathers (or at least families) found the necessary resources to send their sons to college, albeit several of the young men clearly struggled to meet their educational expenses. Two of the ministers were still children when their fathers died. Before the Connecticut Education Society (1814) or the American Education Society (1815) began supporting indigent scholars, these clerical aspirants, as well as other poor youth, depended upon the charity of relatives, local patrons, or most typically the sponsorship of the town pastor to provide the funds for their education.[41] Good will and benevolence, however, were not always enough to pay the balance due. For two New Divinity men, their four years at Yale were punctuated with repeated discouragement due to the strain on family finances.

This collective profile supports broader studies indicating that in eighteenth-century colonial New England fewer men of means and social

39. Jackson Turner Main, *Society and Economy in Colonial Connecticut* (Princeton, N.J., 1985), 330.

40. Quoted in David F. Allmendinger, Jr., *Paupers and Scholars: The Transformation of Student Life in Nineteenth-Century New England* (New York, 1975), 1. For a portrait of the backgrounds of students who attended these new local or regional colleges, see Allmendinger, esp. chap. 1. Significantly, several New Divinity men assumed presidencies of these provincial colleges (Edward Dorr Griffin at Williams, Heman Humphrey at Amherst, Azel Backus at Hamilton)—another indication that the New Divinity was attracted to the backcountry of New England.

41. Allmendinger, *Paupers and Scholars*, 9, 12–13, 28, 46–52; Donald M. Scott, *From Office to Profession: The New England Ministry, 1750–1850* (Philadelphia, 1978), 53.

status were turning to the clerical profession as a life career.[42] According to Main, the proportion of Connecticut ministers lacking any known advantage from birth rose from one-third to one-half in the course of the century.[43] Indeed, the basic qualification for entrance into the New Divinity clerical subgroup was an individual's spiritual, not familial, status. The contention, then, that those who initiated the Second Great Awakening were displaced theocrats whose status was severely reduced by postrevolutionary developments neglects to take into account the social origins of those entering the ministry after 1700. While historians dispute whether the ministry declined as a profession during the eighteenth century, what is clear is that the rise into the ministerial ranks for New Divinity men signaled personal upward mobility.

Correlatively, as the New Divinity movement gained numerical strength in the last decades of the eighteenth century and as revivals ensued, a confidence arose within its ranks that continued efforts could effect sweeping change. The outgrowth was a new evangelical subculture with its own organizations composed exclusively of the regenerate. The numerous mission, benevolent, and publication societies that followed in the wake of revival attest to the emergence of a new evangelical social order. To a large extent, this new order represented those of rising social status who sought an alternative means to Christianize America, not those who felt their status in decline.

Schools of the Prophets

Nearly all Connecticut New Divinity men whose careers fell between 1740 and 1820 graduated from Yale College. Although the curriculum at Yale still favored theological instruction, little professional training was offered to those seeking ministerial careers.[44] Some students intending to become ministers remained at Yale for an additional year or two, and largely by informal, independent theological study were granted the master's degree. However, in nearly every case those young men attracted to the New Divinity sought further training at the home of a New Divinity cleric.

42. James W. Schmotter argues for a decline in professional status, whereas Main "perceives no deterioration in the situation or status of ministers." See Schmotter, "Ministerial Careers in Eighteenth-Century New England: The Social Context, 1700–1760," *Journal of Social History* 9 (Winter 1975): 249–67, and Main, *Society and Economy*, 318. Both studies are confined to the colonial period. For the national period, see Scott, *From Office to Profession*.

43. Main, *Society and Economy*, 330.

44. Gambrell, *Ministerial Training*, 71–79, esp. 74.

The schools of the prophets had their origin in England but came to dominate clerical education in America following the Great Awakening. Apparently introduced spontaneously in America, such boarding schools as William Tennent's "Log College" in Neshaminy, Pennsylvania, trained a new generation of ministers in the piety and theology of the Great Awakening. As an undergraduate at Yale, Samuel Hopkins planned to sit under Tennent's tutelage, but he abruptly changed his mind after an encounter with Jonathan Edwards. "I conceived such an esteem of him, and was so pleased with his preaching, I altered my former determination with respect to Mr. Tennent, and concluded to go and live with Mr. Edwards, as soon as I should have opportunity, though he lived about eighty miles from my father's house."[45] In December 1741, Hopkins arrived unannounced at the doorstep of the Edwards house. Edwards was absent on a preaching tour, but Hopkins was received by Edwards's wife, Sarah. Jonathan's growing fame as a teacher and preacher of revival had by now accustomed her to such unexpected visits.

Joseph Bellamy, who apprenticed himself to Edwards just prior to Hopkins, was the first to establish a school for the training of New Divinity men at his parsonage in Bethlehem in western Connecticut. Over the course of his career he trained some sixty ministers. Other New Divinity leaders followed Bellamy's initiative. Nathanael Emmons of Franklin, Massachusetts, had no intention of beginning a school, and yet over a period of fifty years he put nearly ninety students through the rigors of his brand of New Divinity theology.[46] Two ministers directly involved in Connecticut's Second Great Awakening also trained prospective ministers. Asahel Hooker of Goshen prepared close to thirty students, while Charles Backus of Somers tutored an estimated fifty.[47]

Throughout the last half of the eighteenth century schools of the prophets multiplied, creating a delta effect. Education flowed from Jonathan Edwards to the two main tributaries established by Bellamy and Hopkins, so that by the Second Great Awakening numerous New Divinity men could trace their clerical pedigree back through one or two teachers to Edwards himself (see Figure 1.1). For example, Hopkins trained Edwards's son, Jonathan, Jr., who in turn trained two of the movers of the revival, Edward Dorr Griffin and Giles Cowles. John Smalley, a student of Bellamy's, tutored Ebenezer Porter, a leading revivalist in Washington, Connecticut. And one of Porter's students, Luther Hart, promoted revivals in his church in Plymouth in 1812, 1824, and 1831.

---

45. Quoted in ibid., 104.

46. On Bellamy and Emmons, see ibid., chap. 4; Conforti, *Samuel Hopkins*, chap. 3; Leonard Woods, *History of the Andover Theological Seminary* (Boston, 1885), chap. 1; and Edwards A. Park, *Memoir of Nathanael Emmons; with sketches of his friends and pupils* (Boston, 1861).

47. Augustine George Hibbard, *History of the Town of Goshen, Connecticut* (Hartford, Conn., 1897), 91; Dexter, *Biographical Sketches* 3:310–16.

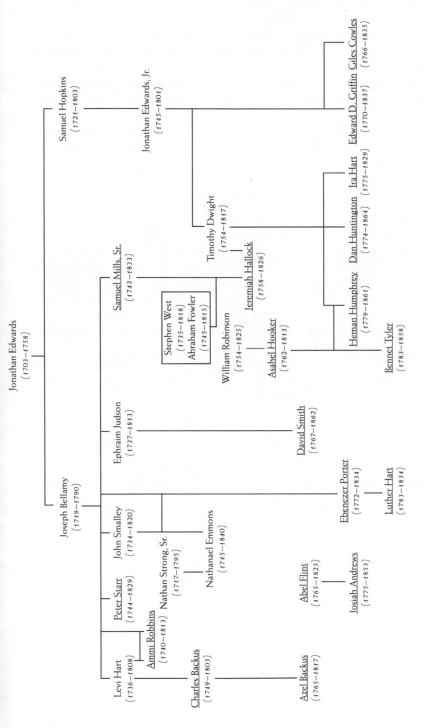

Jonathan Edwards
(1703–1758)

Joseph Bellamy
(1719–1790)

Samuel Hopkins
(1721–1803)

Jonathan Edwards, Jr.
(1745–1801)

Samuel Mills, Sr.
(1743–1833)

Ephraim Judson
(1737–1813)

Timothy Dwight
(1754–1817)

Stephen West
(1735–1818)
Abraham Fowler
(1745–1815)

Jeremiah Hallock
(1758–1826)

William Robinson
(1754–1825)

Asahel Hooker
(1762–1813)

Edward D. Griffin
(1770–1837)
Giles Cowles
(1766–1835)

Ira Hart
(1775–1829)

Dan Huntington
(1774–1864)

Heman Humphrey
(1779–1861)

Bennet Tyler
(1783–1858)

David Smith
(1767–1862)

Peter Starr
(1744–1829)

John Smalley
(1734–1820)

Nathan Strong, Sr.
(1717–1795)

Nathanael Emmons
(1745–1840)

Ebenezer Porter
(1772–1834)

Luther Hart
(1783–1834)

Levi Hart
(1736–1808)

Ammi Robbins
(1740–1813)

Charles Backus
(1749–1803)

Abel Flint
(1765–1825)

Josiah Andrews
(1775–1853)

Azel Backus
(1765–1817)

Sources: Dexter, *Biographical Sketches of the Graduates of Yale College*; Sprague, *Annals of the American Pulpit* (see Appendix 1).

Note: Names underlined represent Connecticut New Divinity ministers whose reports of parish revivals appeared in the *Connecticut Evangelical Magazine* and the *Connecticut Evangelical Magazine and Religious Intelligencer* (1800–1808).

FIG. 1.1   New Divinity Schools of the Prophets

As was the case with Jeremiah Hallock's training, some clerical hopefuls sat under the tutelage of more than one minister. Ammi Robbins, pastor of Norfolk and an older leader of the Awakening, prepared for the ministry under Joseph Bellamy, and then under one of Bellamy's students, Levi Hart. Like Robbins, Asahel Hooker studied first with Bellamy, then with William Robinson.

Training in the schools of the prophets consisted primarily of the study of systematic theology. Students read a variety of theological treatises, both orthodox and heterodox, then discussed assigned readings with their teacher. Often the instructor supplied a variety of questions intended to guide and direct the students in the basics of theology. A rather revealing indicator of the growing theological contentiousness during the last half of the eighteenth century was the increasing number of questions added to the instructor's list. Jonathan Edwards, for example, compiled a list of ninety questions for his students; a generation later, his son's list ran to over three hundred.[48] Maltby Gelston, a student of the younger Edwards, kept a notebook in which he recorded the answers to some five hundred questions, covering the basics of didactic theology. Presumably, all of his answers were committed to memory.[49] No doubt the training of Edward Griffin, another of Edwards's protégés, conformed to this pattern.

The schools of the prophets functioned not only as a theological training ground for clerical aspirants. They also created a sense of social cohesiveness among the New Divinity men. With college acquaintances renewed, friendships made, values shared, and piety enhanced, teacher and students set about their common task. In addition, these prospective pastors were initiated into the private as well as the public side of ministerial life. Their mentor not only disseminated knowledge in the study and preached from the pulpit, but he also provided a model of godly living. In his deportment at home with his wife and children, and in his pastoral relations, the teacher transmitted attitudes and values that his students would take with them into their own ministerial careers.

Not all of the students' time was given to theological studies. Some "seminarians" offset their expenses by regular farm work or by tutoring their instructor's children. On occasion, students took to the fields to assist their teacher in the harvest of his crops. Others were pressed into a different and, to them, a much more important harvest—that of souls. Asahel Hooker of Goshen, whose congregation experienced repeated revivals from 1799 to 1807, regularly enlisted the aid of his students to instruct and counsel

48. See "The Theological Questions of President Edwards, Senior, and Dr. Edwards, His Son" (Providence, R.I., 1822).
49. Gambrell, *Ministerial Training*, 134.

potential converts.[50] Moreover, during the winter months, when few families traveled from outlying districts to the town meetinghouse for Sabbath observance, Hooker sent out his students in pairs to conduct services at small, makeshift churches. These aspiring ministers honed New Divinity sermons on rural families granted "winter privileges."[51]

For some students, the schools of the prophets afforded the opportunity of finding a spouse. As is the case with other social groupings, kinship ties defined the New Divinity group.[52] Josiah Andrews and Jeremiah Hallock each married the sister of his teacher's wife. Others, though not finding a mate within the schools of the prophets, married within the New Divinity social network.[53]

The common life in the schools of the prophets helps to explain the close-knit clerical ties operative during the New Divinity revivals. What emerges from accounts of the Awakening is a pattern of clerical teams initiating and guiding revivals. To be sure, there are continuities with similar efforts made by the clergy during the Great Awakening, when local pastors assisted each other in much the same way.[54] Yet the frequency with which pastors assisted one another during the Second Great Awakening suggests stronger social and spiritual bonds cemented by their common background in the schools of the prophets.

A United Brotherhood

The bonds of fellowship were particularly strong among pastors in Litchfield County and in the area of Hartford County west of the Connecticut River.[55] Among these New Divinity men, the relationship was one of intimate friendship, communal prayer, and mutual encouragement—not unlike that of

50. Sereno D. Clark, *The New England Ministry Sixty Years Ago: The Memoir of John Woodbridge, D.D.* (Boston, 1877), 34.

51. [Zephaniah Moore Humphrey], *Memorial Sketches: Heman Humphrey, Sophia Porter Humphrey* (Philadelphia, 1869), 45.

52. For example, there are parallels between the New Divinity men and early English Puritan leaders. Of the latter, David D. Hall notes that they were bound together by "family intermarriage, familial patterns of recruitment, and a complex set of spiritual relationships" (*The Faithful Shepherd: A History of the New England Ministry in the Seventeenth Century* [New York, 1974], 50).

53. See Appendix 1.

54. Bushman, *From Puritan to Yankee*, 184; J. William T. Youngs, *God's Messengers: Religious Leadership in Colonial New England, 1700–1750* (Baltimore, 1976), 117–18.

55. "Harmony, zeal, and success" characterized the relations between pastors in the Litchfield North Association (*Contributions to the Ecclesiastical History of Connecticut* [New Haven, Conn., 1861], 314).

the "spiritual brotherhood" among early English Puritans.[56] The New Divinity clergy constantly assisted one another during the revivals, taking turns preaching, praying, exhorting, and instructing. After Edward Dorr Griffin left New Hartford in 1800 and settled in Newark, New Jersey, he wrote back to Jeremiah Hallock, his neighboring coworker in Canton Center: "Give my love to . . . Mr. Mills, Mr. Miller, and all the rest of our dear circle of ministers." Griffin then asked to be informed

> of the state of your monthly meetings—of religion—of all dear friends. . . . Brother Washburn writes that your circle love yet to pray, and that Jesus sometimes comes in the midst. I long to be with you. The sweet days of other years, especially the beloved seasons on the well known *mountain*. . . . You know not how much I miss that precious and united brotherhood of ministers. The ministers here are agreeable, friendly, and pious, but I have not prayed and wept, and triumphed with them. I shall never see such another circle. They were my first love.[57]

Griffin's "united brotherhood of ministers" became part of the mainspring whereby revival spread from one congregation to another. The close ties among these ministers may help to explain why the Awakening never spread with the same breadth and intensity among New Divinity churches in the Hartford South Association. There the lines were apparently drawn between the younger generation of ministers and the Rev. Benjamin Trumbull, the renowned historian and New Divinity advocate in North Haven. In a revealing letter written in 1810, Bezaleel Pinneo, a New Divinity pastor from Milford, wrote to Trumbull complaining "of the manner in which you have treated me." The two had disagreed over a number of issues at an association meeting, and now the dispute neared an open rift. "I think," wrote Pinneo, "that at times you have thrown out very heavy and severe charges and insinuations calculated not to convince but to wound. The frequent threats that you have given to withdraw from the Association and Consocation, if we did not do as you wished seem to me calculated to destroy our union, the peace of the Chh and your own influence also."[58]

Pinneo then addressed another issue causing embarrassment to the younger ministers. Evidently Trumbull was in the habit of criticizing what he considered to be the extravagant salaries of younger ministers. He failed to take into account the recent inflationary spiral that necessitated substantially

56. The term is William Haller's, from *The Rise of Puritanism* (New York, 1938), chap. 2, quoted in Hall, *Faithful Shepherd*, 49.

57. Edward Dorr Griffin to Jeremiah Hallock, 3 March 1810, Gratz Collection, HSP.

58. Bezaleel Pinneo to Benjamin Trumbull, 10 September 1810, Benjamin Trumbull (1735–1820) Collection, Correspondence and Papers, Box 5, SML.

higher salaries than what he had received when he had settled in North Haven a half century earlier. "The whole that you gave for your farm," contended Pinneo, "would not now buy, in most of the parishes, within a convenient distance of the meetinghouse, a half dozen acres of land. . . . Many have large families, poor health, and a stingy people to contend with, who think the common comforts of life can be purchased for a trifle and all the rest goes to the score of extravagance." But what most piqued Pinneo was that Trumbull, "having the influence in the Churches that you have, should take sides so much with the people . . . and embarrass . . . the rising hopes of our Churches."[59]

No apparent hostilities existed to the north, where both young and old pastors shared common concerns. A compatibility of interests, not competition, characterized their relations. Pinneo's comments prompt a closer examination of the altered conditions under which the third generation of New Divinity pastors labored, for such conditions fostered attitudes toward the ministry that contrast with the way in which the first two generations viewed their calling. A further inquiry into this perceptual change provides an added dimension by which to view the role of the clergy in the Second Great Awakening.

A Third Generation of New Divinity, 1790–1820

As discussed earlier, the presence of a high concentration of New Divinity men in Litchfield and Hartford counties accounts for the clerical emphasis on revival. Within this group, however, a third generation emerged, represented by Yale graduates after ca. 1790. This younger generation developed a conception of the ministry more suited to the promotion of revivals. Their new outlook evolved from changes within the New Divinity itself, but it also coincided with a general transformation of the New England ministry.

For those such as Joseph Bellamy and Samuel Hopkins who had touched the cloak of the master Edwards, their mentor assumed an exemplary status. Not only did they imbibe his teachings, but their everyday lives were patterned after his as well. Edwards took in students; so did they. Edwards was ousted from his Northampton parish over pure church principles; his followers were dismissed for similar reasons. Edwards's most productive years of scholarship took place on the American frontier; his students followed him into the wilderness. Edwards's preaching stirred his Northampton congregation; his protégés tried to do the same in their parishes. Edwards was a

59. Ibid.

scholar, dedicated to long hours of study; so too, his students applied themselves with equal rigor. Their hours engaged in solitary metaphysical musings and theologizing attest not only to their intense desire to defend the faith but also to their devotion to Edwards. One historian reports that students of such divines as Bellamy, Hopkins, and Emmons "saw their theological mentors spend from thirteen to eighteen hours a day, reading, speculating, and writing upon post-Awakening theological problems. The doctrinal preoccupations of the teachers provided not only a curriculum but a clerical role model for the students." So engaged were these first two generations in theological pursuits that they tended to "deemphasize . . . the pastoral duties of the ministry."[60] Some even retreated from all secular concerns and left such mundane matters as the management of the farm and household expenses to their wives—again, following the example of Edwards. Alexander Gillett, a second-generation devotee of the New Divinity, who pastored the Torrington church during the Second Awakening, "knew [and cared?] as little as Edwards did, respecting agricultural concerns."[61] Dr. Stern, the not-so-fictitious character in Harriet Beecher Stowe's *Oldtown Folks*, epitomized the collective New Divinity identity:

> He was a close student, and wore two holes in the floor opposite his table in the spot where year after year his feet were placed in study. He refused to have the smallest thing to do with any temporal affair of this life. . . . He cared nothing about worldly prosperity; he was totally indifferent to money; he utterly despised fame and reputation and therefore from none of these sources could he be in the slightest degree influenced.[62]

The results of the efforts of Edwards's followers to transmit his (and their) heroic virtues to a third generation were ambiguous, but not without revivalist success. The younger New Divinity men continued to view themselves as defenders of the faith against the emerging Unitarian menace, deistic thrusts, and the new measures that Charles Finney introduced in the 1820s. At the same time, they balanced the traditional long hours of disciplined study with a greater devotion to pastoral duties, and in the process they emerged as harsh critics of former practices. Luther Hart cited infrequent parochial visits as a primary reason for the spiritual "declension"

---

60. Conforti, *Samuel Hopkins*, 36–37, 35; see also Guelzo, *Edwards on the Will*, 91.

61. Luther Hart, "A Sermon, Delivered . . . Jan. 22, 1826, at the Funeral of Reverend Alexander Gillett . . ." (New Haven, Conn., 1826), 34; see also Nathanael Emmons, "Autobiography," in *The Works of Nathanael Emmons, D.D.*, ed. Jacob Ide (Boston, 1842), 1:xix.

62. Harriet Beecher Stowe, *Oldtown Folks*, 40th ed., (Boston, 1869), 380, 382.

between the two Great Awakenings. When visits were made, he contended, they were "too formal, and too little of a strictly pastoral nature."[63] Ebenezer Porter, pastor-revivalist in Washington, insisted that "nothing but systematic and vigorous action can repair the waste places of the church." The problem is, "we have sunk the catechist into the *metaphysician*. Our champions [the older New Divinity men] have not learned the blessed art of building the walls of Jerusalem with one hand while they wield the polemic pen with the other."[64]

The increased attention given to pastoral duties (and the general attention to doing more and thinking less) by the younger generation of the New Divinity largely accounts for the fact that no speculative theologian on the order of a Hopkins or Emmons emerged within their ranks. They did, however, succeed in arousing their churches. Edward Dorr Griffin resolved "to spend as much time as possible in making religious visits to my people . . . and to attend as many religious meetings as are convenient out of season."[65] Older colleagues were not so imbued with his gregariousness and even made opposite resolutions. Jonathan Edwards, Jr., was criticized for spending too much time in the study transcribing his father's writings and too little time laboring to save the souls of his people.[66] Alexander Gillett "was in the habit of visiting them [his parishioners] less than was desirable," and Nathanael Emmons, though familiar with his parishioners, eschewed visitations. They were simply too time-consuming, and moreover, he could never be sure if his parishioners were at home. He preferred to see them at his convenience: they would visit him at his request.[67]

This altered perception of the role of the minister among the younger generation of the New Divinity conforms to the general transformation of the ministry in New England from 1750 to 1850, what one scholar refers to as "from office to profession," and another as "from job-oriented to congregation-oriented."[68] Throughout the eighteenth century, the ministerial office was conceived in terms of a lifelong tenure in a single parish. A minister's "calling" included the understanding that God had set him apart for the ministry, but also implied that within the divine economy, God assigned him to a particular place. "This conception of the sacred office as a calling," notes Donald Scott, "provided a powerful sanction against ambition and

---

63. Hart, "Religious Declension," 226.

64. Quoted in Lyman Matthews, *Memoir of the Life and Character of Ebenezer Porter, D.D.* (Boston, 1837), 195; see also [Humphrey] *Memorial Sketches*, 133.

65. William Buell Sprague, *Memoir of the Rev. Edward D. Griffin, D.D.* (New York, 1839), 14.

66. Robert L. Ferm, *Jonathan Edwards the Younger: 1745–1801* (Grand Rapids, Mich., 1976), 141.

67. Hart, "Sermon at the Funeral of Gillett," 39; Park, *Memoir of Emmons*, 332.

68. Scott, *From Office to Profession*; John A. Andrew III, *Rebuilding the Christian Commonwealth: New England Congregationalists and Foreign Missions, 1800–1830* (Lexington, Ky., 1976), 39. See also Daniel H. Calhoun, *Professional Lives in America* (Cambridge, Mass., 1965), for a similar, though less comprehensive, assessment of the New England ministry.

hence a powerful buttress to permanence."[69] The newer clergy, however, tended to view their calling in terms of their ability to arouse their congregations, make converts, and instill piety. The mark of success was measured not by the respect accorded them due to the office they filled, but by the number of converts gathered. By 1850, "the clergy had become a 'profession' in a modern sense," wherein the pastor "now offered specialized services to a particular clientele," that is, to converts only.[70] Whereas a pastor's sphere of influence once extended to the whole community, it was now restricted to that of his church members.

This altered conception of the ministry among the New Divinity men can be gauged by viewing their pattern of clerical mobility. It appears that the newer generation was caught within and, indeed, contributed to this transformation. For example, salary disputes had been a long-standing issue in New England Congregational life. According to one study, they represented the largest single cause of controversy during the first half of the eighteenth century.[71] Yet contentions over salary were never sufficient grounds alone for severing the union between a pastor and his congregation. Only a gross flaw in the minister's character warranted dismissal.[72]

By the end of the eighteenth century, however, salary disputes reached an impasse, and the younger New Divinity pastors found themselves forced to choose sides. On the one hand, the traditional calling to the ministry presupposed a lifelong tenure with a single congregation; on the other hand, the postrevolutionary inflationary spiral pressured the clergy into taking a market-oriented, supply-and-demand approach to their sacred vocation. Many younger New Divinity men favored the latter choice. The result: a higher percentage of younger ministers were more likely to sever ties with their parish than were the older clergy. Many had legitimate complaints, as Bezaleel Pinneo pointed out to Benjamin Trumbull. Dan Huntington of Litchfield, David Smith of Durham, and Heman Humphrey of Fairfield, all friends of the Awakening, eventually left their churches over salary difficulties.[73] For others, a salary dispute was often reason enough—if not a

---

69. Scott, *From Office to Profession*, 8.
70. Ibid., xi.
71. Schmotter, "Ministerial Careers," 257.
72. Scott, *From Office to Profession*, 5.
73. Dexter, *Biographical Sketches* 5:109–12, 163–67; [Humphrey], *Memorial Sketches*, 133; Dan Huntington, *Memories, Counsels, and Reflections, by an Octogenary* (Cambridge, Mass., 1857), 55–57. The salary issue was taken up by the Litchfield South Association of ministers: "We contemplate with alarm the deficient support of the gospel in many parts of our land. The diversion of pastors from their peculiar employment to minister to their own necessities at a crisis when they need more than ever to be exclusively devoted to their calling" (Original Records of Litchfield County Association and Consociation, 1752–1814, 1 April 1812, CLH). Timothy Dwight observed that because "the price of the means of subsistence . . . doubled" from 1794 to 1814, ministerial salaries were "sufficiently stinted" (*Travels in New England and New York* 4:294).

pretext—for moving on to a more desirable position. In theory, Ebenezer Porter supported a long-tenured ministry, but when the opportunity arose to take a more prestigious appointment as a professor at Andover Seminary, his low salary figured into his decision to leave Washington. In drawing up a list of reasons for and against remaining in his present position, among the "motives for the negative" cited by Porter was an unhappy incident where "my salary was raised by *constraint* rather than by *conviction* and *choice*."[74]

Salary issues also surfaced in Porter's correspondence. Writing to a neighboring pastor, he noted that "Brother [Azel] Backus is in trouble and talks plainly of being dismissed. . . . I do believe however, that the people, on reflection, cannot part with so worthy a minister at *so cheap a rate*"[75] (emphasis added). Backus eventually left his church to accept the presidency of Hamilton College. Porter advised another pastor to "insist on *punctual* payment of salary. Do *set down your foot* on this subject, and *keep it down*."[76] Unlike Porter's generation, pastors of an earlier generation seldom confronted the unpleasant and often acrimonious issue of salary. And on those occasions when the matter created disagreement, it did not become grounds for separation. Nathan Strong, Jr., an older-generation New Divinity fixture in Hartford, amicably settled a salary dispute with First Church and remained there for over forty years.[77] More telling was the case of Alexander Gillett, who, though living on a "very small salary," acquired his property "before that unprecedented increase of the expense of living, which was induced" by the late eighteenth-century wars in Europe.[78] A similar situation held true for Peter Starr, who settled in Warren in 1772. Starr, however, seized a propitious moment—the fiftieth anniversary of his pastoral tenure—to remind his parishioners of their penurious ways. Nearing the end of his "Half-Century Sermon," and immediately after assuring his audience that the dawn of the millennial day was imminent, Starr startled his listeners with something of a rebuke. Millennium or no millennium, in choosing your next minister, he advised, "be not so anxious to obtain a cheap one as a good one." He assured them that they could "obtain a better minister than your old one:—but, you must not expect to obtain so cheap a one."[79]

Ambition, not salary, preoccupied some third-generation New Divinity

---

74. Matthews, *Memoir of Porter*, 55–56.

75. Ebenezer Porter to Asahel Hooker, 14 November 1805, Edward Hooker Letter Collection, No. 11, CLB. On the Consociation's dismissal of Backus, see Original Records of Litchfield County Association and Consociation, 1752–1814, 3 November 1812, CLH.

76. Matthews, *Memoir of Porter*, 294–95.

77. Dexter, *Biographical Sketches* 3:357–63; William Buell Sprague, ed., *Annals of the American Pulpit* (New York, 1857–69), 2:34–41.

78. Hart, "Sermon at the Funeral of Gillett," 33.

79. Peter Starr, "A Half-Century Sermon, delivered at Warren, March 8, 1822, . . ." (Norwalk, Conn., 1823), 18, 19.

pastors. One Sunday evening in 1797, while recording his thoughts in his diary, Edward Dorr Griffin bluntly confessed that he had been "too willing that the people should send me away, under the notion of getting a better place."[80] Griffin's career illustrates the mobile, ambitious generation of pastors emerging late in the century. Following his 1790 graduation from Yale, Griffin served churches in New Hartford, then Newark, New Jersey; taught at the newly established Andover Seminary; pastored Boston's Park Street Church; returned to Newark to take another pastorate; and finally concluded his career as president of Williams College. Griffin's accomplishments were extraordinary, but his vocational path anticipated the route that ministers of his generation would take. For example, Heman Humphrey, one of Griffin's colleagues, prepared for the ministry under Asahel Hooker, pastored churches in Fairfield, Connecticut, and Pittsfield, Massachusetts, and then assumed the presidency of Amherst College.[81]

Several younger New Divinity pastors in northwestern Connecticut left their congregations for reasons unrelated to ambition or financial gain. Josiah Andrews and William F. Miller found home missionary service more attractive than the repeated conflicts they encountered with their churches over New Divinity principles.[82] Both apparently took missionary sabbaticals to frontier settlements in order to escape tension in their home parishes. Perhaps typical of the evolving division of labor in the ministerial profession was Giles Cowles, who, after serving the Bristol church for eighteen years, accepted permanent missionary work in the Western Reserve under the auspices of the Connecticut Missionary Society.[83]

These unsettling issues—disputes over salaries, church factiousness, and personal ambition—contributed to increasing clerical instability in New England. Longitudinal studies spanning the early seventeenth to mid-nineteenth centuries conclude that the late 1790s and early 1800s mark a turning point in clerical mobility patterns, for during this period ministerial terms began to decline dramatically.[84] By tracing the careers of the thirty-seven pastors who provided narratives of the revivals occurring throughout New England between 1798 and 1808 to the *Connecticut Evangelical Magazine* (see Appendix 2), one can gain a more exact picture of clerical

---

80. Sprague, *Memoir of Griffin*, 18. Ambition was by no means a new issue. Philip Jacob Spener, the seventeenth-century Pietist leader, noted, "Behold how they seek promotions, shift from parish to parish, and engage in all sorts of machinations" (*Pia Desideria*, trans., ed., and intro. Theodore G. Tappert [Philadelphia, 1964], 45).

81. On the mobility of New Divinity pastors in Berkshire County, Massachusetts, see Birdsall, *Berkshire County*, 56–57; on Griffin, see Chapter 4; on Humphrey, see [Humphrey] *Memorial Sketches*.

82. Dexter, *Biographical Sketches* 5:239–43; 4:495–98; on New Divinity pastor-parish conflicts, see Chapter 5.

83. Sprague, *Annals* 2:330–31.

84. Scott, *Office to Profession*, chap. 4; Andrew, *Rebuilding the Christian Commonwealth*, chap. 3.

mobility within awakened communities and especially in parishes in north-western Connecticut. All but five of the pastors reporting revivals were Yale graduates. Nineteen graduated from college prior to 1789; eighteen received their degrees between 1789 and 1807. Eighteen of those graduating prior to 1789 held pastorates for thirty or more years, twelve for forty or more, and six for more than fifty years. Three of these pre-1789 graduates changed pulpits once during their career, whereas sixteen remained with one parish. Clearly, stability was the rule. With post-1789 graduates, a strikingly different picture emerges. Eleven of the eighteen held pastorates for twenty years or less; nearly one-half (eight) served more than one pulpit; and well over one-half became either full-time home missionaries or assumed positions of leadership in evangelical institutions following one or more pastorates.

This analysis suggests that those graduating from Yale prior to 1789 viewed the clerical vocation in a traditional manner: their life and pastoral duties centered around the local community. Many graduates after 1789, however, perceived their calling differently. Opportunities for leadership in benevolent societies and mission organizations, seminary teaching posts, college and seminary presidencies—opportunities often based upon prior success as a revivalist—drew these men away from the local community, creating a mobile, fluid generation of Congregational leadership.

Is there any correlation between the newer generation of ministers and their role in fomenting the Second Great Awakening in Connecticut? The younger New Divinity men preferred the active to the sedentary life; they judged their success by the number of converts gathered rather than by their persuasiveness with the pen. The older generation sowed the seed of revival, but the newer one cultivated and reaped it. The older generation desired revivals no less than the newer, but their conception of the ministry impeded their efforts. The younger New Divinity men viewed their vocation in different terms than their older cohorts; less content to spend long hours defending Edwards's theology of revival in writing, they took their case to the people in a forceful and aggressive manner.

A closer examination of the origins of the widespread revivals in north-western Connecticut suggests that a younger minister, Edward Dorr Griffin, created a heightened religious consciousness suitable for the resurgence of piety. As much as can be discerned, Jeremiah Hallock's congregation was the first to be awakened. But of any single individual, Griffin, not Hallock, seems to have been responsible for the general eruption of revival. In 1798–99 revivals broke out in a cluster of seven towns just east of Hartford.[85] In six of these parishes, the same pastor labored for twenty or more years. Further dissection reveals that within these six parishes, five clergy maintained their

---

85. The seven towns were Torringford, Canton Center, New Hartford, Torrington, Bloomfield, Burlington, and West Avon.

pulpits for thirty or more years, and of these, two exceeded fifty years. The impetus for these revivals does not appear to have come from the above six long-tenured ministers. Rather, it came from Griffin, a relative newcomer to the area.[86] As early as 1792 Griffin awakened the people of Derby and then New Salem in Middlesex County with his powerful preaching. Moving northwest into New Divinity territory, Griffin sparked revivals in Farmington in 1793 and then in New Hartford (one of the seven towns mentioned above) in 1798. What a George Whitefield did on a grand scale for the colonial first Great Awakening, an Edward Dorr Griffin did on a smaller scale for Connecticut's New Divinity Awakening. Richard Bushman's contention that "local ministers, adopting Whitefield's style of preaching, started revivals in their own congregations and aided neighboring pastors in theirs"[87] applies to the Griffin-led Awakening: local, *older* ministers, witnessing the success of this young, passionate preacher, adopted his style.

Although Griffin's contributions to the Second Great Awakening await fuller treatment in Chapter Four, what is crucial at this juncture is that he and other young New Divinity pastors energized their congregations and functioned as catalysts of revival without alienating their older peers. The discrepancies between the two generations must not be pressed too far.[88] In this chapter I have stressed the "generational gap" within the New Divinity movement; subsequent chapters emphasize the united efforts and common perceptions among New Divinity men. Shared ideological and theological convictions far outweighed differences in preaching style or clerical mobility. And on one particular issue all apostles of the New Divinity agreed: the spiritual condition of American society was in grave danger, threatened by forces within and without. This unanimous conviction spawned an organized effort to awaken Connecticut churches from their spiritual slumber. Pray one might, but the will of God was carried out not only in a posture of prayer but in pleadings from the pulpit and in the vigorous actions of the united brotherhood of ministers.

---

86. The only contemporary reference to Griffin as the individual at the center of the initial outbreak of revival comes from Heman Humphrey, who, during the winter of 1798–99, attended Griffin's parish and experienced his first religious stirrings. Humphrey noted that the influence of the revival in Griffin's New Hartford parish "extended far and wide" ([Humphrey], *Memorial Sketches*, 30).

87. Bushman, *From Puritan to Yankee*, 184.

88. One exception is Jeremiah Hallock, an older New Divinity man who placed great confidence in his parishioners and extensively utilized laymen during repeated revivals in Canton Center (see Yale, *Godly Pastor*, 2, 156).

2

"ADVANCING THE REDEEMER'S KINGDOM"

The Social Agenda and Institutions of Revival

In addition to a renewed evangelical conception of the ministry and the general conviction that all should come to a saving knowledge of Christ, other issues, more urgent in nature, inspired the New Divinity men to labor fervently for revival in the 1790s, to resuscitate the concert of prayer, engage faithfully in pastoral visitations, and travel continually from village to village in preaching teams. Such objectives and methods, of course, were not unique to the Edwardseans. One can cite precedent for corporate prayer, itineracy, and pastoral visitations as far back as New Testament times. And in the more recent past, various evangelical parties, both in Great Britain and America, employed these methods during the revivals of the eighteenth century. Moreover, simultaneous with New Divinity efforts in Connecticut, Presbyterians in New Jersey adopted nearly the same tactics, and other religious bodies used similar techniques for their own purposes.[1]

What then prompted these New Divinity pastors to engage in such efforts with a heightened spiritual energy probably not witnessed in the half century since the Great Awakening? This chapter examines developments during the

---

1. On Presbyterians in New Jersey, see Martha Tomhave Blauvelt, "Society, Religion, and Revivalism: The Second Great Awakening in New Jersey, 1780–1830" (Ph.D. diss., Princeton University, 1974), esp. 101–10.

crucial decade of the 1790s—one of the most contentious periods in American history—in which the New Divinity clashed with other groups for cultural dominance.[2] The stakes were high. The eternal future of the individual and the temporal future of the young Republic hung in the balance. Because Americans faced clear-cut choices over fundamental issues (the nature of the good life, the structure of the political system, and the meaning of freedom), competing political and religious groups engaged in a frenzy of activity for the hearts and minds of the people. A sense of urgency, born of the conviction that they lived in an era of national and religious crisis, motivated the New Divinity men to shape the course of history according to God's designs. "The present is not a period of indolence and indifference," declared a contributor to the *Connecticut Evangelical Magazine*, but a time "for the most vigorous exertions."[3]

For the New Divinity men, the future of the new nation lay not in an even balance; by 1790 it had tilted sharply to the left. America, they contended, was perched precariously on a slippery slope. No longer a spiritual beacon for the rest of the world, the infant nation was falling from grace. The "sacred cause of liberty" that united the spiritual and political passions of hundreds of New England colonists during the American Revolution dissipated in the aftermath of war. The "sacred cause" reverted to a lost, secular cause; true "liberty" deteriorated into the chaos of libertarianism. A fundamental question confronted the clergy: Could a revolution transpire without religion? Was it possible to break away from political authority and still survive without the authority of the Calvinist God?

Throughout the 1790s the Republic faced severe tests. It was threatened by a quasi-war with France, beset with persistent political factiousness, and continually endangered with domestic instability. According to the New Divinity (and many other clergy as well), the political predicament was merely symptomatic of a more serious problem. The real cause for the present state of decline was a religious malaise. Americans were spiritually backsliding. Infidelity, a catchall term applying to almost anything opposed to New Divinity evangelical Calvinism, struck at the nation's vitals, infecting the soul of the church. A contagious religious apathy sapped Americans of religious energy. Only "the most vigorous exertions," only the redoubled efforts of the New Divinity, could preserve the faith and rescue the nation from imminent destruction.

The intense labor of New Divinity ministers to halt the ominous trend of spiritual decline grew out of a shared interpretative framework. New Divinity

2. As Donald H. Meyer has noted in *The Democratic Enlightenment* (New York, 1976), "The 1790s mark the critical period in American intellectual history. The events of this decade were to determine the course of American thinking for years to come" (171).

3. *CEM* 2 (July 1801): iii.

ideology reflected traces of an inherited Puritan past, yet social and intellectual changes coupled with particular theological convictions impelled the New Divinity men to articulate their own distinct vision. The good society, a truly virtuous society, was a spiritually regenerate society. A revival was the sole prescription, the panacea, for curing the ills of the nation. Although the New Divinity men organized themselves primarily to save individual souls, they expected that the sum of regenerate individuals would save the collective soul of the nation. Hence, a certain ambivalence existed in the New Divinity mind regarding the body politic. On the one hand, because of their heightened stress on individual conversion and obedience to a universal moral law, the New Divinity men repudiated the corporate or civic sense of covenant theology that conceived church and society as inclusive.[4] On the other hand, they were Americans, new Americans, with a keen interest in the welfare of the new republic. As a result, the New Divinity men were politically interested observers, convinced that political stability was an important by-product—but surely not the goal—of their religious activity.[5]

Challenges to Clerical Authority

In the years following the Revolution, and, more immediately, in the wake of the Constitutional Convention in 1787, American life followed a course of political, economic, and social differentiation hitherto unknown. In their successful fight for republican ideals, longtime political leaders undermined their own standing among the populace.[6] Prior deference to community leaders gave way to popular electioneering and factional politics, so that by 1800, democracy proved to be no respecter of persons.[7] Also, America's preindustrial economy reached maturation, assuming a complexity and

4. This position was consistent with prior New Divinity views. During the Revolution, such stalwarts as Joseph Bellamy, Samuel Hopkins, Levi Hart, and Jonathan Edwards, Jr., employed the concept of universal moral law, not the concept of corporate covenant, to clarify a Christian's relationship to the body politic. Although these New Divinity men were deeply involved in politics, they repudiated the idea of American chosenness or American divine election. On Hopkins, see Mark A. Noll, *One Nation under God? Christian Faith and Political Action in America* (New York, 1989), 49–51; on Bellamy, Hart, and Edwards, Jr., see Mark Valeri, "The New Divinity and the American Revolution," *William and Mary Quarterly*, 3d ser., 46 (October 1989): 741–69.

5. For a discussion of the implications of political ideology on theology in this period, see Mark A. Noll, "Revival, Enlightenment, Civic Humanism, and the Development of Dogma: Scotland and America, 1735–1843," *Tyndale Bulletin* 40 (1989): 49–76.

6. Gordon S. Wood, "The Democratization of Mind in the American Revolution," in *The Moral Foundations of the American Republic*, ed. Robert H. Horowitz (Charlottesville, Va., 1979), 103–28.

7. See David H. Fischer, *The Revolution of American Conservatism: The Federalist Party in the Era of Jeffersonian Democracy* (New York, 1965).

dynamism stimulated by a network of banks and corporations, federal tariffs, and state aid.[8] Finally, the colonial form of social organization, based on "vertical institutions" of family, church, and community, gave way to new "horizontal" relations based on economic class and social status.[9] The older social order, characterized by hierarchical and authoritarian structures, was eventually displaced by the voluntary organization. Hence, membership was based not on compulsion, constraint, or law, but on consent, interest, and personal choice.

The impact of these changes on Connecticut's clergy was not altogether uniform. For some, a flattening of the social pyramid led to a loss of status. At least the Rev. David Daggett of New Haven thought as much. In 1787 he outlined the nature of this change and its implications for the ministry:

> The ministers, with two or three principal characters were supreme in each town. Hence the body of the clergy, with a few families of distinction, between whom there was a most intimate connection, in effect, ruled the whole state. The loss of this happy influence of the clergy, in this country, is deeply to be regretted, and is to be ascribed to two causes—*the increase of knowledge and growing opposition to religion. Knowledge has induced the laity to think and act for themselves, and an opposition to religion has curtailed the power of its supporters.*[10] (Emphasis added)

Daggett's assumption of declining clerical influence was reinforced by Henry Adams's comment in 1800 that "lawyers, physicians, professors, and merchants were classes, and acted not as individuals, but as though they were clergymen and each profession was a church."[11] But neither Daggett nor Adams spoke for the whole. Their assessments require qualification when applied to Litchfield and Hartford counties during the formative years of the Second Great Awakening. In general, the transition from a "vertical" to a "horizontal" society occurred more quickly in northern urban areas than in rural and southern sections of the country. The 1780s witnessed the emergence of purely secular political leadership on the national level, yet in the relative backcountry of northwestern Connecticut controlled by the New Divinity, the pastor remained the primary leader and confidant of the people. He was, recalled Harriet Beecher Stowe, "the intellectual centre of his

8. For an overview of these developments, see James A. Henretta, *The Evolution of American Society, 1700–1815* (Lexington, Mass., 1973), chap. 6.

9. Ibid., 206–7.

10. David Daggett, "An Oration, Pronounced at the Brick Meeting-House, in the City of New Haven, on the Fourth of July AD 1787" (New Haven, Conn., 1787), quoted in Richard D. Brown, "Spreading the Word: Rural Clergymen and the Communications Network of Eighteenth Century New England," *Proceedings of the Massachusetts Historical Society* 94 (1982), 12–13.

11. Quoted in Henretta, *Evolution of American Society*, 210.

own district."[12] It is reasonable to conclude that the successful efforts of the clergy to rouse their congregants derived in no small part from the respect they still commanded within their community. Among the institutions that shaped values and attitudes, the family remained first and foremost, followed by the minister and the church, the town meeting, and the school.[13] The transformation of the ministry from office to profession, then, did not necessarily imply an immediate decline in status vis-à-vis the rise of other professional groups. With the exception of the Hartford area, the outbreak of the Second Great Awakening occurred in rural, homogeneous villages largely untouched by the social differentiation more characteristic of urban areas.

The "causes" Daggett noted were more perceptive and truer to the mark than the effect of "the loss of this happy influence of the clergy." The "increase in knowledge" to which he referred was reflected in the multiplication of newspapers and post offices during the 1790s. During this decade all major trading towns in Connecticut (except Farmington) had newspapers at one time or another, while post offices increased from nine in 1790 to sixty-three in 1804.[14] This proliferation and accessibility of newspapers contributed to what Gordon Wood has called the "democratization of the American mind": the populace, having ready access to the printed word, competed with and eventually displaced the intellectual elites as the shapers and purveyors of ideas in American life.[15] Whereas once the clergy gathered and conveyed information to their parishioners, now the laity participated in a free marketplace of ideas.[16] This broad-based access to information undercut the minister's role as not only *a* word-bearer but also as *the* Word-bearer. Again, however, when Daggett's judgments are applied to northwestern Connecticut, the results are ambiguous. Like other parts of Connecticut, Litchfield and Hartford counties felt the explosion of the printed word, much of which was set off in the 1790s by the incursion of a market and commercial economy into these rural areas. But this increase in print did not necessarily undermine clerical strength. To their credit, the New Divinity clergy seized the opportunities that lay before them and challenged competing forces through their own organizational tactics and

12. Harriet Beecher Stowe, *Oldtown Folks*, 40th ed. (Boston, 1869), 453.

13. Douglas H. Sweet, "Church Vitality and the American Revolution: Historiographical Consensus and Thoughts toward a New Perspective," *Church History* 45 (September 1976): 349; see also Chapter 6.

14. Gaspare J. Saladino, "The Economic Revolution in Late Eighteenth-Century Connecticut," (Ph.D. diss., University of Wisconsin, 1964), 353; see also Donald H. Stewart, *The Opposition Press of the Federalist Period* (Albany, N.Y., 1969).

15. Wood, "Democratization of Mind."

16. See Nathan O. Hatch, "The Christian Movement and the Demand for a Theology of the People," *Journal of American History* 67 (December 1980): 547–67; idem, "Evangelicalism as a Democratic Movement," in *Evangelicalism and Modern America*, ed. George Marsden (Grand Rapids, Mich., 1984), 71–82; and William J. Gilmore, *Reading Becomes a Necessity of Life: Material and Cultural Life in Rural New England, 1780–1835* (Knoxville, Tenn., 1989).

theology. The clergy sought to retain or reestablish the premises of 'vertical' institutions while utilizing a modern, 'horizontal' concept—the voluntary organization—as well as their own printed sources to realize their goals. The publication of the *Connecticut Evangelical Magazine*, the touring clerical teams, and the conference meetings manifest this emerging voluntarism. At the same time, it is important to emphasize that neither clerical teams nor conference meetings were novel. The use of both in some form can be traced to English Puritanism and to the more recent Great Awakening and writings of Jonathan Edwards. Viewed in the broadest sense, these 'modern,' voluntary expressions have their origins in the sixteenth-century Protestant Reformation.

Infidelity, Liberty, and Virtue

Related to the increase of independent lay thought was Daggett's second cause for clerical displacement: "opposition to religion." The free marketplace of ideas not only led to religious convictions made independent of clerical influence but might also have led to outright rejection of orthodox Christianity. 'Infidelity' was the shibboleth employed by the clergy as shorthand, or a code word, to describe staunch opposition, while terms such as 'asleep,' 'dull,' 'stupid,' and 'indifferent' were used to portray a milder form. In short, infidelity epitomized all that was wrong with America.

Throughout the 1790s the decline of Christianity was a universal theme among the new Republic's clergy. Baptist, Congregational, Methodist, and Presbyterian leaders bemoaned the loss of religious fervor, the preoccupation with worldly concerns (particularly commercial interests), and the concomitant spread of infidelity.[17] As Martin Marty has shown, infidelity took many forms, including "imported intrusions, British deism, French Enlightenment thought, German idealism, along with liberal theology, immorality, popular disaffection with the churches, and the formal indigenous attack on religion."[18]

All New Divinity ministers railed at the declining state of spiritual affairs, but Timothy Dwight's well-known "Discourse on Some Events of the Last Century" (1801) represented the classic exposition. An overblown, hyperbolic lamentation over America's fall from grace, Dwight's account articulated contemporary clerical perceptions and captured the many-layered meanings of infidelity. The president of Yale College began by tracing the changes in

17. For a Southern response, see John B. Boles, *The Great Revival, 1787–1805: The Origins of the Southern Evangelical Mind* (Lexington, Ky., 1972).

18. Martin E. Marty, *The Infidel: Freethought and American Religion* (Cleveland, Ohio, 1961), 21.

the religious character of America that emerged after the Revolution. First, "the loose conduct and manners" of British officers and soldiers infected Americans. Then came "immoral doctrines and practices" such as profanation of the Sabbath, swearing, drunkenness, gambling, and lewdness; these were followed by "a light, vain method of thinking, concerning sacred things, a cold, contemptuous indifference toward every moral and religious subject." All of this prompted "a new and intimate correspondence with corrupted foreigners introducing a multiplicity of loose doctrines." Finally, "infidelity began to obtain in this country, an extensive currency and reception."[19]

Reflecting upon the effects of war in his later published *Travels in New England and New York,* Dwight dated the incursion of infidelity back to the French and Indian War, when a deistic English army actively proselytized unsuspecting colonists and undermined the divine inspiration of Scripture.[20] And yet the English were no match for the French. At least English infidelity could be countered with sound logic, but the French philosophy was "a system of abstract declarations which violated all just and sober criticism." Together from France, England, and Germany, "the dregs of infidelity were vomited upon us at once."[21] To Dwight, America's native innocence was violated by corruptions imported from across the Atlantic. The corrupt world that prompted the seventeenth-century exodus from England could not be escaped. Furthermore, an underground scheme hatched recently to spread irreligion and disrupt sound government in Europe now reached the shores of America. A group known as the Bavarian Illuminati allegedly organized secret clubs in America bent on subverting its religion and government. The Illuminati already inaugurated the cult of reason in Paris, and now its members in the United States hoped to turn the new republic into a shambles. Although there was no substance to the Illuminati's presence in America, the hoax exacerbated conservative clerical fears.[22]

Of course, one need not go beyond America's borders to discover other sources of irreligion. The writings of three Americans epitomized the infidelity and revolutionary potential of French thought as well as the free trade of ideas that Daggett so feared. Ethan Allen's *Reason the Only Oracle of Man* (1784), Thomas Paine's *Age of Reason* (1794), and Elihu Palmer's *Principles*

19. Timothy Dwight, "A Discourse on Some Events of the Last Century, delivered . . . January 7, 1801" (New Haven, Conn., 1801), 19.
20. Timothy Dwight, *Travels in New England and New York,* ed. Barbara M. Solomon (Cambridge, Mass., 1969), 1:259.
21. Ibid., 265.
22. Dwight, "Discourse," 51. The Bavarian Illuminati was founded in 1776 by Adam Weishaupt, a professor of law at the University of Ingolstadt. Its teachings consisted of Enlightenment rationalism spiced with anticlerical animus. See Vernon Stauffer, *New England and the Bavarian Illuminati* (New York, 1918), and Richard Hofstadter, *The Paranoid Style in American Politics and Other Essays* (New York, 1967), esp. chap. 1.

of Nature (1802) attacked revealed religion by substituting a natural, deistic theology. Of this triumvirate, Paine's notoriety was foremost, and conservative and liberal clergy alike attacked his work. Even William Bentley, the Unitarian of Socinian stripe, while a friend to Paine's political views, called the religious contents of the *Age of Reason* "contemptible."[23]

The clearest, most recent, and most discussed example of infidelity's triumph was the French Revolution, an event that played heavily into the clergy's interpretation of declension in America. Prior to 1798, most clergy welcomed the French Revolution. The happy triumph of republican ideals and the defeat of Catholicism appeared imminent. There was much in contemporary French events with which Americans could identify—at least for a time. But once it became clear that no gains in Protestantism would transpire, and that rationalist creeds would displace the ancient Christian creeds, the clergy forswore their earlier allegiance. The French now assumed the guise of infidels, agents of the Antichrist, and the Revolution represented the natural culmination of a nation mired for over a century in apostasy and infidelity.[24]

Like Dwight, other clergy fashioned a conspiratorial view of French history. Samuel Hopkins made great stock of the secret societies that had infiltrated the French schools, colleges, and courts.[25] In a "Review of the events in the last century," an editor for the *Connecticut Evangelical Magazine* asserted that "conspiracies have been formed against all religion and good government, which have produced the French Revolution, filling Europe, and other parts of the world with blood and carnage."[26] The Rev. Nathan Perkins of West Hartford offered a sweeping view of infidelity's triumph:

> For several years past, errors and heresies have prevailed in the United States, to an astonishing degree; owing no doubt to a variety of causes, and among others to the corruption of morals during our revolutionary war; and to the amazing scenes unfolded on the theatre of Europe; and to the number of loose, infidel and atheistic publications scattered over this country, in its whole length and breadth, by the votaries of MODERN PHILOSOPHY, and the NEW THEORIES of Liberty and

23. William Bentley, *The Diary of William Bentley, D.D., Pastor of the East Church, Salem, Massachusetts* (1905–14; reprint, Gloucester, Mass., 1963), 3:208.

24. For general background to the shift from Francophilia to Francophobia, see Gary B. Nash, "The American Clergy and the French Revolution," *William and Mary Quarterly*, 3d ser., 22 (July 1965): 392–412; and Henry F. May, *The Enlightenment in America* (New York, 1976), 252–77.

25. Samuel Hopkins, "A Serious Address to Professing Christians in the name, and from the words of Jesus Christ, recorded in Revelation 16:15" (1793) in *Sketches of the Life of the Late, Rev. Samuel Hopkins, D.D.*, ed. Stephen West (Hartford, Conn., 1805), 182–85.

26. *CEM* 1 (January 1801): 244; see also *CEM* 5 (January 1805): 244–45, and Dwight, "Discourse," 24–33.

Equality. Piety seemed to be flying away from our land—Religion declined—morality languished—vice grew bold—profaneness, revelling, dishonesty, and sinful amusements rapidly increased—universalism—infidelity—atheism—scoffing at all serious godliness—contempt of the holy sabbath—desertion of public worship—omission of family religion—and disregard of divine ordinances have spread, in a degree, which call for tears of grief, threatening, in their progress, to lay waste all the most valuable interests of society.[27]

In drawing the connection between new political theories and infidelity, Perkins was making a statement self-evident to Americans. Liberty, as Americans knew from their own experience, meant many things, and it was imperative for the survival of the Republic that they get it right. Dwight was quick to point out that *"the liberty of Infidels was not the liberty of New England."* What was the difference? On the one hand, the person who embraced the liberty of infidels was "a mere beast of prey." Infidel liberty was "licentiousness, . . . the spring of continual alarm, bondage, and misery." On the other hand, the true liberty of the American republic was characterized by restraint, by "equitable laws, by the religion of scriptures." This kind of liberty was "far less burthensome and distressing than the boasted freedom of Infidels."[28]

Dwight's general analysis of the nature of liberty, however bombastic in rhetoric, reflected the thinking of both New Divinity ministers and conservative political leaders. The two groups might disagree over whether infidelity led in fact to the kind of liberty Dwight thought it did, but they could agree on the necessity of the kind of liberty Dwight espoused. True liberty was restrained liberty, by which citizens understood "the perfect consistency of being free and being governed."[29] Enlightened political leaders, steeped in classical authors and in seventeenth-century English radical Whig political theorists, and evangelical Calvinists immersed in Scripture, while drawing their views from different sources, reached similar conclusions. Together they embraced the classical republican definition of liberty. The New Divinity contributed to the larger national debate that

---

27. Nathan Perkins, "Two Discourses on the Grounds of the Christian's Hope . . ." (Hartford, Conn., 1800), 38–39; see also Benjamin Trumbull, "A Century Sermon; or, Sketches of the history of the eighteenth century . . ." (New Haven, Conn., 1801), 8.

28. Dwight, "Discourse," 33; see also Asahel Hooker, "The Moral Tendency of Man's Accountableness to God . . . A sermon, preached on the day of the general election . . . May 9, 1805" (Hartford, Conn., 1805), 34, and Joseph Washburn, *Sermons on Practical Subjects* . . . (Hartford, Conn., 1807), 214. Even Ezra Stiles, Dwight's antagonist, agreed on the connection between deism and anarchy. He cites two instances where deism (infidelity) led to the ultimate of licentiousness, suicide (see *The Literary Diary of Ezra Stiles*, ed. Franklin B. Dexter [New York, 1901], 3:50, 348).

29. Dwight, "Discourse," 14.

raged in the 1790s over competing visions of liberty. How was the nation to interpret republican ideals? All agreed that liberty was the prized possession of the people. But according to the classical republican view, the will of the people was not "every man doing that which was right in his own eyes," but the expression of virtuous behavior. Liberty was ultimately grounded in virtue—the willingness of individuals to sacrifice selfish desires for the good of the community. A more liberal, Lockean conception of liberty clashed with this conservative, classical view. "Instrumental, utilitarian, individualistic, egalitarian, abstract, and rational, the liberal concept of liberty," notes Joyce Appleby, "was everything that the classical republican concept was not."[30]

Infidel liberty was liberty run wild—antinomianism at its worst. It had no place for virtue, no place for the moral character.[31] But why? From the New Divinity perspective, infidelity was more than a simple rejection of evangelical Christianity. Infidelity, like deism, was based upon the naturalistic assumptions of philosophical materialism—a position, argued Charles Backus, "inconsistent with the idea of an infinite spirit." If the universe is composed of matter, he reasoned, then "God and nature are synonymous terms."[32] And because nature can only reveal what the eye can see, the concept of life beyond the grave is spurious. From these assumptions, then, infidels rejected a state of future rewards and punishments. Without a hell, without the fear of having to answer ultimately to God for one's conduct, the New Divinity and other clergy concluded that all moral restraint collapsed. Was it any surprise that the infidel lived "in the practice of gross impiety, and in all those sensual and worldly lusts"?[33] Without the conviction that God would punish offenders of the moral law, governments could not endure—witness the recent events in infidel-ridden France. If infidels rejected God's eternal laws, then they certainly could not be trusted to uphold man's civil law. According to Noah Porter, "They have emancipated themselves from this bond of civil society by denying the punitive justice of God."[34] Porter reasoned that atheists, deists, or universalists—all those who rejected a future punishment—should be denied permission to take an oath of allegiance, for to these infidels

30. Joyce Appleby, *Capitalism and the New Social Order: The Republican Vision of the 1790s* (New York, 1984), 21.

31. For an extended discussion of "virtue" and its meaning during the Revolution and early republic, see Gordon S. Wood, *The Creation of the American Republic, 1776–1787* (Chapel Hill, N.C., 1969), 65–70.

32. Charles Backus, "A Sermon Delivered Jan. 1, 1801, containing a brief review of . . . the Eighteenth Century" (Hartford, Conn., 1801), 13.

33. Asahel Hooker, "The Immoral and Pernicious Tendency of Error. Illustrated in a Sermon, delivered . . . Jan. 1st, 1806 . . ." (Hartford, Conn., 1806), 8.

34. Noah Porter, "Perjury Prevalent and Dangerous: A Sermon, delivered in Farmington . . . September, 1813" (Hartford, Conn., 1813), 11; see also Jonathan Edwards, Jr., "A Future State of existence, and the immortality of the soul . . . ," in *Sermons on Important Subjects: Collected from a number of ministers, in some of the Northern States of America* (Hartford, Conn., 1797), 125; Backus, "Review of the Eighteenth Century," 11–13; and Hooker, "Moral Tendency of Man's Accountableness," 27–28.

an oath was "nugatory," "an insignificant ceremony."[35] Thus, the very patriotism of infidels was suspect, for "neither honor, constitutions, covenants nor oaths can have any binding influence on such men; and that in such people no confidence can be placed."[36]

From the perspective of the clergy the logic was clear: the spread of infidelity ultimately undermined the integrity of the new Republic. True religion not only offered individual salvation but provided the moral underpinnings upon which the republic was based. Nations have come and gone, said Asahel Hooker, because "they wanted that divine cement, the religion of Jesus, which unites man to man, and men to God."[37] How then was true virtue obtained? For the New Divinity men and other Evangelicals, virtue was the habit of a remade heart. Modifications in the institutional framework, which enlightened liberals of the early republic thought might check selfish pursuit and resuscitate virtue in a backhanded way, were ultimately futile.[38] No, true virtue was a love for God, a disinterested love of God, even to the point, as Samuel Hopkins and other New Divinity adherents reasoned, of being willing to be eternally damned for the glory of God. Ironically, while the threat of everlasting punishment was sufficient to deter natural man from crimes against his neighbor (functioning as supernatural positive law), such a threat was never the proper motivation for loving God. True religious affections, as all New Divinity men learned from Jonathan Edwards, were "primarily founded on the loveliness of the moral excellency of divine things."[39] Ultimately, God was not loved for the benefits he provided—in this case, escape from hell—but for his lovely and holy nature.

For the New Divinity, true virtue was supernatural virtue implanted by God in the act of regeneration. Charles Backus rejected the notion that recent advances in politics and science brought Americans any closer to true virtue. "In what light will posterity look upon the idea which contemplates a compleat recovery of the human race to virtue by political regenerations and the progress of science? . . . It will not be found that civil freedom or science, will regenerate the heart; nor that man can escape the dissolution of

35. Porter, "Perjury Prevalent and Dangerous," 11.
36. *CEM* 5 (January 1805): 244–45.
37. Hooker, "Moral Tendency of Man's Accountableness," 32.
38. As Wood points out, "the events of the 1780s forced a separation between those who clung to moral reform and regeneration of men's hearts as the remedy for viciousness and those who looked to mechanical devices and institutional contrivances as the only lasting solution for America's ills" (*Creation of the American Republic*, 428). The calling of the Constitutional Convention was, in part, a response to the recognition that under the Articles of Confederation, virtuous behavior was a scarce commodity. The framers of the Constitution were convinced that a restructuring of federal powers would promote virtue.
39. Jonathan Edwards, "A Treatise concerning Religious Affections," in *WJE: Religious Affections*, ed. John E. Smith (New Haven, Conn., 1959), 253.

this mortal frame."[40] Only through conversion, then, could one become a truly virtuous citizen. Every social malady—be it political, economic, or religious—was met with the same prescription: the necessity of a remade heart, or the renewal of a slothful, indifferent heart. In essence, the New Divinity men viewed the vagaries of history from a personal perspective. They knew nothing of a moral (virtuous) man contributing to an immoral (unvirtuous) society, for society's ills were never the result of impersonal forces or institutional malfunctioning. A one-to-one correspondence existed between individual morality and social morality. The lump sum of individual virtue totaled the collective virtue of society.

Federalists, Yes; a Political Clergy, No

A revival, then, was the only hope for escaping the upheavals of France. Turning back infidelity assured both the preservation of the true faith and the stability of good government. The fear of a disordered, atomistic, selfish, and, above all, infidel society naturally attracted Connecticut Congregationalists to embrace conservative or Federalist politics.[41] Indeed, voting patterns reveal that the northwest portion of the state remained overwhelmingly Federalist until the collapse of Connecticut Federalism between 1816 and 1820.[42] On the whole, however, there is little evidence to support the notion that the leaders of Connecticut's New Divinity Awakening preached Federalist politics from the pulpit or were even active in politics. None of the manuscript or printed sermons consulted for this study explicitly mentioned Federalist politics. The New Divinity clergy's concerns were primarily religious, and while Federalist politics reflected their vision of a cohesive, stable, and religious society, personal transformation through revival was their preoccupation.[43] As in so many matters, they heeded the advice of Edwards. In *The Distinguishing Marks* (1741), Edwards expressed an order of

40. Backus, "Review of the Eighteenth Century," 28; see also Nathan Strong, *Sermons on Various Subjects, Doctrinal, Experimental, and Practical* (Hartford, Conn., 1800), 60.

41. Ironically, the New Divinity's departure from covenant theology and stress on the individual contributed to the very atomism they decried and assisted in the eventual fusion of democratic Evangelicalism and democratic liberalism in the 1840s. See Noll, "Revival, Enlightenment, Civic Humanism, and the Development of Dogma," esp. 56–61.

42. See Edmund B. Thomas, Jr., "Politics in the Land of Steady Habits: Connecticut's First Political Party System, 1789–1820" (Ph.D. diss., Clark University, 1972), 218, 233, 269.

43. For a similar conclusion applying to Republican as well as Federalist clergy, see Ruth H. Bloch, *Visionary Republic: Millennial Themes in American Thought, 1756–1800* (New York, 1985), 214–15, 219–20. For exceptions to the rule of the New Divinity apolitical approach, see Allen C. Guelzo, *Edwards on the Will: A Century of American Theological Debate* (Middletown, Conn., 1989), 127.

priorities that the New Divinity apparently took to heart: "We are to consider that the end for which God pours out his spirit, is to make men holy, and not to make them politicians."[44] The *American Mercury* (Hartford) and other Republican newspapers accused the clergy of being a "political clergy," and clearly, Timothy Dwight and Jedidiah Morse filled issues of the *Palladium* with anti-Jefferson propaganda, but their writings are expressions of a social vision, not of political sermonizing.[45] Moreover, both Dwight and Morse were closer to moderate Calvinists, who differentiated less between church and society than did New Divinity men, whose pure church principles generally led them to make clearer distinctions between the two spheres.[46]

The New Divinity clergy consistently used public election-day and fast-day sermons—those occasions on which one would expect to find explicit partisan political pronouncements made—to preach the gospel. Because they viewed regenerate people as the basis of good government, rather than tout the blessings of a particular form of government, they preached that the origin of good government was rooted in the Christian faith. Piety, the proper relationship to God, lay at the basis of morality, the right behavior of citizens. "Indeed," announced Dan Huntington, "nothing but piety gives proper security for morality."[47] Put another way, law by itself was

44. Edwards, "The Distinguishing Marks of a Work of the Spirit of God," in *WJE: The Great Awakening*, ed. C. C. Goen (New Haven, Conn., 1972), 241.

45. The quote from the *American Mercury* is found in Stephen E. Berk, *Calvinism versus Democracy: Timothy Dwight and the Origins of American Evangelical Orthodoxy* (Hamden, Conn., 1974), 162–63. Historians' treatment of the issue ranges from Conrad Wright's comment in *The Beginnings of Unitarianism in America* (Boston, 1955) that "the congregational clergy . . . preached Federalism as well as Christianity" (249), and Kenneth Silverman's similar estimate that the clergy "openly preached politics from the pulpit" (*Timothy Dwight* [New York, 1969], 101), to Charles Keller's contention that there was "no evidence for believing that religious means were used for political ends" (*The Second Great Awakening in Connecticut* [New Haven, Conn., 1942], 56; see also 66, 146). Most scholars agree that politics and religion were inseparable during the early national period. For examples, see Richard J. Purcell, *Connecticut in Transition, 1775–1818* (Washington, D.C., 1918), 324–25; Alan E. Heimert, *Religion and the American Mind, from the Great Awakening to the Revolution* (Cambridge, Mass., 1966), 541; James M. Banner, Jr., *To the Hartford Convention: The Federalists and the Origins of Party Politics in Massachusetts, 1789–1815* (New York, 1970), 156–64; Paul Goodman, *The Democratic-Republicans of Massachusetts* (Cambridge, Mass., 1964), 91–96; and Charles I. Foster, *An Errand of Mercy: The Evangelical United Front, 1790–1837* (Chapel Hill, N.C., 1960), 133–34.

46. On Dwight's moderate, or "old," Calvinism, see Mark A. Noll, "Moses Mather (Old Calvinist) and the Evolution of Edwardsianism," *Church History* 49 (September 1980): 473–85, and Guelzo, *Edwards on the Will*, 221–29. On Morse, see Joseph W. Phillips, *Jedidiah Morse and New England Congregationalism* (New Brunswick, N.J., 1983). On the shared political views of Dwight and Morse, see K. Alan Snyder, "Foundations of Liberty: The Christian Republicanism of Timothy Dwight and Jedidiah Morse," *New England Quarterly* 56 (September 1983): 382–97.

47. Dan Huntington, "The Love of Jerusalem, the Prosperity of a People: A sermon, preached . . . May 12, 1814" (Hartford, Conn., 1814), 25; see also Backus, "Review of the Eighteenth Century," 27; Nathan Perkins, "The Benign Influence of Religion on Civil Government and National Happiness. Illustrated in a sermon, preached . . . on the Anniversary Election, May 12th, 1808" (Hartford, Conn., 1808), 17; and idem, "The National Sins, and National Punishment in the

insufficient to establish and maintain good government. Christianity was its sole guarantor. So Ammi Robbins in a 1789 election sermon urged his listeners "to leave the paths of sin . . . to become friends of the Lord Jesus. . . . This will make us good citizens and good subjects."[48] So Nathan Perkins took sixty pages in his 1808 election sermon—the longest of its kind between 1792 and 1830—to reiterate "the benign influence of religion on civil government and national happiness."[49] Naturally, the New Divinity targeted civil rulers with the gospel message. According to Nathan Strong, the Christian faith would "prepare men to rule, to ordain wise laws and execute them faithfully when called to high office."[50] Charles Backus confronted the Connecticut legislature with the claim that in order for rulers to exhibit true virtue, "the religion of Jesus Christ can have no substitute."[51]

Advice is one thing, political meddling and intrigue quite another. During the bitter presidential contest between Thomas Jefferson and John Adams in 1800, the Hartford North Association advised the clergy to "exercise great candor, moderation and prudence, and avoid such an interference as shall tend to destroy their usefulness as ministers of the gospel."[52] Given this cautious advice, William Bentley's complaint that "nowhere were the clergy so insolent as in Connecticut" in their Federalist politics seems unwarranted.[53] The rise of political parties, accompanied by some of the most virulent and libelous propaganda in the history of American politics, was viewed by the clergy in general and the New Divinity men in particular as draining spiritual energies and detracting from the primary goal of personal regeneration. "I fervently wish," confided Nathan Perkins to Jonathan Trumbull, that "the virulence & malignity of party might soon subside."[54] Samuel Hopkins wrote that involvement in political or civil concerns weakened the cause of Christ and was "in itself but a temporal, worldly matter, and comparatively of small

Recently Declared War, considered in a sermon, delivered July 23, 1812 . . ." (Hartford, Conn., 1812), 11.

48. Ammi Robbins, "The Empires and Dominions of this World, made Subservient to the Kingdom of Christ . . . A sermon, delivered . . . on the day of the anniversary election. May 14, 1789" (Hartford, Conn., 1789), 39; see also Nathan Strong, "A Thanksgiving Sermon, delivered November 27th, 1800" (Hartford, Conn., 1800), 11.

49. Richard A. Harrison, ed., *Princetonians, 1769–1775: A Biographical Dictionary* (Princeton, N.J., 1980), 100. Nathan Perkins, "A Preached Gospel, the Great Instituted Means of Salvation . . ." (Hartford, Conn., 1808), 6.

50. Nathan Strong, "On the Universal Spread of the Gospel: A sermon . . ." (Hartford, Conn., 1801), 32.

51. Charles Backus, "A Sermon, preached . . . on the Day of the Anniversary Election. May 9, 1793" (Hartford, Conn., 1793), 20; see also Robbins, "Empires and Dominions," 19, and Hooker, "Moral Tendency of Man's Accountableness," 37–38.

52. Consociation Records, Hartford North Association, 1790–1820, 136, CLH.

53. Bentley, *Diary* 3:208. In addition to his Unitarian sympathies, Bentley was also an ardent Jeffersonian.

54. Nathan Perkins to Jonathan Trumbull, 19 July 1806, Jonathan Trumbull, Jr., Collection, CHS.

importance." At best, a Christian "will be on that side in politics, which in his best and most mature judgment will most promote the cause of Christ."[55] During one of his stints for the Missionary Society of Connecticut, William F. Miller declined an invitation to address the Federalist-founded Washington Benevolent Society, claiming the missionary society had "no desire to meddle with politics" and alienate Democrats.[56] Stephen West of Stockbridge, Massachusetts, warned his flock in 1805 that inordinate political involvement was "one of Satan's snares—one of his baits to draw you off from religion."[57] Edward Dorr Griffin's view that "party spirit, whether in religion or politics, or whatever else, is a selfish spirit" represented the general consensus among the New Divinity clergy.[58] Not that they remained neutral in their political preferences. Shortly after Jefferson's election, Joseph Washburn left this amusing yet revealing account of a Hartford North Association meeting:

> The ministers all appear to feel that we have occasion to look out for perilous times—that persecution may yet take place in our day—that we may have to *abjure, flee,* or *die.* Mr. Miller (Bristol) says, if when we are together thus to pray a Jacobin mob should come upon us he don't know what he should do—He thinks he should not dare to deny Christ, and fears he could not *die* for him—he believes he should be one of the first *to Jump out of the window & run.*[59]

Redemptive History and the Millennium

The New Divinity men's perceptions of the past and present were linked inextricably to their view of the future. How, they repeatedly asked, did political factiousness and infidelity fit into God's sovereign plans? Why would a God who controlled the futures of peoples and nations permit such wickedness? From their theological perspective, theodicy was linked to the larger context of redemptive history. "Though we see infidelity spreading its baneful influence," wrote Alvan Hyde,

55. Hopkins, "Serious Address," in *Sketches of the Life,* 208–10.

56. Quoted in Ronald Harold Noricks, "'To Turn Them from Darkness': The Missionary Society of Connecticut on the Early Frontier" (Ph.D. diss., University of California, Riverside, 1975), 22.

57. Quoted in Donald Weber, *Rhetoric and History in Revolutionary New England* (New York, 1988), 145; see also Stephen West, "A Sermon, delivered on the Public Fast, April 9th, 1801" (Stockbridge, Mass., 1801), 22–25.

58. Edward Dorr Griffin, *Sermons not before published, on various subjects* (New York, 1844), 305; see also 123; idem, *Sermons by the Late Rev. E. D. Griffin, to which is prefixed a Memoir of his life, by W. B. Sprague, D.D.* (New York, 1839), 2:267; and idem, "Dr. Griffin's Letter to Deacon Hurlbut, on the subject of Open Communion" (Williamstown, Mass., n.d. [1829?]).

59. Joseph Washburn to Edward Dorr Griffin, 5 February 1801, Gratz Collection, HSP.

the adversaries of religion triumphing, and the cause of Christianity despised and persecuted; though nations are spilling the blood of each other, and the Kingdoms of the world are plunging into wars, and confusion, yet we may confide in the thought, that all things are designed to answer, and that they will certainly answer, some *important ends* . . . the wrath of man shall surely praise him. . . . If all events are under the control, and brought about by the agency of God, it is certain that the changes and revolutions which take place in the world, will, in some way or other, advance the Redeemer's kingdom.[60]

For the New Divinity, a knowledge of God's purposes in history offered hope for renewal. The Old Testament paradigm offered a cyclical model of spiritual awakening where popular apostasy and national affliction were followed by popular repentance and restoration. If the people turned from their sin, God would honor their act of repentance with blessing and spiritual renewal. In times of declension there was cause for alarm, dismay, and jeremiads—but always a concurrent glimmer of hope, hope for regeneration, hope that God would intervene and turn the wheel of history to another cycle of restoration.

This schema, or view of history, pressed the very limits of understanding, for in the human drama there was much more than met the mortal eye. The outworking of human history was veiled history, a mere prelude to things to come. Whereas human history contained periods of backsliding and renewal, providential history subsumed human history within a teleological framework. God would eventually intervene in the cyclical historical process and inaugurate the millennium, a thousand years during which, according to the New Divinity interpretation, Christ's rule and kingdom would spread throughout the earth. Exactly when this golden age would take place was unknown. Though seeing through a glass darkly, the New Divinity clergy had the tools at their disposal at least partially to illumine the picture. Since the Reformation, not a few English and American Protestant clergy and laymen preoccupied themselves with the millennial timetable, issuing forecasts and prognostications about eschatology and the millennial reign according to their reading of the prophetic passages of Scripture, especially those found in Isaiah, Daniel, and Revelation. Unraveling these prophetic utterances perplexed the best theological minds; then forging them into a coherent pattern

---

60. Alvan Hyde, "The Purpose of God displayed in abasing the pride of nations," in *Sermons on Important Subjects* (Hartford, Conn., 1797), 289. According to Hyde, it was necessary to look beyond "secondary causes"—e.g., calamity, revolutions—to the "first cause," viz., God's sovereign plan (280–89).

proved a formidable task, yet the mental world of the New England clergy was built upon such an eschatological framework.[61]

Within the drama of salvation history, according to the apocalyptic Book of Revelation, the end of time is characterized by a period of tribulation for Christians. During this time, the angels of the Lord pour out seven vials, or plagues, indicative of God's wrath upon the world (Revelation 15). Following the outpouring of the seventh vial, Satan is bound and cast into a bottomless pit for a thousand years, at which time, according to New Divinity calculations, a spiritual Christ and his saints rule for the millennium. Next, Satan emerges again to do battle, only to be once and for all crushed. The Last Judgment of Christ then follows.

The clergy generally agreed that five vials had been poured out and that the French Revolution precipitated the outpouring of the sixth. Samuel Hopkins predicted that "we live in the time of the sixth vial," and an author in the *Connecticut Evangelical Magazine* confidently asserted, "Doubtless a considerable part of the prophecies under the sixth vial have had their completion."[62] Others, convinced that the end was even closer, posited the appearance of the seventh vial. Nathan Strong thought that "we are come to . . . the last days," for "it is the sixth and the seventh vials in combination that are running."[63] And William F. Miller, the eccentric pastor at Windsor who wrote lengthy treatises on prophecy, concluded in 1808 that "the seventh vial was now pouring out."[64]

61. See James West Davidson, *The Logic of Millennial Thought: Eighteenth-Century New England* (New Haven, Conn., 1977), and Bloch, *Visionary Republic*, for a full account of eighteenth-century New England clerical views. In his *Roots of Fundamentalism: British and American Millenarianism, 1800–1930* (1970; reprint, Grand Rapids, Mich., 1980), Ernest Sandeen noted that early nineteenth-century Americans were "drunk on the Millennium" (42). Bloch estimates that from 1793 to 1796, the number of works printed per year in America on eschatological themes was five to ten times that of the years 1765 to 1792 (*Visionary Republic*, 121). For articles and references in early issues of the *CEM* dealing with eschatological themes, see 1 (July 1800): 91–94; 1 (October 1800): 125–29; 1 (November 1800): 161–65; 1 (January 1801): 249; 1 (February 1801): 291–99; 1 (May 1801): 412–13; 2 (January 1802): 243–47, 252; 2 (May 1802): 407; 4 (July 1803): 22–24; 4 (August 1803): 50–53, 55–59; 4 (November 1803): 178. For a discussion of Southern millennial views, see Boles, *Great Revival*, 100–110.

62. Hopkins, "Serious Address," in *Sketches of the Life*, 181; *CEM* 1 (January 1800): 248.

63. Nathan Strong, "Political Instruction from the Prophecies of God's Word: A sermon, preached . . . Nov. 29, 1798" (Hartford, Conn., 1798), 14, 23; see also Trumbull, "Century Sermon," 34; Strong, "On the Universal Spread of the Gospel," 35; and Timothy Dwight, "A Discourse, in Two Parts, delivered July 23, 1812, on the National Fast . . ." (New Haven, Conn., 1812), 8.

64. William F. Miller, "A Dissertation on the Harvest of Mystical Babylon" (Hartford, Conn., 1808), 41; see also his earlier "Signs of the Times, or the Sure Word of Prophecy: A Dissertation on the Prophecies of the Sixth and Seventh Vials . . ." (Hartford, Conn., 1803). Miller's prophetic scheme dated the coming of the millennium around the year 2000. More bizarre than Miller was the Edwardsean David Austin (Yale, 1779), who held a Presbyterian pastorate in New Jersey (1788-97) and later served the Congregational church in Bozrah, Connecticut (1815–31). Austin not only rejected the more conventional postmillennial views of the day, but, after a severe bout with scarlet fever left him partially deranged, he prophesied that Christ would visibly return on 15 May 1796.

A precise dating of the end of the sixth or seventh vials depended on the unfolding of contemporary historical circumstances, as well as which set of prophetic symbols one manipulated. In general, however, as the late eighteenth-century revivals advanced in both place and duration, fears subsided and confidence grew that the millennium was an approaching reality. This evolution in prophetic understanding can be seen in statements made over a period of three decades. Readings of the signs of the times ranged from Samuel Hopkins's gloomy forecast in 1793 that "the time of greatest suffering is yet to come," to the cautious optimism of a writer for the *Connecticut Evangelical Magazine* in 1803 "that the events of the times are favorable to the hypothesis of an increasing of the church of Christ both in numbers and graces," to Edward Dorr Griffin's ebullience a decade later that "we have already seen . . . that period of which is to extend the morning of the millennium."[65] Hopkins's views represent the predominant thinking about the millennium by New Divinity men and other New England Congregationalists in the last half of the eighteenth century. He minimized the efficaciousness of human activity in the present period of declension and found spiritual consolation in knowing that such a high concentration of infidelity portended the millennium. James West Davidson has called this view "the afflictive model of progress," in which, out of evil, God brings good. This model expressed the paradox of hope amid despair, or optimism in light of God's wrath. In short, the advance of Christ's kingdom was preceded by or coincided with the raging of a loosed Satan.[66] The Rev. Charles Backus, delineating these views in a 1791 sermon, stated:

> We are on the stage in one of the most eventful periods the world ever saw. The spirit of free inquiry which was roused a few centuries ago, after slumbering a thousand years, has of late made an amazing progress. Civil and ecclesiastical tyranny have received a fatal wound, and we hope will soon be banished from the earth. The world is swiftly preparing for the general spread of light and truth as predicted long ago in the oracles of God. An acquaintance with human nature, and the history of the church, will not permit us to look for the accomplishment of Zion's hopes, without great convulsions in the

Dismissed by the New Jersey presbytery, Austin returned to New Haven in 1797 and purchased buildings and a wharf to be used by American Jews as a way station to the Holy Land to await the Messiah's imminent return. See William B. Sprague, ed., *Annals of the American Pulpit* (New York, 1857–69), 2:195–206, and James W. Davidson, "Searching for the Millennium: Problems for the 1790s and the 1970s," *New England Quarterly* 45 (June 1972): 241–61.

65. Hopkins, "Serious Address," in *Sketches of the Life*, 215; *CEM* 4 (August 1803): 51; Edward Dorr Griffin, "A Sermon, preached October 20, 1813, at Sandwich, Massachusetts, at the Dedication of the Meeting House . . ." (Boston, 1813), 12–13.

66. Davidson, *Millennial Thought*, 129, 131–32, 136–41, 270–76, 279–80.

kingdoms of the world. Great abuses of reason and the passions in matters of religion are also to be expected, before Jerusalem shall become the joy of the whole earth.[67]

On the other hand, Griffin's view represented a fundamental shift in the millennial paradigm, a shift that took place in the late 1790s and early 1800s.[68] He utilized the afflictive model of progress to explain the past, but given the recent gains from the Awakening and its outgrowth in foreign missions, millennial expectations rose. Griffin infused his postmillennial outlook with a more optimistic and progressive view of the future than prophetic interpreters rendered in the 1790s. He instructed graduates of Williams College to

> open to any page of Isaiah's prophecy and you will see the destruction of the enemy and the upbuilding of the Church put together as contemporaneous parts of one work. . . . Thus through all the book the prophet goes backwards and forwards from mercy to wrath and from wrath to mercy, as inseparable parts of one whole. He every-where exhibits God as coming with mercy in one hand and the sword in the other to build up Zion and to crush his enemies in one great campaign. And it is plain that these predictions ultimately relate to the day which is now opening on the world.[69]

Speculation as to which came first—a postmillennial eschatology that shaped human events, or events that gave credence to postmillennial views—must remain just that.[70] It is clear, however, that as revivals spread and as the

67. Charles Backus, "The Faithful Ministers of Jesus Christ Rewarded: A sermon, delivered . . . April 6, 1791" (Litchfield, Conn.: [1791]), 12; see also CEM 6 (July 1805): 10.

68. For a discussion of this shift, see Davidson, Millennial Thought, chap. 7, and Bloch, Visionary Republic, chap. 9.

69. Edward Dorr Griffin, Sermons (1844), 316, 317, 319. For Griffin's prophetic calculations and millennial expectations, see "Sermon Preached At Sandwich, Massachusetts"; "Living to God: A sermon, preached June 16, 1816 . . ." (New York, 1816); "A Plea for Africa: A sermon preached October 26, 1817 . . ." (New York, 1817); "An Address to the Public, on the subject of the African School . . ." (New York, 1816); "Foreign Missions: A sermon, preached May 9, 1819 . . ." (New York, 1819); "The Claims of Seamen: A sermon, preached November 7, 1819 . . ." (New York, 1819); "The Kingdom of Christ: A missionary sermon preached . . . May 23, 1805" (Andover, Mass., 1821); "A Sermon preached before the Annual Convention of the Congregational Ministers . . . May 29, 1828" (Boston, 1828); and Sermons (1844): 239–42.

70. Davidson contends that events, particularly the modern foreign-missions movement, preceded a coherent postmillennial eschatology: "The idea that Christ would come only after the millennium, for instance, was common enough at the end of the seventeenth century, but it was not used as a linchpin on which to hang a rationalized psychology of motivation. Postmillennialism thus came into its own only when divines consciously argued that Christ's figurative millennial reign demanded human action; that natural catastrophes were inappropriate means of providential accomplishment in such a scenario; and that

missionary enterprise expanded, bolder predictions were made to fit a more coherent postmillennial prescription. These predictions, in turn, gave great confidence to many that they could play a part in building up Zion. Prophecy, in a sense, was self-fulfilled.

According to Richard Shiels, the New Divinity expedited prophecy by creating the "myth of the second great awakening."[71] That is, before the actual outpouring of revival in the late 1790s, a number of clergy announced the inauguration of an awakening. The myth functioned as a sacred story, as a powerful rhetorical or narrative device (not as "fiction"), harking back to the Great Awakening and anticipating what lay head. The myth provided coherence and assurance—a heuristic tool by which to gauge the future— that even in the midst of infidelity, spiritual declension, and the seeming loss of clerical authority, God would break through. The myth gained its real potency, however, within the wider context of the clergy's view of history. For the New England divines, theodicy was linked to their view of redemptive history ascertained and calculated through biblical prophecy. The precise point at which God would reverse the trend of infidelity was unclear, but Connecticut's New Divinity clergy expressed confidence in two things: first, a sovereign God controlled the world, contemporary events notwithstanding; second, the increase in what they perceived as unprecedented evil portended a historical turning point in which God would turn back Satan's minions. "From the history of divine providence in past ages," wrote Giles Cowles following the 1799 revival in Bristol, "it appears, that the most dark and gloomy season in the moral world often immediately precedes times of great light and joy."[72] Were not the walls of Zion built up in troublesome times?

Organizing for Revival

As agents of God's sovereign design, the clergy believed they had to seize the moment. The cry of the New Divinity votaries for human exertion to repair the crumbling walls of Zion was increasingly heard. "That which is now

---

consequently, history was to be seen as a series of gradual, progressive steps toward this-worldly perfection" (*Millennial Thought*, 262) (emphasis added).

71. Richard D. Shiels, "The Connecticut Clergy in the Second Great Awakening" (Ph.D. diss., Boston University, 1976), chap. 1. Shiels is indebted to Mircea Eliade's definition of myth in *Myth and Reality*, trans. Willard R. Trask (New York, 1963). On the New Divinity's creation of the "myth" of the Great Awakening, see Joseph Conforti, "The Invention of the Great Awakening, 1795–1842," *Early American Literature* 26 (1991): 99–118.

72. CEM 1 (August 1800): 56. This view reflects the afflictive model of progress, which, despite receding into the background as a sole explanatory model, continued to play an important rhetorical role. It also provided a much simpler way of viewing history.

opening," declared Edward Dorr Griffin, "is to be an age of action, of energy, of enterprise, of devotedness, generosity, of which . . . former generations had no conception."[73] Charles Backus, Griffin's neighboring colleague in Somers, insisted that

> the present attritions and shaking in the religious world loudly call upon us to gird on the armor of righteousness on the right hand and on the left, and to maintain the simplicity of gospel faith and practice, amidst the sallies of enthusiasm, the licentiousness of luke-warm Christians, and the scoff of open infidels. . . . Let us think and act on the great scale of Christian benevolence.[74]

Backus's pleas were carried forward on two fronts: first, on a formal level within the county associations and consociations and the Connecticut General Association;[75] second, and more significantly, on an informal, local level where the united brotherhood of ministers worked together to promote revival.

In 1794, Walter King of Norwich—primarily at the instigation of David Austin, a fervent premillennialist and Presbyterian minister in Elizabethtown, New Jersey—circulated a letter throughout the consociations of Connecticut recommending the reinstitution of the quarterly concert of prayer. Broached originally by Edwards in "Some Thoughts concerning the Revival" (1743) and then detailed in "An Humble Attempt" (1747), the concert of prayer consisted of the united efforts of "praying societies" to implore God for mercy and to pour out his Spirit.[76] Now, once again, at the behest of King and Austin, a

---

73. Griffin, *Sermons* (1844), 319.

74. Backus, "Faithful Ministers," 13.

75. Connecticut Congregational polity remained based on the Saybrook Platform (1708), despite the fact that the platform had had no binding legal authority since 1784, when it was removed from the state laws. The platform provided for three forms of organization: (1) county associations, composed exclusively of ministers, which dealt with issues of collective concern to ministers and licensed new ministers; (2) consociations, composed of both ministers and laymen, which dealt primarily with local church problems; and (3) the General Association, composed of delegates or representatives from county associations, which advised and oversaw ministers and churches. The present study focuses on the four associations of Litchfield and Hartford counties—Hartford North and Hartford South (both formed in 1709), and Litchfield North and Litchfield South (both formed out of the original Litchfield Association in 1792). See Keller, *Second Great Awakening*, 9–10; and *Contributions to the Ecclesiastical History of Connecticut* (New Haven, Conn., 1861), 307–8, 313–14. For the text of the Saybrook Platform, see Williston Walker, ed., *The Creeds and Platforms of Congregationalism* (1893; reprint, Philadelphia, 1969), 463–523.

76. Edwards, "Some Thoughts concerning the Present Revival of Religion in New-England," in *WJE: The Great Awakening*, 518–21. According to Emerson Davis, the concert of prayer had its origins in early eighteenth-century Great Britain and was used extensively in the Cambuslang revivals in Scotland in the 1740s. After Edwards received a published memorial of these revivals, he wrote "An Humble Attempt." See Davis, *The Half Century; or, A History of the Changes that have taken place, and events that have transpired, chiefly in the United States, between 1800 and 1850* (Boston, 1851), 299–300. As noted by Alan Heimert, Edwards suggested using the concert of prayer in "Thoughts Concerning the Revival"

concert was called. The Hartford North Association, including the towns of Simsbury, Farmington, Hartford, and Windsor, responded quickly and affirmatively. At its October 1794 meeting, the association drafted a letter to the General Association of Connecticut, the General Assembly of the Presbyterian Church, and the Convention of Clergy in Massachusetts, stating that the ministers "would wish to contribute their assistance in a regular and authorized manner, to a proposal for a general concert of prayer . . . for the revival of religion and the copious effusions of divine grace and spirit." In the meantime, the churches of the Hartford North Association would conduct "stated sessions of public prayer, once a fortnight, on Wednesday afternoon."[77] Apparently, these prayer meetings had the desired effect, as nearly every church within the association shared in the revivals of 1798–99.

The Hartford North Association also took the lead in the formation of the Connecticut Missionary Society. The haunting fear of the "seduction of infidelity" on the frontier inspired this initiative. Especially frightful was the knowledge that the settlers "are our old neighbours; our brothers, our sisters, our children," who "are gradually forgetting the religious habits and truths received in their youth."[78] As early as 1788, the association sent settled ministers on brief missionary tours to the New England frontier region. Nine years later, its members formed a missionary society "for the purpose of collecting funds from the pious and benevolently disposed, to support missionaries, who may carry the glad tidings of salvation among our brethren, in the borders of the wilderness."[79] Recognizing that the consociation might be accused of "precipitance or arrogance" by the General Association, its ministers urged a statewide missionary society under the auspices of the General Association. Other consociations agreed with the suggestion, and in 1798, the General Association took control of the Connecticut Missionary Society.

These and other institutional consolidations of the Second Great Awakening have received thorough treatment by historians, while the behind-the-scenes efforts of individual clergy have been overlooked.[80] Clerical exertions to secure revival at the parish level have been bypassed in favor of the more

---

before its popular use in Scotland (*Religion and the American Mind*, 80–81). For a recent discussion of the transatlantic use of the concert of prayer, see Michael J. Crawford, *Seasons of Grace: Colonial New England's Revival Tradition in Its British Context* (New York, 1991), 229–31.

77. Hartford North Association, Minutes, 1714–1800, CLH; see also *CEM* 2 (January 1802): 268–70. At its 16 June 1795 meeting, the General Association adopted a recommendation for "seasons of prayer for the revival of religion." See *Records of the General Association of Connecticut, 1800* (Hartford, Conn., [1890]), 159, 163.

78. *CEM* 1 (March 1801): 324.

79. Consociation Records, Hartford North Association, 119–20, CLH.

80. For the institutional consolidations in Connecticut, see Keller, *Second Great Awakening*, esp. chaps. 4–7, and Shiels, "Connecticut Clergy."

visible official pronouncements and activities. Yet without the clergy's success at the grass-roots level, the Awakening in Connecticut would have assumed a decidedly different character. The revivalist here today, gone tomorrow, may offer immediate excitement and a quick spiritual boost, but the long-term effects of his short stay are often negligible, and in some cases, disruptive.[81] The indigenous revivals in northwestern Connecticut enabled the New Divinity ministers to maintain decorum, consolidate gains, and follow up new converts with instruction and encouragement. At the parish level, these evangelical pastors labored individually and collectively to promote revival. Following his conversion in 1791, Edward Dorr Griffin displayed his enthusiasm for revival by conducting frequent meetings for the purpose of arousing sinners. He explained, "I felt it to be a principal recommendation of a place as my residence that the people would allow me to hold as many meetings as I pleased. I held extra meetings in every place I preached, which was a new thing in that day. What then appeared strange, bating some youthful indiscretions has long since become the general usage."[82] Other clergy sought to heighten spiritual concern among their parishioners by calling extra meetings. In 1799, Nathan Perkins began holding an "anxious meeting" for those "inquiring what they should do to be saved."[83] Similarly, Israel Day and Timothy Cooley met with seekers at their parish homes, and Jeremiah Hallock conducted house-to-house visitations.[84]

Individual efforts, however, were not nearly as effective as clerical visitation teams. The exchange of ministers for Sunday services was a common practice in New England, necessitated by a pastor's dual responsibility to tend his farm as well as to shepherd his flock of parishioners. The five or six weeks of the haying season, between late June and early August, were the busiest. During this time the rural clergy (as well as craftsmen and merchants and their help) reluctantly abandoned their regular vocations for the fields.[85] In response to the time-consuming and exhausting demands of labor, ministers developed a system of exchanges in order to minimize sermon preparation.[86] If organized

---

81. On the questionable long-term effects of revivalists, see William G. McLoughlin, *Modern Revivalism: Charles Grandison Finney to Billy Graham* (New York, 1959), esp. 524–30; on the disruptive effects of itinerating revivalists during the Great Awakening, see Clarence C. Goen, *Revivalism and Separatism in New England: Strict Congregationalists and Separate Baptists in the Great Awakening* (New Haven, Conn., 1962).

82. Quoted in William B. Sprague, *Memoir of the Rev. Edward D. Griffin, D.D.* (New York, 1839), 10.

83. Nathan Perkins, "A Half-Century Sermon . . ." (Hartford, Conn., 1822), 21.

84. *CEM* 3 (December 1802): 227; *CEM* 2 (January 1802): 270; *CEM* 1 (October 1800): 138.

85. [Zephaniah Moore Humphrey], *Memorial Sketches: Heman Humphrey, Sophia Porter Humphrey* (Philadelphia, 1869), 35; Jack Larkin, *The Reshaping of Everyday Life, 1790–1840* (New York, 1988), 19.

86. Farmington diarists made constant mention of these exchanges. For examples, see Julia Cowles, *The Diaries of Julia Cowles, 1797–1803*, ed. Laura Hadley Mosley (New Haven, Conn., 1931); Diary of Mary Treadwell Hooker, CSL; David Gleason Diary, Farmington Room, Pamphlets, FVL; and Mary Ann Cowles Diary (1819–24), Farmington Room, Pamphlets, FVL.

properly, a pastor could travel the summer circuit preaching a single sermon. The idea of clerical visitation, then, was not entirely novel but the outgrowth of the Sabbath-day exchange system. And yet the organization of clerical *teams* went beyond the utility of exchanges, for the very purpose of visitation teams was to spiritually reenliven parishioners, not to relieve pastors from onerous paravocational responsibilities. In "Some Thoughts concerning the Revival," Edwards encouraged ministers to continue to "act as fellow helpers in their great work . . . and with united strength, to promote the present glorious revival of religion: and to that end [they] should often meet together and act in concert." For "as had been found by experience," ministers with "united zeal . . . would have a great tendency to awaken attention."[87] Over a half century after ministerial teams lit the fires of the Great Awakening, the fire was reignited.

Ebenezer Porter reported that ten ministers once visited him, none ever having had a revival in his church. Together they resolved to renew the system of preaching by twos utilized during the Great Awakening. Once deployed, revivals followed,[88] as is verified by most accounts of the Connecticut revivals appearing in the *Connecticut Evangelical Magazine*. For example, Simon Waterman recounted that little spiritual activity occurred in his parish until visiting ministers spoke at an evening lecture.[89] Some stirrings of revival were evident in Harwinton, but when a team of neighboring pastors visited, one hundred people were "impressed" about their condition.[90] Ammi Robbins, longtime minister at Norfolk, claimed that his colleagues "were undoubtedly . . . a means of promoting the work."[91] Other pastors participated in revivals in West Avon, Bristol, and Farmington.[92] Following his entry, "A Yr. Never to be forgotten," in the Bristol church records for 1799, the Rev. Giles Cowles noted that Joshua Williams of Harwinton and Joseph Washburn lent assistance during that year of divine outpouring.[93]

In their private correspondence and journals, the clergy emphasized the importance of mutual assistance. Writing to three colaborers about the recent revival in Torringford, Samuel Mills exuded, "We live in a wonderful day!! The Lord, this great Lord of Heaven and Earth hath visited this place." He then requested "friendly assistance from all that can afford it to me."[94] In the same way, Edward Griffin implored the Rev. Lynde Huntington to "come over

87. Edwards, *WJE: The Great Awakening*, 508.
88. Ebenezer Porter, *Letters on Revivals of Religion* (Boston, 1833), 18.
89. *CEM* 2 (July 1801): 25.
90. *CEM* 1 (June 1801): 463.
91. *CEM* 1 (February 1801): 313.
92. *CEM* 1 (September 1800): 102; *CEM* 1 (August 1800): 56; *CEM* 1 (April 1801): 380.
93. Bristol First Congregational Church Records (1742–1897), CSL.
94. Samuel J. Mills to Asahel Hooker, Weston, and Bordwell, 3 January 1799, Edward Hooker Letter Collection (8a), CLB.

into our Macedonia and help us."[95] Because poor health and the responsibilities of a theological school consumed much of Asahel Hooker's energy, he relied upon the help of others during seasons of revival. "I have been for some time," he wrote, "much assisted by neighboring ministers, and have reason to expect, that their assistance will be continued."[96]

In the journal of Jeremiah Hallock the outburst of united activity emerges in full force. During the week of 24 June 1799, Hallock and several neighboring pastors toured the westernmost villages of Litchfield County on horseback. Hallock and Alexander Gillett preached at meetinghouses in North and South Canaan, Salisbury, Cornwall, Kent, and Warren from Monday through Friday. On Saturday, they were joined by Peter Starr and Joshua Knapp in Milton. The group then split up, with Hallock and Gillett doubling back to Warren on Sunday and then completing their tour on Monday at Goshen.[97]

These numerous visitation teams heightened expectations among the people. Jonathan Miller of the West Britain Society reported that when two ministers visited, "the people . . . expected something unusual."[98] And as the news of revival spread from town to town, those yet unblessed expected spiritual renewal in their own parishes. Clearly, this expectation contributed to the clergy's effectiveness. When Edward Dorr Griffin returned from a revival in West Simsbury and relayed the news to his New Hartford congregation, "Christians began to break their minds to each other; and it was soon discovered that there had been for a considerable time fomenting in each breast a secret and increasing desire for a revival of religion; and while all were the subjects of the same exercises, each one supposed himself to be singular."[99] The results of this religious effervescence did not escape the Harwinton church, where "an uncommon effect" was reported after news of a nearby revival reached the parishioners.[100] Likewise, after hearing of divine visitations at an adjacent parish, the Norfolk church was "induced . . . to pray that we might have a gracious visit also."[101]

The primary vehicle for the transmission of revival was the conference meeting. The conference had long been a part of Puritan devotional piety, dating back to Puritan lay practices of sixteenth-century England. These

95. Edward Dorr Griffin to Lynde Huntington, 14 March 1799, p. 3, BL.

96. Asahel Hooker to Samuel J. Mills, 16 July 1807, Lavius Hyde Letter Collection (18), CLB.

97. Cyrus Yale, The Godly Pastor: Life of the Rev. Jeremiah Hallock, of Canton, Conn. (New York, [1854]), 134–35.

98. CEM 1 (July 1800): 22.

99. Edward Dorr Griffin, "Letter on religious revival in about forty adjacent parishes" (copy), 1 August 1799, CSL; see also reports on other local revivals in CEM 1 (March 1801): 342; CEM 2 (January 1802): 271; and CEM 2 (December 1801): 225.

100. CEM 1 (June 1801): 462.

101. CEM 1 (February 1801): 312; see also reports on other local revivals in CEM 1 (January 1801): 269; CEM 1 (April 1801): 379; and CEM 1 (June 1801): 464.

private meetings continued in America, where devout laypeople and occasionally a minister gathered in homes on a weekly, biweekly, or monthly basis.[102] Whether initiated by the clergy or by others with awakened sensibilities, the religious conference functioned as the basic organizational unit and transmitter of the revival among Congregationalists in northwestern Connecticut.

The nature of these conferences varied in format. Some were "praying conferences," synonymous with the concert of prayer. Whether organized at the behest of the General Association in 1794 or simply the result of pious Christians gathering on their own for corporate prayer, some praying conferences preceded the outbreak of revival by several years. Five years before the awakening in Norfolk, the devout met regularly, petitioning God for a divine outpouring.[103] Jeremiah Hallock reported that at a weekly praying conference, "the work began, and here it has been the greatest."[104] At other times, a concert of prayer was initiated when the alert detected signs of spiritual awakening.[105]

The most common type of religious conference was the "lecture" conducted either by a settled or a visiting pastor. The revival lecture was an extension of the traditional Wednesday or Thursday public lecture intended for religious instruction, but its tone and frequency differed markedly. In the throes of revival, people gathered "at all times" of the day, two to five times per week.[106] At strategic locations throughout the parish, pastors instructed, exhorted, and prayed with earnest Christians, those under conviction, or, in some cases, curious onlookers attracted by the novelty of religious excitement.[107] The cooperative endeavors of revival-minded New Divinity men are revealed in the diary of fourteen-year-old Julia Cowles of Farmington. On a Thursday afternoon in May 1799, young Julia attended a lecture where she "heard a very good sermon by Mr. Griffin of N. Hartford, and another by Mr. Mills of Torringford."[108]

---

102. Charles E. Hambrick-Stowe, *The Practice of Piety: Puritan Devotional Disciplines in Seventeenth-Century New England* (Chapel Hill, N.C., 1982), 137–38; for a general discussion, see 137–43.

103. *CEM* 1 (February 1801): 312; see also the report of revival at Torringford in *CEM* 1 (July 1800): 27, and Oliver W. Elsbree, *The Rise of the Missionary Spirit in America, 1790–1815* (Williamsport, Pa., 1928), 37.

104. *CEM* 1 (October 1800): 182. Hallock noted the continuation of the weekly concert of prayer (Yale, *Godly Pastor*, 156).

105. See *CEM* 1 (June 1801): 462.

106. Luther Hart, "A View of the Religious Declension in New England, and of its Causes, during the latter half of the Eighteenth Century," *Quarterly Christian Spectator*, 3d ser., 5 (June 1833): 217.

107. *CEM* 1 (July 1800): 22; *CEM* 1 (September 1800): 101, 102; *CEM* 1 (January 1801): 269; *CEM* 1 (March 1801): 341; *CEM* 2 (July 1801): 26; *CEM* 3 (April 1803): 389; Mills to Hooker, Weston, and Bordwell, CLB; Nathan Perkins, "Two Discourses," 41. In 1807, as an eighteen-year-old, John Mason Peck, the famous Baptist missionary in Illinois and Kentucky, attended a meeting at Litchfield South Farms out of curiosity. He was converted. See *Forty Years of Pioneer Life: Memoir of John Mason Peck, D.D.*, ed. Rufus Babcock, introd. Paul M. Harrison (Carbondale, Ill., 1965), 16.

108. *Diaries of Julia Cowles*, 23. For other references to exchanges in Hartford recorded by another

Some conferences were held under the tight scrutiny of the pastor, as at Farmington First Church, where Joseph Washburn neither issued invitations to conversion nor allowed "hopeful" converts to testify.[109] Other pastors permitted more spontaneity of expression. Ammi Robbins described a typical meeting in Norfolk: "They begin and end with prayer, and besides singing of hymns, they converse on some texts or passages of holy scripture—read some pious discourses."[110] Frequently, an article in the *Connecticut Evangelical Magazine* was the pious discourse read. An "A.Z.," writing to the periodical's editors, gave assurance that the magazine "has been already read and will continue to be read in religious meetings and conferences. Those who read it will converse of it to others; one pious friend will hand it to another, and thus its usefulness will become more and more extensive."[111] This printed news, as well as correspondence of revivalist successes elsewhere, was an important means for exciting audiences and transmitting revival, not only in Connecticut but throughout the country.[112] Lyman Beecher, for example, wrote to Edward Dorr Griffin in 1807, asking him to "communicate by letter an account of God among your people" because "such communications from brethren . . . are many times blessed to extend to other regions the same blessed work."[113] Clearly, a revival publicized was a revival expanded.

Finally, religious conferences were often inspired, organized, or even conducted by pious youth. The young turned out in overwhelming numbers at several conference meetings. At Warren, the young people of the church set up their own weekly conferences, where they prayed, sang psalms and hymns, and read printed sermons in lieu of a personal appearance by the pastor.[114] At his Northington parish in West Avon, the Rev. Rufus Hawley was approached by the youth and invited to attend a religious conference they had initiated.[115] On yet other occasions, the outbreak of revival began

young female, see Nancy Maria Hyde, *The Writings of Nancy Maria Hyde, of Norwich, Conn., connected with a Sketch of Her Life* (Norwich, Conn., 1816).

109. *CEM* 1 (April 1801): 383.

110. *CEM* 1 (March 1801): 341; see also *CEM* 2 (December 1801): 225, and Alvan Hyde, *Memoir of Rev. Alvan Hyde, D.D. of Lee, Mass.* (Boston, 1835), 350.

111. *CEM* 1 (October 1800): 124; see also *CEM* 1 (March 1801): 341, and *CEM* 1 (May 1801): 439.

112. Such practices date back to the lively transatlantic exchange between Evangelicals in the eighteenth century. These communications—in published narratives and private correspondence—provided much of the fuel for revivalist successes of the British Revival and the American Great Awakening, successes that continued well into the nineteenth century. See Crawford, *Seasons of Grace*, 141. Gilmore, *Reading Becomes a Necessity of Life*, discusses frequent public readings in the context of "the first age of mass literacy" (1780–1835) in America (132, 20).

113. Lyman Beecher to Edward Dorr Griffin, 6 December 1807, Mellen Chamberlain Collection, BPL.

114. *CEM* 1 (September 1800): 100.

115. *CEM* 1 (September 1800): 102.

among the young.[116] The Rev. Simon Waterman recounted a typical pattern where two "lads or young men" met in the school house for religious conversation. Others joined them, including Waterman, who witnessed the presence of both sexes between the ages of eight and eighteen, numbering up to 140. They met for prayer, readings, and singing, and eventually attracted adults to their conference.[117]

For many youth, the schoolhouse was the vortex of revival. In fact, according to one New Divinity minister, schoolhouses "were far more instructive and moving than the more labored and elevated services of the Sabbath."[118] Samuel Mills of Torringford could not recall "any schools in the place where there are not children impressed."[119] During recess, pious children elected to read their Bibles rather than engage in frivolous play. The "greatest number" of those who "obtained hope" ranged between twelve and eighteen years.[120] To the south of Torringford, schoolmaster Erastus Scranton "talked on the new birth" and noted "some serious awakenings in my School Rocky Hill."[121] Legislation passed by the Connecticut General Assembly in 1795 and 1798 established "school societies," separate from parish or ecclesiastical control. These societies were independent of town limits and town authorities and received their finances from the state-subsidized school fund.[122] One historian considered this transfer of authority "a blow to the clergy" because it removed public education from parish control.[123] Some contemporary clergy, however, drew different conclusions. The Rev. Edward Dorr Griffin surmised that one section of the new laws was

116. Nathan Strong to Jedidiah Morse, 21 February 1799, Morse Family Papers, SML; CEM 1 (July 1800): 27; CEM 1 (October 1800): 137; CEM 4 (January 1804): 271; Yale, Godly Pastor, 216–17.

117. CEM 2 (August 1801): 61; see also CEM 5 (September 1804): 110.

118. Hyde, Memoir, 342.

119. Mills to Hooker, Weston, and Bordwell, CLB.

120. CEM 1 (July 1800): 30.

121. Erastus Scranton Diary, SML. Scranton taught at Rocky Hill for six months before accepting a pastorate; see Franklin B. Dexter, ed., Biographical Sketches of the Graduates of Yale College with Annals of the College History (New York, 1885–1912), 5:534–35.

122. George C. Stewart, Jr., A History of Religious Education in Connecticut to the Middle of the Nineteenth Century (New Haven, Conn., 1924), 160–62. From 1717 to 1793, towns, parishes, and occasionally churches controlled local schools (see M. Louise Greene, The Development of Religious Liberty in Connecticut [1905; reprint, Freeport, N.Y., 1970], 390–92). A state appropriations act in 1793 stipulated that monies collected from the sale of land in the Western Reserve would fund the public schools. In its final, 1795 form, the act stipulated that either all the monies would go to the local school fund or, if a two-thirds majority of the district so voted, a portion or all of the monies would be divided among the churches for the support of the ministry. The latter alternative was rarely invoked, except in Farmington, where from 1799 to 1808 the school society voted consistently to use its money for the support of the ministry. On the appropriations act, see James R. Beasley, "Emerging Republicans and the Standing Order: The Appropriations Act Controversy in Connecticut, 1793 to 1795," William and Mary Quarterly, 3d ser., 29 (October 1972): 587–610. On Farmington, see Christopher P. Bickford, Farmington in Connecticut (Canaan, N.H., 1982), 267.

123. Keller, Second Great Awakening, 64.

an unmitigated blessing, for it required teachers to subscribe to the doctrine of God's ordaining decrees. In one instance a teacher who previously rejected this doctrine underwent a radical change when confronted with the new law: "Soon after this his conscience was seized," he was convicted, and became a Christian.[124] According to Griffin, the law "led the way to important benefits to the children of this and neighboring towns," for the newly appointed teachers became transmitters of revival:

> School-masters of a serious cast have been employed, who have taken upon themselves, in earnest, the business of instructing, and praying with the children; especially three which were under the care of men professedly and apparently pious. Out of those three, nearly 20 children, in the course of the winter, obtained hopes. Small children of 10 or 12 years old used to meet for conferences. And by their order, conversation, and prayers, astonished those who happened to be among them. . . . The blessings of many children, ready to perish, will come on our legislature for their late benevolent act.[125]

Griffin's special interest in the common schools, legislation notwithstanding, led to his appointment as chairman of the board of "Schools Inspectors."[126] In this privileged position he exerted influence to secure pious teachers who would conduct conference meetings during the school day. Once hired, evangelical teachers prayed with and offered catechetical instruction to the children—all in the name of public education. In what might be construed as "release time," twenty-four "children" from two nearby schools met in the study of the Rev. Samuel Mills for religious instruction.[127] In other instances the local minister simply visited the schools within his parish.[128]

James Morris was a fitting New Divinity example of the kind of schoolmaster engaged in nurturing young minds. After his theological training with Joseph Bellamy was interrupted by the American Revolution, Morris returned to Litchfield in 1780, made a profession of faith in 1790, and opened his own academy at Litchfield South Farms in the same year.[129] Concerned with the spiritual condition of the town's young people, Morris established the school "for the purpose of improving the manners and morals

---

124. *CEM* 1 (December 1800): 220.
125. Griffin, "Letter on religious revival," CSL, 10–11.
126. Parsons Cooke, *Recollections of Rev. E. D. Griffin; or, Incidents Illustrating his Character* (Boston, 1855), 134.
127. Mills to Hooker, Weston, and Bordwell, CLB.
128. Asahel Hooker, "Funeral Sermon for Joseph Washburn," in Washburn, *Sermons on Practical Subjects*, 344.
129. Morris's career is discussed briefly in John A. Andrew III, *Rebuilding the Christian Commonwealth: New England Congregationalists and Foreign Missions, 1800–1830* (Lexington, Ky., 1976), 87–90.

of youth, and of attracting their attention from frivolity and dissipation."[130] A friend of revival, he proffered spiritual guidance and counsel, and conducted interviews with converted adults and students from his school after the Awakening swept the community in 1814.[131]

The religious conference, then, whether held at the parsonage, meeting house, or school house, occupied a prominent place in the revival. From the clergy's perspective, its primary purpose was to detail the "hard sayings" of Calvinism and to rouse the spiritually lax. Yet on another level the conference performed quite another function. In a ritual departure from formal institutionalized structures, the conference meeting brought into being an entirely new community. In an atmosphere combining intense spiritual searching with mutual encouragement, a new communal consciousness demarcated saints from sinners. Here, the spiritually indifferent but curious were brought under conviction; here, anxious seekers witnessed a community of saints hitherto unknown. This heightened conviction among the unsaved led one observer to exclaim, "I never saw such conferences before. People seemed to be attending as for their lives."[132] For youth and women, the conference meeting created a new or an alternative form of spiritual intimacy. The young drew upon the strength of others to combat "vain amusements"; women, relegated to the domestic sphere, found a socially acceptable form of emotional release and voluntary participation.[133] Here, saints encouraged others and shared their common joys and fears. In short, these *ecclesiolae in ecclesia* provided insularity and community for those seeking fellowship and a temporary safe haven from infidelity and threatening change.

Historians have been quick to assert the communal nature of the nationwide Second Great Awakening, but they have done so only in broad, general terms. Perry Miller called the literature of the revival unabashedly "communal," and Carey McWilliams concurred, asserting that the revival "sought to create a national community, a fraternal policy that could give moral direction to the forces of the age."[134] Similarly, Donald Mathews referred to the Awakening as "an organizing process that helped give meaning and direction to people."[135] Richard Birdsall came closest to the mark when

130. Quoted in Alain C. White, comp., *The History of the Town of Litchfield, Connecticut, 1720–1920* (Litchfield, Conn., 1920), 180–81.

131. Dexter, *Biographical Sketches* 3:576–77; James Morris, "Revival of Religion in South Farms, beginning March, 1814," James Morris MSS, SML; see also *CEM* 7 (April 1807): 392.

132. *CEM* 1 (October 1800): 133.

133. See Chapter 7 for an extended discussion of youth and women in the Awakening.

134. Perry Miller, *The Life of the Mind in America: From the Revolution to the Civil War* (New York, 1965), 11; William Carey McWilliams, *The Idea of Fraternity in America* (Berkeley and Los Angeles, 1973), 237.

135. Donald G. Mathews, "The Second Great Awakening as an Organizing Process, 1780–1830: An Hypothesis," *American Quarterly* 21 (Spring 1969): 27.

he noted the reemergence of religion with "a new community of mutual concern."[136] Yet none of these historians has emphasized that the basic unit for community was the conference meeting. Less public than the formal Sabbath service, where attendance often proceeded from habit, the conference represented a private, voluntary religious association. Anxious sinners attended to find salvation—"to get more feeling," as Luther Hart put it.[137] Distraught saints attended to reconfirm their commitment to the faith. And dedicated Christians attended to provide leadership and lend encouragement. Together they created an intense community of support. Together they prayed, sang hymns, and heard testimonies of God's work of grace. Often they heard a pastor-awakener deliver an impassioned sermon, urging immediate repentance before it was too late. They trembled at the repeated warning: "This may be your last chance. What then is your answer?"[138] To be saved or to be lost forever to the clutches of infidelity and eternal damnation. To save the Republic or to see it go to ruin. The choice was theirs—within the sovereign plans of God.

Carl Becker once remarked that while the American Revolution settled once and for all the issue of home rule, it was left to future generations to determine who would rule at home. If left to the New Divinity men, those who embodied the evangelical conception of virtue would hold the spiritual reins of power. The very problems confronting American society, they contended, could be traced to the loss of virtue, a loss triggered by the spread of infidelity. This lamentable condition prompted them to press vigorously for spiritual renewal. Recognizing that the social fabric rested ultimately upon the virtue of its citizens, and theorizing (or theologizing) that true virtue was implanted by God in the individual soul, they sought revival as a means to halt the nation's moral decline. True religion was, after all, the moral backbone of the new Republic.

The New Divinity clergy countered spiritual laxity by taking their message of regeneration to the people. Thus, the Second Great Awakening in Connecticut was a grass-roots movement let by a group of relatively obscure clergy who traveled from town to town and ignited a populace receptive to their message. Through their shared experiences and a willingness to offer mutual spiritual assistance, the New Divinity men constituted a formidable presence in northwestern Connecticut. Conference meetings, the basic units of communal revival, provided a forum where the clergy prayed and preached, and where the laity both responded to and initiated revival.

---

136. Richard D. Birdsall, "The Second Great Awakening and the New England Social Order," *Church History* 39 (September 1970): 357.
   137. Luther Hart, "View of the Religious Declension," 217.
   138. Edward Dorr Griffin, *Sermons* (1844), 77.

Critics of the New Divinity awakeners expressed wonder and even incredulity that anyone would listen to their message. How could disputatious "Farmer Metaphysicians" speak a language apprehended by laypeople, much less ignite the flames of spiritual passion through conversion? In an age of recent independence and self-determination, who would listen to the New Divinity message of absolute dependence upon a sovereign God? In fact, many. Many listened, many understood, and many responded. The New Divinity clergy fashioned a theology drawn essentially from the tenets of traditional Calvinism yet revised to meet their critics as well as to arouse the people. Charged by their enemies with obscurantism, intolerance, and inconsistency, the New Divinity created America's first indigenous theology—a theology of revival.

3

"THE HEART GOVERNS THE HEAD"

A Theology of Revival

In 1800, after a generation of taking (and giving) verbal abuse, the New Divinity men felt vindicated. Opponents had pronounced them "metaphysic-mad," claiming that their teaching was a "chaos of divinity" and "the very essence of pagan fatality."[1] Now, for over a year, revival had raged throughout the villages of Hartford and Litchfield counties. Finally, a half century after the Great Awakening, the "hard sayings" of New Divinity Calvinism achieved their desired effect. While utility was never the full measure of truth, the New Divinity eagerly touted their brand of Calvinism as the spark that lit the fires of revival. Whatever it was—metaphysical madness, pagan fatalism, or chaotic theology—the teachings of the New Divinity bore the fruit of revival.

The New Divinity comprehended all religious expression as an outgrowth of theology. Ritual, ecclesiastical, or devotional practices—these refracted the light of theological conviction; words defined and words set limits on

---

1. The terms are from the English Baptist, Andrew Fuller; the Old Calvinist, William Hart of Saybrook; and the Liberal Arminian, Charles Chauncy of Boston. The quotes from Fuller and Chauncy are found in Allen C. Guelzo, *Edwards on the Will: A Century of American Theological Debate* (Middletown, Conn., 1989), 88, 89; from Hart, in Joseph Haroutunian, *Piety versus Moralism: The Passing of the New England Theology* (1932; reprint, New York, 1970), 67.

religious expression.[2] In the same way, the New Divinity understood and interpreted religious revivals—that phenomenon that became the American Protestant *ritual* in the early nineteenth century—first and foremost in theological terms. The basic goal of revivalism—the new birth—was clear enough. And the plan of salvation was essentially the same for all evangelical groups: humanity is sinful, in need of redemption; through belief in Christ's death, redemption is accomplished, humans are reconciled to God, and they gain eternal life. But explicating the gospel message, even in the most rudimentary way, raised questions.

Throughout the last half of the eighteenth century and well into the nineteenth, the fundamental question with which pastors, revivalists, and theologians wrestled was Who did it? Did God alone save, or did humans make a decision (or somehow "will") to follow Christ? By the late eighteenth century, the rub for the New Divinity had come to this: on the one hand, in *Freedom of the Will* (1754), Edwards argued creatively and forcefully for moral determinism—the notion one could not of his or her own will, turn to God; on the other hand, nearly a half century later, the Edwardseans found themselves confronted by moderate Calvinists and those of Arminian sympathies—whether elitist Unitarians, popular Methodists, or other radical evangelical sects—who cited abundant evidence from experience as well as from Scripture that God endowed humans with the ability (to a lesser or greater degree) to accept or reject the gospel offer. To complicate matters further, God "the Creator" endowed humans with inalienable rights, among which were life, liberty, and the pursuit of happiness. These endowments—whether theological or political—point to the momentous changes that occurred in American society since Edwards's death in 1758, changes related to thought and action, changes that included continued permeation by Enlightenment ideas and the American victory in the War of Independence. Some observers portray the ideas of the Enlightenment and those of evangelical Calvinism as polar ideological opposites: the Enlightenment stressed reason, moralism, measure, and control, whereas Evangelicalism stressed the emotions ("affections"), piety, millennial fervor, and sometimes political radicalism.[3] Others, however, although they affirm points of contrast

2. Richard Rabinowitz, *The Spiritual Self in Everyday Life: The Transformation of Personal Religious Experience in Nineteenth-Century New England* (Boston, 1989), refers to the New Divinity preoccupation with intellect as "the orthodoxy of doctrinalism" (15; and part 1 passim)—an accurate phrase, but at times exaggerated. Rabinowitz's portrait of the New Divinity fails to fill in some important details: the role of the affections in their theology, their evangelical preaching, their indebtedness to Edwards's "Narrative"—all important components in New Divinity heartfelt religion.

3. William G. McLoughlin, *Revivals, Awakenings, and Reform: An Essay on Religion and Social Change in America, 1607–1977* (Chicago, 1978); Alan E. Heimert, *Religion and the American Mind, from the Great Awakening to the Revolution* (Cambridge, Mass., 1966).

between these two ideologies, also demonstrate their complex interaction.[4] Indeed, the New Divinity men, while seeking to remain Edwardsean Evangelicals, appropriated the language and even, at times, the assumptions, of the Englightenment. They created a revivalist theology—expressed in simple, evocative terms to their auditors—but not before their hearty theological appetites had fed upon and digested a main course consisting of Calvinist meat marbled throughout with Edwardseanism and seasoned with the salt of Enlightenment rationalism and humanism. Though restricted to regional popularity, this New Divinity entrée created a sensation. The hundreds who fed upon it professed to changed lives.

The Dimensions of the New Divinity Dilemma

"It is of unspeakable importance," wrote Ammi Robbins in his account of the 1799 revival in Norfolk, "that the means of grace be used with impenitent Christless sinners."[5] Otherwise, he feared, the unsaved would rely on the excuse that God's electing decrees paralyzed any human effort to make themselves a new heart. Robbins's plea accentuated an apparent dilemma of New Divinity revivalists. On the one hand, they called the unsaved to repent, to turn immediately from a sinful past, and to embrace the offer of salvation. On the other hand, they assured the unregenerate that because of their inherent corruption they could not fulfill the will of God. Moreover, in God's sovereign design, some were elected to salvation, the rest were reprobated to damnation. Within such a scheme, critics asked, where was human freedom? Without the freedom to choose, how could one be held accountable for sin? Why attend to the means of grace—often called the means of regeneration—if attention to such means went for naught anyway? And if one granted some connection between human freedom and divine initiative, what precisely was it?

Such questions, of course, were not new. The apostle Paul, St. Augustine, the Protestant Reformers, Puritan divines—all those who made the sovereignty of God the centerpiece of their theology—wrestled with these issues.[6] And yet these questions acutely challenged the New Divinity men. Unlike their Puritan forebears, they encountered stiff competition and the stinging

---

4. Henry F. May, *The Enlightenment in America* (New York, 1976); John Corrigan, *The Prism of Piety: Catholick Congregational Clergy at the Beginning of the Enlightenment* (New York, 1991); Michael J. Crawford, *Seasons of Grace: Colonial New England's Revival Tradition in Its British Context* (New York, 1991), 81.

5. *CEM* 1 (March 1801): 339.

6. On the Puritans, see Norman Pettit, *The Heart Prepared: Grace and Conversion in Puritan Spiritual Life* (New Haven, Conn., 1966).

accusation that their views deviated from mainstream New England Calvinism. The New Divinity also carried the extra burden of reconciling divine
sovereignty with human freedom and responsibility in a postrevolutionary
climate that increasingly emphasized human self-determination. Old (or
moderate) Calvinists and Arminians were less troubled with this issue, for
their theologies were more in concert with enlightened thinking. Their
understandings of human freedom and ability coincided with those of a
nation optimistic about the potential of Americans to shape their destiny
both on this earth and in the world to come. To varying degrees, Old
Calvinists and Arminians repudiated New Divinity conceptions of human
depravity, divine sovereignty, and human responsibility. The New Divinity
advocates, reasoned their critics, could not have it both ways: they could not
uphold the utter sovereignty of God and his electing decrees *and* support
human freedom and responsibility. Something had to give. The paradox and
perennial problem of Calvinism had reached an impasse where the retreat to
mystery was insufficient to resolve the quandary.

By the end of the eighteenth century, two distinct versions of theological
liberalism (or "Arminianism," as opponents called it) challenged the hegemony of Calvinists in New England. What united both was a willingness to
admit a greater role for human initiative in the process of salvation. The
newer and more populist version, comprised of Methodists, Free-Will
Baptists, "Christians," and others, was viewed (inaccurately as it turned out) by
the New Divinity to be less of a threat than the in-house, elitist version of
liberals centered primarily in Boston. This latter group, which developed
within and then splintered from Calvinism, had carried on since the Great
Awakening a long and often bitter debate with the Edwardseans. By 1790, the
liberals rejected the Calvinist conception of the world out of hand.
Embracing the heady ideas of the European Enlightenment, they denied the
notion that humans were born in sin. Their humanism blunted the effects of
the fall of Adam and stressed the role of nurture in the spiritual process.
Viewing humans in Lockean terms as neutral entities—blank slates upon
which the vicissitudes of life shaped character—liberals such as Charles
Chauncy and Jonathan Mayhew advanced moral teaching and a constructive
environment as the path to salvation. Nurture by nature replaced conversion
by supernatural grace. A new view of human nature became the linchpin upon
which other Calvinist doctrines tumbled. If humans were not as bad off as the
New Divinity assumed, then what of God as an avenging judge who
pronounced condemnation on the lost? A new view of humanity supplanted
an old view of God: the God of the liberals was a God of love who, because
he sought the greatest happiness for his creatures, would not condemn the
impenitent to everlasting hell. The worst of sinners, as Chauncy expressed in
The Salvation of All Men (1784), would suffer temporal punishment, not eternal

punishment in the next world. A God of love was a God of universal salvation. John Murray reached the same conclusion, but from a Calvinist view of human nature. According to Murray, whose Universalism was popular among a vocal minority in New England, Christ bore the punishment of all humanity in his atoning death, and because he paid the price for all, all would be saved ("for by the obedience of one man all were made righteous," Romans 5:19).

The liberals' optimistic view of human nature led naturally to the conviction that individuals played a larger role in their salvation than was previously granted. As free, self-determining agents, they cooperated with God. God left it to his creatures to work out their salvation, not with fear and trembling, but with reason and confidence, so that the means of grace were theirs for the taking. The Fall had not so blighted human effort that exertions were futile; rather, a causal connection existed between a nurtured faith, an upright life, and salvation.

Both moderate Calvinists and New Divinity men rejected the cheery liberal view of human nature, contending that the means of grace were useful and needful but that God was under no necessity to save those who pursued them. They exhorted the impenitent to "believe on the Lord Jesus Christ and be saved" (Acts 16:31), but parted over what encompassed true belief and the place of the means of grace in the process of regeneration. According to the moderates, the new birth did not require a sudden, agonizing, or cataclysmic experience; it was acceptable and normal that regeneration proceeded gradually within the preparationist model of traditional Puritanism. The process of regeneration, where God drew sinners to himself, began as the Holy Spirit illuminated the mind. This intellectualist view of the "effectual call" took place when the sinner appropriated the means of grace, for "faith comes by hearing, and hearing by the word of God" (Romans 10:17). Common, or prevenient, grace enabled the impenitent, through prudence and sound judgment, to wish to repent. This desire, known as "next power," resulted in the new birth. Though God was under no obligation to save, he ordinarily gave a new heart to those who prepared for salvation. In all probability, those who heard the Word and obeyed it would be saved.

For the New Divinity the critical issue surfaced where the moderates left off. How could the totally depraved obey the word to repent? If indeed all were mortally infected with sin, then was it just, much less consistent, to hold sinners accountable for their eternal destiny? However abstract and insoluble such questions appeared, the New Divinity men devoted much of their constructive theological efforts to answering their critics. In the process they developed an evangelical theology cast within the "hard sayings" of Calvinism but stamped by a peculiar New Divinity imprimatur. Though convinced themselves that rational truth or "speculative knowledge" alone could not save, the New Divinity men expended a great amount of intellectual energy to prove it to others.

As I have shown, New Divinity ministers in northwestern Connecticut had a great deal in common. They were raised in modest social settings, educated at Yale, tutored in schools of the prophets, united by common spiritual goals and aspirations, and were moderate republicans of Federalist sympathies. Above all, however, the New Divinity shared the same theological views—a "new" kind of divinity as their Old Calvinist opponents had derisively named it in the 1760s. This New Divinity theology represented the lengthening shadow of Jonathan Edwards's influence, for all who claimed a New Divinity connection affirmed Edwards as their theological mentor. In the last half of the eighteenth century and well into the nineteenth, Edwards's reputation as a spokesman for true Christianity grew to heroic proportions. In fact, between 1780 and 1800, his works were published more extensively in America than in the twenty years following his death.[7] On both sides of the Atlantic, his name was invoked with reverence as the popularity of his writings on heartfelt religion spread through the Calvinist community, both lay and clerical.[8] Samuel Hopkins had anticipated this acclaim when he wrote in 1765 that "President Edwards was one of those men of whom it is not easy to speak with justice without seeming . . . to incur the guilt of adulation."[9] And guilty he and others would so plead. Alexander Gillett confessed that he "read Mr. Edwards with as much greediness as ever the luxurious person glutted his appetite."[10] In his "century sermon" of 1801, Charles Backus predicted that Edwards's "memory will be precious to the friends of pure religion, in ages to come."[11] A generation later, Luther Hart referred to the

7. Note the following American reprints (in parentheses) of Edwards's works: *History of the Work of Redemption* (1786, 1792, 1793); *Sinners in the Hands of an Angry God* (1786, 1796, 1797); *Thoughts on Revival* (1784); *Religious Affections* (1784, 1787, 1794); *Freedom of the Will* (1786, 1790); *Faithful Narrative* (1790); *True Grace* (1790, 1791, 1799); *Humble Attempt* (1789, 1794); *A Divine and Supernatural Light* (1795); *The Justice of God in the Damnation of Sinners* (1799). In addition, nearly thirty separate editions or parts of Edwards's works were issued between 1800 and 1819. See Charles L. Chaney, "God's Glorious Work: The Theological Foundations of the Early Missionary Societies in America, 1787–1817" (Ph.D. diss., University of Chicago, 1973), 139n; Crawford, *Seasons of Grace*, 239.

8. Iain H. Murray, *Jonathan Edwards: A New Biography* (London, 1987), 458–62; for references to Edwards's writings among Connecticut laity, see *CEM* 1 (March 1801): 335; *CEM* 4 (March 1804): 353; Mary Treadwell Hooker Diary, CSL; and Joan Jacobs Brumberg, *Mission for Life: The Story of the Family of Adoniram Judson* (New York, 1980), 25.

9. Quoted in the editor's introduction to Jonathan Edwards, *WJE: Freedom of the Will*, ed. Paul Ramsey (New Haven, Conn., 1957), 1.

10. Luther Hart, "A Sermon, delivered . . . Jan. 22, 1826, at the Funeral of Reverend Alexander Gillett . . ." (New Haven, Conn., 1826), 23.

11. Charles Backus, "A Sermon Delivered Jan. 1, 1801; containing a brief review . . . of the Eighteenth Century" (Hartford, Conn., 1801), 17.

man deceased for nearly seventy years as "the immortal Edwards."[12] Other disciples titled him "the great Edwards" or "the great and pious President Edwards."[13]

The New Divinity men embraced Edwards's "logic and tears" approach to the faith by insisting that the demands of reason must be coupled with a remade heart. Not all of Edwards's followers, however, reflexively imitated his views. Backus admitted that "the principles which have been considered as fundamental in the Calvinistic system, have been pursued farther in their consequences, within the last fifty years, than they had been in any former period."[14] He was referring, in part, to the very doctrines that made the New Divinity appear to be so repugnant. By 1790, critics had had their heyday with the exaggerated theological positions of Samuel Hopkins (that one must be willing to be damned for the greater glory of God) and Nathanael Emmons (that the saved in heaven should rejoice in God's just condemnation of the unrepentant to hell). These statements, even if uttered with a certain relish (as some interpreters suggest), have caricatured the New Divinity movement, detracted from its other innovative theological formulations, and have often led to a neglect of other New Divinity contributions in ecclesiology and homiletics. Moreover, the New Divinity did not always speak with one voice: distinctive emphases emerged that gave the movement an inner vitality apart from its unified front against detractors.

The third generation of New Divinity men pursued the dogmatics of Edwards himself or identified with one of his principal interpreters—Samuel Hopkins, Joseph Bellamy, or Nathanael Emmons.[15] The primary transmitters of New Divinity theology to leading clerics of Connecticut's Second Great Awakening were Hopkins, Bellamy, and a few of their first wave of students, such as Jonathan Edwards, Jr., a pupil of Hopkins. No speculative theologian of the stature of a Hopkins or an Emmons emerged among the awakeners in Connecticut's formative period of revival, who, in an "age of action," were more dedicated to reviving the lost than reflecting long and deeply on

12. Hart, "Sermon delivered at the Funeral of Gillett," 39.

13. Levi Hart of Preston, Connecticut, cited in Donald Weber, Rhetoric and History in Revolutionary New England (New York, 1988), 75; Edward Dorr Griffin, Sermons not before published, on various practical subjects (New York, 1844), 53. On the New Divinity "reinvention" of Edwards and the "canonization" of his works, see Joseph Conforti, "The Invention of the Great Awakening, 1795–1842," Early American Literature 26 (1991): 107–12.

14. Backus, "Review of the Eighteenth Century," 17.

15. On the various positions within the New Divinity spectrum, see George N. Boardman, A History of New England Theology (Chicago, 1899); Frank H. Foster, A Genetic History of the New England Theology (Chicago, 1907); Haroutunian, Piety versus Moralism; Robert C. Whittemore, The Transformation of the New England Theology (New York, 1987); and Guelzo, Edwards on the Will. For recent revisionist views on the connection between Edwards and the New Divinity, see William Breitenbach, "Piety and Moralism: Edwards and the New Divinity," in Jonathan Edwards and the American Experience, ed. Nathan O. Hatch and Harry S. Stout (New York, 1988), 217, and Guelzo, Edwards on the Will, esp. chaps. 3, 4.

theological issues. Still, in occasional theological treatises and more often in sermons and popular writings, they faithfully defended New Divinity views. Among these lesser theological lights, Edward Dorr Griffin stands out as one of the more astute, productive, and contentious. New Divinity views also found expression in the published sermons of Joseph Washburn of Farmington and in a trio of editors and contributors to the *Connecticut Evangelical Magazine*: Charles Backus of Somers, Nathan Perkins of West Hartford, and Nathan Strong of Hartford. The sovereignty of God, the moral freedom of humans, and the affectional nature of religion preoccupied the New Divinity men's agenda. Theirs, as much as Edwards's, was a theology of a sound mind and a revived heart.

The Context of New Divinity Theologizing

The theological issues that engaged the minds of American divines—whether Arminian, Old Calvinist, or New Divinity—largely reflected eighteenth-century Europe's general concern in reconciling the demands of authority with the pleas of liberty. While political theorists revised the basic political structures of their time and in some cases rejected the ancien régime by asserting the right of peoples to determine their own political destinies, so theologians gave increasing attention to the issue of divine sovereignty and human freedom, to the conundrum of what Griffin called "order and happiness."[16] Given these broad common concerns, the rhetorical worlds of political theorists and religious systemizers overlapped. Thus, New Divinity expressions of God's nature and work in the world closely paralleled their views of an ideal political world.

The New Divinity formulated what might be called a "theology of proportionality," based on the Enlightenment premise of God as the Moral Governor of the universe. Eighteenth-century Western thought was preoccupied with balance, proportion, and symmetry—whether in art, ethics, jurisprudence, politics, domestic relations, or theology. Edwards had warned of "deformed" and "maimed" Christians whom Satan deceived through a "lack of proportionality" by uplifting some of Christ's attributes to the exclusion of others. For the believer to experience Christ truly was to experience a "proportional manifestation of justice and mercy, holiness and grace, majesty and gentleness, authority and condescension."[17] Perhaps more than Edwards did, the New Divinity men cast their theology within the conceptual mold of proportionality. They observed, for example, that an infinite evil deserved an

16. Griffin, *Sermons* (1844), 184.
17. Edwards, "Some Thoughts concerning the Present Revival of Religion in New-England," in *WJE: The Great Awakening*, ed. C. C. Goen (New Haven, Conn., 1972), 463.

infinite punishment; that enmity against God and his law rose in proportion to one's conscience being convinced of sin; that the fall of Adam brought the greatest glory to God, for "the sin of man was the occasion of higher advances in holiness"; that "nothing is in vain: All things answer to his benevolent purposes"; that the atonement of Christ for the sins of the world satisfied the demands of public justice; that repentance, faith, love, and obedience were "altogether rational and fit"; and, finally, that the plan of redemption displayed "the greatest order, proportion, and beauty."[18]

At the same time, the New Divinity inherited from Calvinism and most directly from Edwards the conviction that God's sovereignty was "the main doctrine of Christianity."[19] Since sovereignty connoted rule, the New Divinity men typically described God in legalistic, governmental terms— terms used predominantly in eighteenth-century political discourse, and terms that mirrored their own Federalist sympathies with a firm and resolute political order. If forced to choose between freedom and authority in the civil realm, there was no question of their allegiance. So too, in the cosmic realm, the ultimate authority ruled as the Moral Governor, the "glorious Monarch," the "glorious sovereign," and the "great and powerful monarch."[20] Like any benevolent ruler, God desired the happiness and good of his creatures. Yet, as the Moral Governor, God was the "Supreme Legislator to his creatures."[21] He gave to his subjects "some principle, or law by which . . . they are to be directed."[22] "Law is the eternal rule of righteousness," wrote Joseph Bellamy, "which is essential to the being and glory of God's moral government and kingdom."[23] As in the political realm, so in the heavenly realm of God's moral world, the governed were held accountable for their actions, and as such they were culpable. When the law was broken in the civil realm, appropriate penalties were meted out. When God's infinite law was broken, the appropriate and proportional response was an infinite punishment, the everlasting torment of hell. No one justly deserved to escape hell, but God, in an act of mercy consistent with his justice, offered Christ—his

18. Edward Dorr Griffin, "God Exalted and Creatures Humbled by the Gospel" (New York, 1830), 26; CEM 1 (September 1800): 95; Sermons, on Various Important Doctrines and Duties of the Christian Religion (Northampton, Mass., 1799), 143; Jonathan Maxcy, "A Discourse designed to explain the Doctrine of the Atonement," in The Atonement: Discourses and Treatises by Edwards, Smalley, Maxcy, Emmons, Griffin, Burge, and Weeks, With an Introductory Essay by Edwards A. Park, ed. Edwards A. Park (Boston, 1859), 107.

19. CEM 1 (September 1800): 98.

20. Sermons on Doctrines and Duties, 84; Sermons on Important Subjects; Collected from a number of ministers, in some of the Northern States of America (Hartford, Conn., 1797), 499.

21. Asahel Hooker, "The Moral Tendency of Man's Accountableness to God . . . A sermon, preached on the day of the general election . . . May 9, 1805" (Hartford, Conn., 1805), 7–10; Nathan Perkins, "The Doctrines Essential to Salvation," The American National Preacher 7 (January 1833): 115; John Smalley, "Two Sermons," in Atonement, ed. Park, 60; Maxcy, "Discourse," in ibid., 101, 106.

22. Sermons on Doctrines and Duties, 80.

23. Quoted in Haroutunian, Piety versus Moralism, 94.

"viceregent"—as an atonement for fallen humanity.[24] Finally, the exact number ultimately redeemed by God was congruent with "the highest happiness of his moral kingdom."[25]

Another prominent emphasis in New Divinity thought was its assumption of the "reasonableness of Christianity." Unlike deists, who invoked reason to discredit traditional Christianity, the New Divinity utilized it to defend their "Consistent Calvinism," to make it ultimately rational. God, after all, did everything for a reason, and "nothing is in vain." To the accusation that God was unreasonable in his condemnation of sinners or that the doctrine of divine election was the design of a capricious tyrant, the New Divinity men responded that "the Divine Disposer" had "good and sufficient reasons" for predestining some to salvation and the rest to condemnation. In fact, the electing decrees of the Moral Governor ensured "the highest happiness of his moral kingdom."[26] When questioned about the divine permission of sin, they retorted that God could have prevented sin, but he chose not to in order to display "the double glory of justice and mercy."[27] Sin was "the occasion of immeasurable good," for if there had been no sin, "the universe would have lost all the glorious results of redemption, which . . . was the great end for which God built the universe."[28] For reasons that humans could not entirely fathom, sin entered the world by God's permission and became the occasion for humanity's greatest good through the work of Christ's redemption.[29] By squarely accepting the Enlightenment agenda, namely, that God must be reasonable and that one of his purposes (but not his sole purpose) was the happiness of humanity, the New Divinity men consciously placed themselves in conversation with their liberal opponents. Juggling divine sovereignty with human happiness, they never tired of trying to make their Calvinist version of Christianity eminently reasonable and compelling.

Above all, New Divinity theology was conversionist. Christianity was not merely a system to be grasped intellectually but a faith imparted supernaturally and embraced passionately. In this respect, the New Divinity position sided with the "voluntarist" tradition of Christian thought, wherein between the two main faculties of the mind (so conceived in seventeenth-century Protestant scholastic thought), the will had primacy over the intellect in the choice of good or evil. Though traceable to St. Augustine and the Puritans, Jonathan Edwards infused the voluntarist concept with "heart" language.

24. Griffin, Sermons (1844), 138.

25. Asahel Hooker, "The Divine Sincerity in the free and indiscriminate offer of salvation to sinners," in Sermons on Important Subjects, 309.

26. Ibid.

27. Griffin, "God Exalted," 26.

28. Edward Dorr Griffin, The Doctrine of Divine Efficiency, defended against certain Modern Speculations (New York, 1833), 195.

29. Griffin, Sermons (1844), 190; CEM 1 (September 1800): 95.

According to the Edwardseans, the true work of redemption was wrought in the affections—the heart, the will—"the real seat of all moral good and evil."[30] At best, the intellectualist approach of the Old Calvinists—called "speculative knowledge" by the New Divinity—was preparatory. It could neither save nor contribute efficaciously to salvation. Instead, its sole purpose was to lay the groundwork for the Holy Spirit to awaken and enlighten the sinner to God's work of regeneration, and subsequently to assist in the appropriation and expression of the faith.

In their theological expressions, New Divinity adherents primarily emphasized the relation of God to man. Their transformational theology accentuated the exalted sovereignty of God and the dependent yet wholly accountable nature of humans. How they construed the nature of each and its relation to the other is explicitly seen in their views of human nature and the will, the process of salvation, and the atoning work of Christ. The propagation of these doctrines was not merely confined to the learned ministry or to the printed page, but was vigorously preached to congregations of believers and crowds of anxious sinners. Such dogma was, in fact, the driving force, or, as Ammi Robbins of Norfolk put it, "the powerful engine, in the hands of the holy spirit," behind the New Divinity revivals in Connecticut.[31]

Human Nature and the Will

With other Calvinists, the New Divinity assumed a radical disjunction between human nature and divine grace. According to Charles Backus, people were not born as malleable agents "with a heart clear of any moral bias, like a piece of paper which has nothing written on it," for humans naturally despised the things of God and were inclined toward sinful habits rather than holy virtue.[32] They were, echoed Griffin, "destitute of *holiness*," totally depraved.[33] Yet, depravity did not mean, wrote Nathan Strong, "that the heart breaks out into all possible enormity of vice," or that people's actions were always wrong, or that they could not love their fellow men.[34] God

---

30. Edward Dorr Griffin, *A Series of Lectures, delivered in Park Street Church, Boston, on Sabbath Evening* (Boston, 1813), 66.

31. Ammi Robbins, "A Half-Century Sermon," in *History of Norfolk, Litchfield County, Connecticut,* comp. Theron Wilmot Crissey (Everett, Mass., 1900), 135.

32. Charles Backus, *The Scripture Doctrine of Regeneration Considered, in Six Discourses* (Hartford, Conn., 1800), 16.

33. Griffin, *Lectures in Park Street Church,* 10.

34. Nathan Strong, *Sermons, on Various Subjects, Doctrinal, Experimental, and Practical* (Hartford, Conn., 1798), 115.

extended a common grace to all, enabling them to do good, to behave properly, and to love others. But such grace applied to human, not divine, relations. Human depravity originated in a skewed relation to God. In words reminiscent of Augustine, Griffin described depravity as essentially privative, a "love to a *private circle or object*," a limited affection, an "opposition to the interest of God and the universe."[35] Conversely, holiness consisted of a conformity to the moral character of God, or, in Edwardsean terms, to a "love of being in general."

That the present human condition began with Adam's first sin no good Calvinist would deny. However, in a significant departure from the traditional Puritan view, the New Divinity asserted that Adam's sin was neither genetically transmitted nor imputed. They rejected Puritan creedal affirmations, expressed in the Westminster Confession and Saybrook Platform, of imputed sin in order to place the responsibility for sin squarely upon the shoulders of each person as well as to avoid the Arminian criticism that a cruel God delighted in condemning sinless, innocent babies to the everlasting torments of hell.[36]

According to Edwards, Adam was the "federal head" of his posterity.[37] The divine constitution provided that if he stood, all humanity stood, and if he fell, all humanity fell. God viewed Adam's posterity as one with Adam, coexisting together, "like a tree with many branches."[38] When Adam fell, so too all humanity fell, in that the disposition of the heart was turned away from God. It was not so much a matter of genetically inheriting Adam's sin as it was a disposition to approve of Adam's sin, to join with him in rebellion against God. In this sense, all individuals participated in the sin of Adam.

Edwards's revision of the link between Adam and his posterity was taken a step further by his devotees. Nathanael Emmons and Jacob Catlin of New Marlborough, Massachusetts, abandoned the concept of imputation altogether, dismissing it as an "absurd idea" and "antiscriptural."[39] The whole human race could not be held accountable for the sin of one man; individuals could not be condemned wholesale because of Adam's first sin. Because "sin and guilt are personal matters," reasoned a contributor to the *Connecticut Evangelical Magazine*, they could not be transferred to become the sin and guilt of another.[40] Edward Griffin, whose views on original sin more closely

35. Griffin, *Lectures in Park Street Church*, 93–94; see also Strong, *Sermons on Various Subjects* (1798), 125.

36. *Creeds of the Churches*, rev. ed., ed. John H. Leith (Atlanta, 1973), 201; Williston Walker, ed., *The Creeds and Platforms of Congregationalism* (1893; reprint, Philadelphia, 1969), 374.

37. Edwards, *WJE: Original Sin*, ed. Clyde A. Holbrook (New Haven, Conn., 1970), 260.

38. Ibid., 389.

39. Emmons is quoted in James Hoopes, "Calvinism and Consciousness from Edwards to Beecher," in *Jonathan Edwards and the American Experience*, ed. Hatch and Stout, 217; Jacob Catlin, *A Compendium of the System of Divine Truth, contained in a series of essays* . . . (Middletown, Conn., 1824), 105.

40. *CEM* 5 (March 1805): 342.

resembled Edwards's, refused to speculate on when exactly infants sinned, but of this he was certain: "They will by the free consent of the heart, eventually sin as soon as they are able."[41] Adam's fall, then, produced the occasion for sin. "In consequence of his apostasy," declared the *Connecticut Evangelical Magazine*, "we come into existence with a sinful temper."[42] As I will show later, this occasionalist view of sin profoundly altered the traditional Reformed view of the atonement, for just as Adam's sin could not be imputed to mankind, so neither could mankind's sin be imputed to Christ.

If humans were constitutionally unable to love God, then in what sense could they be held accountable for their sinful disposition? Arminian critics contended that with such a bleak view of human nature, individuals could not be held responsible for wrongdoing. In response, Edwards and his followers were inspired not only to rethink the idea of original sin but also to clarify the nature of God's sovereignty and human responsibility. Holy Writ, of course, provided the context for all thinking about God and man, and the New Divinity marshaled proof text upon proof text to support their claims. But the content of Scripture was neither self-evident nor self-interpreting; the human-divine dilemma was never systematically reconciled in its pages. One could muster passages supporting each side of the equation. Some passages of Scripture upheld divine sovereignty ("no one cometh to God except he be drawn," John 6:44); other passages supported human freedom ("And whosoever will, let him take the water of life fully," Revelation 22:17). And how one understood the dynamic between the two defined the basics of one's theology. Arminians believed that sinners could, of their own free will, accept or reject God's grace. Moderate Calvinists reasoned that sinners could utilize the means of grace to good effect and make progress toward salvation. New Divinity men rejected both positions, contending that humans were totally depraved and yet responsible, that the use of means were commendable and yet essentially unholy exercises, and that salvation was an immediate transformation of the heart wrought by God alone.

In their discussion of the divine-human encounter the New Divinity acknowledged the enormity of the issue and admitted that they could merely apprehend, never fully comprehend, what was essentially the mystery of God's sovereign intentions. "The disposing hand of God over moral agents while they remain free and accountable," confessed one New Divinity supporter, "is a process in the divine government attended with obscurity and incapable of explanation by the limited powers of men."[43] In some mysterious way, the Creator and his creatures operated in distinct spheres. Griffin

---

41. Griffin, *Lectures in Park Street Church*, 13.

42. *CEM* 5 (March 1805): 343.

43. *Sermons on Doctrines and Duties*, 83; see also Jonathan Edwards, Jr., "Future State of Existence," in *Sermons on Important Subjects*, 139.

appealed to the metaphor of "a wheel within a wheel," where human agency "has complete motion in itself, while moved by the machinery without."[44] "We sustain two relations to God," he wrote, "in a great measure independent of each other; namely, . . . that of beings *acted upon* and that of beings *acting*. And if, on the one hand, we are *none the less* dependent for being bound, and on the other *none the less* under obligations for being dependent, then each of these relations is entire without reference to the other."[45] Like a fish within a bowl, whose sustenance and care depended upon its owner but whose movements were nevertheless free (though restricted), so humans were dependent and yet free.

Challenged by the mystery of it all and yet threatened by Arminian counterclaims and dismayed by Old Calvinist lethargy, the New Divinity did not shirk from offering explanations for God's ways with man. As the first generation had defended its views in intermittent "pamphlet wars" from the 1750s through the 1770s, and as the second and third generations engaged in their own theological reformulations, the New Divinity men approached their task as much more than an ivory tower debate among a handful of prosaic theologians. At stake was not simply intellectual respectability but truth itself—the very character and government of God, his gospel, and, ultimately, human salvation. New Divinity partisans roundly condemned "that dreadful dogma, the invention and trick of modern infidelity . . . THAT IT IS NO MATTER WHAT A MAN BELIEVES, PROVIDED HIS CONDUCT IS RIGHT." Such thought, "profanely baptized by the name of Charity . . . has an infidel heart."[46] Right belief and right behavior were linked inseparably. The piety of Jonathan Edwards did not give way to the bland moralism of the New Divinity, as Joseph Haroutunian once suggested; rather, right belief was the precondition of true holiness.[47] Theology properly understood was crucial to the affective appropriation of the faith—the very stuff of which religious revivals were made.

Edwards's philosophical treatise, *Freedom of the Will* (1754), provided the framework for all New Divinity theological discussions of the will. As Allen

---

44. Edward Dorr Griffin, "A Humble Attempt to Reconcile the Differences of Christians respecting the Extent of the Atonement," in *Atonement*, ed. Park, 265.

45. Griffin, *Divine Efficiency*, 188–89.

46. Griffin, *Lectures in Park Street Church*, 310–11; see also Asahel Hooker, "The Immoral and Pernicious Tendency of Error. Illustrated in a Sermon, delivered . . . Jan. 1st, 1806 . . ." (Hartford, Conn., 1806), 16–17; and idem, "The Use and Importance of Preaching the Distinguishing Doctrines of the Gospel. Illustrated in a sermon . . . Oct. 30, 1805" (Northampton, Mass., 1806), 10–11.

47. This is Haroutunian's thesis in *Piety versus Moralism*. In the introduction to an exhaustive study of colonial New England sermonizing, Harry Stout concludes that "no shift from piety to moralism was evident" (*The New England Soul: Preaching and Religious Culture in Colonial New England* [New York, 1986], 6). For a similar assessment, see Breitenbach, "Piety *and* Moralism," in *Jonathan Edwards*, ed. Hatch and Stout, 217.

Guelzo has demonstrated, the primary corpus of New Divinity theology represents little more than an extended footnote on this work.[48] Indeed, well into the nineteenth century the New Divinity replicated Edwards's view of the will. From Charles Backus's *Scripture Doctrine of Regeneration* (1800) to Edward Dorr Griffin's *Doctrine of Divine Efficiency* (1833)—probably the last sustained restatement of Edwards's views—the New Divinity defended, preached, and popularized Edwards's view of the will as a way to undercut spiritual indifference and spark revival. Against all detractors—be they moderate Calvinists, liberal Unitarians, Arminian Methodists, or Free-Will Baptists—the New Divinity declared that Edwards's views on the will represented the only logical way to construe God's sovereign pleasure and man's moral responsibility.

Edwards's treatise was a response as well as a response to a response. First, *Freedom of the Will* was a reply to the naturalistic determinism implicit in the scientific revolution of the seventeenth century and made explicit in the materialistic philosophy of Thomas Hobbes. Second, and more to its actual content, *Freedom of the Will* was a rebuttal of Christian responses given to date. Edwards attacked the knee-jerk reaction of Old Calvinists as well as the misinformed ideas of Arminians, both of whom advanced indeterminist views of the will in order to retain the existence of spiritual substance. Edwards rejected as well the atheistic determinism of Hobbes. The latter view denied the existence of God; the former denied the sovereign pleasure of God. Through an idealist metaphysic that posited that "all thought and conception are created by, and contained in, the mind of God," Edwards affirmed a limited freedom of the will within the sovereign designs of God.[49] In effect, he offered a new Christian worldview.

To begin, Edwards advanced the notion that individuals were both free and determined. He approached this apparent contradiction by distinguishing between natural and moral determinism (or necessity).[50] Many aspects of life, said Edwards, are governed by natural necessity. Such necessity refers to actual physical hindrances, or conditions, which, no matter what we may wish, are out of our control and for which we cannot be held responsible. To offer examples

48. Guelzo, *Edwards on the Will*, esp. 14–16. Cf. James Hoopes, *Consciousness in New England: From Puritanism and Ideas to Psychoanalysis and Semiotics* (Baltimore, 1989), who argues that *Freedom of the Will* and *Original Sin* were "coda" to the *Religious Affections:* "Had he [Edwards] been unable to uphold the possibility of religious conversion, maintaining orthodox doctrine on will and sin would have been to no purpose to an evangelical like Edwards" (87).

49. Edwards, "Personal Narrative," in *Works: The Life of President Edwards*, by Sereno Dwight (New York, 1830), 1:133, quoted in Hoopes, *Consciousness in New England*, 70.

50. Edwards, *WJE: Freedom of the Will*, 156–59. My discussion of Edwards's and the New Divinity's views on the will are informed by Bruce Kuklick, *Churchmen and Philosophers: From Jonathan Edwards to John Dewey* (New Haven, Conn., 1985), 34–39, 48–55, and William Breitenbach, "The Consistent Calvinism of the New Divinity Movement," *William and Mary Quarterly*, 3d ser., 41 (April 1984): 255–58.

often cited by the New Divinity: someone commanded to move a mountain cannot be held responsible for not carrying out the order. Neither can a crippled girl be held accountable for her inability to walk, for there is nothing in her power to prevent her incapacitated condition. In the world of nature, physical limitations preclude a person's will from affecting the outcome.

But in another area of human experience the will influences the outcome. There was another kind of determinism, said Edwards, a moral determinism distinguishable from its physical counterpart. Moral determinism inclined people to act in certain ways for which they were held accountable. The crippled girl could not be held accountable for not walking, but a healthy girl was entirely accountable for her refusal to walk. Nothing but, say, her stubbornness prevented her from walking. Such an inclination (or disinclination) was entirely voluntary and prompted by the will. The girl was capable of choosing, but she was not free to choose *what* she chose. Put simply, concluded Griffin, "If we are willing we are free."[51] The ability to love God, then, had nothing to do with the origin or cause of one's disposition, but only with the ability to perform or to exercise such love if so inclined.[52]

Moreover, individuals possessed the freedom to do as they pleased and as they judged to be the greatest good. The problem was that sin had so blighted moral capacity that people preferred to act contrary to God's law. Humans had freedom—a freedom that always led to wrong choices and sinful behavior. So, while sinners were morally unable to change their ways, and while their depravity was morally determined, they nevertheless preferred and freely chose to sin. "We admit that men have a capacity or power to love God with the application of divine efficiency," declared Griffin, "otherwise none could be punished. But they never will."[53] No physical ailment or natural necessity stood in the way of a sinner's ability to love God; rather, the sinner voluntarily willed not to love God, and in so doing was culpable. Thus, moral inability was a necessary *and* voluntary condition. "The unregenerate," preached Charles Backus to his Somers congregation, "are not under the same kind of inability of loving and serving God, as a deaf man is of hearing sounds, or as a blind man is of discerning colors; but their inability arises from

---

51. Griffin, *Lectures in Park Street Church*, 163. In philosophical terms, the Edwardsean view of the will is known as "soft" determinism. The soft, or "reconciliationist," view of the will is the middle position between "hard" determinism (all events are caused, there is no free choice, and hence the will is not free) and "libertarianism" (some events are caused, but some are also uncaused, free, and spontaneous; and hence, in the latter case, the will is free). The reconciliationist view, as Griffin's statement indicates, does not deny that there are causes, but restricts the definition of a cause to a physical hindrance; where there is no compulsion the will acts freely. For a summary of these views, see Guelzo, *Edwards on the Will*, 7–8.

52. Griffin, *Lectures in Park Street Church*, 165; idem, 'Humble Attempt,' in *Atonement*, ed. Park, 264, 283.

53. Griffin, *Divine Efficiency*, 61.

a heart which is opposed both to the law and the gospel."[54] The doings of the unregenerate were not analogous to natural deafness or blindness, in which case the plea of inability to hear or see was legitimate. Rather, individuals were infected with a "sinful temper," and a "bad disposition" for which they were "wholly to blame and altogether inexcusable."[55]

Critics of the Edwardseans refused to accept these distinctions, contending that Edwards never really developed an acceptable notion of freedom. Freedom to do only wrong was a circumscribed, incomplete view of freedom. A sinner who could not do otherwise than sin did not have genuine freedom and therefore was not accountable, that is, worthy of praise or blame. Edwards responded by appealing to the natures of God and Christ. Were they not necessarily holy and virtuous and yet worthy of praise? No physical impediment kept them from sinning, yet they did not sin. Could it not be the same with humans? Nothing stood in their way, and yet they sinned.[56]

According to Edwards and the New Divinity, any other scheme diminished God as the efficient cause of salvation and erroneously shifted the focus to secondary causes such as human action and response. Alvan Hyde neatly summarized their position: "Besides God, there is nothing in the universe, which may not be properly denominated an *effect*."[57] In sermons, lectures, and essays, the New Divinity defended Edwards's notion of the will against Arminians, Pelagians, semi-Arminians, semi-Pelagians, and semi-Calvinists—in short, against any and all who impugned the sovereignty of God. In point of fact, however, those who most often felt the brunt of New Divinity ire were those of like Calvinist ilk, especially those like the Old Calvinists who often claimed Edwards's legacy (i.e., his support for revival) as their own.[58] Amid astounding Methodist gains in the 1820s and 1830s, the New Divinity directed the bulk of their formal theological writings not against these explicit Arminians but toward the Old Calvinists, especially Nathaniel William Taylor, whom they concluded was a closet Arminian. As a result, their conversation remained predominantly a Reformed one, confined to an ever-shrinking Calvinist orbit in New England. To be sure, Methodists incurred the wrath and condescension of the New Divinity, but because they had gone so far beyond the pale theologically, they were deemed irredeemable. On the other hand, Taylor, a self-proclaimed Calvinist, had not so much rejected as betrayed the tradition, threatening to destroy Calvinism from within.

---

54. Backus, *Scripture Doctrine*, 20; see also Perkins, "Doctrines Essential to Salvation," 118; idem, *Twenty-four Discourses on Some of the Important and Interesting Truths, Duties and Institutions of the Gospel . . . .* (Hartford, Conn., 1795), 485; and Maxcy, "Discourse," in *Atonement*, ed. Park, 95.

55. *CEM* 5 (March 1805): 342; Griffin, *Lectures in Park Street Church*, 257; *Sermons on Doctrines and Duties*, 81.

56. Edwards, *WJE: Freedom of the Will*, 277–94.

57. Alvan Hyde, "The Purpose of God displayed . . . ," in *Sermons on Important Subjects*, 285.

58. Guelzo, *Edwards on the Will*, 149–50, 153–54, 243, 254.

One gains some measure of the extent of New Divinity reaction to Taylor by considering briefly not the chief protagonists in the highly publicized Tyler-Taylor controversy (1829–33) but Griffin's overlooked contribution to this debate. After nearly a decade of formulating the "New Haven Theology," a system of dogmatics in the broad tradition of Old Calvinism and at odds with Edwards's view of the will, Taylor finally made plain his explicit departure from Edwards in his *Concio ad Clerum* address of 1828. In response, Bennet Tyler, then a pastor in Portland, Maine, and one of a handful of third-generation New Divinity men still on the scene, initiated an attack on Taylor.[59] Soon, Asahel Nettleton and Leonard Woods joined Tyler in the New Divinity fight against Taylor by employing tactics ranging from Nettleton's gentle personal persuasion to Tyler's public accusations of heresy. Griffin, because he was geographically removed from the center of the controversy, followed a somewhat different, yet conventional, New Divinity course of action. He confined himself to his presidential study at Williams College, where, at a feverish pace, he turned out a 220-page treatise, *The Doctrine of Divine Efficiency* (1833).

According to Griffin, Taylor's "grand object" was "to put sinners upon exertion, not merely by urging their obligations," as did the New Divinity, "but by telling them that they may succeed and can succeed, and that God may be ready to regenerate them at once."[60] Indeed, Taylor rejected Edwards's view of the will (he referred to Edwards's definition of natural ability as "an essential nothing"), and, in Griffin's judgment, spouted nothing less than the "radical principle of Arminianism," that the will was self-determined.[61] Taylor had converting intentions in mind: he wished to undercut sinners' pleas of "inability"—the excuse that because God alone saved, they had no obligations or responsibilities toward God. To treat the impenitent as if they could do nothing, said Taylor, was ill-advised and theologically mistaken. God granted salvation to those who exerted themselves toward that end. Human initiative arising from "self-love" meant something in the cosmic scheme of redemption.

Griffin took issue. Taylor removed God's efficient causative power in salvation by erroneously inserting human secondary power. Here, Griffin was not only responding directly to Taylor but also to the widespread complaint from Congregational liberals (by now, a Unitarian denomination) and Arminians that the New Divinity views vitiated the sinner's response to God's grace. To answer these critics, Griffin recapitulated the same distinctions

---

59. On Taylor, see Sidney E. Mead, *Nathaniel William Taylor, 1786–1858: A Connecticut Liberal* (Chicago, 1942). For a nuanced treatment of Taylor's views within the context of the views of Edwards and New Divinity, see Guelzo, *Edwards on the Will*, chap. 8.

60. Griffin, *Divine Efficiency*, 45.

61. Edward Dorr Griffin, "The Causal Power in Regeneration Proper . . ." (North Adams, Mass., 1834), 10.

made by Edwards three-quarters of a century earlier in *Freedom of the Will*. First, Griffin challenged the very idea that the will is self-determined, contending that the will corresponds to its object through the strongest motive, for motives control "the affections, the will, and conduct."[62] And yet "a motive will only move the will when it agrees with the temper of the heart"—which is precisely the problem, for "the glory of God is no motive to an opposing heart."[63] The will is not competent to resist motives, and motives alone cannot induce one to turn from sin.[64] God does more than simply lay truths before the mind, which the sinner then accepts or rejects, for the sinner never wills to accept God's promises.

Similarly, Griffin continued, Taylor's semi-Arminian position, which allowed for the illumination of the Spirit upon the motives and subsequent free human decision in view of the motives, was deficient, for it failed to uphold God's sovereign initiative in regeneration.[65] Taylor had cozied up to the Arminian position of what Edwards called "liberty of indifference."[66] According to this view, the will was suspended in a neutral state without the influence of an antecedent motive or bias, and therefore was free to decide of its own power. But God did not merely place before the sinner the proper motives for abandoning the destructive impulses of self-love and then leave it to the sinner to decide; he went a step further by empowering the sinner to love him.[67] The sinner was indeed free—he willed, yet only God could make the sinner "will" him.[68] Humanity was determined yet free, and God alone was the author of salvation.

In their unrelenting frontal attack upon the notion of self-determination, the New Divinity exposed their flanks to a barrage of criticism. Liberals claimed that New Divinity views obviated human freedom and led to "inability," a spiritual paralysis brought on by the deadly combination of human depravity and God's electing decrees. They argued that the harsh, Calvinist doctrine of election made God a whimsical tyrant who condemned some to hell and granted heaven to others. With moral agency destroyed, individuals were rendered helpless. In addition, both Old Calvinists and

62. Griffin, *Lectures in Park Street Church*, 256.

63. Ibid., 152.

64. Edward Dorr Griffin, *Sermons by the Late Rev. E. D. Griffin, to which is prefixed a Memoir of his life*, by W. B. Sprague, D.D. (New York, 1839), 2:506. Because Edwards never clearly defined what he meant by "motive," his followers disagreed among themselves over his intended meaning. Griffin joined Hopkins and Asa Burton in viewing motives as external influences, but not as causes: "The disposition of the heart is never produced by motives, even as a second cause" (Griffin, *Sermons* [1839], 2:152). Stephen West and Samuel Spring, to the contrary, considered motives intrinsic to the individual mind, so that motives arise as one wills (see Guelzo, *Edwards on the Will*, 106–7).

65. Griffin, *Divine Efficiency*, 43.

66. See Edwards, *WJE: Freedom of the Will*, esp. 195–203.

67. Griffin, *Lectures in Park Street Church*, 202.

68. Griffin, "Causal Power," 19.

Arminians accused New Divinity men of antinomianism—a kind of lawless and reckless attitude that took the view "What I think or do matters little, for God, regardless of my behavior, by the supernatural infusion of grace, saves those whom he will." In answering their critics, the New Divinity reaffirmed that individuals were solely dependent upon God's election to salvation and yet were obliged to turn immediately from sin.

From the pulpit—not merely the study—the New Divinity went on the offensive. They baited those who promoted the efficaciousness of human endeavor: If sinners wanted to control their own destiny, then why did they refuse to do anything about it when proffered salvation? When the gospel was set before them, they retreated to the excuse that they were not able, that they could not change their own hearts. The very people who rejected the doctrine of election and called it unfair were the very ones who did nothing about their condition. To those "without an anxious thought of God or eternity," remarked Griffin in an obvious reference to his Unitarian critics in Boston, the plea of inability was "nothing but a pretence to protect [their] stupidity."[69] They refused to take the necessary steps to renounce the world and throw themselves at the feet of the Savior. Because they "will not," Arminians retreated to the very doctrine they purportedly rejected. But they could not have it both ways. "If you say you have power," contended Griffin, "you will not have it so because that would lay you under obligations; if we say you are dependent, you resist because that puts your fate out of your own hands. How then would you have it? . . . You cannot support the plea of inability and at the same time deny the doctrine of election."[70] Arminians, not the New Divinity, fell into the clutches of fatalism.

And so falling led to another error—antinomianism. Old Calvinists were especially fond of accusing the New Divinity of this haunting New England heresy, but the New Divinity rejected any truck with heedless behavior. The antinomianism implicit in fatalism, reasoned Asahel Hooker, was nothing less than a disdain for the obligations incumbent upon the impenitent, a rationalization to riotous, "licentious" behavior.[71] "No mind so stupid ever received the true religion" with this approach. Although the New Divinity viewed the use of means to salvation as an unholy act, sinners nevertheless had obligations, for without effort or anxious feeling on their part, sinners could not expect God to grant his "infinite blessing."[72]

In a final effort to uphold moral agency, Griffin suggested abandoning any connection between the doctrine of election and the "vulgar notion of

69. Griffin, *Lectures in Park Street Church*, 264; see also idem, *Sermons* (1844), 66, 154, and idem, *Sermons* (1839), 2:512.

70. Griffin, *Sermons* (1839), 2:500–501; see also idem, *Lectures in Park Street Church*, 265–66.

71. Asahel Hooker, Sermons by Connecticut Ministers, Box E-L, CLH; see also Eliphat Steele, "Absolute Dependence on God," in *Sermons on Important Subjects*, 172.

72. Griffin, *Sermons* (1839), 2:512.

succession."[73] God was not bound by human categories of time; his existence was "one eternal now," so that no ancient decree prevented a sinner from coming to him. "His present choice," noted Griffin, "is to save you if you sincerely pray, and to reject you if you do not; and everything turns on his present choice unshackled by any former decree; because his present choice is the purpose of one eternal now."[74] The decree of election, then, was not a hindrance to human liberty, for the decree touched none until it was actually executed. God "did *not* create [humans] to be damned. He created them to be *saved.*"[75] In the order of nature (not in time), God's decree to save some came after all refused his invitation.[76] To God, the decree and the execution were simultaneous. In short, those who drew fatalistic conclusions from this doctrine did so at their own eternal risk.

The Head and the Heart, the Means of Grace, and Regeneration and Conversion

To be saved by grace meant that a sinner had a radical change of heart. Edwards had, after all, remarked that the people of Northampton did not so much need their heads stored as their hearts touched. He reiterated time and time again that true virtue "has its seat chiefly in the heart, rather than in the head. . . . The informing of the understanding is all vain," in so far as "it affects the heart."[77] One of the distinctions of New Divinity revival theology was its overriding emphasis upon the heart as the seat of the will, the core of the moral self. During his more explicit New Divinity days, Timothy Dwight aptly expressed this heart sentiment in his well-known poem, 'Greenfield Hill':

> Vain hope! by reason's power alone,
> From guilt no heart was ever won.
> Decent, not good, may reason make him;
> By reason, crimes will ne'er forsake him.[78]

In emphasizing the heart as the seat of sinful inclinations, the New Divinity rejected the Old Calvinist conviction that regeneration was preeminently a

---

73. Griffin, *Lectures in Park Street Church*, 230.
74. Griffin, *Sermons* (1844), 161.
75. Griffin, *Lectures in Park Street Church*, 227.
76. Griffin, *Sermons* (1844), 85; idem, "Humble Attempt," in *Atonement*, ed. Park, 332–34.
77. Edwards, "Some Thoughts concerning the Revival," in *WJE: The Great Awakening*, 297–98.
78. Quoted in Peter Dobkin Hall, *The Organization of American Culture, 1700–1900: Private Institutions, Elites, and the Origins of American Nationality* (New York, 1982), 156.

matter of the intellect. For Edwards and for his followers, the divine image was placed in the heart, not the understanding.[79] No Edwardsean admitted that the natural and moral faculties functioned in isolation from each other, but some New Divinity men, in their defense of natural ability, went as far as to say that the understanding was a neutral faculty, devoid of moral sense, and untouched by the Fall. For example, when John Smalley, a leading second-generation New Divinity man from Berlin, Connecticut, presented Nathanael Emmons for ordination in 1769, a conversation ensued about the extent of Adam's fall. Did it affect his understanding, asked Edwards Eels of Emmons? No, replied Emmons. Smalley jumped in, saying that "the divine image was no more upon Adam's Understg. than upon his Fingers & Toes."[80] In point of fact, the New Divinity recognized the pervasiveness of the heart's depravity. Four decades after Smalley's utterance, a contributor to the *Connecticut Evangelical Magazine and Religious Intelligencer* reiterated the standard New Divinity view: "A corrupted heart corrupts the judgment, biases the reason, and blinds the understanding of men."[81]

Often called "speculative knowledge," understanding led to an intellectual affirmation of the faith, but had only an indirect bearing upon the heart. Through natural ability, or by an act of the intellect, one gained knowledge of God and even became aware of a dependence upon God. Given rudimentary instruction, all people had a natural ability to understand God's nature, his creation, and plan of redemption. Yet "the fact is, that the heart governs the head more than the head the heart."[82]

Moral inability hindered the full, personal appropriation of God. "Wherever there is a rational soul with competent light," averred Griffin, "there is one who can certainly love God if his heart is well disposed."[83] But without an alteration in the disposition, all the rationality and understanding in the world amounted to naught. Joseph Washburn expressed the contrast plainly: "A speculative or historical faith is that which the devil and the wicked men are professors of and is not saving faith . . . but saving faith is that wich [sic]

---

79. Edwards distinguished between the head and the heart, between the intellect and will, but did not hypostatize them. He viewed them as interconnected aspects of the mind, although in conversion and in the true apprehension of faith, the heart had priority (see Stout, *New England Soul*, 206; and Guelzo, *Edwards on the Will*, 32–34).

80. This quote from Smalley was originally taken down by Edwards Eels and appeared in his "Protest" of 6 October 1769; from here it was subsequently copied by Ezra Stiles (*Extracts from the Itineraries and Other Miscellanies of Ezra Stiles . . . With a Selection from his Correspondence*, ed. Franklin B. Dexter [New Haven, Conn., 1916], 365); see also Strong, *Sermons on Various Subjects* (1798), 106.

81. *CEMRI* 2 (September 1809): 336; see also *CEMRI* 3 (April 1810): 121–27, and *CEMRI* 5 (November 1812): 417–24.

82. Griffin, *Divine Efficiency*, 90.

83. Griffin, *Sermons* (1839), 2:507; see also Perkins, *Twenty-four discourses*, 27, and Strong, *Sermons on Various Subjects* (1798), 103.

inspires the heart to love God."[84] In the heart was lodged the affections, the will, the moral taste, and here regeneration began. "The difference in taste," noted a writer in the *Connecticut Evangelical Magazine*, "forms the first, and the most essential difference of moral character, between the saint and the sinner."[85] Only when the heart was renewed to a "holy mental taste" could the understanding fully grasp God's ways, for a sense of the heart consisted of "the truths and excellency of things of the gospel."[86]

One might pile precept upon precept but remain unregenerate, for "God does not work by truth."[87] In fact, "the increase of doctrinal or speculative knowledge," warned Nathan Strong, "be the degree ever so great, hath no tendency to regenerate a person."[88] More and more knowledge, even of things Christian, could not alter a heart of stone or "convert a devil." The truly regenerate not only knew about God, but personally experienced gracious affections toward him.

Such views on the nature of regeneration had implications for what was commonly known as the means of grace—or in more accurate New Divinity parlance, "unregenerate doings." The New Divinity men rejected the moderate Calvinist idea of "next power," for not only was the mind illuminated by

84. Joseph Washburn, "Regester," Joseph Washburn Family Papers, SML; see also *CEMRI* 3 (January 1810): 12–16.

85. *CEM* 5 (September 1804):83. See also *CEM* 5 (November 1804): 170–75; Strong, *Sermons on Various Subjects* (1798), 159–74; Stephen West, "The Testimony of God to the truth of Christianity," in *Sermons on Important Subjects*, 54; and Nathan Perkins, "Two Discourses on the Grounds of the Christian's Hope . . ." (Hartford, Conn., 1800), 50.

86. *CEMRI* 3 (January 1810): 12; Samuel Hopkins, *Sketches of the Life of the Late, Rev. Samuel Hopkins, D.D.*, ed. Stephen West (Hartford, Conn., 1805), 126. The New Divinity men agreed that in some sense God created the temperament or disposition, and that individuals acted freely according to their disposition. Critics noted that it follows from this position that God is responsible for sin: i.e., God is responsible for my disposition; my disposition is sinful; therefore, God is responsible for sin. God is evil and man is let off the hook of responsibility.

To answer their critics, the New Divinity devised two responses—the "taste" and "exercise" schemes. "Tasters," such as Hopkins, John Smalley, and Asa Burton, claimed that the propensity to sin was innate (though not a physical trait) and yet was wholly man's. They thus posited a spiritual substance, independent in humans, distinct from the immediate agency of God. Regeneration, then, was an alteration of the bias of the heart, or a "physical" change of the soul. "Exercisers" like Nathanael Emmons and Griffin claimed that tasters indeed portrayed the sinful nature as physical and hence as a creation of God's (and hence, the view reinforced "inability"). Emmons rejected the tasters' idea of a sinful nature and proposed that God created "exercises" (the heart's desire, intentions, etc.), which in natural man were sinful. Sin arose from actual sinning, not from a morally corrupt nature. But even Emmons could not escape the notion that, in an ultimate sense, God was the author of sin—a position that he even came to articulate. Although Griffin opted for the exercise scheme, he refused to engage in Emmons's kind of speculation. For a more extensive treatment of the taste/exercise controversy, see Foster, *Genetic History*, 347–50; Kuklick, *Churchmen and Philosophers*, 55–59; Guelzo, *Edwards on the Will*, 106–11; Hoopes, *Consciousness in New England*, 102–18.

87. Griffin, "Causal Power," preface.

88. Strong, *Sermons on Various Subjects* (1798), 167; see also Perkins, "Doctrines Essential to Salvation," 117; idem, *Twenty-four Discourses*, 43; and idem, "A Sermon delivered at the Ordination of Rev. Hezekiah N. Woodruff . . . July 2, 1789" (New London, Conn., 1790), 9.

the Holy Spirit, the heart also required radical transformation. Although moderates concluded that the means of grace were not converting ordinances per se, they nevertheless believed that the unregenerate could "seek God and pray to him acceptably" and that God would gradually bless their efforts, "even to obtain regenerating grace."[89] The means of grace were not to be held in contempt, nor did their appropriation worsen the sinner's condition. If unregenerate sinners exercised the means of grace with sincerity and persistence, God would honor their efforts. There were, in fact, degrees of sinning. If a sinner followed the lesser of two sins, truth might grow more and more in his mind and heart to the point where he gradually entered the kingdom of God.

From the New Divinity perspective, the use of means as converting ordinances, or duties to be performed within a spectrum of gradations of sin, was essentially vain. Any dependence upon means merely led to false security, for there were no degrees of moral worth. Charles Backus denied there was a "latent spark of moral virtue" in the hearts of the unregenerate.[90] Scripture made plain that "they that are in the flesh cannot please God." And those who thought they could were "no better than the devils, and damned . . . to all eternity."[91] Moreover, renouncing evil habits, attending divine worship, and reading Scripture only worsened, not bettered, one's sinful state by making the impenitent all the more culpable. And that was the way it should be, said the New Divinity, for at that point the sinner realized all the more that he could not save himself. Only when the impenitent exhausted all natural possibilities, to the point of casting himself "dead at his Master's feet,—to die," was he ripe for regeneration.[92] Anything that smacked of preparationism or "the doctrine of progressive regeneration" was "built on principles which deny the full extent of man's depravity," and "the necessity of an essential change of character."[93] What Old Calvinists and other opponents failed to grasp were the either/or preferences of the heart. The transition from an unregenerate to a regenerate state was neither a growth experience nor "a gradual change of reason which triumphs over passions and appetites," for "there is an *essential* difference between the two."[94] Either one was saved or damned, and no gray area could cloud the difference. "The man is either under the dominion of sin,"

89. Ezra Stiles, *The Literary Diary of Ezra Stiles*, ed. Franklin B. Dexter (New York, 1901), 1:352.

90. Backus, *Scripture Doctrine*, 53; see also Griffin, *Sermons* (1839), 2:511, and Nathan Strong, "A Sermon, delivered at the Consecration of the New Brick Church in Hartford, December 3, 1807" (Hartford, Conn., 1808), 13.

91. Edwards, Jr., "A Future State of Existence," in *Sermons on Important Subjects*, 143.

92. Griffin, *Divine Efficiency*, 53.

93. Backus, *Scripture Doctrine*, 25.

94. Griffin, *Lectures in Park Street Church*, 114; Backus, *Scripture Doctrine*, 65; Samuel Austin, "True Obedience to the Gospel," in *Sermons on Important Subjects*, 361.

contended Samuel Hopkins, "as vile as ever, dead in trespasses and sin, or his heart is humble and penitent."[95]

Sinners, then, were instructed to repent immediately, while God regenerated instantaneously.[96] God demanded "the immediate duty of sinners, to hear the voice of Christ, and comply with his gracious proposals."[97] And God never asked the impossible, for he gave to sinners the natural ability to obey. Only their obdurate, incorrigible, but voluntary will kept them from carrying out their duties. Once sinners repented, an instantaneous regeneration followed. "There is no intermediate space. . . . No time is taken up in passing from death unto life."[98] Scripture (along with Edwards's Lockean application of a "simple idea") amply supported the "great and signal revolution" of instantaneous regeneration through its vivid imagery. The transit from sin to salvation was described by such biblical metaphors as "from darkness to light," "from a heart of stone to a heart of flesh," "the opening of a blind man's eyes," "a new creation," and "a new birth."

New Divinity theology and preaching did not undercut human activity in the process of the new birth but stressed that sinners had the natural ability to reform their lives. In the eyes of the New Divinity men, Old Calvinists fashioned a theology that ignored immediate repentance. By stressing duties within the means of grace without the immediacy of repentance, Old Calvinists encouraged a gradualism that could only bring discouragement, laxity, and eventual ruin. "God commandeth all men everywhere to repent," to make themselves a new heart, and to that end they must seek. Every prop must be removed and all obligations stressed. "From what I have seen in past revivals," surmised Edward Dorr Griffin at the close of his career, "I am ready to say of this method, as David said of Goliath's sword, 'There is none like that; give it to me.'"[99] In their evangelical teaching and preaching, New Divinity ministers exhorted the unregenerate to forsake sin posthaste and "take the kingdom by violence" (Matthew 11:12). To passively wait and do nothing was tantamount to committing spiritual suicide.[100]

What then precisely was the role of the means of grace in the New Divinity scheme? To clarify their position, the New Divinity men distin-

---

95. Quoted in Foster, *Genetic History*, 18; see also Steele, "Absolute Dependence," in *Sermons on Important Subjects*, 149–59.

96. Backus, *Scripture Doctrine*, 22; CEM 4 (March 1804): 345–48; Edwards, Jr., "A Future State of Existence," in *Sermons on Important Subjects*, 141; Ebenezer Porter, *Letters on the Religious Revivals* . . . (Boston, 1858), 16.

97. Joseph Washburn, *Sermons on Practical Subjects* . . . (Hartford, Conn., 1807), 299; see also CEM 4 (March 1804): 345–48; CEM 4 (April 1804): 380–82; and CEM 4 (August 1804): 76–79.

98. Griffin, *Lectures in Park Street Church*, 115; Perkins, "Doctrines Essential to Salvation," 117; see also Edwards, Jr., "A Future State of Existence," in *Sermons on Important Subjects*, 141, and Catlin, *Compendium*, 123–24.

99. Griffin, *Divine Efficiency*, 53–54.

100. See Griffin, *Lectures in Park Street Church*, 206.

guished between regeneration and conversion. Regeneration was "the work of God in giving a new heart," "the forming of a holy disposition," "the energy of the Holy Spirit in changing the heart."[101] Conversion was "the holy exercises of the heart which follow; such as love, repentance, faith, and other graces."[102] In short, God regenerated, humans converted, and only after God seized the heart were the means of grace efficacious. By so differentiating the process of salvation, by using separate vocabularies to describe the mysterious workings of God and the verifiable, self-conscious efforts of humans, the New Divinity once again reiterated a two-tiered understanding of events. Or, to use Griffin's concentric circles metaphor of a "wheel within a wheel," the New Divinity asserted that human agency had complete motion within, while moved by divine machinery without. In the process of salvation, humans sustained two relations with God: that of being acted upon (regeneration) and that of acting (conversion). One relation involved the supernatural order of grace, which interrupted the natural course of events; the other involved the order of nature, which ran according to Newtonian mechanistic principles. Strictly speaking, then, means were not truly means in the regenerative process; they were not converting ordinances but part of the process of conversion and progress in the Christian life. So Griffin in his *Park Street Lectures* placed the discussion of "regeneration supernatural" before "the means of grace." "Put bluntly," concluded the biographer of Jonathan Edwards, Jr., "the New Divinity men did not view the 'means of regeneration' as a means of regeneration at all."[103]

Though not always consistent, the New Divinity appeared to suggest that the use of means be understood in a dual sense: first, in the sense of an attention to truth that resulted in conviction *prior* to regeneration; and second, in the sense of a gracious performance of spiritual truth *after* regeneration.[104] In the first, the sinner had duties and obligations to perform. Technically, duties and obligations were not the means to the end of regeneration (for only God could regenerate), but they nevertheless played a preparatory role.[105] As the Moral Governor, God operated "a rational kingdom" by the "instruments of reason and motives."[106] Reason, or speculative knowledge, was God's instrument for clarifying a sinner's true condition. Next, when God directly addressed the motives, the sinner, in a "passive" condition, was regenerated. Finally, once regenerated, the Christian "actively" engaged in the exercise of converting former sinful habits and attitudes into holy exercises and love of God.

101. Hopkins quoted in Foster, *Genetic History*, 135; Jonathan Marsh, Archives and MSS, Misc. Personal Papers Collection, Group 3, Box 214, YDL; Backus, *Scripture Doctrine*, 15; see also Perkins, *Twenty-four Discourses*, 485, and Strong, "Consecration of the New Brick Church," 12.

102. Backus, *Scripture Doctrine*, 16; see also Griffin, "Causal Power," preface. Some New Divinity men viewed the two as synonymous; see *Sermons on Doctrines and Duties*, 141–49.

103. Robert L. Ferm, *Jonathan Edwards the Younger: 1745–1801* (Grand Rapids, Mich., 1976), 103.

104. Porter, *Letters on Revivals*, 17.

105. *CEMRI* 7 (February 1814): 54–56.

106. Griffin, *Lectures in Park Street Church*, 181.

During the initial stage in which the means of grace were utilized, the rational faculties enabled the impenitent to attend to the truths of Scripture. The spoken and written words of Scripture—the "grand instrument of converting the world"—were conveyed through the secondary natural operations of God.[107] Knowledge of Scripture did not arouse holy affections, but it did disclose God's nature and declare the sinner's obligations. In this way, clarified Nathan Perkins, "knowledge always precedes right affections of the heart."[108] The use of Scripture prior to regeneration "prepares the sinner for greater humility, love and gratitude" after regeneration, and "produces a lasting impression of the greatness of mercy and power."[109] It also showed sinners how far they strayed from God's command to love him with all their hearts. The truths of Scripture convicted sinners of guilt, helplessness, and ruin. And the more convicted they became, the more they hated God. "Light," announced Griffin, "so far as extinguishing the flame of rebellion, is only oil cast on the fire. . . . So it is with convicted sinners. Never was their enmity this inflamed until they came to have clear ideas of the God of the law. I have seen them ready to gnash with their teeth but a few hours or even minutes before they began the immortal song."[110]

Complementing the convicting words of Scripture was the simultaneous, inspiring work of the Holy Spirit. Through ministers and other Christians, the Holy Spirit imparted more light. "Though we cannot tell" how this is done, the Holy Spirit excites the mind, and "increases the liveliness of speculative faith."[111] "It pours light upon the mind," and is the "great and immediate agent in renewing the heart."[112] In this preregenerative stage God's Spirit worked through secondary causes, for, again, only in regeneration was the efficient cause of God brought to bear. In the preregenerative period, while sinners "work out" their "own salvation," God "works in" them "to will and to do." In the end, "it is God using means upon the sinner, and not the sinner using means for himself."[113]

By attending upon means in this preparatory sense, God ordinarily gave grace to the sinner.[114] In typical down-to-earth fashion, Asahel Hooker observed that just as a farmer prepares and tends the soil in anticipation of the necessary rain, so the sinner must prepare his heart. The farmer cannot produce rain, and yet he tends to his crop; so too, the sinner cannot save himself, and yet he must attend to the means of grace.[115] "It does appear,"

107. Ibid., 173.
108. Nathan Perkins, "The Gospel Glad Tidings of Good Things . . ." (Herkimer, N.Y., 1810), 8; see also idem, *Twenty-four Discourses*, 17–24, and Strong, *Sermons on Various Subjects* (1798), 109–10.
109. Griffin, *Lectures in Park Street Church*, 180, 182.
110. Griffin, "Regeneration Not Wrought by Light," *The National Preacher* 6 (February 1832): 327.
111. Griffin, *Lectures in Park Street Church*, 194; see also CEMRI 3 (January 1810): 15–16.
112. Griffin, *Lectures in Park Street Church*, 119; Strong, *Sermons on Various Subjects* (1798), 159.
113. Griffin, *Lectures in Park Street Church*, 208.
114. CEMRI 7 (March 1814): 91.
115. Asahel Hooker, "Divine Sincerity," in *Sermons on Important Subjects*, 311–12.

wrote "Eusebius" in the *Connecticut Evangelical Magazine*, "as if a degree of awakening and diligent attendance on means were, ordinarily, necessary to God's giving renewing grace to sinners. It appears from fact, that this is the *ordinary* way." But lest he concede too much, the author inserted a caveat: "There is no established connection, between their attending on means, as they do attend, and regeneration." Scripture teaches that "there is a certain connection between attending on means of grace, in a certain qualified sense, and *salvation*."[116] The author then lent himself to ambiguity by reverting to the other sense of the use of means by concluding that "such an attendance on means never precedes regeneration."[117]

In the supernatural act of regeneration, convicted sinners "leap from one state to the other in a moment."[118] They now have a new feeling and disposition toward God, a new taste for the things of God. The regenerate delight in God's law; they have a love of "being in general"—that is, toward all of existence—rather than a limited, selfish love. They love God not for anything that he does on their behalf (even their own salvation!), but for who and what he is. They have a disinterested benevolence wherein their own personal interest is gladly sacrificed for the glory and good of God's kingdom. Samuel Hopkins's famous and misunderstood statement—a statement, in fact, derived from Edwards's *Faithful Narrative*—that one must express a theoretical "willingness to be damned for the [greater] glory of God," found its logic in this unconditional love of God.[119] Edwards admitted that no words of Scripture "require such a denial as this." And yet "the truth is, as some have more clearly expressed it, that salvation has appeared too good for them, that they were worthy of nothing but condemnation, and they could not tell how to think of salvation's being bestowed upon them, fearing it was inconsistent with the glory of God's majesty, that they had so much contemned and affronted."[120] This emphasis on the primacy of a disinterested love of God led the New Divinity to alter the traditional Puritan morphology of conversion. In the Reformed *ordu salutis*, justification preceded regeneration. But the New Divinity reversed the scheme, observes William Breitenbach, to guarantee "that saints would love God for what he was rather than out of gratitude for pardon."[121]

Conversion accompanied regeneration. It was neither synonymous nor

116. *CEM* 1 (February 1801): 288, 289, 290; see also Catlin, *Compendium*, 124, and *CEMRI* 7 (February 1814): 54.

117. *CEM* 1 (February 1801): 289.

118. Griffin, "Regeneration Not Wrought by Light," 331.

119. See Hopkins, "A Dialogue Between a Calvinist and a Semi-Calvinist," in *Sketches of Hopkins* 142–50, and his syllogism: "We should submit to God's will. It is God's will that some should be damned. Therefore, we should be willing to be damned for God's will" (ibid., 166).

120. Edwards, "Faithful Narrative," in *WJE: The Great Awakening*, 170–71.

121. William Breitenbach, "Unregenerate Doings: Selflessness and Selfishness in New Divinity Theology," *American Quarterly* 34 (Winter 1982): 491.

necessarily simultaneous with regeneration. At times, the New Divinity men interchanged the two concepts, or spoke of them as one and the same, or referred to them as occurring concurrently.[122] In regeneration, God gave the sinner a new disposition; it was "an impression made upon a passive subject," so much so that one might not be aware of the transformation.[123] This unconscious occurrence meant that one might be regenerated without actually knowing it and therefore should make every effort to seek conversion.[124] In conversion, gracious affections were exercised by the regenerate and represented the actual self-conscious turning to God. As such, the regenerate "are not merely acted upon, but do themselves act," by "exercises of evangelical repentance, faith, love, and new obedience."[125] Conversion, then, in the strict theological sense, was the actual application of the means of grace to good effect. It was the progress of sanctification.[126] If prior to regeneration the use of means was a futile, unholy exercise, now its performance became a useful, holy act, the display of gracious affections.

A General Atonement

Because the exaltation of God's sovereign pleasure lay at the core of their theology, the New Divinity more often emphasized God's work of regeneration than Christ's work of redemption. References to the person and work of Christ in redemption were consistently subordinated to God's salvific purposes: Christ carried out the plan of redemption according to the secret counsel of God. Even the atoning work of Christ was subsumed within the context of God's sovereign rule. As the New Divinity stressed repeatedly, the atonement was an occasion for humanity's redemption, but a necessity for God's moral government. Rather than stress what God in Christ did for humanity (compare Wesley's highly personalized expression that Christ "had taken away *my* sins, even *mine*, and saved *me*"), the New Divinity depersonalized the atonement, observing it as a spectator would observe a transaction drawn up between two parties (God and Christ).

The New Divinity theory of the atonement reflects the continuing effort to render consistent the sovereignty of God and the moral freedom of man.

122. *Sermons on Doctrines and Duties*, 149. Connecticut New Divinity men generally followed Hopkins's view that regeneration was passive and even imperceptible, whereas conversion was active.
123. Ibid., 329; see also *CEM* 1 (March 1801): 339; *CEM* 6 (May 1806): 431; Nathan Perkins, "Two Discourses," 54–55; and Porter, *Letters on Revivals*, 61–63.
124. Griffin, *Lectures in Park Street Church*, 114; see also idem, "Regeneration Not Wrought by Light," 322–23, and Edwards, "Faithful Narrative," in *WJE: The Great Awakening*, 173.
125. *Sermons on Doctrines and Duties*, 143; see also Catlin, *Compendium*, 145.
126. Griffin, *Lectures in Park Street Church*, 176.

To hold these together, the New Divinity rejected both the accepted Calvinist model of the atonement and the traditional understanding of the extent of the atonement. In repudiating both, they sought to steer clear of the antinomianism of the Universalists, the fatalism of the Old Calvinists, and the self-determinism of the Arminians.[127]

Old Calvinists, like their Reformed and Puritan ancestors, endorsed the "five points of Calvinism," one of which was a limited atonement. Christ's death, they held, was a substitutionary sacrifice that atoned for the sins of the elect only—those whom God in his secret, inscrutable will chose to save. The merits of Christ's death did not extend to all humanity, but only to those whom God predestined to eternal life. Conversely, those to whom the merits of Christ's death did not extend were reprobate—predestined to everlasting punishment. Liberal Arminians attacked the theory of a limited atonement, arguing that it made God out to be implacable, insensitive, and deceitful. With one hand, the offer of salvation was freely extended to all; with the other, it was purposely withdrawn from some. God's offer, they said, lacked sincerity and promoted fatalism. Better to view God's offer as genuinely extending to everyone, and allow all people to determine their future through the exercise of their own self-determining will.

Another reply to traditional Calvinism came from the Universalists. In the 1770s, John Murray, an American apostle of the Englishman James Relly, trumpeted the Universalist theme throughout New England. The Universalists were Calvinists in some respects (they conceded human depravity) but were very uncalvinistic in others (they believed all would be saved). They considered their view a logical outgrowth from the Calvinist position on the atonement. When Christ died he stood in the place of all sinners, taking upon himself the sins of the human race. Through the merits of his atoning sacrifice, salvation was not only offered to all and sufficient for all but given to all. The atonement was general and, hence, universal.

The New Divinity men once again found themselves on the horns of a dilemma. How to skirt the accusation that God was unfair and humans were "impotent machines," while at the same time to avoid the unscriptural view of a universal salvation?[128] In short, how could they maintain the integrity of God's sovereignty and human accountability? In responding to these issues, the New Divinity replaced a limited atonement with a general one, rejected the debt model of the atonement in favor of a penal one, and severed the traditional connection between the decree of election and the doctrine of the atonement.

---

127. For a comprehensive treatment of New Divinity views on the atonement, see Dorus Paul Rudisill, *The Doctrine of the Atonement in Jonathan Edwards and His Successors* (New York, 1971), and *Atonement*, ed. Park. For helpful, shorter summaries, see Kuklick, *Churchmen and Philosophers*, 62–63; Breitenbach, "Consistent Calvinism," 247–50; and Guelzo, *Edwards on the Will*, 129–35.

128. Griffin, "Humble Attempt," in *Atonement*, ed. Park, 359.

To answer Arminian critics, the New Divinity agreed with the Universalist premise of a general atonement. Christ indeed atoned for the sins of all humanity, not for the elect only. However, they rejected the conclusion that a universal atonement implied a universal salvation. While the atonement extended to all, God was not obliged to save all. Universalists, contended the New Divinity, constructed their position upon the flawed debt model of the atonement accepted by traditional Calvinism. According to this model, Christ's atonement was akin to a commercial transaction in which Christ paid a debt owed by sinners to God. Christ satisfied the debt by taking upon himself the sins of humanity. Accepting this view led logically to the conclusion that if the debt for all sin was satisfied, sinners owed nothing more to God, and in fact they could justly demand that God owed them salvation. "If an equivalent price be paid for their redemption," wrote a New Divinity sympathizer, "may they not on the ground of justice demand salvation?"[129] If a third party (Christ) paid a creditor (God) in full for an incurred debt (sin), then is not the creditor obliged to release (save) the debtor from prison (hell)? No mercy is exercised; the scales of justice are merely balanced. The Universalist argument, concluded John Smalley, "turns the table entirely respecting obligation and grace between God and man. According to it, all the obligation is now on God's part; all the grace is on ours!"[130]

Furthermore, the consequences of the Universalists' doctrine were disastrous, for they led to the "gross error of Antinomianism."[131] Without the threat of eternal punishment, what prevented individuals from behaving in any way they pleased? "The doctrine of universal salvation," reasoned a New Divinity adherent in the *Connecticut Evangelical Magazine*, "tends to take off those restraints and to open the floodgates of iniquity." Wrong belief led to wrong behavior. The author told the tale of a young man who was once "amiable and promising," but after drinking from the poisoned barrel of Universalism, he became "ferocious in his manners,—profane—contentious."[132]

In place of the commercial model of the atonement, the New Divinity substituted a governmental model—a model that comported with the general New Divinity theological conception of God as a moral governor. In a plan that "conforms to the nature of things," God created a moral law and a moral government for moral (i.e., responsible, accountable) creatures. When the law is broken, the Moral Governor must inflict punishment on those who transgress; otherwise the law becomes "mere advice," "falls into contempt," the lawgiver is

129. Maxcy, "Discourse," in *Atonement*, ed. Park, 104; see also John Smalley, "Two Sermons," in ibid., 58.

130. Smalley, "Two Sermons," in *Atonement*, ed. Park, 59.

131. Nathanael Emmons, "Two Sermons on the Atonement," in *Atonement*, ed. Park, 133.

132. *CEM* 2 (November 1801): 186.

"mocked," and the divine government is "totally annihilated."[133] The legislative and executive parts of God's government must coincide; laws promulgated must be carried out. When God's laws are broken, the punishment is death, for the breaking of an eternal or infinite law deserves an infinite punishment. Ergo, "there must be a hell or there is no moral government."[134]

From this perspective, an atonement was necessary not for the human race but "entirely on God's account."[135] The atonement assured humanity that the Moral Governor would uphold the law and punish those who broke it. Christ's atonement was not a literal payment for debt—"we had not robbed the treasury of heaven"—but a public example to the human race of what lay in store for those who disobeyed the law.[136] As manager of the estate and glorious sovereign, God demonstrated in a visible way that sin would not go unheeded. "By the atonement," wrote Jonathan Edwards, Jr., "it appears that God is determined that his law shall be supported; that it shall not be despised or transgressed with impunity."[137] Christ's suffering and death were a public example to all that the wages of sin were death. The demerits of sin were not removed by the merits of Christ, nor were the sins of humanity imputed to Christ. Unlike a pecuniary debt, merit and guilt were personal and nontransferable, inhering in the subject. All individuals still deserved punishment, but by the sufferings of Christ, God lifted the penalty. Christ's atonement made possible the exercise of God's grace—"the bestowment of good where evil is deserved"—without impugning his justice. "Christ's sufferings rendered it right and fit, with respect to God's character and the good of the universe, to forgive sin."[138] The cross became a deterrent, calculated to restrain sin, to incite obedience to the law, and to increase appreciation for God's aversion to sin.[139]

133. Jonathan Edwards, Jr., "Three Sermons on the Necessity of the Atonement," in *Atonement*, ed. Park, 6; Maxcy, "Discourse," in ibid., 101–2; Griffin, "Humble Attempt," in ibid., 153; see also *Sermons on Important Subjects*, 241.

134. Griffin, *Sermons* (1844), 190; see also Stephen West, "The necessity of atonement for sin," in *Sermons on Important Subjects*, 116. To get around this logic is to deny the premise, viz., that human sin is an infinite evil because it is perpetrated against an infinite God—which is precisely the tack taken by "Uncle Bill" in Harriet Beecher Stowe's *Oldtown Folks*, 40th ed. (Boston, 1869). After "grandmother," the New Divinity protagonist, rehashes the argument that the infinite evil against an infinite God deserves an infinite punishment, Uncle Bill responds, "No act of a finite being can be infinite. No finite evil deserves infinite punishment. Man's sins are finite evils; therefore man's sins do not deserve infinite punishment." And so, concludes Stowe, "when the combatants had got thus far, they generally looked at each other in silence" (377).

135. *CEMRI* 5 (September 1812): 332.

136. Edwards, Jr., "Three Sermons," in *Atonement*, ed. Park, 18; see also Smalley, "Two Sermons," in ibid., 55–58; Emmons, "Two Sermons," in ibid., 131; and Griffin, "Humble Attempt," in ibid., 172, 223.

137. Edwards, Jr., "Three Sermons," in *Atonement*, ed. Park, 6.

138. Maxcy, "Discourse," in *Atonement*, ed. Park, 105, 106; see also Smalley, "Two Sermons," in ibid., 70–71, and Emmons, "Two Sermons," in ibid., 123.

139. Perkins, "Doctrines Essential to Salvation," 116.

Along with the governmental view of the atonement, the New Divinity advocated a general atonement devoid of Universalist conclusions. Their view of moral agency prompted them to depart from traditional Calvinism's "darling doctrine of a limited atonement" in order to sidestep the accusation that God was arbitrary and predestined humans without the exercise of free choice.[140] Actually, the New Divinity did little more than shift the emphases in the traditional Reformed understanding of the sufficiency, design, and effectiveness of the atonement. That is, they stressed the unlimited *sufficiency* of the atonement (Christ's death was sufficient to save each and every sinner; salvation was freely offered to all) and de-emphasized the limited *design* of the atonement (Christ's death was designed to save only God's elect or chosen people). So Asahel Hooker reasoned "that the gospel makes a free and impartial offer of salvation, to all who hear it, appears not only from the plain-meaning of scripture expressions, but from this important fact, that men, considered as rational and moral beings . . . are fully capable of accepting the blessings proposed."[141] In sermons, systematics, and selected pieces, the New Divinity emphasized repeatedly that the atonement was "sufficient for the whole world—offered indiscriminately to all."[142] The doctrines of predestination and election were misunderstood to restrict the sufficiency of the atonement, for God "never decreed that any man should be saved, who should not, upon just gospel grounds, be entitled to the kingdom of heaven."[143] Even the cursed "Simon Magus, had Simon Magus believed . . . would have found a provision ready for him."[144] A general atonement, then, made a genuine provision of salvation for any and all who believed.

To emphasize the primacy of human accountability, some New Divinity men revised their vocabulary. They eschewed the term *reprobate* and replaced it with *nonelect*.[145] *Reprobate* implied that some were rejected by God and excluded from salvation on account of the limited design of the atonement; *nonelect* implied that provision was made for salvation (the atonement was "sufficient" for all) but that some rejected it and were then left to themselves. The offer extended to all: God did not exclude or reject sinners; he simply left some to their own devices, others to his regenerating influence. He did not consign the impenitent to hell so much as allow them to follow the dictates of their own hearts.

---

140. Emmons, "Two Sermons," in *Atonement*, ed. Park, 132.

141. Hooker, "Divine Sincerity," in *Sermons on Important Subjects*, 293.

142. Samuel J. Mills, "The Religious Sentiments of Christ," in *Sermons on Important Subjects*, 8; see also Alexander Gillett, Sermons by Connecticut Ministers, CLH; Washburn, *Sermons*, 269; CEM 1 (July 1800): 33; CEM 1 (April 1801): 407–8; CEMRI 4 (July 1811): 242, 244; Griffin, *Sermons* (1839), 2:504; idem, *Sermons* (1844), 70, 83–86; idem, *Lectures in Park Street Church*, 226; idem, "Humble Attempt," in *Atonement*, ed. Park, 366, 388–89; Smalley, "Two Sermons," in ibid., 80, 81; Emmons, "Two Sermons," in ibid., 119; and Catlin, *Compendium*, 117–18.

143. Washburn, *Sermons*, 408.

144. Griffin, "Humble Attempt," in *Atonement*, ed. Park, 348.

145. Ibid., 384; see also Smalley, "Two Sermons," in *Atonement*, ed. Park, 80.

The "grand mistake" of hyper-Calvinism, contended Edward Griffin, was its neglect of moral agency. These Calvinists construed humans as "passive blocks under the hands of the engraver," rather than free moral agents under the moral government of God. In an effort to uphold both the secret decrees and human passivity, traditional Calvinists could not "conceive that God had any serious aim to provide a means of salvation for the non-elect."[146] Once again, this view laid Calvinists open to the Arminian criticism that God commanded the impossible: he called upon all to repent but then limited the sufficiency of the atonement to the elect. How could the nonelect be held accountable and then eternally punished for having no power to alter their situation?

To further ensure human accountability, Griffin disconnected the decree of election from the doctrine of the atonement. These doctrines, he believed, reflected two different aspects of the way in which God related to his creatures. Individuals sustained two relations to God, one as passive and dependent upon God, the other as active moral agents with obligations to God. Similarly, God related to humans in two independent ways. "As he stands related to the moral agent, he is the Moral Governor; as he stands related to the mere passive receiver, he is the Sovereign Efficient Cause."[147] As the Sovereign Efficient Cause, God elects and regenerates; as Moral Governor, he acts "without the least apparent reference" to his sovereign designs "and constructs his measures just as though men were indepen-dent."[148] And since the atonement involved God's moral government, it must extend to all, for all creatures by nature are moral agents who live under God's moral government. By freeing the doctrine of the atonement from the decree of election, Griffin liberated it from the perceived limiting effect of an unchangeable decree. According to the New Divinity, the consequences of a limited atonement were no less disastrous than a universal salvation.[149] By destroying human agency, the doctrine of a limited atonement made sinners and even Christians "stupid" and "careless"; it deadened a sense of obligation and inexcusableness and made salvation a thing passively hoped for rather than actively sought after. It engendered an indifference that led to worldliness. In fact, the ramifications of a limited atonement reached into the everyday lives of American citizens with the result that "their farms, their merchandise, their luxuries, diversion, and pleasure, engross their whole time; their Bibles they rarely read, and God is not in all their thoughts."[150]

"And why," asked Edward Dorr Griffin in a typical fit of rhetorical flourish, "is a

146. Griffin, "Humble Attempt," in *Atonement*, ed. Park, 339, 343.
147. Ibid., 269; see also idem, *Divine Efficiency*, 188–90.
148. Griffin, "Humble Attempt," in *Atonement*, ed. Park, 273.
149. Ibid., 346.
150. Smalley, "Two Sermons," in *Atonement*, ed. Park, 82.

whole town roused, and hundreds converted in a few weeks, by an influence whose beginning had been working for months in twenty different minds unknown to each other, and without the possibility of being traced to any natural cause?"[151] His unequivocal answer: revival comes by the supernatural work of God. According to Griffin, the Second Great Awakening came not through predictable, natural causes but through inscrutable, divine ones. But to recognize the sovereign efficient cause in regeneration in no way diminished human responsibility. Sinners were accountable for their condition by virtue of their moral freedom. Indeed, "perhaps ninety-nine hundreths" of Scripture treated humans as responsible agents.[152] By stretching the tension between God's sovereignty and human accountability to its limit, by carefully delineating that humans both acted and were acted upon, the New Divinity awakened sinners to acknowledge a present condition for which they were fully responsible and a future salvation only God could bestow. With an appeal to "common sense delivered from the shackles of metaphysics" (the New Divinity was repeatedly accused of being too metaphysical), revival-minded ministers led sinners to the brink by removing excuses, decrying lethargy, stressing immediate repentance, and extending the invitation of salvation to all.[153] In so doing, they continued the Edwardsean repudiation of Puritan covenant theology. No longer was a gathered people buffered from the Almighty through corporate covenants with God. "External covenant relations" of a nation or church, insisted Nathan Strong, "will prepare no one for heaven."[154] There was no refuge in solidarity, for what mattered was the solitary soul's direct encounter with the Moral Governor.

In leading New Englanders "from the covenant to the revival," the New Divinity employed the sermon as the primary means of communication. Right theology delivered "affectively" from the pulpit lay at the basis of their successful efforts to awaken those "dead in trespasses and sin." Content and style were inseparable. Without a theology that emphasized God's laws and sovereignty as well as human duties and freedom, the impenitent would live in ignorance or shirk from confronting their voluntary sinful ways. And without impassioned, personal preaching, New Divinity preachers would lose the attention of their audience. A renewed style of evangelical preaching was just as crucial as a new kind of divinity in generating a spiritual revival.

151. Griffin, "Regeneration Not Wrought by Light," 331.

152. Griffin, "Humble Attempt," in *Atonement*, ed. Park, 298; see also *CEM* 5 (February 1805): 288, and Mills, "Religious Sentiments of Christ," in *Sermons on Important Subjects*, 12, 24.

153. Griffin, *Lectures in Park Street Church*, 202; see also *CEM* 1 (September 1800): 95, and Mills, "Religious Sentiments of Christ," in *Sermons on Important Subjects*, 12.

154. Strong, "Consecration of the New Brick Church," 11.

4

"EXHORT, EXPOSTULATE, PLEAD"

The Preaching of Revival

The New Divinity men knew their own history. At the very least they remembered the excesses of the past Great Awakening in order not to repeat them. Reflecting upon the differences between the first and second major awakenings, a New Divinity contributor to the *Connecticut Evangelical Magazine* wrote:

> Without any disparagement to our venerable ancestors, may we not conclude that the doctrines of the gospel are more distinguishingly taught and better understood, than they were in general in this country, a little above half a century past? I think this inference may be fairly drawn from the different manner in which religious awakenings are now conducted and treated, from what they then were.[1]

New Divinity ministers "conducted and treated" the revivals of the Second Great Awakening with a restraint learned from the hard lessons of the past. Noticeably absent during the village revivals in northwestern Connecticut

---

1. *CEM* 1 (October 1800): 157. For similar evaluations, see *CEM* 2 (October 1801): 129–34; Nathan Perkins, "A Preached Gospel, the Great Instituted Means of Salvation . . ." (Hartford, Conn., 1808); David Smith, "The Disposition and Duty of a Faithful Minister . . ." (New London, Conn., 1811); and *Contributions to the Ecclesiastical History of Connecticut* (New Haven, Conn., 1861), 240.

was the "enthusiasm"—literally, a God-inspired madness—that characterized the early phases of the Great Awakening. No ranting itinerants worked up the people into a frenzy; no New Divinity pastor attacked lukewarm ministers or called for separation from compromising churches. God's Spirit worked through the clergy's decorous methods, sober theology, and clear, simple, heartfelt preaching.

Evangelical Homiletics: The Eighteenth-Century Background

The New Divinity preaching style owed its origins to a mode of sermonizing developed in the early 1730s and popularized by New Lights during the Great Awakening. In his exhaustive study of New England colonial preaching, Harry Stout has shown how two distinct styles of preaching emerged by the mid-eighteenth century.[2] Traditionally, Puritan preaching emphasized the balance between the head and the heart, between rational understanding and emotional appropriation. By the 1730s, this balance gave way to extremes, with each pole represented at Harvard and Yale colleges. The teaching at Harvard reflected the "intellectualist" approach, which retained the traditional emphasis on the understanding; at Yale the "voluntarist" approach placed greater emphasis on sentiment.

The Edwards-Chauncy debates in the 1740s, arising out of the disturbances of the Great Awakening, magnified these two approaches and, in so doing, more clearly defined opposing clerical parties. New Lights embraced the affectional or "evangelical" style of preaching, whereas Old Lights (including Old Calvinists) and liberals adopted the "rational" style. New Lights constructed sermon outlines, inserted brief notes under various headings, and spoke extemporaneously. John Cleaveland's extant sermons, for example, reveal that from 1750 to 1775 this New Light minister relied on skeleton outlines from which to preach Sabbath-day sermons.[3] Unlike their counterparts, Old Lights created elaborate written-out sermons, replete with literary allusions, and often read to their congregations.

Underlying these rhetorical divisions was the widening divergence between enlightened and evangelical Christianity. Each side appealed to ancient models in order to advance its cause. Liberals aspired to the felicity, elegance, and reason of Cicero, Quintilian, and Demosthenes. Evangelicals, like Timothy Dwight, invoked the simplicity of Paul. In "Dissertation on the

---

2. Harry S. Stout, *The New England Soul: Preaching and Religious Culture in Colonial New England* (New York, 1986), 187, 218–21. The paragraph summary of colonial preaching is indebted to Stout's insights.

3. Christopher M. Jedrey, *The World of John Cleaveland: Family and Community in Eighteenth-Century New England* (New York, 1979), 107–8.

History, Eloquence, and Poetry of the Bible" (1772), Dwight endorsed "the natural, unstudied language of affection" in Paul over the artificial eloquence of the ancient rhetoricians.[4] Liberal oratory was intended to impress learned audiences and to move them to moral rectitude. Evangelical oratory was aimed at the general population and was intended to be the instrument of salvation. The debate between these two very different styles—which was rooted in the theological debate about the nature of God, humanity, and salvation—persisted throughout the remainder of the eighteenth century and well into the nineteenth.[5]

Moreover, these differing styles of preaching reflected contrasting "tastes" among the people. In mid-eighteenth-century New England, those living on the frontier, or in areas such as Litchfield County where the population was less concentrated than coastal regions, tended more toward the New Light heartfelt preaching; those residing in well-established urban areas found polished, urbane discourses more to their liking. As the century progressed, however, the divisions between city and country preaching styles broke down. In Hartford, the ministers, not the region, defined the style of preaching. A triumvirate of New Divinity men—Nathan Strong of First Church, Nathan Perkins of Fourth Church (West Hartford), and Abel Flint of South Church—embodied the voluntarist, evangelical approach toward preaching. Perkins used ordination and installation sermons as a platform from which to expound the merits of New Divinity heartfelt preaching—an approach toward preaching that set "the Evangelical Ministry" apart from other forms.[6] In typical Puritan fashion he emphasized that the "preached gospel" was the divine method of bringing the human race to salvation.[7] But he then drew distinctions over the style and content of that gospel message. He attacked Old Light and Arminian preaching: "The style proper for the pulpit is . . . not laboured, formal and flowery—loaded with pomp of metaphor and false ornament." Rather, the correct style is "highly evangelical," "pure and clear," and "reaches the heart."[8] Moreover, formal differences merely indicated the deeper theological divisions separating the two camps. Consider, said Perkins, how the two groups invoke distinct vocabularies to communicate diametrically opposed theologies. Those of the intellectualist

4. Quoted in Kenneth Silverman, *Timothy Dwight* (New York, 1969), 26.

5. Alan E. Heimert, *Religion and the American Mind, from the Great Awakening to the Revolution* (Cambridge, Mass., 1966), 217; see also 159, 170–71, and 215–24 for a further explication of these rhetorical divisions.

6. Nathan Perkins, "A Sermon delivered at the Ordination of Rev. Hezekiah N. Woodruff . . . July 2, 1789" (New London, Conn., 1790), 26.

7. Nathan Perkins, "A Preached Gospel," 16; idem, "The Gospel Glad Tidings of Good Things . . ." (Herkimer, N.Y., 1810), 3.

8. Nathan Perkins, "A Sermon, preached at the Installation of the Rev. Mr. Solomon Wolcott . . . May 24th, 1786" (Hartford, Conn., [1786]), 32.

school "avoid touching upon the distinguishing truths of Christianity." A minister of this ilk avoids the use of "gospel terms, but instead of regeneration, uses the phrase, moral habits, instead of grace, virtue, instead of holiness of life, good morals." These emphases, concluded Perkins, "are certainly censurable," for they betray the very heart (or heartfelt nature) of the gospel.[9] Put simply, he reiterated in another discourse, "there must be the *regenerate principle.*"[10]

On the eve of the Second Great Awakening, as a third generation of New Divinity pastors came of age, the New Light tradition of evangelical preaching had fully matured. In an era of increasing clerical mobility where pulpit effectiveness and audience orientation claimed a higher priority than ever before, the New Divinity maintained a preaching style congruent with a theology of the heart. Within their ranks, as well as in the larger orbit of American Evangelicalism, there emerged two gifted revivalists. Edward Dorr Griffin, exalted as "the prince of preachers," was unrivaled in his ability from the pulpit to move and awaken sinners.[11] Asahel Nettleton excelled in the more informal conference meeting, where "he seemed to come into direct contact with the mind of his hearers."[12] Whereas Griffin was the preeminent preacher during the formative period of revival, Nettleton followed a decade later to become the New Divinity's prized revivalist.

The Evolution of New Divinity Homiletics

The efforts of the first two generations of New Divinity ministers to urge the impenitent to immediate repentance and newness of life had mixed results.[13] Samuel Hopkins, one of the architects of the New Divinity, was thrilled at the outpouring of divine grace in the late 1790s, but he could not count himself among the successful revivalists. Some scholars have attributed his failure to rouse his constituents to a penchant for metaphysical disquisitions from the pulpit.[14] Assuming that Hopkins is a fair representative of New

9. Ibid., 26.

10. Nathan Perkins, "A Minister of the Gospel Taking Heed to Himself and Doctrine; illustrated in a discourse delivered . . . 15th of May, 1816 . . ." (New Haven, Conn., 1816), 8.

11. Gardiner Spring, "Death and Heaven: A Sermon preached at Newark at the interment of the Rev. Edward D. Griffin, D.D." (New York, 1838), 32.

12. Bennet Tyler, *Memoir of the Life and Character of Rev. Asahel Nettleton, D.D.*, 2d ed. (Hartford, Conn., 1845), 206.

13. See Stephen E. Berk, *Calvinism versus Democracy: Timothy Dwight and the Origins of American Evangelical Orthodoxy* (Hamden, Conn., 1974), 49–73.

14. Joseph Haroutunian, *Piety versus Moralism: The Passing of the New England Theology* (1932; reprint, New York, 1970), 71; Herbert W. Schneider, *The Puritan Mind* (1930; reprint, Ann Arbor, Mich., 1958),

Divinity preaching, these critics then generalize that the New Divinity men failed in their efforts to transmit the experimental religion of Jonathan Edwards to their generation. A revisionist biographer of Hopkins rightly counsels the need to discriminate between oral proclamation from the pulpit and written discourse from the study.[15] Hopkins and his confreres intricately defended their theological position against moderate Calvinists and Arminians in their writings, but in their preaching they retained the evangelical fervor of the Great Awakeners. They understood that they were engaged in two different modes of communication and adjusted accordingly.

This reasoning seems consistent with the broad New Divinity influence in the Second Great Awakening, but it fails to emphasize sufficiently the personal or human factor in the making of an effective revivalist. Hopkins's failure as a preacher did not necessarily stem from his pulpit theologizing. His stress upon "Hopkinsian" doctrine to the exclusion of a heart-searching style reveals only part of the story.[16] By temperament, he was unsuited to become an effective soul winner. He confessed that he "loved retirement" and would rather be "alone, than in any company." His greatest pleasures "have taken place in my retirement," whereas his "public performances, praying and preaching have generally been low."[17] Part of his discomfort in public was due to a speech impediment that rendered his voice low, nasal, and monotonal. Still, Hopkins was so haunted by his ineffectiveness that he doubted the validity of his own conversion. He expressed his misgivings in his *Autobiography*:

> It has been a matter of doubt and discouragement to me, that I have little or no success by my preaching, in being made the instrument of awakening and converting sinners. . . . I came upon the stage and began to preach when there was a great and general revival of religion in New England; many were awakened, and thought to be converted, and many ministers were successful in this, and had great revivals in their congregations; but no such thing has appeared under my preaching. . . . I should expect that a good minister of Christ would

---

208; Edmund S. Morgan, "The American Revolution Considered as an Intellectual Movement," in *Paths of American Thought*, ed. Arthur M. Schlesinger, Jr., and Morton White (Boston, 1963), 11–33; and, less so, Sydney E. Ahlstrom, *A Religious History of the American People* (New Haven, Conn., 1972), 404–5. No doubt Ezra Stiles's comment that Hopkins "preached his own Congreg.ᵃ almost away or into an Indifference" prejudiced scholars' views of the New Divinity men in general (see *The Literary Diary of Ezra Stiles*, ed. Franklin B. Dexter [New York, 1901], 2:504).

15. Joseph A. Conforti, *Samuel Hopkins and the New Divinity Movement: Calvinism, the Congregational Ministry, and Reform in New England between the Great Awakenings* (Grand Rapids, Mich., 1981), 175.

16. Samuel Hopkins, *Sketches of the Life of the Late, Rev. Samuel Hopkins, D.D.*, ed. Stephen West (Hartford, Conn., 1805), 91.

17. Ibid., 86, 85.

be successful in this respect especially when others round him were successful, more than I have appeared to be. This has led me to fear, especially at times, that there is some essential defect in me, and that I had not the true spirit of Christ, and his real presence and approbation.[18]

In addition, Hopkins and other New Divinity men lacked the spontaneity necessary to arouse and sustain widespread revivals. As creatures of habit, given to long hours of study, active, time-consuming evangelism was foreign to their nature. Nathanael Emmons's opposition to hastily called religious conferences stemmed not only from his conviction that such gatherings smacked of contrived evangelism but also from the fact that they disrupted his personal life.[19] Both Emmons and Stephen West witnessed periodic revivals in their parishes in rural Massachusetts, but in neither case did the revivals coalesce into wider movements until caught up in the spiritual upheaval of the late 1790s.

In style and content, the preaching of Joseph Bellamy provided the connecting link between generations of the New Divinity.[20] Although he was every bit a Consistent Calvinist, his pragmatic Evangelicalism employed heart-searching preaching to rouse the impenitent. Because Bellamy was the most effective preacher among Edwards's protégés, his approach was passed on to a second and then a third generation of New Divinity men in the 1790s and early 1800s. The preferred solitude of Hopkins and other New Divinity "metaphysicals" was foreign to them. The new activism of the postrevolutionary age, coupled with the view that history was approaching a turning point, inspired an aggressive, vigorous attitude toward pastoral duties. The use of conference meetings, organized preaching tours, and the appeal to sinners to appropriate the means of grace testify to this mentality. As heirs of Edwards and the evangelical temper of Bellamy, the leaders of the Awakening sought to remain true to New Divinity dogma within the context of an active Evangelicalism. While preaching the "hard sayings" of Calvinism, they urged sinners to repent immediately. They envisioned their preaching as an instrument, not the cause, of divine regeneration.

Heartfelt preaching was not entirely confined to the younger clerical leaders of the New Divinity revivals, but it was among their ranks that a style of preaching aimed at the affections was most pronounced.[21] These clergy

18. Ibid., 124.
19. Edwards A. Park, *Memoir of Nathanael Emmons; with sketches of his friends and pupils* (Boston, 1861), 58, 108, 174, 332.
20. Berk, *Calvinism versus Democracy*, 54, 59; Conforti, *Samuel Hopkins*, 178.
21. Cf. Richard D. Shiels, "The Second Great Awakening in Connecticut: Critique of the Traditional Interpretation," *Church History* 49 (December 1980): 401–15, who contends that statements by Lyman Beecher regarding a new style of evangelical preaching are exaggerated and that

reasserted the affective, "experimental" preaching of George Whitefield, Edwards, and Bellamy. Not content that sinners sit idly by and passively wait for divine intervention, they urged human initiative: that sinners had the duty and natural ability to repent. As a later revivalist put it, "I believe fully that we are no longer to trust Providence, and expect that God will vindicate his cause while we neglect the use of appropriate means."[22]

One discovers, however, a certain ambivalence in clerical appraisals of their own efforts and in their attributions of revival to divine operations through doctrinal preaching alone. That the New Divinity was uneasy about uplifting human effort and undermining divine sovereignty is clearly seen in their written accounts of local revivals. In a letter written in 1799, Edward Griffin related how, prior to the outbreak of revival in New Hartford, he preached a "plain . . . and very indifferent sermon."[23] Yet upon closer examination, these self-effacing words cannot conceal his mighty efforts to awaken his congregation. Griffin mentioned that his sermon text was Matthew 20:30—the healing of the two blind men by Jesus. The same text appeared in Griffin's published sermons under the title "Jesus of Nazareth Passing By." A note to an asterisk appearing next to the title indicated "preached in a revival."[24] No doubt the sermon was revised for publication, but surely the basic content remained unaltered. In this sermon, Griffin captured the broad themes of revival sermonizing. By a direct, personal appeal, he exhorted his listeners to use the means at their disposal: perhaps it would be their last chance; death stalks all; and procrastination would lead to "stupidity"—the byword for indifference and hardness of heart.[25]

Griffin introduced his topic by noting that it was necessary for the blind men to be by the side of the road in order for Jesus to notice them. "However fixed the event was in the counsels of heaven, their being by the wayside was an established link in the chain leading to the happy change. Without that means, the end was never to be accomplished." In the same way, "it is necessary for ruined men to attend solemnly and earnestly and sincerely on all the means of grace." Just as the blind men called out for the mercy of Jesus,

---

one must look elsewhere for the origins of the revival. I argue not for a qualitatively different form of preaching but for a self-conscious, renewed commitment to evangelical preaching among New Divinity ministers. For a contemporary view similar to Beecher's, see Luther Hart, "A View of the Religious Declension in New England, and of its Causes, during the latter half of the Eighteenth Century," *Quarterly Christian Spectator* 5 (June 1833): 220–25.

22. Lyman Beecher, *The Autobiography of Lyman Beecher*, ed. Barbara M. Cross (Cambridge, Mass., 1966), 1:248.

23. Edward Dorr Griffin, "Letter on religious revival in about forty adjacent parishes" (copy), 1 August 1799, CSL.

24. Edward Dorr Griffin, *Sermons by the Late Rev. E. D. Griffin, to which is prefixed a Memoir of his life, by W. B. Sprague, D.D.* (New York, 1839), 2:2.

25. Ibid., 7, 10, 12.

so must sinners call upon him for salvation. "Is there a poor sinner in all these seats who has been raising his anxious cry to the Son of David? Blessed tidings my friend. Put thine ear to the Gospel and listen. He calleth thee."[26] Griffin closed with an impassioned plea: "If you have deliberately resolved to lie down in eternal burnings, arise and take the kingdom of heaven by violence. Delay not a moment. . . . By the worth of our ever-dying souls I entreat you,—by the love and sorrow of Calvary I adjure you, not to reject this mission of the Holy Spirit. Your everlasting all is at stake. It is likely to be your last chance."[27] This is hardly the kind of language that makes for a "plain" and "very indifferent sermon," but the juxtaposition of Griffin's declamations and his actual sermon reveal what one historian calls a "theological schizophrenia" embodied in the revival reports to the *Connecticut Evangelical Magazine* from 1800 to 1808.[28] After 1808, clerical accounts displayed a utilitarian bent, blurring the distinction between divine sovereignty and human initiative. Now confident that God blessed their efforts, the authors emphasized human effort and the dawn of a new millennial day.

Although one could make a case for the origins of extemporaneous preaching as far back as Peter's Pentecost sermon in Acts 2, the particular paradigm employed during the revivals of the Second Great Awakening is traceable to seventeenth-century English Puritanism and, more immediately, to George Whitefield and Jonathan Edwards during the Great Awakening.[29] Primitive Christians, Puritans, and leaders of the Awakening purposely constructed sermon outlines or fragments in order to allow for the inbreaking of the Holy Spirit—that moment when the Spirit unloosed the speaker's tongue and torrents of inspired words poured forth. At such times when the Spirit controlled speech, a rapt audience responded to the invitation for salvation or renewal, and a revival ensued. Edwards offered a profound psychological insight into the nature of this Spirit-driven preaching. "The main benefit," he noted, came from the "impression made upon the mind in the time of it, and not by the effect that arises afterwards by a remembrance of what was delivered." The proper value of preaching was in the excitation of the mind through the divine operation of the Spirit, not in the auditor's ability to recall a sermon in its detail. What truly endured was "an impression of words made on the heart in the time of it," for it was the experience—the encounter with

26. Ibid., 2, 2–3, 5–6.
27. Ibid., 12–13.
28. Berk, *Calvinism versus Democracy*, 168; see also Edward Dorr Griffin, "An Oration delivered June 21, 1809 . . . in the Divinity College at Andover" (Boston, [1809]), where he writes, "[The apostle] Paul saw no connection between his preaching and the salvation of men" (23).
29. On the Puritans, see David D. Hall, *The Faithful Shepherd: A History of the New England Ministry in the Seventeenth Century* (New York, 1974), 50–54.

the divine—that forever altered the affections.[30] Remembering yielded speculative knowledge only, whereas experiencing produced saving heartfelt knowledge.

Whitefield and Edwards, then, bequeathed to their disciples the extemporaneous mode of preaching whose style was primarily to "impress the conscience, as well as enlighten the understanding."[31] But "extemporaneous" in Edwards's use of the term did not refer to Whitefield's spontaneous preaching, utterly dependent upon the inspiration of the Spirit. Rather, it meant a spoken, not read, sermon; an outlined, not fully written-out, text. The sermon was to be so well prepared—Jeremiah Hallock spoke of a craving to "eat my sermons before I preach them" (probably an allusion to Jeremiah 15:16)—that the minister could establish a psychological bond with his audience through direct eye contact.[32]

During the 1790s and early 1800s, New Divinity pastors reaffirmed their commitment to evangelical, extemporaneous preaching. Discussion arose over the most appropriate preaching style for reaching the lax and the lost. The topic was broached during a Hartford North Association meeting in 1795, when the clergy resolved to spend time at each meeting discussing "the best method of composing and delivering sermons."[33] An article appearing in the *Connecticut Evangelical Magazine* considered "the best manner of preaching the gospel."[34] And the Litchfield South Association took up the same issue in a 19 October 1802 meeting. The minutes recorded two questions for consideration: What was "the best method of preaching?" and What was "the most profitable manner of preaching?" To the first question, the reply came, "the plain, practicle [sic] preaching of christian duties, founded on the doctrines of the gospel." To the second question, the association concluded that "memoriter, or extempore preaching is calculated to have best effect, where it is practicable and can be done with propriety."[35]

The progression from older to younger New Divinity leaders of the Second Great Awakening is from a group of evangelical ministers uneven in their preaching abilities to a group whose talents in the pulpit outshone their predecessors. The trend points toward a self-conscious effort among the

---

30. Edwards, "Some Thoughts concerning the Revival," in *WJE: The Great Awakening*, ed. C. C. Goen (New Haven, Conn., 1972), 397.

31. Park, *Memoir of Nathanael Emmons*, 276.

32. Quoted in *Historical Sketch of the Congregational Church and Parish of Canton Center, Conn., formerly West Simsbury*, comp. Frederick Alvord and Ida R. Gridley (Hartford, Conn., 1886), 35. The text of Jeremiah 15:16: "Thy words were found, and I did eat them." Samuel Hopkins noted that he wrote out his sermons and then memorized them "with allowance to extemporize in some cases." If memorization was practiced diligently, a minister would be able to preach without writing out his sermons (see *Sketches*, 90–91).

33. Consocation Records, 1790–1820, Hartford North Association Minutes, CLH.

34. *CEM* 2 (October 1801): 129–34.

35. Original Records of Litchfield County Association and Consociation, 1752–1814, CLH.

younger ministers to develop and refine their homiletic skills. As discussed earlier, a new definition of a successful minister emerged in the early nineteenth century. Within the clerical profession—in part stimulated by increasing demands of the laity—a minister's preaching ability was no longer considered as one among several criteria of equal value in selecting a pastor. A candidate's preaching ability assumed a higher priority than other pastoral skills. The long-tenured parson, represented by the older generation of pastors, was eventually displaced by the mobile preacher whose very reputation—and in some cases his job—depended upon his success as a revivalist.[36]

Second-Generation New Divinity Homiletics

Some of the older New Divinity men became progressively aware of the ineffectiveness of finely nuanced sermons and so altered their preaching style over time. Charles Backus pastored the First Congregational Church of Somers in Tolland County, an area torn by Separatism during the third quarter of the eighteenth century. Initially he favored the abstract, ideational sermon as the appropriate way to avoid the excesses of Separatism, but eventually he adopted a more practical style.[37] In a 1795 ordination sermon, Backus clarified his new approach. He urged ministers to preach with "great plainness" and to direct their message to the "heart."[38] Acknowledging the social basis of religious commitment—and unwittingly affirming the social distinctions between the intellectualist and voluntarist preaching traditions— Backus noted that historically the Christian faith has been more attractive to the "unlettered peasant" than to the "man of penetration and science." Accordingly, ministers should accommodate their sermon style to suit their audience: they "had better sacrifice elegance than fail of giving light to the minds of men."[39] With this audience-oriented approach, the preacher must address his listeners personally, and "with glowing warmth," "animation," and "zeal" make them feel "that he is speaking to them."[40]

On the periphery of the intense revivals sweeping Litchfield and Hartford

---

36. For the broad context of this change, see Peter Dobkin Hall, *The Organization of American Culture, 1700–1900: Private Institutions, Elites, and the Origins of American Nationality* (New York, 1982), chap. 3; on the clergy, see 47–53.

37. See "Charles Backus" in Appendix 1.

38. Charles Backus, "Qualifications and Duties of the Christian Pastor: A Sermon, delivered . . . October 29, 1795 . . ." (Boston, 1795), 18.

39. Ibid., 19; see also idem, "The High Importance of Love to Jesus Christ in the Ministry of the Gospel: A sermon, delivered . . . October 31, 1799" (Amherst, N.H., 1799), 26–27.

40. Backus, "Qualifications and Duties," 20, 19.

counties during the Second Great Awakening, Backus's own church underwent four revivals during his thirty years as pastor. A classmate of Timothy
Dwight and Nathan Strong at Yale—two revivalists in their own right—
Backus mirrored the normal vocational attitudes of New Divinity men come
of age before American nationhood. He spent long hours in the study,
decried unsupervised conference meetings, and left the management of the
home to his wife. Yet he proved adaptable to change in the pulpit and
realized that unadorned, passionate preaching moved the unregenerate to
seek salvation. "As a preacher," Dwight wrote in his *Travels*, "Dr. Backus was
calm, affectionate, solemn, interesting, and persuasive. His style and elocution were artless [i.e., they lacked artificial elegance], manly, and pleasing.
His sentiments were in a high degree evangelical, and without a suspicion
seated in the heart."[41] His affectionate preaching is evident at the conclusion
to one of his sermons. Employing images of civil disorder, Backus urged the
rebellious subjects to relent and yield to the divine ruler:

> Tremble at the thought of maintaining a controversy with God!
> Throw down the weapons of your rebellion, and submit yourself to
> him. . . . O ye sinners, of every description, let not a deceived heart
> any longer turn you aside. Do not flatter yourselves with the hope of
> finding peace while you remain God's enemies. You must become
> reconciled to him or you must perish forever.[42]

Among the other older clergy participating in the local Connecticut
revivals, Nathan Strong, Samuel Mills, and perhaps Ammi Robbins stand out
as exceptional preachers. Others, such as Simon Waterman, Rufus Hawley,
Nathan Perkins, Peter Starr, Joshua Williams, Jonathan Miller, Jeremiah
Hallock, and Alexander Gillett, could be classified as godly, pious supporters
of the Awakening but undistinguished as revivalists until caught up in the
spiritual outpouring of the 1798–99 revivals. Then, emboldened by the
success of others, these pastors adopted the rhetorical conventions of
evangelical sermonizing.

Prior to this *volte-face* of the clergy during the revivals of the late eighteenth
century, precedent for sermon adaptation had been firmly established. The
example of Philemon Robbins, the controversial New Light–New Divinity

41. Timothy Dwight, *Travels in New England and New York*, ed. Barbara M. Solomon (Cambridge,
Mass., 1969), 2:190.
42. Backus, "Qualifications and Duties," 19–20. For other references to Backus's emphasis upon
evangelical preaching, see his "Afflictions Improved: The substance of a discourse
delivered . . . February 28, 1790 . . ." (Springfield, Mass., 1793); "Ministers Serving God in the
Gospel of His Son: A sermon delivered . . . February 3, 1796" (West Springfield, Mass., 1796); and
"The Principal Causes of the Opposition to Christianity Considered; in a sermon,
delivered . . . January 10, 1798" (Worcester, Mass., 1798).

pastor from Branford, Connecticut, is instructive. During the first decade of his ministry, Robbins constructed his sermons along conventional lines: many were written out in full, and by his own admission, his preaching was dull, didactic, and uninspiring. In the summer of 1741, however, Robbins radically altered his style of preaching. Caught up in the fervor of the Great Awakening, he adopted the extemporaneous, evangelical style of itinerant revivalists. No longer did he write out his sermons, but he assembled abbreviated sermon notes arranged in vertical fragments.[43] In similar fashion, during the 1790s, many New Divinity pastors delivered fully orthodox but lackluster sermons until bitten by the bug of revival; once infected, they employed the feverish evangelical mode of preaching. Even Nathan Strong, recognized for his forceful evangelical preaching before the outbreak of the revival, discarded his formal, "scholastic" approach for a "simple, . . . terse, direct, and perspicuous style" when he sensed heightened spiritual interest among his parishioners.[44]

An accurate evaluation of the preaching abilities of the New Divinity clergy must rely on both the reading of their extant sermons and contemporary opinions of their homiletic skills. The contrasting styles of two older clergy, Samuel Mills, Sr., and Alexander Gillett, offer a case in point. The two were close friends and labored together for revival in their contiguous parishes, but their personalities, pulpit demeanor, and success as awakeners differed markedly. Governor Roger Griswold considered Mills the most eloquent preacher he had ever heard. "Father Mills," as he was known to his congregation, was a popular preacher with a notable ability to illustrate and describe the points he sought to stress.[45] Outpourings of revival were experienced five times during the more than fifty years he served Torringford's Congregational church. Writing to Gillett during the outburst of revival in 1798, Mills urged that active measures be taken to further the cause: "It is time for everyone, even the whole world to awake from their slumberings. A little more sleep, a little more folding of the hands, will not answer. It ought not to answer."[46] In his contributing piece to Sermons on Important Subjects, Mills held up Christ as an exemplary preacher who "was a remarkable advocate for the use of means" and probably a "very plain, striking, intelligible, and pathetic preacher."[47] No doubt he believed he embodied those same traits in his own preaching.

43. On Robbins's sermonic alterations, see Donald Weber, Rhetoric and History in Revolutionary New England (New York, 1988), chap. 1, esp. 14–24.

44. Samuel H. Riddel, "Memoir of the Rev. Nathan Strong, D.D.," American Quarterly Register 13 (November 1840): 136.

45. Samuel Orcutt, History of Torrington, Connecticut (Albany, N.Y., 1878), 546–47.

46. Quoted in Orcutt, History of Torrington, 538.

47. Samuel J. Mills, "The Religious Sentiments of Christ," in Sermons on Important Subjects (Hartford, Conn., 1797), 19, 25.

Gillett was nearly fifty years old when revival came to his Torrington congregation in 1799. His name often appears along with Mills and Griffin as a coleader of revivals in the Torrington area. That may be true, but Gillett's leadership did not evolve from recognized preaching skills, for his effectiveness in the pulpit was hampered by a speech impediment—shades of Hopkins!—which probably contributed to his reclusive nature. In his account of the revival in Torrington, Gillett observed that "the most plain, pungent preaching" was attended with great success, but he did not mention exactly *who* was doing the preaching.[48] In all probability, the awakener was one of his itinerating cohorts.

While Gillett's colleagues described his preaching as "fervid," they also conceded that "he possessed not the graces either of style or elocution."[49] Moreover, Gillett's dour mien and love of the study did not endear him to his parishioners. Ironically, the content of his manuscript sermons read as though they could arouse the most wayward of sinners. The substance of these sermons was "doctrino-practical" and consistently emphasized the stock-in-trade images of revival preaching. Gillett frequently employed the "death to life" or "asleep to awaken" image. At the close of one sermon whose text was Ephesians 2:5—"even when we were dead in sins, God hath quickened us together with Christ"—he scribbled the following plea: "O impenitent, dead sinners. I would try one more effort to awaken you to 'hearken to the voice of the Son of God and you shall live.' Now I bid you and invite you to Christ."[50]

Perhaps his effectiveness in the Awakening is resolved when the anticipation and heightened expectations of convicted sinners are taken into account. This aspect of the revival will be fully explored later, but it is worth stating here that many clergy reported that their preaching was no different when revival erupted than in the past. Clerical accounts attribute the revival to an increased sense of audience receptivity as well as to a supernatural and therefore unpredictable act of God.

One of Gillett's sermons that evidently triggered revival was delivered at a conference meeting. His text was Jonah 1:1–6, where Jonah was fast asleep in the bow of the ship. Preached at least six times during the 1799 revivals, Gillett emphasized that "now is the only time to be saved. . . . If we are asleep, we're condemned."[51] The conference meeting enabled a preacher such

---

48. *CEM* 1 (October 1800): 136.

49. See "Alexander Gillett," Appendix 1, and Luther Hart, "A Sermon, delivered at Torrington . . . Jan. 26, 1826, at the Funeral of Reverend Alexander Gillett . . ." (New Haven, Conn., 1826), 29. For a more positive contemporary assessment of Gillett's preaching abilities, see Thomas Robbins, *Diary of Thomas Robbins, D.D., 1796–1854*, ed. Increase N. Tarbox (Boston, 1886), 1:21, 297.

50. Alexander Gillett, Sermons by Connecticut Ministers, Box E-L, CLH.

51. Ibid. Gillett listed the parishes where he preached this sermon.

as Gillett to exercise a freer style than would otherwise be exhibited in a Sabbath-day sermon or a more formal setting.[52] Moreover, in those cases where the minister repeated a sermon—and this happened often with pulpit exchanges and even more frequently during itinerant revival preaching—he relied less and less on notes, to the point where he spoke entirely from memory.[53] Where a pastor is known to have preached at a conference meeting, the sermon outline is generally shorter than the normal Sunday sermon.[54] This abbreviated format allowed for extemporaneous preaching in its pristine form: personal, audience-oriented, spontaneous, and inspired by the Spirit. Such seemed to be the case with Gillett and, indeed, was the case with Nathan Strong, who "always spoke extemporaneously" at conference meetings.[55]

In the manuscript sermons of Burlington's Jonathan Miller this contrast between formal Sunday sermons and informal conference meeting exhortations is clear. Miller was "not an eloquent preacher," and the content of his sermons delivered during the 1780s and 1790s appears dull and didactic.[56] Sermons marked "conference meeting," however, exhibit a passionate, evangelical flavor. "Exhort-Expostulate-Plead" he scribbled boldly in the margin of his conference sermon notes dated 1806–7. Urging his audience "toward the duty of immediate submission to Christ," Miller used such phrases as "fly to Christ," "ye must be born again," and "be not seduced by Delay."[57] The informal setting of the conference meeting, with its focus on revival, allowed New Divinity preachers the freedom to discard usual pulpit etiquette and speak fervently and directly to their audience.

Third-Generation New Divinity Homiletics

The heart-searching, evangelical style of preaching characterized by the Great Awakeners and transmitted through the schools of the prophets with

---

52. This contrast is particularly evident in Gillett's sermon, "On the Proper Mode of Preaching the Gospel . . ." (New Haven, Conn., 1808). The thrust of the sermon is doctrinal, toward preaching "things new and old" (10), i.e., the "whole counsel of God," rather than homiletical skills.

53. For other examples of New Divinity ministers' repeated use of a single sermon in the late eighteenth-century revivals, see Weber, *Rhetoric and History*, 23, 52.

54. Thomas Robbins made several references to differences in style and composition that set conference meeting sermons apart from sabbath day sermons (see Robbins, *Diary* 1:414, 580, and esp. 600, where he records that he spoke at Nathan Strong's Hartford church conference with "short notes.")

55. Riddel, "Memoir of Strong," 140.

56. [Zephaniah Moore Humphrey], *Memorial Sketches: Heman Humphrey, Sophia Porter Humphrey* (Philadelphia, 1869), 35; Jonathan Miller, Sermons, CHS.

57. Jonathan Miller, Conference Books, CHS.

varying degrees of success was applied more consistently by the younger leaders of the Second Great Awakening. Such adjectives as "evangelical," "edifying," "simple," "plain," "pungent," "searching," "perspicuous," and "popular" were used by clerical peers to describe the preaching of third-generation New Divinity men. Although reports from lay people hearing the sermons of these men are scanty, the impressionistic evidence gathered confirms clerical estimations.

The contents of the diary of John Fitch reveal contrasting impressions of two ministers involved in the village revivals. In December 1804, Fitch heard the elderly Simon Waterman of Plymouth preach on the subject of humility. According to Fitch, the topic was inconsistent with Waterman's character. "I think," he wrote, "he ought to have a little more experimental knowledge to give their precepts their full force."[58] He was right. Waterman had a history of belligerence with his congregation and was eventually dismissed for "alleged petulance and willfulness."[59] Fitch thought differently of Josiah Andrews. A 1797 graduate of Yale, Andrews studied under Abel Flint, served as a missionary to new settlements in Pennsylvania and New York before candidating in 1801, and accepted a permanent settlement in Killingworth the following year. When Fitch heard Andrews speak, he was impressed by his "two excellent discourses, methodical, and in good language."[60] Others judged him an "animated, popular preacher of high Calvinism."[61]

The Rev. Asahel Hooker of Goshen typified the kind of younger preacher whose sermons penetrated the heart and conscience of his listeners. "An edifying and searching preacher," Hooker grew up in Bethlehem under the evangelical preaching of Joseph Bellamy.[62] He graduated from Yale in 1789 and accepted a settlement in rural Goshen in 1791. Like Bellamy, he established a school for the prophets—the last of its kind in New England.

Only one of Hooker's surviving manuscript sermons is known to have been delivered at a conference meeting. The format and content closely resemble Jonathan Miller's. With a rough outline before him, Hooker hit upon the central theme of salvation: sinners must undergo "an improved change, called in the scriptures, 'being born again.'"[63] After the Goshen church added eighty converts to its membership roll following the 1799 revival, Hooker pressed for another significant ingathering. In the fall of 1800 he chose an apt text for his rural congregation: "The harvest is past, the summer is ended, and we are not saved" (Jeremiah 8:20). Hooker introduced his sermon by describing the

58. Jonathan Fitch, Diary, CSL.
59. Franklin B. Dexter, ed., *Biographical Sketches of the Graduates of Yale College with Annals of the College History* (New York, 1885–1912), 2:630.
60. Fitch, Diary, CSL.
61. See Joseph Andrews, Appendix 1.
62. Ibid.
63. Asahel Hooker, Sermon Collection, 1640–1875, Box 1, No. 48, AAS.

"similitudes of harvest."[64] Just as in autumn the fruit of the earth is gathered, "so is the time of special outpouring—divine spirit, to the revival of religion." Just as the earthly harvest comes at regular intervals, so comes the spiritual harvest, though in times of difficulty or declension. In both kinds of harvest there is "rejoicing." Unfortunately, Hooker continued, the analogy breaks down: all who witness spiritual harvests are not always gathered in. "Some remain at ease in Zion. The truths they hear are without spiritual benefit." Others, whose consciences are enlivened, "grow careless." Hooker concluded by decrying the lamentable state of those who remain unmoved.[65] Clearly, this was the kind of sermon aimed at reaching a large audience. Replete with everyday images familiar to his Goshen auditors, Hooker set forth the terms of salvation with simplicity, clarity, and—critics would add—crudity. The contrasting homiletical styles of liberals and Evangelicals were set in stark relief by the *Monthly Anthology's* review of Hooker's 1805 election sermon. Hooker's sermon "might be deemed a good one," noted the reviewer, if delivered "before ordinary assemblies." Which is to say, it might find favor in rural Goshen, but not in sophisticated Boston. "To a scholar . . . Mr. Hooker will seem a vapid performance, distinguished for neither richness of matter, fire of fancy, nor elegance of style."[66]

Nearly every New Divinity preacher took up the theme of "inability." One Sunday in July 1800, Hooker preached on this topic in order to leave sinners without any excuse for rejecting the gospel. To Hooker, the unawakened often retreated into the shelter of fatalism to escape responsibility for their eternal destiny. Using the text, "But we are bound to give thanks always to God for you . . . because God hath from the beginning chosen you to salvation" (2 Thessalonians 2:13), Hooker dismissed the notion that God's election was arbitrary. Rather, "we are to understand by this, that God did not choose *any* of mankind, to salvation absolutely, so as to leave out of his precious purpose those *conditions* and *qualifications*, which are essential to their being saved."[67] Hooker made no mention of the difference between God's act of regeneration and human conversion, but in unadorned, simple language he set before the impenitent their responsibility to fulfill certain conditions by appropriating the means of grace.

64. Asahel Hooker, Sermons by Connecticut Ministers, Box E-L, CLH. Evidently this was a popular text. One diarist noted that Noah Porter of Farmington spoke from the same text in November 1803 (see Mary Treadwell Hooker Diary, CSL, p. 33).

65. Hooker, Sermons, CLH.

66. *Monthly Anthology and Boston Review* 2 (July 1805): 382. Lyman Beecher wrote to Hooker regarding the latter's success in "extempore speaking" and went on to contrast extempore preaching, where inevitably grammatical mistakes are made, with written sermons. Beecher concluded: "If we felt less concern about our own reputation, and more of the love of Christ and of souls, we should oftener, I am persuaded, speak with fluency and power." Mr. Beecher to the Rev. Asahel Hooker, 22 January 1811, in Beecher, *Autobiography* 1:174–75.

67. Hooker, Sermons, CLH.

A revival sermon of Bennet Tyler's accentuated the continual New Divinity concern to clarify the relationship between divine sovereignty and human responsibility. A staunch New Divinity apologist throughout his career, Tyler defended Connecticut theological conservatism against Nathaniel Taylor of Yale Divinity School in the "Taylor-Tyler Controversy." Later, he became president and professor of theology at the Theological Institute of Connecticut in East Windsor—the New Divinity answer to the liberal influences at Yale Divinity School and Charles Finney's "new measures." Earlier in his career, following ministerial preparation under Asahel Hooker, Tyler had itinerated throughout Connecticut and New York. He developed a prize revival sermon that he preached nearly twenty times during his tour of 1806–7.[68] "A revival of religion desired" abounds with the personal address ("O friends") and exclamations throughout, and yet Tyler made clear who brings revival:

> Ministers may preach with earnestness and pungency till they are almost ready to faint with discouragement—they may warn the wicked with tears in their eyes to turn from their evil ways, describe to them in the most glaring colors their alarming situation, unveil to their view the awful pit into which they are rushing—But in vain. . . . No my friends, nothing but the Spirit of God can make any useful impression on the mind which will be permanent.[69]

Yet dependence upon the Spirit did not imply passivity. "Go to your heavenly father," implored Tyler, "and bare yourselves in his presence and resolve that you will give him no rest until he appears for the upbuilding of Zion in this place."[70]

Edward Dorr Griffin: The Prince of Preachers

According to those who favored revivals and heard him preach, Edward Dorr Griffin was the greatest revivalist of his day. Such an accolade raises Griffin to the status of the prime clerical mover during the formative period of Connecticut's Second Great Awakening. And the results of his preaching did not bely such claims. In all but one of his appointments, whether stated supply or settled pastorates, numerous conversions took place. Even Lyman Beecher, the whirl at the center of the institutional phase of the Awakening,

68. Bennet Tyler, MS Sermons, Box 15, 8a, CLB.
69. Ibid.
70. Ibid.

envied Griffin's success.[71] Griffin's formula was simple: prepare to preach, he suggested, "with a sense of absolute dependence on God . . . and a strong desire in your heart for the salvation of men." Then preach "such as would most please and affect an audience in the revival of religion."[72]

In oratorical skills, Griffin closely resembled George Whitefield, the grand itinerant of the colonial Great Awakening.[73] Both men set before their audience in the starkest terms possible that life's ultimate purpose pointed to the hereafter. Both dealt bluntly yet intimately with their listeners. As Whitefield put it, "every preacher should be a Boanerges, a son of thunder, as well as a Barnabas, a son of consolation."[74] Both mastered such rhetorical devices as repetition, the imperative, the use of a series of short and pointed questions, and the drawing of contrasts between the old life and the new. An urgency with their audience sprang from their own personal experience of sin and the release from its clutches through the new birth. Finally, both were either enthusiastically received or rejected. Their styles brooked no ambiguity: those opposed to their heartrending preaching decried them as enthusiasts; those gratified by their promotion of revival praised them as instruments of God.

Griffin struck a commanding presence in the pulpit. A man of imposing stature, he stood six feet, three inches tall and, though not corpulent, weighed a hefty 260 pounds. His preaching, he remarked, was designated "to strike the conscience" and to engage not merely the intellect but the whole being.[75] He believed that the preacher "must address the whole man by a powerful appeal to the conscience and the heart. Without passion the soul cannot act. Passion will move."[76] The result of such preaching was "a living, experimental religion . . . which fits the soul for the enjoyment of God."[77]

Born into a prosperous East Haddam farming family in 1770, Griffin attended Yale with his sights set on the ministry.[78] He succeeded in the classroom, graduating with highest honors in 1790, but he failed to attain the

71. Beecher, *Autobiography* 1:113.

72. Edward Dorr Griffin, "A Sermon on the Art of Preaching, delivered . . . May 25, 1825" (Boston, 1825), 10, 21.

73. On Whitefield, see Stuart C. Henry, *George Whitefield: Wayfaring Witness* (Nashville, Tenn., 1957), esp. chap. 5; James Downey, *The Eighteenth Century Pulpit* (Oxford, Eng., 1969), 156–88; Stout, *New England Soul*, 189–94; and idem, *The Divine Dramatist: George Whitefield and the Rise of Modern Evangelicalism* (Grand Rapids, Mich., 1991).

74. Quoted in Downey, *Eighteenth Century Pulpit*, 162.

75. Griffin, *Sermons* (1839), 1:50.

76. Edward Dorr Griffin, *Sermons, not before published, on various practical subjects* (New York, 1844), 246.

77. Griffin, *Sermons* (1839), 1:50.

78. Biographical data on Griffin are drawn from three accounts, the last two derived largely from the first: William Buell Sprague, *Memoir of the Rev. Edward D. Griffin, D.D.* (New York, 1839); Parsons Cooke, *Recollections of Reverend E. D. Griffin; or, Incidents Illustrating his Character* (Boston, 1855); and Ansel Nash, "Memoir of Edward Dorr Griffin," *American Quarterly Register* 13 (May 1841): 365–85. No full-length critical biography of Griffin has been written.

requirement of an evangelical minister—namely, an experience of God's saving grace. With his career path to the ministry stalled, Griffin pondered the practice of law and began to prepare for that end while teaching at an academy in Derby.

Then came the turning point in his life. In July 1791, a debilitating illness confined Griffin to bed for several weeks, during which he struggled with body and soul. He lay literally under conviction but did not immediately experience confidence in God's work of regeneration. For nearly three months Griffin agonized over his eternal destiny. Finally, one day, released from nagging doubts, he concluded "that I was a child of God." For several more months he worried over the prospect of entering the ministry. Then, after "the whole character of Christ as a *preacher*" appeared to him during a meditation on the Sermon on the Mount, Griffin reaffirmed his commitment to the ministry. Convinced of his calling, he studied with Jonathan Edwards, Jr., pastor at the White Haven Church in New Haven. At the same time, he regularly attended a prayer meeting in Derby, where he quickly distinguished himself "by his fervent prayers and thrilling addresses."[79] On 31 October 1792, he was licensed by the New Haven West Association.

Sometime in late 1792, Griffin returned home to fill the vacant pulpit at the Congregational church in New Salem. His witness to family members precipitated the conversion of his mother, sister, and sister-in-law, and it was from this time that Griffin later dated the beginning of a grand revival that ran uninterrupted for forty years. His dynamic preaching soon resulted in a revival that extended to the nearby towns of East Haddam and Lyme, adding one hundred "hopeful converts" to church membership rolls within a seven-month period.

The lure of a permanent position and perhaps larger and more prestigious church prompted Griffin to candidate at Farmington First Congregational Church in 1793. A revival quickly ensued, with fifty new births reported. The church extended a call and Griffin accepted. Soon after his acceptance, however, he found himself in the midst of a long-standing conflict between the forces for and against the New Divinity. In the face of strong minority opposition, Griffin requested and was granted a release.[80]

In the aftermath of the Farmington controversy, the small country parish of New Hartford, seven miles to the northwest, extended an invitation to Griffin to candidate for a pulpit vacancy. It was to this church in Litchfield County—the stronghold of New Divinity clergy—that the twenty-five-year-old Griffin was called and ordained in June 1795. Once again the fruits of his labors were rewarded with an ingathering of fifty converts in the fall of that year. "The neighboring towns were not then visited," he noted later, until

---

79. Sprague, *Memoir of Griffin*, 4, 5, 7.
80. See Chapter 5 for a thorough discussion of this controversy.

October 1798, when a revival erupted in West Simsbury and spread west to Torringford and other surrounding communities including his own, where one hundred new births were reported in 1799.[81]

In 1800 Griffin left New Hartford for Orange, New Jersey, hoping the milder climate of the highlands would allay his wife's health problems. Although he initially viewed the move as a temporary expedient, he never returned to Connecticut in a professional capacity. At Orange, revival ensued under his preaching. At Newark First Presbyterian Church, to which he accepted a call as an assistant to the aging Alexander McWhorter, 372 were converted under his preaching—97 of whom joined the church on one Sunday in 1807.

By the end of the first decade of the nineteenth century, Griffin's popularity as a pulpit orator and defender of Edwardseanism reached its height. In 1809, a year after Andover Seminary was formed to counter Unitarian influences at Harvard, Griffin accepted an invitation to fill the Bartlett Chair of Sacred Pulpit Rhetoric. At the same time, beleaguered conservatives in Boston enlisted his services to lead the newly formed Park Street Church.[82] What Andover was to Harvard, Park Street was to the rest of the Unitarian Congregational churches in Boston: a bastion of conservative, trinitarian Calvinism against liberal, antitrinitarian Arminianism.

Serving in dual capacities consumed so much of Griffin's time and energy that he resigned from Andover in 1811 and assumed full-time responsibilities at Park Street.[83] It was not a good match. According to some of Park Street's leaders, Griffin's fervid New Divinity preaching drove off potential members—the very people desperately needed to contribute monies to an overextended building program, as well as to Griffin's inflated salary. Internal conflicts and attacks from the Unitarian *Anthology* severely tested Griffin's character. He could elucidate the verities of New Divinity theology in his famous *Lectures in Park Street Church* (1813), but he could not rouse his people to his own heights of passionate faith. He confessed, "Boston folks will be Boston folks still. They will not retrench their habits nor lose a nap at church to save their lives."[84]

---

81. *CEM* 1 (January 1801): 265.

82. On the origins of Andover, see Leonard Woods, *History of the Andover Theological Seminary* (Boston, 1885); on Park Street Church and Griffin's role, see H. Crosby Englizian, *Brimstone Corner: Park Street Church, Boston* (Chicago, 1968).

83. Parsons Cooke offered another reason for Griffin's exit from Andover. William Bartlett, who endowed the chair Griffin filled, offered to finance a house that Griffin himself designed. When Griffin's plan amounted to twice the cost expected, many felt he exploited an already sweetheart deal. While the expense did not apparently offend Bartlett, the resentment of others contributed to Griffin's departure (see Cooke, *Recollections*, 19). See also William Bartlett to Dr. Griffin, 29 December 1809, Historical Manuscripts, SML.

84. Quoted in Cooke, *Recollections*, 29. Several of Griffin's sermons clearly addressed what he considered to be the lethargic state of Park Street (see esp. *Sermons* [1844], 61–62).

Frustrated and discouraged, Griffin resigned from Park Street in 1815 and returned to Newark as pastor of the newly formed Second Presbyterian Church. Following a six-year tenure that was the "most tranquil" of any pulpit he had filled, Griffin accepted the presidency of Williams College in 1821. For the next fifteen years, he devoted his energies to providing administrative and spiritual leadership to this small, struggling school in the Berkshires of Massachusetts.[85] Competition from newly established Amherst College siphoned off one-half of the student body and nearly led to the closing of the college, but under Griffin's vision, Williams was saved from financial collapse and slowly built back its enrollment.

The attraction of presiding over Williams was an intensely personal one for Griffin. As a fervent supporter of missions, he was attached to Williams as the birthplace of the modern missionary movement in the United States. Here, at the famous Haystack Prayer Meeting in 1806, Samuel Mills, Jr., Gordon Hall, and James Richards vowed to carry the gospel abroad. Griffin hoped to extend this vision by training more foreign missionaries at Williams. He had a particular fondness for Mills, whom he had known as a lad. "Father Mills" had been Griffin's erstwhile colleague during Griffin's ministry in New Hartford; and Samuel junior, knowing of Griffin's keen interest in missions, studied theology with him in order to gain an influential supporter for his missionary vision.[86]

Griffin's career had come full circle. "It filled me with gratitude and wonder," he wrote, "to discover that the religious destinies of the college, which are now opening with such unspeakable interest upon my age, received such an impression from the revivals in which I spent the labors of my youth."[87]

A colleague put it simply: Edward Dorr Griffin was "unequal as a preacher."[88] Other peers reached the same conclusion. In a eulogy to his predecessor at Williams, President Mark Hopkins remarked that "probably the labors of no preacher in his day were blessed to the conversion of more persons than were his."[89] Another college president, Heman Humphrey of Amherst, reiterated Hopkins's sentiments. "Few ministers," he wrote to Griffin's children, had been

---

85. On the origins of Williams College and Griffin's role, see Calvin Durfee, *A History of Williams College* (Boston, 1860); Frederick Rudolph, *Mark Hopkins and the Log: Williams College, 1836–1872* (New Haven, Conn., 1956); and Cooke, *Recollections*.

86. Gardiner Spring, *Memoir of Samuel John Mills*, 2d ed. (New York, 1842), 25–26, 29–30; Edward Dorr Griffin, "A Sermon preached September 2, 1828, at the Dedication of the New Chapel . . ." (Williamstown, Mass., 1828), 24.

87. Quoted in Cooke, *Recollections*, 41.

88. Spring, "Death and Heaven," 31.

89. Mark Hopkins, "A Discourse occasioned by the death of the Rev. Edward Dorr Griffin . . ." (Troy, N.Y., 1837), 17.

as "instrumental of awakening and saving more souls" as their father.[90] Gardiner Spring elevated Griffin to the rank of a Great Awakener. "I doubt whether the minister can be named," he claimed, "since the days of Edwards and Whitfield [sic], to whom God has given more seals of his ministry. God had eminently fitted him for usefulness in revivals."[91]

In the composition of sermons, Griffin worked within the Reformed–Puritan–New Divinity tradition. Like Whitefield, however, he reversed the customary emphasis in the expository and applicatory parts of the sermon. Exposition was no longer the centerpiece of the sermon. Instead of "opening the text" or explicating its various levels of meaning at length, Griffin offered several cursory paragraphs of exposition and then devoted the bulk of the sermon to its application. Given that his "ruling passion" included "love to the cause of Christ, exhibited in earnest endeavors to promote revivals of religion," this emphasis was natural.[92] In nearly every sermon, regardless of the text, Griffin pled with sinners, cajoled or frightened them, and demanded that they immediately turn to Christ. When engaged in revival preaching— which was often—he attenuated the last subject of the "sin-salvation-service" triad of traditional Reformed sermonizing and uplifted the themes of law (sin) and gospel (salvation).[93] Typically, Griffin began by preaching the terrors of the law "with a force of thought that made his hearers tremble."[94] The auditors' attention was riveted on their own willful lost state. "By beginning with obligation you get to their sense of guilt," remarked Griffin.[95] It produces "attention" followed by "conviction." After reducing the audience to despair—Griffin and other New Divinity men were fond of reminding their listeners that "you richly *deserve* to die"—he offered the love of God in Christ poured out to humanity as the only escape.

In preaching style, Griffin mastered the rhetorical conventions of his day. He invoked the imperative in his revival sermonizing, especially as he pressed his listeners to see their lost condition. He confronted them with the demands of God:

> You must feel your need of a Savior. This sense cannot be obtained till your eyes are opened to see *what God is.* . . . You must see the claims which God has upon his creature, as Being of infinite perfection; as

90. Quoted in Griffin, *Sermons* (1839), 1:168.
91. Spring, "Death and Heaven," 32–33.
92. Quoted in Cooke, *Recollections*, 121. On the Christ-centered preaching theme, see also Perkins, "Sermon preached at Installation of Wolcott," 27.
93. See Stout, *New England Soul* (180), for developments leading to the dropping of the "service" aspect of the sermon.
94. Spring, "Death and Heaven," 31.
95. Edward Dorr Griffin, *A Series of Lectures, delivered in Park Street Church, Boston, on Sabbath Evening* (Boston, 1813), 212.

their Creator, Preserver, and Redeemer. You must see the reasonableness and excellence of His holy law. You must see the amazing
wickedness of rising up against such a God and such a government.
You must see the justice of your condemnation to eternal death. You
must justify God in all His sovereignty—must take all the shame and
blame to yourselves, and clear our Maker.[96]

At other times, Griffin mixed the imperative with a series of pointed
questions. "O sinners," he pled at the conclusion of one sermon,

can you reject such a Savior! Will you plunge into eternal burnings
rather than receive him? Will you stand and sport with his agonies?
Will you trample his blood under foot? Will you break your way to
hell over his mangled body? Stop, stop your mad career. O turn, and
let the blood which your sins have shed wash out every stain. Turn
before justice allows his patience to work no longer. Turn before the
Lamb is changed into a lion.[97]

Griffin wielded these rhetorical devices with "tenderness and tears."[98] With
a voice of "remarkable compass and flexibility," he preached New Divinity
truths in the language of the people.[99] Noah Porter, whose ministry at
Farmington First Church spanned the first five decades of the nineteenth
century, had occasion to hear Griffin preach as a candidate in that church. He
perceived that Griffin's ability to awaken souls "was *not another system*" apart
from New Divinity dogma; rather, Griffin preached these doctrines "with a
clearness and a force that were new. There was also a simplicity, a vividness,
and an affection in his manner, which gave the truth access to the mind."[100]
All who heard Griffin—the young and the old, the ignorant and the
intelligent—apprehended a message expressed with unmistakable clarity and
"irrepressible tenderness."[101]

Underlying the force of Griffin's rhetoric and emotional appeals was the
same dependent attitude he enjoined upon the unregenerate. In a "Sermon on
the Art of Preaching" (1825) he advised his colleagues to enter the pulpit in
full submission to God, desiring the salvation of all hearers.[102] Individual
conversion and widespread revival were predicated upon both the preacher

96. Griffin, *Sermons* (1844), 11; see also 21–26, 30–36, and Spring, "Death and Heaven," 32.
97. Griffin, *Sermons* (1839), 2:141; see also 480, and idem, *Sermons* (1844), 7.
98. Spring, "Death and Heaven," 31.
99. Cooke, *Recollections*, 79.
100. Rev. Noah Porter to William Buell Sprague, 12 March 1832, in the appendix to William Buell
Sprague, *Lectures on Revivals of Religion*, 2d ed. (New York, 1833), 290.
101. Spring, "Death and Heaven," 31.
102. Griffin, "Sermon on the Art of Preaching," 10.

and his audience acknowledging their utter dependence. "We shall never be revived," Griffin concluded, "until we realizingly feel our absolute and entire dependence on God—until we can heartily and without reserve say, 'My soul, wait thou only upon God, for my expectation is from him.'"[103]

This state of dependence was reached by plumbing the depths of one's conscience. "Consult your joys or trials or necessities," urged Griffin, "to know what to say in what order. Copy your own heart and views. These are the most interesting sermons. Here heart answers heart."[104] In the tradition of evangelical piety, Griffin and other New Divinity revivalists scrutinized their own hearts through the exercise of "self-examination."[105] Echoing the sentiments of John Wesley, they confessed, "Every time I look inside myself I see hell." Some might call this morbidity, and indeed, such a condition could be reached; but the primary goal of rigorous self-searching was to uncover selfish motives in order to lead to a selfless reliance upon God.[106] Moreover, such introspection reflected the continual struggle of the heart's affection for God. The more that holy emotions filled the soul, the more heightened the sense of internal corruption. Sensitized by the chasm separating God's holiness from their own, New Divinity ministers often expressed a sense of self-loathing. Griffin's expressions were typical: "What an awful examination shall I sustain," he recorded in his journal in 1803, "when all the sins of my life shall be collected together and an account taken of them. Black has been my life; I need seas of blood to wash me clean. . . . Awful! Awful!"[107] Yet, several days later, consoled by Christ's provision of salvation, he exuded: "All free, rich, astonishing grace."[108] Such preparatory self-examination on a personal and intimate scale vivified the law-gospel themes of revival sermonizing. Having thoroughly examined his own heart, the preacher now communicated "heart to heart" with his audience, guiding them on a tour of their spiritual condition. By pressing his thoughts and experiences upon their consciences, the revivalist elicited a passionate, heartfelt response.

According to Griffin, preaching was on an altogether different level from other forms of oral communication, for its goals and methods were altogether different. To demonstrate the "material difference" between heartfelt preach-

---

103. Griffin, *Sermons* (1839), 2:287.

104. Griffin, "Sermon on the Art of Preaching," 11.

105. Griffin, *Sermons* (1839), 1:12–21; idem, *Sermons* (1844), 324–26; Perkins, "Sermon delivered at the Ordination Woodruff," 27; Cyrus Yale, *The Godly Pastor: Life of the Rev. Jeremiah Hallock, of Canton, Conn.* (New York, [1854]), 26–30 (for Hallock's reflections bordering on morbidity, see 162–65); Lyman Matthews, *Memoir of the Life and Character of Ebenezer Porter, D.D.* (Boston, 1837), 160–65; Hart, "Sermon at the Funeral of Gillett," 26–27. For the colonial practice of self-examination, see Stout, *New England Soul*, 35–38.

106. In the early years of his ministry, Griffin suffered with bouts of depression (see Cooke, *Recollections*, 117–18).

107. Griffin, *Sermons* (1839), 1:63; see also Hart, "Sermon at the Funeral of Gillett," 27, 38.

108. Griffin, *Sermons* (1839), 1:72.

ing and other forms of elocution, Griffin contrasted the oratorical styles of two men of the ancient world—the Roman orator Cicero and the apostle Paul. Griffin's choice of Cicero was not by happenstance, for the Puritan/Reformed tradition borrowed heavily from this ancient orator's rhetorical paradigm, as did early nineteenth-century Unitarians.[109] Thus, in pitting Paul against Cicero, Griffin set himself squarely against traditional Puritan sermonic techniques, as well as against the contemporary highbrow Unitarian embrace of the ancients known only too well by Griffin from his unpleasant years in Boston. On account of Cicero's "wonderful sweetness; his inexhaustible copiousness; his tenderness; [and] the sharpness of his irony," Boston's *Monthly Anthology* proclaimed him "the orator of the world and the instructor of every age."[110] The same periodical that found Asahel Hooker's sermon wanting, inveighed against other New Divinity sermons. One reviewer called Levi Hart's style of discourse "too often incorrect, vulgar, and colloquial," while another concluded that one of Griffin's sermons was "deformed by frequent confusion of images, and unpardonable inaccuracy of style."[111]

According to the Puritan adaptation of Ciceronian rhetorical theory, sermons progressed sequentially as the preacher moved from a rational apprehension of divine truths to a personal application of that truth. The preacher's duties included "opening the text," drawing out doctrinal truths, providing rational underpinnings for those truths, and then concluding with a brief "application" where he sought to persuade his auditors of the truths just proven. In this way Puritan sermons combined Ciceronian rhetorical organization with faculty psychology; that is, they moved in an orderly fashion from intellect to emotion.

In point of fact, the real foil to the Puritan approach was not Paul, as Griffin suggested, but such Great Awakeners as Whitefield and Edwards. Because Edwards viewed the faculties of understanding and will in a unitary way, he (in the words of Eugene White) "negated the Ciceronian duties of the speaker. Instead of consisting of separate duties, Edwards's sermonic persuasion tended toward being unitary in its rhetorical functions and its exhortative effect."[112] Thus, for Edwards and then for evangelical preachers such as Griffin, the parts of the sermon retained their traditional skeletal structure, but they were modified toward unitary exhortation. In the same way, the duties of the minister were modified toward stimulating and altering the affections. The understanding is addressed, but as Griffin put it, "there is a

109. My discussion of the Puritan use of Ciceronian rhetoric and Edwards's departure from this paradigm follows Eugene E. White, *Puritan Rhetoric: The Issue of Emotion in Religion* (Carbondale, Ill., 1972), 17–48.

110. "Cicero," *Monthly Anthology and Boston Review* 6 (March 1809): 161–62.

111. *Monthly Anthology and Boston Review* 3 (March 1806): 156; *Monthly Anthology and Boston Review* 8 (February 1810): 135.

112. White, *Puritan Rhetoric*, 46.

conscience to be affected. Men must . . . feel the pungency of divine truth."
And so, whereas Cicero "addressed himself only to the natural feelings," Paul
set out "to create new tastes, and to awaken feelings" brought about solely by
supernatural influence. Whereas Cicero's objective was to "make men *act*" by
arousing "*selfish* passions," Paul's goal was to enable men to act "from *holy
motives.*" Cicero appealed to "the prejudice of judges," but Paul "presented
nothing but the truths of God."[113]

Such truths, of course, were contained in Scripture—unrivaled as the book
addressed to the passions and imagination. When coupled with the work of
the Holy Spirit, conditions were ripe for revival. The Spirit "does not enlarge
the understanding" but "impresses divine truths upon the heart and awakens
those affections which are suited to the truths impressed."[114] Revivals, then,
were ignited and sustained by the combination of two forces—Word and
Spirit. And the primary conduit through which they moved was audience-
oriented preaching.

In the throes of revival, Griffin was the master of extemporaneous
preaching, and notably so in cases where the same sermon was preached
repeatedly. According to one biographer, Griffin used "On the Worth of the
Soul" more than one hundred times.[115] The practice of "*writing* sermons" out,
Griffin stated, often led to the reading of sermons—a sure way to deaden an
audience. Equally disastrous was the "cold, abstract, essay style" of religious
rationalists and others who failed to recognize the necessity of a remade
heart. "It is the rightful property of bookworms," noted Griffin, "but not of
pastors."[116] Those whose sermons fixed only on the understanding betrayed
an insincerity that "spread stupidity and infidelity among our hearers and
children."[117] Theological fellow travelers were not immune from this faulty
preaching practice, though it often assumed the guise of didactic or doctrinal
preaching. Instruction in New Divinity dogma had its rightful place, but
sermons confined solely to doctrine failed to reach the affections.[118]

Griffin astutely observed that the theologian in the study and the preacher in
the pulpit engaged in two different forms of discourse. "I care not how closely
you distinguish and reason in your study," he explained, "but in the pulpit it were
better in general to present the *results* than the *processes* which led to them."[119] The

113. Griffin, "An Oration," 18, 22–23.

114. Griffin, "Sermon on the Art of Preaching," 21; see also idem, *Lectures in Park Street Church*, 195.

115. Cooke, *Recollections*, 48; Griffin also preached "The importance of working in the day" at least
twenty-four times. See Williamsiana, Misc. MSS, vol. 12, Box 5F5, WC.

116. Griffin, "Sermon on the Art of Preaching," 30; see also idem, *Sermons* (1844), 245.

117. Griffin, "Sermon on the Art of Preaching," 31.

118. Ibid., 30. Nathan Perkins offered the same counsel, urging ministers to "avoid metaphysical
subtleties. Dwell on the plain, peculiar, and distinguishing doctrines of the gospel" ("A Preached
Gospel," 24).

119. Griffin, "Sermon on the Art of Preaching," 30.

Rev. Nathan Strong of Hartford's First Church said essentially the same thing to Jonathan Edwards, Jr., during the latter's tumultuous years as an unsuccessful revivalist at the White Haven Church in New Haven. During a revival in Hartford, Edwards asked Strong, "Why does the influence of the Holy Spirit attend your preaching so much more than mine, when our congregations are so much alike, and we preach the same system of truth?" Strong replied, "The reason is that you present Gospel truth as a proposition to be proved, and go on to prove it; whereas I endeavor to exhibit it as something already admitted and to impress it upon the hearts and conscience."[120]

Successful revivalists such as Strong and Griffin acknowledged that doctrine to the exclusion of passionate appeals reflected a gross misunderstanding of human psychology.[121] Truth, though unitary, had two dimensions. On the one hand, intellectual truths were laid before the mind as rational verities, unassisted by supernatural inspiration. On the other hand, heartfelt truths took hold of the whole being and were only fully grasped after submission to God. This passionate kind of truth was subordinate to reason—a handmaid, not a mistress, as Griffin put it—but its appropriation was essential in the process of regeneration.

Few of those who heard Edward Dorr Griffin preach knew or understood the specifics of his theory of preaching. What they did grasp, however, was that there were two kinds of people—the saved and the unsaved. A great gap separated the everlasting torments of hell from the eternal bliss of heaven. In graphic language reminiscent of Edwards's sermon "Sinners in the Hands of an Angry God," Griffin described the fate of humanity: "You hang over the grave by a thread on which the flame has seized. Were a man literally suspended over the eternal pit, in full view of it, only by a brittle thread, what horrors would seize him."[122]

Like all charismatic preachers, Griffin's very presence in the pulpit evoked an aura of expectation and excitement. He began his sermons in moderate, conversational tones, then slowly built to a simple but urgent plea at the close. Employing the standard revival metaphors of wakefulness and sleep, he set before his listeners the alternative of life or death:

> My poor dear hearers, start from your slumbers; the Judge is at the door. You will have time enough to sleep in your graves; but while heaven is suspended on your vigilance, sleep no longer. O now awake suddenly and finally out of your sleep. Awake or you will soon sleep the sleep of death. Awake and live forever.[123]

120. Quoted in William Buell Sprague, ed., *Annals of the American Pulpit* (New York, 1857–1869), 1:38.
121. Griffin, "Sermon on the Art of Preaching," 31.
122. Griffin, *Sermons* (1844), 7; see also 46–53.
123. Ibid., 154–55; see also 10–15, 36–40, 53–58, and 227–37.

They were fully responsible: "You are altogether to blame for your unbelief."[124] Finally, at the closing invitation, with direct, personal, and impassioned pleading, Griffin entreated his hearers to make an immediate choice:

> The great God is now looking on to receive your answer. The holy angels are listening. What *is* your answer? . . . There is now an opportunity to decide. You have a chance to be saved. I know not what an hour may bring forth. You may open your eyes in hell before I have done speaking. This may be your last chance. What then is your answer?[125]

Moved by Griffin's preaching, hundreds responded to the call for salvation.

Asahel Nettleton: The Curer of Souls

In 1812, twenty years after the inauguration of the Second Great Awakening in New England (as Griffin calculated it), Asahel Nettleton accepted a temporary appointment as an evangelist to the "waste places" of eastern Connecticut. Shortly thereafter, when revival followed revival, Nettleton abandoned his overseas missionary aspirations and permanently entered into an evangelistic career at home. During the next decade, he became the New Divinity's greatest revivalist. Bennet Tyler, Nettleton's longtime associate and laudatory biographer, claimed he was instrumental in the salvation of thirty thousand souls.[126] Francis Wayland, Baptist leader and president of Brown University, summarized Nettleton's success: "I suppose no minister of his time was the means of so many conversions."[127] And Lyman Beecher, Nettleton's revivalist friend and sometimes theological foe, concluded that he was "beyond comparison, the greatest benefactor which God has given to this nation."[128] Indeed, Nettleton's success compared to Griffin's was clearly "beyond comparison." Griffin, the prince of preachers, was simply no match for Nettleton, the curer of souls.

These two revivalists offer an instructive contrast in New Divinity career paths and preaching styles. They illustrate the variety within the New

---

124. Ibid., 67; see also 12.
125. Ibid., 77; see also idem, *Sermons* (1839), 2:480.
126. Bennet Tyler, *The Life and Labours of Asahel Nettleton*, ed. Andrew Bonar (1859; reprint, London, 1975), 19. By John F. Thornbury's "conservative estimate," twenty-five thousand were converted under Nettleton's ministrations (*God Sent Revival: The Story of Asahel Nettleton and the Second Great Awakening* [Grand Rapids, Mich., 1977], 233).
127. Quoted in Thornbury, *God Sent Revival*, 55.
128. Quoted in ibid., 23.

Divinity movement, as well as the overlapping connections of people and events that gave the movement its particular character. Griffin could be confrontational, exceedingly formal, and autocratic; Nettleton was shy, retiring, and irenic. Whereas Griffin excelled in rhetorical skills before large audiences, Nettleton mastered pastoral techniques of personal counsel in small groups. Griffin chased fame in the cities of Newark and Boston, but Nettleton contented himself with itinerating in the villages of New England. Whereas Griffin's ambition got him into salary troubles at Park Street, Nettleton—by far the wealthier—had a "pious indifference to worldly wealth."[129] What united these two very different men of mutual respect was their devotion to New Divinity theology—especially to Edwards's view of the will as the driving force of revival. As the New Divinity waned in popularity in the late 1820s, both men defended Edwardsean views against Charles Finney and Nathaniel Taylor. When Griffin was informed about the founding of the Theological Institute of Connecticut—a foil to Taylor's New Haven Theology at Yale and an institution to which Nettleton gave time and money—he responded: "I vote for the new school with all my heart."[130]

Nettleton was a product of the village revivals in Connecticut. His conversion accorded precisely with New Divinity theology, and it became the standard by which he gauged the spiritual pilgrimage of others. He was born in 1783 in rural Killingworth to parents who embraced the Half-Way Covenant. A sensitive, impressionable lad, Nettleton recalled that as an adolescent he once "stood for some time and wept alone" in a field after contemplating human mortality. In the fall of 1800 he was overcome with permanent conviction after attending a Thanksgiving ball. Like any anxious sinner, he appropriated the standard means of grace. For ten tortuous months he "mourned in secret," beseeching God out in the fields and in the "closet," and yet "God seemed to pay no regard to his prayers." He read the Bible. He pored over Edwards's *Narrative of Revival* and the *Memoir of David Brainerd* but still found no relief. Eventually, in true New Divinity fashion, he came to realize the futility and sinfulness of unregenerate doings—that "he had been prompted by selfish motives. He saw that in all which he had done, he had had not love to God, and no regard to his glory; but that he had been influenced solely by a desire to promote his own personal interest and happiness." Finally, after being seized by "an unusual tremor" during which the "horrors of mind were inexpressible" and thinking he was about to die, Nettleton "felt a calmness for which he knew not how to account." He

129. Tyler, *Memoir of Nettleton*, 339.

130. Quoted by Asahel Nettleton in a letter to Milo L. North, 13 November 1833, Thompson Autograph Letters, Case Memorial Library, Hartford Theological Seminary; quoted in George Hugh Birney, Jr., "The Life and Letters of Asahel Nettleton, 1783–1844" (Ph.D. diss., Hartford Theological Seminary, 1943), 363.

thought he had lost all conviction, but then "a sweet peace pervaded his soul. The objects which had given him so much distress, he now contemplated with delight." Even so, for several days he did not consider himself to be saved. Not until he discovered that his views and feelings corresponded to those of others who were converted to the New Divinity way did he begin to "think it possible that he might have passed from death unto life." God had given Nettleton a new heart and a new taste for spiritual things. And so (note the order), first, "the character of God now appeared lovely." And then "the Saviour was exceedingly precious; and the doctrines of grace, towards which he had felt such bitter opposition, he contemplated with delight." The months of Nettleton's spiritual travail, culminating in regeneration and conversion, confirmed in his mind the truth of New Divinity theology and gave him, according to Tyler, "a knowledge of the human heart which few possess."[131]

During the next four years, Nettleton tended the family farm (his father and brother died in the smallpox epidemic of 1801), filled his head with the standard New Divinity reading list of Edwards, Bellamy, and Hopkins, and studied with his pastor, Josiah Andrews. After reading thrilling tales of overseas missionary exploits in American and British religious periodicals, he set his sights on the mission field. To that end, Nettleton entered Yale in 1805 as a sober, mature twenty-two-year-old who had little time for the frivolity of college life that beckoned most of Yale's entering teenagers. He was an ordinary student, but he began to cultivate those extraordinary skills that would make him a renowned revivalist. In 1807, when a revival broke out among the freshmen, Nettleton was in the center of the spiritual storm, counseling those under conviction. In the following year, however, he required counseling himself, after nagging doubts about the genuineness of his own religious experience put him in a deep funk. Plagued with hypochondria, depression ("melancholy"), and an inability to eat—symptoms of those nearing a nervous breakdown—Nettleton went to see President Dwight. No stranger to revivals, Dwight prescribed Edwards's *Religious Affections*, as well as his own "Evidences of Regeneration." A sick, shaken Nettleton soon recovered.

In his junior year, Nettleton met Samuel Mills, Jr., a recent graduate of Williams, who was passing through New Haven on his way to prepare for missionary work at Andover Seminary. The two discussed missionary plans, and Nettleton agreed to follow Mills to Andover following graduation. College debts, however, prevented Nettleton from carrying out his plans. Following graduation in 1809, he stayed on at Yale as college butler, worked off his debt, and decided against Andover—but remained firmly committed

131. Tyler, *Memoir of Nettleton*, 12–22.

to missionary work. He studied with Belazeel Pinneo, a New Divinity pastor at Milford, and then, following licensure and ordination as an evangelist in 1811, he accepted an interim position as traveling minister to the "waste places" (pastorless churches) of eastern Connecticut until his plans for missionary service were finalized. Nettleton put his plans on hold after the initial outpourings of revival under his ministrations. Eventually, after repeated revivals, he abandoned his plans for the mission field altogether. He had discovered his own field "white unto harvest."

During the next decade (1812 to 1822), Nettleton itinerated primarily in Connecticut and also ventured into Rhode Island and New York. He turned parts of northwestern Connecticut into a "burned-over district," rekindling the flames in such villages as Torrington and Farmington, where the revival had burned brightly in the formative period between 1798 and 1808. It was Nettleton who, on the invitation of Lyman Beecher, roused Litchfield in 1813 and then contiguous South Farms in 1814 at James Morris's academy.

A severe bout with typhus in 1822 forced Nettleton into semiretirement. He remained, however, active in the cause of the New Divinity, compiling a hymnal suited to revival (*Village Hymns*, 1824), challenging the new measures of Charles Finney at the Lebanon Conference in 1827, and opposing vigorously Nathaniel Taylor's teachings on the will in the late 1820s. Consequently, Nettleton helped form the Connecticut Pastoral Union in 1833 and supported its Theological Institute formed a year later. He turned down a professorship, but lectured occasionally, and stipulated in his will that income from the *Village Hymns* provide an annual income to the institute.

There are four major reasons for Nettleton's spectacular success as a revivalist. First, he understood others. According to Belazeel Pinneo, Nettleton had "an uncommon insight into the human character."[132] Like all great revivalists, he drew from his own experience of doubt and confidence, rebellion and submission, sorrow and joy, anxiety and relief. From these valleys and peaks, as well as from persistent self-examination, Nettleton derived the ability to discern the thoughts and spiritual states of others. As Tyler observed, "By knowing his own heart he knew the hearts of others."[133]

Second, Nettleton perfected the use of the conference meeting as the catalyst of revival. His sermons, noted Beecher, "would have been compara-tively feeble but for the ubiquity and power of his personal attention where exigencies called for it, and the little *circles* which he met daily, when many were interested, to instruct and guide, and often press submission with a success unsurpassed any where."[134] Nettleton excelled in the personal

132. Quoted in Tyler, *Memoir of Nettleton*, 200.
133. Ibid., 205.
134. Beecher, *Autobiography* 2:365.

encounter. His audience knew Nettleton and Nettleton knew his audience. They both came together intending to transact spiritual business. Nettleton began the conference (or inquiry) meeting with a short extemporaneous address. During his delivery, recalled Heman Humphrey, Nettleton "seemed to look every hearer in the face, or rather to look into his soul, almost at one and the same moment."[135] Following prayer, he spoke briefly to each inquirer. He would evaluate the inquirer's state of mind, offer counsel, and then advise him or her to quietly depart the meeting and deal with God alone.

He insisted on silence, for in silence the God of the New Divinity was revealed to the understanding. Silence, broken only by Nettleton's words or conversation with individuals under conviction, ensured the elimination of noisy distractions. He decried excessive conversation with others, for it either confused the mind or resulted in a false sympathy toward the anxious that soothed the sting of conviction. Nettleton advised an awakened audience in Harwinton to "go alone, & be alone, but the business must be settled before God and their souls."[136] He instructed the convicted at Newington to leave the conference meeting without making any noise, adding: "I love to talk to you, you are so still. It looks as though the Spirit of God was here. Go away as still as possible. Do not talk by the way, lest you forget your own hearts. Do not ask how you like the preacher; but retire to your closets—bow before God and give yourselves to him this night."[137] Nettleton promoted a "love of stillness" to secure salvation the New Divinity way.[138]

A third reason for Nettleton's success lies in the support he received from local pastors. No minister would abide another James Davenport, the itinerant of the Great Awakening whose rantings and ravings against sin and settled ministers wreaked havoc and led to divided churches. Indeed, the vacancies or "waste places" that Nettleton filled were attributed to the carnage left in the wake of Davenport's harangues some sixty years earlier. Davenport's divide-and-conquer tactics were anathema to Nettleton, who never conducted meetings without an invitation from and the unqualified endorsement of the local pastor. Thus, for example, Nettleton accepted invitations from Bennet Tyler at South Britain, Beecher at Litchfield, Gillett at Torrington, Heman Humphrey at Pittsfield, Massachusetts, and Noah Porter at Farmington. These ministers welcomed Nettleton, knowing that his one- or two-month stay would cost them nothing (Nettleton never asked remuneration for his services), create heightened spiritual concern, and ultimately boost church membership rolls.

Finally, Nettleton excelled as an evangelist because he embraced a

135. Quoted in Tyler, *Memoir of Nettleton*, 358.
136. Quoted in Birney, "Life and Letters of Nettleton," 247.
137. Tyler, *Memoir of Nettleton*, 208.
138. Beecher, *Autobiography* 2:270.

theology of revival. The empathy and near-instant rapport he established with his auditors in the conference meeting were the means to understanding the New Divinity way to salvation, which was, he averred, the "basis of all genuine religious experience."[139] Nettleton preached and taught all of the New Divinity verities. He insisted on the duty of immediate repentance; he distinguished between natural ability and moral inability; he invoked the term "regeneration" to describe the new birth, meaning that "there is an actual new creation, . . . a new spiritual taste . . . implanted by a sovereign creative operation, and not simply a new direction given to old faculties."[140] When Nettleton, the master of the conference meeting, filled anxious heads full of New Divinity theology, the work of the Spirit did not return void.

As I have shown, New Divinity theologians elucidated and defended dogma primarily through the written medium. In their role as evangelical pastors and revivalists, however, New Divinity preachers sought to arouse and elicit a response from their audience through oral proclamation. Given these two different modes of communication, not all New Divinity pastors easily made the transition from the study to the pulpit. A minister's temperament, training, and view of his calling largely determined the nature of his preaching. In general, the first two generations of New Divinity men (i.e., Edwards's students and the students of Edwards's students) were better theologians than revivalists, whereas the third generation featured better revivalists than theologians. The latter's forceful preaching went hand in hand with the message of salvation, for revivalists understood that without an appropriate medium, the message fell on deaf ears. By simple, direct, and personal appeal, New Divinity preachers roused their audience from indifference, exhorting them to make an immediate decision. The Sabbath day continued to remain the conventional time for communicating the Word, but the conference meeting proved to be a more effective environment for personal salvation. No social pressure forced people to attend these meetings. They came of their own free will (in the Edwardsean sense, of course), anxious to be spiritually inspired or transformed by the preaching of their own pastor or, more often, by the exhortations of assisting New Divinity ministers. Hitting upon a successful, evocative sermon, New Divinity itinerants preached the same sermons again and again, to the point where they personally engaged their listeners with direct eye contact throughout the duration of their discourse. Unencumbered by extensive notes, often without elevated pulpits to separate

139. Tyler, Memoir of Nettleton, 327.
140. Quoted in Sherry Pierpont May, "Asahel Nettleton: Nineteenth-Century American Revivalist" (Ph.D. diss., Drew University, 1969), 141. For specific references to Nettleton's view on the will, see ibid., 137–46, and Remains of the late Rev. Asahel Nettleton, D.D., comp. Bennet Tyler (Hartford, Conn., 1845), 56–70, 314–18.

them spatially from their audiences, the revivalists broke down formal barriers in order to unleash the moving of the Spirit. In clear, unadorned language, the New Divinity preached the doctrines of human depravity, the unregenerate's natural ability to repent, the duty of immediate repentance, the free offer of salvation, and the atoning death of Christ for the whole human race—all within the sovereign purposes of God.

God continued to move in mysterious ways, and yet New Divinity revivalists were on to something. They discovered—or rediscovered—an unmistakable connection between their own convictions expressed in evangelical preaching and the response of their audience. When eyes met eyes and heart met heart, when, in the inspiration of the moment, New Divinity ministers spoke extemporaneously and the Spirit moved, then sinners were convicted and the unregenerate were saved. Though no New Divinity man would admit as much, Charles Grandison Finney, harbinger of another era, did: "Mere words will never express the full meaning of the gospel. The *manner* of saying it is almost everything."[141]

141. Quoted in Leonard I. Sweet, "Views of Man Inherent in New Measures Revivalism," *Church History* 45 (June 1976): 212.

5

"AN UNHAPPY CONTENTION"

Farmington First Church
and the
Second Great Awakening

Gardiner Spring could be forgiven for not speaking the whole truth about Edward Dorr Griffin. He was, after all, delivering a eulogy at Griffin's funeral. In his encomium, Spring alleged that no one was "more eagerly sought by the churches" than Griffin.[1] As I have shown, Griffin was indeed an effective revivalist and a renowned preacher, but his popularity was not universal. Spring failed to mention the intense opposition Griffin encountered early in his career as a stated supply minister at Farmington First Church. Only twenty-three years old, Griffin barely survived the thicket of a long controversy that preceded his arrival at Farmington in 1793. While he pleased a majority of First Church's members who voted him a permanent settlement, a dissenting minority vote was large enough to dissuade him from accepting the position. Truth be told, not all at First Church "eagerly sought" the prince of preachers.

The serious difficulties Griffin experienced at Farmington reveal something about the nature of New England ecclesiastical life in the last half of the eighteenth century, as well as something about the overall receptivity of the New Divinity message. Neither the preponderance of New Divinity pastors in northwestern Connecticut nor the success of their revival efforts indicates

---

1. Gardiner Spring, "Death and Heaven: A Sermon preached at Newark at the interment of the Rev. Edward D. Griffin, D.D." (New York, 1838), 2–3.

the true measure of their acceptance among the laity.[2] There was a morsel of truth to Ezra Stiles's exaggeration in 1793 that "none of the Chhs. in New Engl are New Divy"—to his thinking, only the clergy were so inclined.[3] Invariably, at some point in their history, congregations with New Divinity pastors quarreled over New Divinity dogma and matters of "church discipline."

Frequently, disagreements led to long-standing battles where opposition to a New Divinity pastor culminated in his dismissal. Stiles, with something of a sanctimonious "I told you so" attitude, dutifully chronicled New Divinity conflicts and terminations in New England. From 1790 to 1795, Stiles recorded martyrs to the New Divinity cause in Connecticut: Alexander Gillett of Farmingbury, Jonathan Edwards, Jr., of North Haven, Joshua Perry of Hamden, Samuel Austin of Fairhaven, and Allen Olcott of Farmington. In some of these cases, the conflict between a New Divinity pastor and his congregation consisted of a vocal, obstreperous minority—often parish or society residents, but not full church members—pitted against the pastor and a majority of the church members. The dissatisfied minority often created disruptions and mobilized opposition to the extent that an outside ecclesiastical council intervened and voted for a dismissal. On other occasions, a clear majority of church members voted to dismiss the New Divinity pastor.

By the close of the eighteenth century, the pure church principles of the New Divinity men prevailed more often than not (especially in Litchfield County, where they controlled the formal ecclesiastical machinery), and yet their victories exacted a price—the price of church harmony. Continual disputes between opposing parties characterized church meetings; factions worked behind the scenes to offset each other; those filled with rancor expressed their hostilities openly; and the battle between parties became an endurance contest. The end result, according to both sides, debilitated spiritual vitality within the church.

Two ecclesiastical practices that the New Divinity found particularly offensive centered around qualifications for church membership. The first was the Half-Way Covenant. Although New Divinity men succeeded in overthrowing half-way practices in Connecticut by 1800, they did so at the

2. For an example of divisiveness and outright separation of a nonrevived Litchfield County church society, see Stephen Foster, "A Connecticut Separate Church: Strict Congregationalism in Cornwall, 1780–1809," New England Quarterly 39 (September 1966): 309–33.

3. Ezra Stiles, The Literary Diary of Ezra Stiles, ed. Franklin B. Dexter (New York, 1901), 3:506n. There are recorded cases of lay support for New Divinity principles. For example, when Ebenezer Garnsey (Yale 1757) discovered that the proprietors of Pittsfield, Massachusetts, supported New Divinity tenets, he withdrew his candidacy from the church. Garnsey had studied theology with the Rev. Robert Breck, a well-known "Arminian," and thus "was somewhat a subject of suspicion." See Franklin B. Dexter, ed., Biographical Sketches of the Graduates of Yale College with Annals of the College History (New York, 1885–1912), 2:462–63.

risk of dividing their congregations.[4] Scars remained and wounds festered among those whose religious preferences did not comport with New Divinity convictions. A second divisive issue, the practice of open communion, or "Stoddardeanism," was just as repugnant as the Half-Way Covenant. In the late seventeenth century, Solomon Stoddard, the grandfather of Jonathan Edwards, abandoned the traditional "fencing of the table," and opened the communion table to all comers in his Northampton congregation. Stoddard was convinced that this practice could be used effectively as a "converting ordinance." When Edwards later followed in his grandfather's footsteps as Northampton's pastor, he fought hard to do away with the practice. In so doing, he incurred the wrath of his congregation and triggered his eventual dismissal.

The practices of both the Half-Way Covenant and open communion, though related to ecclesiology, ultimately involved issues of doctrine. Although few could argue with the New Divinity conviction that the visible church should be composed of Christians, contention arose over how the New Divinity men defined a Christian. In effect, they said that a true Christian was one who was saved the Edwardsean way. The New Divinity doctrine of regeneration set forth unmistakable criteria regarding the saved and unsaved. In that instant when individuals crossed from a sinful condition into sainthood, they were given a whole new taste for spiritual things. There were indeed, as Edwards had so carefully catalogued, "distinguishing marks" of a saint. No gray area clouded the difference between the regenerate and unregenerate. Ultimately, the elect were known to God alone; nevertheless, God gave saints with gracious affections the ability to discern, however imperfectly, the affections of others. Nathan Perkins conceded that there never was or ever would be a pure church in this world, that is, "a collection of real saints without one hypocrite"; still, this condition did not lessen the responsibility to "strive for purity in doctrine and worship." To those who complained, "You make the way too strict," Perkins replied, "Give up yourselves to God."[5] As another New Divinity supporter expressed it, the qualifications for membership into the visible church of Christ were "right

---

4. James P. Walsh, "The Pure Church in Eighteenth Century Connecticut" (Ph.D. diss., Columbia University, 1967), fully documents the overthrow of half-way practices in Connecticut from 1750 to 1800, noting that the combined weight of New Divinity and strict (i.e., separated) Congregationalist views won out. Walsh calculates that by 1800 the ratio of pure to open churches was four to one (218). Among New Divinity men in Connecticut, Joseph Bellamy emerged as the most vociferous defender of pure church principles (see Walsh, chap. 6). For a sample of New Divinity statements on the proper criteria for baptism, see Ammi Robbins, "A Half-Century Sermon," in *History of Norfolk, Litchfield County, Connecticut*, comp. Theron W. Crissey (Everett, Mass., 1900), 126; Jacob Catlin, *A Compendium of the System of Divine Truth, contained in a series of essays* . . . (Middletown, Conn., 1824), 242–44; Charles Backus, "Qualifications and Duties of the Christian Pastor: A sermon, delivered . . . October 29, 1795 . . ." (Boston, 1795), 20; and Nathan Perkins, *Twenty-four Discourses on Some of the Important and Interesting Truths, Duties and Institutions of the Gospel* . . . (Hartford, Conn., 1795), 221–24.

5. Perkins, *Twenty-four Discourses*, 354, 356, 224.

affections of heart toward God and divine things."[6] Old Calvinist cant about admitting those into the church who lived "blameless" or morally upright lives but who could not with conviction testify to God's work of regeneration was at best an oxymoron and at worst blasphemous. What Ezra Stiles called the "ltd. Charity" of the New Divinity was simply Consistent Calvinism put into practice.[7] It was also a further rejection of the Puritan vision of an amalgamated church and society.

New Divinity scruples on matters of church discipline and doctrine were well known. Asahel Hooker had his "Goshen enemies," Giles Cowles encountered "considerable opposition" from his Bristol parishioners over his "Calvinistic doctrines," and Heman Humphrey endured salary difficulties as his Fairfield parishioners by their parsimony protested his stand against the Half-Way Covenant.[8] These three were young New Divinity ministers whose devotion to purity illustrated the rambunctious idealism of the third generation. It was this group who encountered "much opposition" because they preached "the distinguishing doctrines of Calvinism . . . more fully and pointedly than that had been in some of the preceding years."[9] And it was also this group who, according to Ellen Larned in her history of Windham County, "led a division of the [Windham County] Association in 1799."[10]

New Divinity pure church practices often transcended the local congregation and extended to the relations among Connecticut Congregational

6. John Stevens, "The Church of Christ essentially the same in all ages," in *Sermons on Important Subjects* (Hartford, Conn., 1797), 68.

7. Stiles, *Diary* 3:286.

8. Timothy Edwards to Asahel Hooker, 27 November 1810, Park Family Papers, Box 18, Letter Book of Timothy Edwards, SML; Hooker is quoted in *Bristol, Connecticut* (Hartford, Conn., 1907), 191; [Zephaniah Moore Humphrey], *Memorial Sketches: Heman Humphrey, Sophia Porter Humphrey* (Philadelphia, 1869), 49, 64.

Two of the more infamous cases of New Divinity principles colliding with the views of parishioners occurred in Massachusetts. In Stockbridge, the celebrated "Fisk affair" pitted Stephen West against Mrs. John Fisk. A former captain in the Revolutionary army who became a schoolmaster in Stockbridge, John Fisk married the widow Deane in 1779. Whereas she was a member of West's church, he was not, and by all appearances, he had no intention of joining. For becoming "unequally yoked with an unbeliever," West excommunicated Mrs. Fisk. She considered it a travesty of justice, appealed her sentence, and chose the Old Calvinist, Joseph Huntington of Norwich, Connecticut, to defend her—all to no avail. She eventually moved to Vermont. See Richard D. Birdsall, *Berkshire County: A Cultural History* (New Haven, Conn., 1959), 59–61, and Allen C. Guelzo, *Edwards on the Will: A Century of American Theological Debate* (Middletown, Conn., 1989), 140–43.

In Fitchburg, the Rev. Samuel Worcester encountered stiff opposition from Universalists and other liberals when he attempted to reform the church along New Divinity principles. For five years a widely publicized controversy raged, until in 1802 a church council dissolved the pastoral relationship. The term "Hopkinsian" became such a derogatory term that schoolboys used it as an epithet. See William B. Sprague, ed., *Annals of the American Pulpit* (New York, 1857–69), 2:398–99, and Samuel M. Worcester, *The Life and Labors of Rev. Samuel Worcester, D.D.* (Boston, 1852), 1:282.

9. Timothy Tuttle, "A Permanent Ministry," in *Contributions to the Ecclesiastical History of Connecticut* (New Haven, Conn., 1861), 240.

10. Ellen D. Larned, *History of Windham County, Connecticut* (Worcester, Mass., 1874–1880), 2:391.

ministers. On some occasions, New Divinity men refused to share the sacrament of Communion with fellow Congregational brethren who did not embrace their theological views.[11] On others, they refused to attend the ordination of non–New Divinity men who accepted calls from churches clinging to half-way practices.[12] They, of course, also refused to baptize the children of unregenerate parents and to conduct what the acerbic Stephen West called "mongrel marriages," in which one of the partners was unregenerate.[13] In yet other matters of discipline, the New Divinity shunned churches practicing open communion.[14] Perhaps most exasperating to Old Calvinists was the issue of church membership transfers. Petitions to transfer membership from New Divinity churches to Old Calvinist churches were granted pro forma. However, New Divinity pastors refused the transfer of membership from a non–New Divinity church to their own without unmistakable proof of regeneration from the transferee.[15] "Endless were the confusions," wrote a bitter critic, "which resulted from their efforts to reduce the people to Edwardean rules."[16]

The history of the First Church of Farmington illustrates the uneven acceptance of New Divinity practices within a local congregation. Its history also underscores the fact that church disputes were seldom purely doctrinal or ecclesiastical. Plots, subplots, and intrigue make for a fascinating but convoluted tale that defies the simple ecclesiastical issue of "purity" versus "charity." Clashing personalities, family loyalties, class antagonisms, and disputes over religious style intruded into the fray, creating a situation in which the underlying or original issues merged with subsequent or less substantive issues.

Farmington was one of nearly thirty parishes caught up in the village revivals of the Second Great Awakening in northwestern Connecticut. Sixty-eight converts joined the church in 1799–1800. Yet for over a decade before the outbreak of revival, divisiveness reigned. Few of the awakened churches experienced this kind of intense, prolonged discord, but the history of Farmington illumines several aspects characteristic of religious life in late eighteenth-century Connecticut. One was the tradition of religious dissent within the Congregational churches. Another was the persistence of piety, expressed most demonstrably in religious awakenings but exhibited at other times by the seriousness with which Congregationalists engaged in religious discourse, theology, and devotional life. Finally, the inauguration of the

11. Stiles, *Diary* 3:355.
12. Ibid., 132, 378.
13. West quoted in Birdsall, *Berkshire County*, 60; Stiles, *Diary* 2:335; 3:7, 208, 343, 358.
14. Stiles, *Diary* 3:208, 562.
15. Ibid., 284, 344.
16. [John Ogden], "A Short History of late Ecclesiastical Oppressions in New England and Vermont" (Richmond, Va., 1799), 5.

Second Great Awakening in Farmington demonstrates that local New Divinity ministers, sometimes working individually, but often in concert, created the conditions ripe for revival.

A Century of Dissent, 1652–1752

When Farmington First Church was organized in 1652, its requirement for full church membership upheld the principle of the necessity of regeneration. Only the elect—only those who could satisfactorily testify to a conversion experience—were allowed the privilege of church membership. This requirement closely reflected the views of Thomas Hooker, the colony's founder and guiding light. In 1634, Hooker and a band of followers left Boston and the Bay Colony to settle Hartford and a cluster of towns along the lower Connecticut River valley. Several issues prompted Hooker's departure, but a major one was his disagreement with John Cotton and others over the problem of nature and grace. Hooker was a "preparationist," convinced that God's elect could prepare their hearts for the "effectual call" of the Spirit. His views enlarged the role of the minister to include not only the nurture of his flock but also the ingathering of lost sheep—tasks equally necessary and fitting for a faithful shepherd. Cotton disagreed: the work of regeneration was unconditional and arbitrary. God in his own good pleasure, through the Holy Spirit and unaided by human contrivance or preparation, effected the work of grace. Such views mitigated, if not obliterated, Hooker's conception of an evangelical ministry. Furthermore, Hooker was less restrictive in his views of church membership than his Boston counterpart. Though no less desirous of church purity, Hooker urged "rational charity" to the more exclusivist tendencies of Cotton.[17]

Few churches or ministers in the Connecticut Valley shared Hooker's views. In *Valley of Discord*, Paul Lucas exposed the erroneous conception of cohesive, homogeneous, gathered churches insulated from internal bickering and intrachurch disagreements. In Hooker's case, "rigid" and "moderate" Congregationalists challenged his views. Despite a shared body of Puritan belief and practice, the first generation of clergy and laity brought to the valley different visions of church order.[18] Rigid Congregationalists held views similar to Cotton's, whereas moderates rejected visible sainthood as a requisite for full church membership. Moreover, competing visions of church

---

17. Quoted in Paul R. Lucas, *Valley of Discord: Church and Society along the Connecticut River, 1636–1725* (Hanover, N.H., 1976), 29. On Hooker, see Frank Shuffelton, *Thomas Hooker, 1586–1647* (Princeton, N.J., 1977); Lucas, *Valley of Discord*, chap. 1; and Norman Pettit, *The Heart Prepared: Grace and Conversion in Puritan Spiritual Life* (New Haven, Conn., 1966), chap. 3.

18. Lucas, *Valley of Discord*, 31.

polity compounded disagreements within and between churches. Finally, the laity clashed with their pastor and among themselves over these same issues.

That Farmington bore Hooker's imprimatur was no accident. From its inception to the close of the seventeenth century, the church's pastors maintained familial ties to the patriarch of the colony. Roger Newton, Farmington's first pastor (1652–57), married Hooker's daughter; Samuel Hooker, the son of Thomas, served the church from 1661 to 1697. Samuel's ability to maintain his father's ideals, however, was challenged by the laity of the church.

During Samuel Hooker's tenure the laity of First Church assumed the right to judge the validity of a church applicant's conversion experience—a practice that Thomas Hooker held was the exclusive prerogative of the minister. In addition, the laity altered the conditions for church membership. Not only were applicants required to convince the laity of the integrity of their conversion experience, but they were now expected to present evidence of strict moral probity. In one membership interview in 1673 at the home of "Deacon Hart," the laity who participated in the vote accepted James Bird's testimony to the work of grace. A majority of the elders present, however, abstained from voting. Their abstention sent its own message. More was required of Bird than a simple testimony to the work of grace: the standards of First Church were high, and in the estimation of the laity, Bird fell short.[19] The necessity of the conversion experience was not overturned, but its place as a sole yardstick in determining admission to full communion receded into the background. Although the required conversion narrative was not deleted from membership requirements until 1707,[20] the Bird case indicates that moral behavior emerged as the primary criterion of judgment in the 1670s.

During these same years Connecticut's churches debated and divided over the Half-Way Covenant. Farmington was the only church in the colony to reject its provisions (at least for the remainder of the seventeenth century), primarily because it obscured the issue by replacing the spiritual experience with moral uprightness. "Farmington could maintain the orthodoxy of the first generation," wrote Robert Pope in his study of the Covenant, "because it softened the harshness of the practice which made the Half-Way Covenant necessary."[21]

Although First Church society never physically separated over the issue of church membership qualifications, following Hooker's death in 1697, a nine-year controversy ensued over the calling of a new pastor. Perhaps

19. For Hooker's transcription of these proceedings, see Farmington, Connecticut, Records of the First Church of Christ, vol. 2 (manuscript copy), 15 June 1673, CSL (hereafter cited as Records of First Church); see also Lucas, Valley of Discord, 127–28.

20. Records of First Church, vol. 2, 15 December 1707, CSL.

21. Robert G. Pope, The Half-Way Covenant: Church Membership in Puritan New England (Princeton, N.J., 1969), 123–24.

dissent among the laity and conflicting opinions among town residents over the membership views of a prospective minister created this prolonged quarrel. Or perhaps, in keeping with another traditional area of dispute in New England churches, a salary issue divided the church. Records from the General Court intimate that the church was reluctant to pay a salary on a parity with Samuel Hooker's.[22] In 1702, at the request of some Farmington residents, the court intervened and ordered the town "to seek counsel and help" from a group of ministers, "to nominate and appoint a minister for them, and in case the minister so nominated and appointed will undertake the work, this assembly doth hereby order that said inhabitants of Farmington shall entertain him for one year, and also pay to him such salary as hath been usual and customary among them."[23] Two years later, the General Court directed these ministers to find a pastor for the town and to "pay him as formerly until this court do otherwise, or until they agree among themselves."[24] In 1705, a group was sent to Nantascot, near Boston, to consult with the Rev. Samuel Whitman. Whitman accepted the generous salary offer and settled in 1706.

Early in his career, Whitman stood in the evangelical preaching tradition of Thomas Hooker. An advocate of the primacy of the conversion experience, Whitman labored to revive First Church, and he cooperated with neighboring ministers in their efforts to awaken their congregations. Three decades prior to the Great Awakening, Whitman called for revival to cure the ills of New England society. "Suffer me to remind myself and you," he instructed his colleagues in a 1714 election sermon, "of the Necessity lying upon us to Endeavor the Revival and Flourishing of Religion among the people." The reason for the present religious indifference, he continued, was his fellow ministers' "coldness and want of zeal in the Delivery of the Lord's message." It was the clergy's responsibility "to endeavor the Revival of Religion."[25] Whitman's wishes were granted, though not until three decades later, when the Great Awakening swept through the Connecticut River valley. But he got more than he bargained for. No friend to itinerant preaching and enthusiasm, Whitman soon joined the antirevivalist Old Light party.[26]

Two actions taken by First Church during Whitman's early tenure indicate

22. Hooker was one of Farmington's wealthiest inhabitants. In 1672/73, his name topped the tax list among Farmington's eighty-four proprietors (see Christopher P. Bickford, *Farmington in Connecticut* [Canaan, N.H., 1982], 65–66).

23. Quoted by Noah Porter, "Farmington," in *The Memorial History of Hartford County, Connecticut, 1633–1884*, ed. James Hammond Trumbull (Boston, 1886), 1:173.

24. Trumbull, *Memorial History*, 173–74.

25. Samuel Whitman, "Practical Godliness the Way to Prosperity: A Sermon preached before the General Assembly of the Colony of Connecticut . . . May 13, 1714 . . ." (New London, Conn., 1714), 33.

26. Noah Porter, "Half-century discourse . . ." (Farmington, Conn., 1857), 14; see also Michael J. Crawford, *Seasons of Grace: Colonial New England's Revival Tradition in Its British Context* (New York, 1991), 79. Crawford mistakenly identifies Whitman as the pastor of Framingham.

the persistence of lay-inspired reform efforts. In 1707, the church dispensed with the conversion narrative as a condition of full church membership and, the following year, adopted the Half-Way Covenant. The church "agreed that such persons as own the covenant personally shall be accounted under the watch and discipline of the church though not admitted to full communion."[27] Why the unconverted children of full members were now granted permission to offer their children for baptism is something of a mystery, considering the action taken the year before to remove the conversion experience from the church covenant. Apparently, they did not fulfill the church's behavioral standards for full church membership. Church discipline was further tightened in 1730, when a rule was adopted requiring those proposing to own the covenant but who had committed a scandalous sin to publicly confess repentance by naming the sin and agreeing to "submit . . . to the discipline and government of Christ in his church, . . . promising not to rest in present attainments, but to be laborious after a preparation for the enjoyment of God in all his ordinances."[28]

The Rev. Timothy Pitkin, 1752–1785

In 1752, Timothy Pitkin succeeded Whitman as pastor of First Church. The son of Governor William Pitkin, Timothy maintained the family's high social standing by marrying Temperance Clap, the daughter of Yale President Thomas Clap.[29] Well-bred and well-wed, Pitkin cut a dignified presence among his parishioners. The parson's elevated social status, however, meant little to laity bent on constraining his power. At a church meeting in January of 1760, the church dropped Article Seven (i.e., 1:7) of the Heads of Agreement (1691), as well as Article Seven of the Saybrook Platform (1708).[30] These articles gave to the pastor the general "Administration of Church Power" (as the Heads of Agreement put it) and, more specifically, the power and exercise of church discipline. Accordingly, the laity were restricted to a consensual role.[31] First Church now overturned these provisions, asserting that discipline was "given jointly to the pastor and church."[32] The

27. Records of First Church, vol. 2, "Relation of those owning the covenant," 1708, CSL.
28. Ibid., 26 November 1730.
29. Dexter, Biographical Sketches 2:129–31.
30. Records of First Church, vol. 2, Miscellaneous Papers, no. 2, CSL.
31. On the Heads of Agreement and the Saybrook Platform (which includes the Heads of Agreement), see Williston Walker, ed., The Creeds and Platforms of Congregationalism (1893; reprint, Philadelphia, 1969), 418, 503.
32. Records of First Church, vol. 3, Miscellaneous Papers, no. 2, CSL.

laity also altered other articles of the Saybrook Platform in order to give the church more latitude in its own affairs without consociational or associational interference.

Unlike his predecessor, Pitkin was an ardent New Light Evangelical. He invited George Whitefield, the greatest awakener in the colonies, to preach at Farmington. In 1774 he welcomed Levi Hart, the New Divinity minister from Preston, to deliver a sermon before the town's freemen. In articulating the New Divinity support for the Revolution, Hart pled for "the sacred cause of liberty" against British depradations by applying Edwards's views on the will (moral liberty) to the political realm (civil liberty).[33] Pitkin not only identified with the "black regiment" of New Divinity clerical supporters of the Revolution, but also embraced New Divinity ecclesiastical principles. Nathan Perkins, Pitkin's son-in-law, remembered Pitkin's vehement opposition to the Half-Way Covenant:

> His ideas of church communion, order, and discipline were most strict. In admissions to the communion of the Churches; the Lord's Table; and the baptismal water, he deemed real piety, or heart-experience of divine things, the *principle* upon which the churches of New England were formed, the ESSENTIAL term. None but the infant seed of professing believers had a right, in his opinion, to baptism on account of their parents.[34]

At Pitkin's insistence, the covenant question was broached in 1770, but not until 1782 did he and a core of church leaders succeed in persuading the rest of the church to overturn the covenant.[35] Later in life, Pitkin remarked that "the breaking up of that half-way covenant nearly cost me my ministerial life."[36] In some respects it did. In 1785, due in part to the serious divisions created over this issue, Pitkin resigned.[37]

Another factor also figured into Pitkin's retirement: he was losing touch with his congregation. The younger generation in the society found his sermons less than inspiring. "A popular address was his province," observed John Treadwell.

> Hence there was a want of variety in his sermons, which many excellent qualities could not fully compensate. The reverse which

---

33. Levi Hart, "Liberty Described and Recommended; in a sermon, preached . . . Sept. 20, 1774" (Hartford, Conn., 1775), esp. 7–9.

34. Nathan Perkins, "A Sermon Delivered at the Interment of the Rev. Timothy Pitkin . . ." (Hartford, Conn., 1812), 18.

35. Records of First Church, vol. 3, Miscellaneous Papers, nos. 4, 7–10, CSL.

36. Quoted in Trumbull, *Memorial History*, 176.

37. Failing health also plagued Pitkin (see Stiles, *Diary* 3:166).

took place some years before he resigned his ministry was painful to him and his people. *Another generation had arisen which knew not Joseph.* They regarded him indeed with affection; still, Mr. Pitkin saw, or thought he saw, a wide difference between that affection and the admiration of the former generation.[38]

Following Pitkin's resignation, the church society erupted into ten years of chaos. Old resentments, smoldering for years, surfaced with a vengeance. New issues, debated with acrimony, added more fuel to the fires of controversy. Farmington's pastors collided with society and church members, and the laity divided over membership qualifications, preaching styles, theological convictions, and church polity.

The Olcott Controversy, 1786–1791

The resentment created by Timothy Pitkin over the issue of the Half-Way Covenant spilled over into the calling and subsequent settlement of Allen Olcott. Pitkin's opposers became Olcott's opposers because they detected the same force at work behind both men. In their eyes, a handful of respected church and community leaders virtually controlled the church society, swaying and influencing votes in their favor.

The rebellion against longtime control of church affairs by the town's elite was partially rooted in the political turmoil of the day. On the national level, the 1780s represented a decade of constitutional crisis, as leaders tested and found wanting a confederated government and then turned to a strong federal government to help resolve critical postwar social and economic issues. On a local level, citizens responded to the crisis in various ways depending upon their convictions and interests. A crisis that energized the citizens of Connecticut, and particularly those of Farmington, involved a 1780 proposal by the federal government to compensate army officers who agreed to remain in the army until the war's end. An initial plan called for officers to receive one-half-pay pensions for life, but after great popular protest, Congress modified the plan in 1783. The new offer "commuted" the one-half-pay-for-life proposal to an outright grant of five years full pay.[39]

One incident that inflamed the passions of Farmington's citizens occurred when Captain William Judd obtained government securities for the commutation of half pay for officers of the Connecticut Line. On 4 August 1783,

---

38. Jonathan Treadwell Papers, 1706–1870, Box 2, "Sketches of the Town of Farmington," CSL.
39. For a discussion of the commutation issue, see Jackson Turner Main, *The Antifederalists: Critics of the Constitution, 1781–1788* (Chapel Hill, N.C., 1961), 106–9.

anticommutation leaders held an informal town meeting to protest Judd's actions. When John Treadwell and other town committee leaders heard of the meeting, they quickly took control and in an effort to calm the "riotous proceedings" unanimously disapproved of Judd's actions. A "Republican" in the *Connecticut Courant and Weekly Intelligencer* attacked Treadwell's intrusion by claiming that Treadwell's behavior was inconsistent with the New Divinity principles he was known to espouse so fervently. The writer sarcastically wrote that he once had "doubts whether providence ever encouraged villainy to help out the ends and designs of the Deity" until the pious Treadwell proved otherwise.[40] The editors of the *Courant* allotted Treadwell ample space to respond, and in fact, they filled an entire front page (a rarity) with an article in which Treadwell defended both his actions and the federal government's rationale for commutation. He opposed commutation on the grounds that it was unjust on "the scale of distributive justice," but nevertheless counseled calm and renewed confidence in the national government.[41]

Although the commutation issue faded from public consciousness by 1785, the underlying issue did not. In Farmington, the debate apparently moved from the political to the ecclesiastical arena. The controversy at First Church over a successor to Timothy Pitkin was at least partially rooted in prior political tensions. And the principle at stake was identical: whether an elite—be it army officers or church leaders (often one and the same)—should benefit at the expense of the people. Farmington residents had rejected the offer of commutation, for it was "founded on Principles Subvertive of a Republican Government," and it favored "a proper Aristocracy: wherein the Body of the People are excluded from all share in the Government, and the Direction & management of the state is committed to the Great & Powerful alone."[42] Likewise, as the controversy at First Church raged in the early 1790s, one parishioner expressed no personal objections to Edward Dorr Griffin as a minister; rather, his republican convictions transcended a personal like or dislike of the prospective pastor. Griffin was simply allied with the wrong cause. Because the elite supported Griffin, the dissident did "not want that two or three men shall rule the society."[43]

When Allen Olcott entered the scene in the mid-1780s he was identified with the same elitist clique that supported Griffin several years later. For Olcott's (and the elite's) opponents to marshal an attack appealing to political principles alone was undoubtedly deemed inappropriate in a hallowed ecclesiastical setting. Some other issue—a spiritual issue—was needed. And

40. *Connecticut Courant and Weekly Intelligencer* (Hartford), 2 September 1783.
41. Ibid., 16 September 1783; see also the 23 September issue for the conclusion of Treadwell's article.
42. Quoted in Main, *The Antifederalists*, 108, 109.
43. Julius Gay Collection of Farmington Manuscripts, MS. 92, CHS.

so the opposition immediately went for broke, claiming that Olcott was an unfit minister of the gospel. His preaching style was deficient; he lacked the ability to arouse his audience from spiritual laxity; he was "a son of consolation," not "a son of thunder."[44] Perhaps Olcott was a little too consoling: during his five years at First Church less than ten members were added to the church.

First Church called Allen Olcott as pastor in December 1786. Despite substantial opposition (the vote was 88 for, 33 against),[45] he accepted the call. Why he did can only lead to speculation, for typically, candidates eschewed settlements without a unanimous or near unanimous vote. A man of rigid New Divinity sympathies, he had been without a permanent settlement or ordination for nearly twenty years.[46] No doubt his overweening desire for a pastorate got the better part of wisdom. Perhaps he was impressed by the support he received from such prominent men as the Hon. John Treadwell (then state representative and circuit judge, and later governor of the state) and Noah Porter, the leading deacon of the church. Perhaps his budding romance with Cynthia Hooker, the daughter of the respected Roger Hooker and at whose home he boarded, figured into his decision. In the end, it seems, Olcott believed that God spoke through the majority, however strong the minority opposition. Whatever the reason, his decision to settle at First Church proved catastrophic.

Olcott candidated for a year before he received an official call to serve First Church. Despite significant minority opposition, the church proceeded and, by a slim margin of 47 to 35, voted to hold Olcott's ordination council. A misunderstanding surrounding this decision set the tone for the following four years of acrimonious debate. Due to the close vote, several anti-Olcott men believed that Olcott's ordination would be postponed, if not canceled. The date set to take up this issue was 18 January 1787—or so some thought. Olcott supporters assumed the meeting would be necessary only if he was not ordained. Olcott opponents presumed the date was set as a forum for continued discussion regarding his ordination. When the pro-Olcott ordination committee proceeded to set 17 January as the ordination date, the anti-Olcott forces became infuriated. Clearly, in their eyes, the slim majority conspired to force through Olcott's ordination without any more discussion. "As soon as the committee announced the day," wrote an Olcott partisan, "the opposition appeared to be greatly agitated," contending that the committee

44. Farmington, First Congregational Church Documents concerning the controversy over the Rev. Allen Olcott, 1786–1791 (hereafter cited as Olcott controversy documents), CHS, p. 12. The entire controversy is detailed in these papers.

45. Olcott controversy documents, CHS, p. 1.

46. Dexter, Biographical Sketches 3:291–92.

had set the date "on purpose to prevent any further deliberation of the subject."[47]

Acceding to pressure from the anti-Olcott forces, the church leaders held a special meeting for the church society on 10 January in order to hear grievances and to correct misunderstandings. The turnout "was fullest that has ever been held." To the opposition's dismay, the Olcott forces prevailed, and by a vote of 88 to 50, they retained the original ordination date. Undeterred, the anti-Olcott men circulated a petition and "through gross misrepresentation of Mr. Olcott's character and conduct" obtained seventy signatures of protest, "including some sectaries and others, who either did not belong to the society or had never heard Mr. Olcott preach."[48] So began a series of petition drives extending over the next four years in which each group garnered signatures for the retention or the dismissal of Olcott.

On 17 January 1787, Allen Olcott was ordained as minister of First Church. In protest, the opposition met the following day at a private home adjacent to Olcott's, "as if with design to wound his feelings."[49] There they appointed a committee to confer with the new pastor and to issue him the ultimate coup de grace: because the church was so "destitute of preaching" and "thirsted for the Word," would Olcott call in a neighboring minister? To demonstrate their hostility, the anti-Olcott faction hired a Baptist preacher for a series of services at the meetinghouse.

"Destitute of preaching . . . thirsted for the Word"—these phrases summarize the minority's ostensible grievances against Olcott from the beginning. When they initially discovered that Olcott's ordination would proceed, they hurriedly lodged a protest with their first petition. They did not question Olcott's orthodoxy; rather, they castigated his sermons, which "are not Rousing and Awakening nor Delivered with the Energy which we think Necessary in this day of Coldness and Indifference in Matters of Religion." In addition to citing Olcott's homiletical deficiencies, they continued, "the Suddenness and Hurry with which the Business has been conducted by a Small Majority to us appears very Extraordinary. The Appointing the Ordination the day Before the Adjourned Society Meeting which was for the purpose of Giving fair and full Opportunities to all parties is unaccountable."[50]

These objections, first directed against Olcott's preaching style and then against the maneuverings of his supporters, persisted until Olcott's dismissal in August 1791. For four years, Olcott's detractors marshaled more and more evidence in support of their claims. He lacked prudence, he was infected with

47. Olcott controversy documents, CHS, p. 2.
48. Ibid., 2–3.
49. Ibid., 4.
50. Ibid., Letter, 9 January 1787.

a "party spirit," he had contempt for the society, he was an inept teacher, and he neglected pastoral visitations in favor of closeting himself in his study for twelve hours at a time.[51] Olcott fit the critical description of the New Divinity men offered by President Ezra Stiles of Yale: "The difficulty of New Haven, Carmel, and Farmington," he wrote, "is New Div^y and rigid Discipline. No objections against the Moral Character of these Ministers, who are pious and conscientious Men, but very fixt and contentious in some novel Peculiarities."[52] Foremost in the minds of Olcott's Farmington opposers, however, was his flawed performance in the pulpit. Put simply, his sermons were "too general to be clearly understood, ineffectatious, uninstructive, and unentertaining."[53] Such critical evaluations of a pastor's preaching abilities were increasingly heard in the early Republic and attest to the emerging importance of popular opinion in the making and breaking of a minister. As one Farmington resident put it in 1811, the "essential part of a perfect minister's character" is "that animation and delivery which is so well calculated to move an audience." To Edward Hooker's dismay, nearly all of the ministers he heard were "too dull" and "want rousing."[54]

Olcott was one of these dull ministers. His defenders acknowledged a peculiarity in his preaching, yet they asserted that such a liability could just as easily be seen as an asset. They admitted that "Mr. Olcott's manner of speaking is not the most engaging; the fact is, Mr. Olcott's defect consists principally in making too frequent pauses." But even this mannerism had its benefits, as it offered "the hearer time to anticipate the speaker and to dwell a moment upon the sentences as they pass." To answer the objection that Olcott's sermons reached only a homogeneous audience (i.e., the converted), his supporters replied that sermonizing gauged to reach a larger audience (i.e., the unconverted as well) "was popular in the last age, but now the judicious seldom use this method."[55]

One member of the majority party perceptively contrasted Olcott's style of preaching with that for which the minority clamored:

> He seems less calculated to plant a church, than to build up one that has made some progress in divine knowledge and dwells with more entire delight upon the grace of the gospel, than the terrors of the law. . . . It is more congenial to his feelings to lead men to repentance by a sense of God's goodness, than by the terrors of his wrath, but still makes use of both considerations. His discourses are

51. Ibid., 10.
52. Stiles, *Diary* 3:374.
53. Olcott controversy documents, Church Minutes, 1786–1790: Letter, 20 January 1790, CHS.
54. Edward Hooker to William Hooker, 27 October 1811, Edward Hooker Letter Book, CHS.
55. Olcott controversy documents, CHS, pp. 7, 9.

full of sentiment; they are addressed to the understanding and not to the passions; they are instructive; but not pathetic; they delight the mind but not the senses.[56]

Clearly, Olcott favored a pedantic style. He appeared incapable of doing what every successful evangelical minister considered prime of place in preaching: engaging his listeners' understanding *and* emotions.

Beyond (or behind) the quarrel over Olcott's homiletic skills lay issues of power and control over church politics. The popular forces of democracy challenged an elite group that traditionally controlled both ecclesiastical and civil affairs. The composition of the groups on either side of the controversy indicates the extent to which the entire parish was caught up in the fracas. Society members involved in the Olcott controversy far outnumbered church members. Society members included adults living within the geographical boundaries of the parish set by law. They were required to pay a tax for maintaining the church and the minister's salary. Although not as influential in church affairs as full members, society members could make known their wishes through their control of the purse strings. In the case of Olcott, they tried to starve him out. Stiles noted that "Farmington . . . voted indeed a salary to Revd Mr. Olcott, but voted no collector."[57] If a majority vote could not remove Olcott, then economic pressure might.

Church members, those who had given an acceptable testimony to a conversion experience and who agreed to live by the standards of the church, normally nominated a ministerial candidate. The entire parish of adult males (including church and society members) then voted on the calling of a candidate. In the Olcott petition of 1789, only 27 percent (18 of 67) of those favoring the pastor were church members, whereas an even smaller percentage (20 percent, or 11 of 55) of those dissenting fully owned the covenant. Church members cast a mere 7 out of the 49 neutral votes (14 percent).[58] This low ratio of church members to society members was not uncommon in Connecticut, for during the seventeenth and eighteenth centuries this ratio steadily declined, though at a relative, not an absolute, rate. That is, church membership on the whole increased, but not at the same pace as the increase in town or parish residents.

Despite the low number of church members voting in the Olcott controversy, church members most often exercised influence and controlled the vote. Interestingly, the controversy was perceived (somewhat inaccurately) as pitting the church against the society. The church minutes of 10 February 1790 record that it was "voted, that this church cannot concur with

56. Ibid., 12.
57. Stiles, *Diary* 3:374.
58. Olcott controversy documents, CHS, p. 5 and voting lists, December 1789.

the society in opinion, as relative to Mr. Olcott's conduct or qualifications as a Christian minister."[59]

Olcott's key supporters consisted of Farmington's power elite: Noah Porter, Sr., the respected deacon of First Church; the Hon. John Treadwell, deacon, probate judge, state representative, and, later, state governor; Roger Hooker, justice of the peace; Martin Bull, deacon, church moderator, and town clerk; and Seth Lee, deacon, tavern keeper, apothecary, and New Divinity sympathizer who studied theology under Joseph Bellamy after graduating from Yale in 1759. With these, the opposition had its greatest quarrel. Anti-Olcott forces included both church and society members who embraced democratic principles and rejected the automatic deference paid to the elite. Standing for or against Olcott was not based on individual conviction alone but involved entire family networks. Petition lists reveal a general split along familial lines as sons and fathers, often united in business concerns, consistently voted in a unified bloc. Surnames such as Cowles, Hooker, Richards, Porter, and Hawley repeatedly appear on the lists of those supporting Olcott, while the names of Wadsworth, Thompson, and North consistently appear on opposition lists.

This basic conflict of interests did not escape the notice of the pro-Olcott forces. In the preface to their last petition, circulated in August 1791, the writer addressed the nature of the conflict. The problem, he contended, related to "old political grievances and jealousies, struggles of remaining anarchy, resentments from supposed affronts offered by individuals and the society, in sundry proceedings in the settlement and matters subsequent." These conflicts, in turn, were triggered by a "competition of interests—inattention to Gospel truths and prevalence of error."[60] Mature Christians, the writer implied, would overlook their own objections, submit to the majority's choice, and support Olcott.

Olcott himself did little to heal the agonizing division. In the face of stiff opposition that culminated in a majority vote against him in August 1791, he remained inflexible and refused to accept a dismissal. Long before the vote, as early as January 1791, his supporters began deserting the cause. "The friends of the settlement," wrote an Olcott partisan, "having been worn down with the increasing clamor on this subject, generally neglected to attend this and future meetings."[61] Even John Treadwell acknowledged the impasse: "In the existing state of things his dismissal was indispensible."[62] Not until an official church council was held in late August 1791, when representatives from the Hartford North Association voted for his dismissal, did Olcott finally agree to terminate his contract. The council reluctantly took action.

59. Olcott controversy documents, Church Minutes, 1786–90, CHS.
60. Ibid., Petition list, 1 August 1791.
61. Ibid., p. 14.
62. Memorial Sketch of the Rev. Allen Olcott, in "Sketches of the Town of Farmington," Treadwell Papers, CSL.

While voting for the dismissal in order to heal the schism, the New Divinity–controlled council remained unmoved by the accusations from the anti-Olcott group. Olcott "supported the character of a good, faithful, and able minister of the gospel," it concluded, " and was by no means given any just cause or reason of opposition to the uneasiness under his ministerial administrations."[63]

A Train of Candidates, 1791–1795

With Olcott's departure, the aggrieved minority set about finding a minister in tune with their wishes. They found their man in Jonathan Brown. In the first weeks after Olcott's removal, Brown preached at First Church and received a cordial reception from the former anti-Olcott faction. At the same time, another prospect candidated and was called "with unanimity," but he rejected Farmington's invitation for another settlement. Brown was then recalled, given serious consideration, and "warmly approved by a great majority of the Society."[64] The church, however, dissented from the society's choice. In March 1793, the parish committee voted eighteen to fourteen against extending a call to Brown. A breakdown of the voting list reveals eight former pro-Olcott men among the dissenters, including Treadwell, Noah Porter, and Martin Bull. According to Treadwell, Brown attracted Separatists, Baptists, and church members inclined toward a highly expressive piety.[65] "There seems to be a sympathy between him and them," he wrote, " and all others who are inclined to violent emotions of the mind and agitations of the body." Evidently, what Olcott lacked, Brown possessed in the extreme. As well, Treadwell judged Brown's exegetical and homiletical skills deficient. The candidate "drew the wrong conclusions from text" and "confuses doctrinal and applicatory parts of the sermon." When Brown heard of these criticisms, he embarrassed his detractors by referring to them by name in his prayers and sermons. "Injudicious," wrote a disgusted Treadwell. As a parting shot, Brown chose for his sermon text "The fruit of the spirit is long-suffering." The ploy was intended, concluded Treadwell, "to insinuate that his opposers had treated him ill."[66]

With Brown gone, a young, spirited Edward Dorr Griffin was invited to fill

---

63. Olcott controversy documents, CHS; see also Perkins, "Interment of Pitkins," 23.

64. Records of First Church, vol. 4, John Treadwell, "A Compendious History of the Church," CSL.

65. Treadwell Papers, Box 2, Misc. Correspondence; "Minutes of Jonathan Brown's Candidacy at Farmington," CSL. Following the Great Awakening, a small separatist Baptist group of thirty-eight people withdrew from First Church, though no formal body was established. The spirit of this group lived on. See Farmington Seventh Day Baptist Church, Connecticut. Formerly Bristol, Burlington. Church Book, 1780–1820, Seventh Day Baptist Materials (Microfilm, reel 1, no. 9), HC, SBC; and David Benedict, A General History of the Baptist Denomination in America, and other parts of the world (New York, 1848), 2:508.

66. Treadwell Papers, "Minutes of Brown's Candidacy," CSL.

First Church's vacant pulpit as a stated supply pastor.[67] He seemed an ideal candidate for a settlement. Fresh from reviving several churches in Middlesex County, Griffin's passionate preaching would most likely endear him to many of those who had wanted Brown. New Divinity in theological sympathies, Griffin would gain the support of former Olcott supporters and Brown opposers. But it was not to be. Opposition to Griffin emerged from two sources, both united in their opposition to First Church's ruling triumvirate of Treadwell, Porter, and Bull. One group was composed of those who had complained loudest about Allen Olcott's preaching and who had supported the candidacy of Jonathan Brown. "Dan.l North," recorded an observer, "says he has nothing against Mr. Griffin, but he opposes him because he was opposed in the matter of Mr. Brown." Griffin was simply too closely allied with the ruling oligarchy to be acceptable. "One of Griffin's opposers," noted another, "said he was sorry that Mr. Griffin was not ordained, but that he would not give up his will to Esq. Treadwell." Another response was just as revealing. Asked if he had ever heard Griffin preach, James Andrus replied, "No nor never desier [sic] to as long as old Treadwell likes him."[68]

The second source of opposition to Griffin originated from those objecting to his New Divinity views. Whether this group found the ruling elite as personally repugnant as the other group did is uncertain, but in their theological views they agreed with neither Griffin nor the church leaders. During Timothy Pitkin's tenure, Treadwell, Porter, Bull, and Seth Lee were members of the committee that favored dispensing with the Half-Way Covenant. Griffin took the same position. Although the society "called him almost unanimously" in 1794,[69] theological detractors arose and clashed with him over the nature of baptism and the doctrine of grace. Griffin not only opposed baptizing the children of the unregenerate, but he also insisted that the primary requisite for church membership was a conversion experience.

Even with these two sources of opposition, a church council voted to ordain Griffin, and the society followed with a 71-to-26 vote of approval.[70] Still, as with Olcott, opposition grew and stiffened, and another council convened. There Griffin's enemies "laid an unfounded charge of sundry immoralities against" him.[71] Although Griffin was acquitted of any impropri-eties and was recommended again for ordination, the vote in his favor narrowed to 64 to 41.[72] Sensing a swing of the pendulum, Griffin had the foresight, unlike Allen Olcott, to withdraw his candidacy.

No official church membership records exist for First Church during

---

67. Records of First Church, Treadwell, "Compendious History," CSL.
68. Julius Gay Collection of Farmington Manuscripts, MS. 92, CHS.
69. Records of First Church, Treadwell, "Compendious History," CSL.
70. Ibid., vol. 9.
71. Ibid., Treadwell, "Compendious History."
72. Ibid., vol. 9.

Griffin's stated supply, but according to his successor, the "greater part" of those joining the church in 1795 dated "their hope from that revival" under Griffin.[73] In an account of the 1799 revival, the Rev. Joseph Washburn noted that 55 joined the church in 1795, most of whom were initially aroused during the revival under Griffin in the fall of 1793.[74] (Note: the church records, picking up in 1795, list only 42 admitted in this year, excluding those who transferred their membership from other churches.)

It is striking to note that of those 42 members, 17 (40 percent) had directly voted for or were indirectly associated with (by marriage or offspring) those who had supported Allen Olcott, whereas only 3 (7 percent) had directly voted against or were indirectly associated with those opposing Olcott. These figures seem to suggest that those against Olcott on the ostensible grounds of lacking proper preaching credentials were not moved once a preacher as dynamic as Griffin was found. Political differences continued to obstruct any success Griffin might have had with the anti-Olcott faction. Even Washburn pointed out that the revival under Griffin was soon squelched "due to an unhappy contention" within the society.[75] One constant remained, however; those converted during the revival of 1793 followed a familiar pattern in New England: they were the children or spouses of church members or of those having a long standing in the church.[76]

The Rev. Joseph Washburn, 1795–1805

The settlement of Joseph Washburn brought a welcome peace to First Church. For the first time in nearly a decade, intrachurch rivalries, resentments, and wranglings ceased. No disputes broke out over Washburn's candidacy or ordination, and he was called by a near unanimous vote. With Washburn, the society found a pastor with qualities of character acceptable to all. Irenic in spirit, edifying and evangelical in preaching, he labored at First Church for ten years before his untimely death in 1805.

A Yale graduate of 1793, Washburn matched the profile of those most likely to succeed in awakening a Connecticut Congregational church: young,

73. CEM 1 (April 1801): 379, 382. Mary Treadwell Hooker recorded that under Griffin "there was at this time considerable attention to Religion in this Town" (Diary, CSL, p. 4).

74. CEM 1 (April 1801): 378.

75. Ibid.

76. Ibid., 382. On this long-term trend, see Gerald F. Moran, "The Puritan Saint: Religious Experience, Church Membership, and Piety in Connecticut, 1636–1776" (Ph.D. diss., Rutgers University, 1974).

New Divinity in theological sympathies, and sensitive to the needs of his church. One friend described him as an "ambassador of peace and salvation," "a watchman of souls" at First Church.[77] Under Washburn, First Church experienced its greatest period of growth, as two revivals over a five-year span added more than one hundred members.

On the last page of his "Regester" [sic], Washburn penned the following: "The religion of the world is seated in the head and goes no farther than the brain. . . . But the religion taught by our Blessed Saviour is implanted in the Heart by the Holy Spirit and flows out in Love to God supremely."[78] Washburn based his sermons on heartfelt religion, for like Griffin, he sought to reach the affections of his listeners. Many of his sermons dealt with practical concerns such as family prayer, the follies of youth, the attraction of riches, and the need for self-examination.[79] However edifying and instructive, Washburn based these sermons on the necessity of the new birth.

As a watchman of souls, Washburn devoted a great deal of time to the parish youth. His success with them was borne out by the fact that they composed nearly two-thirds of the converts in the 1799–1800 revival.[80] He often directed his sermons toward this "rising generation," whose pliable hearts made them prime candidates for conversion. "There is still less hope of those in youth," he reasoned, "who are still impenitent, than those in childhood; less still of those in middle age; and least of these in old age."[81] No doubt Washburn's admonitions deeply impressed the young after a 1798 dysentery epidemic took twenty-six lives—twenty-one under the age of fifteen.[82] God's judgment, concluded the frightened youth, was visited upon a community of hardened hearts.[83] But others, like Horace Cowles, a Farmington youth attending Yale College, took little notice of this divine rebuke. Cowles was a bit of a roustabout who evidently enjoyed his share of gaiety at Yale. In a letter to this son of pious parents, Washburn warned Cowles of the words in the catechism and Scripture: "The chief end of man is to glorify God," not "to dance and sing, not to riot upon the goods of Providence, not to make provision for the flesh to fulfill the lusts thereof."[84]

Washburn guarded not only the souls of youth but also the purity of the church. In 1796, this "watchman on the walls of Zion" supported a new

---

77. Asahel Hooker, "Funeral Sermon for the Rev. Joseph Washburn," in Joseph Washburn, *Sermons on Practical Subjects* . . . (Hartford, Conn., 1807), 334–35.

78. Joseph Washburn Papers, SML.

79. See Washburn, *Sermons*.

80. *CEM* 1 (April 1808): 382; see also Isaac and Lucinda Cowles to Horace Cowles at Yale, 22 March 1799, Julius Gay Misc. MSS, Box 6, Farmington Room, FVL.

81. Washburn, *Sermons*, 37.

82. Records of First Church, vol. 5, CSL.

83. Noah Porter to William Buell Sprague, 12 March 1832, in William B. Sprague, *Lectures on Revivals of Religion*, 2d ed. (New York, 1833), 291.

84. Joseph Washburn to Horace Cowles, 16 December 1799, Treadwell Papers, CSL.

confession of faith drawn from New Divinity principles. At first blush, its unanimous approval by the members of First Church on 4 August gave the appearance that all was well and that finally dissension was a thing of the past. However, in the months preceding the approval of the new confession, First Church had ousted the remaining dissenters. On 2 May, Judah Woodruff and John Hosford appeared before a church council. These well-known septuagenarians had joined the church half a century earlier during the tenure of Samuel Whitman. Woodruff was certainly no stranger to the meeting-house. A designer and master builder, he constructed the existing church structure in 1771, and with his own hands he carved the raised pulpit from which the likes of Pitkin, Olcott, Griffin, and now Washburn preached their uncompromising New Light–New Divinity sermons. Now, in a twist of irony, the elders excommunicated the very man who had built First Church. Deacon Noah Porter lodged a complaint against Woodruff on 21 June for failing to attend Sabbath-day services—even Communion services. Unrepentant, Woodruff called First Church "a church without a cross, with a legal preacher." Hosford leveled more severe criticisms by claiming that the church's doctrines were "immoral." He repudiated the "hard sayings" of Calvinism: its decrees, its doctrines of election and perseverance of the saints. He also rejected the New Divinity doctrine "that the unregenerate can do no duty." Finally, in words that hint at his own attraction to some brand of religious perfectionism (perhaps Methodism), Hosford contended that the idea "that no Christian lives without sin" was "false doctrine." On 24 December, 1796 the mop-up operation was completed: the elders formally excommunicated Woodruff and Hosford. In the next fifty years First Church's records remain conspicuously silent on issues of discipline involving deviation from doctrinal or ecclesiastical standards.[85]

Although Washburn played a crucial role in the revival at Farmington, he alone could not take credit for the awakening. The dynamics of revival required more than a young, evangelical minister preaching the word of salvation. Two other factors were operative. First, a network of pastors joined together in prayer, the mutual exchange of pulpits, and team revivalism. Second, lay persons took initiative to spread and sustain revival.

In Washburn's register, kept over a three-year period (1797–1800), he regularly recorded the Sunday sermon text as well as noted the speaker. Though incomplete, the register reveals a pattern of pastoral exchanges common to New England Congregational life and used extensively by New Divinity men in the Second Great Awakening. Particularly striking is the

85. Records of First Church, vol. 4, "A Record of the Votes and Proceedings of the First Church of Christ in Farmington, after 7th May, 1795," CSL.

choice of the texts selected by visiting ministers. The following samples illustrate the evangelical flavor of their preaching:

1. On 12 February 1797, the Rev. Giles H. Cowles from nearby Bristol preached in the morning on Acts 17:30: "But now commandeth all men everywhere to repent." In the afternoon his text was 2 Corinthians 6:2: "Behold, now is the day of salvation."

2. Two weeks later a Reverend Bird preached on justification by grace from the text in Romans 3:4: "Being justified freely by his grace through the redemption that is in Christ Jesus." The afternoon text was John 3:7: "Ye must be born again." Bird also spoke on 25 June 1797, using Matthew 18:11 as his text: "For the Son of man is come to save that which was lost."

3. On that same 25 June 1797, James Richards (who later became a close associate of Griffin in Newark) chose Galatians 2:16 as his text: "A man is not justified by works of the law but through faith in Jesus Christ."

4. Ebenezer Porter from Washington also preached at First Church. He spoke on such themes as salvation by grace alone (Ephesians 2:8) and the new birth—the classic text being John 3:3, where Jesus said to Nicodemus, "Except a man be born again, he cannot see the kingdom of God."

Other visiting preachers uplifted the same themes of salvation. Drawing upon classic New Testament texts that demarcated saints from sinners and demanded immediate repentance, many of these pastors had one goal in mind: to bring the gospel message of salvation. As discussed earlier, an extensive network of exchanges such as occurred at Farmington spread throughout northwestern Connecticut and became a critical device for initiating and sustaining the revival.[86]

In addition, Washburn promoted revival by working closely with the laity. He reported that when word of revival reached Farmington, it "became the subject of conversation among Christians." Soon, however, interest waned, and not until almost six months later, when a spiritual awakening erupted in some nearby churches, did the people "unite in prayer for the divine presence, and a revival of religion."[87] In order to sustain spiritual fervor, Washburn suggested holding conference meetings. The deacons and others agreed and so proceeded to organize fortnightly meetings "for the purpose of special united prayer for a revival of religion."[88] One meeting was held at "Mr. Smith's . . . for Religious conversation and prayer."[89] Religious conference meetings at Farmington, as in other awakened communities, created a

86. See Chapter 2.
87. *CEM* 1 (April 1801): 379.
88. Ibid., 380.
89. Letter to Horace Cowles at Yale from his parents, 11 March 1799, Julius Gay Misc. MSS, FVL.

community of mutual concern, intensified the mood of revival, and offered a "sacred space" for personal edification and God's work of regeneration.

A decade of turbulence at First Church had finally come to an end. The upheaval revealed a typical side of New England church life in the early years of the Republic. Few churches avoided disruptions of one sort or another, be they salary disputes, doctrinal wranglings, or issues of church discipline. Frequently, not one, but many convoluted issues—witness Farmington—divided a parish.

The controversy at First Church pointed to another source of conflict in Connecticut Congregational churches, namely, the tension between parish residers and full church members over the choice of a pastor. This nettlesome issue was not fully resolved until 1818, when the General Assembly voted to disestablish the alliance joining the Congregational church to the state and to do away with the parish system. All religious bodies then became voluntary denominations, unsupported by local taxes and exclusively governed by church members.[90]

With the stated supply ministry of Edward Dorr Griffin and the settlement of Joseph Washburn, the Second Great Awakening came to Farmington. During the first three decades of the nineteenth century, First Church continued to boost its membership through regular seasons of revival. The Rev. Noah Porter, who succeeded Washburn and served First Church for over half a century, calculated that from 1795 to 1831 some 460 members were added to the church as a direct result of revivals—with over half (250) coming in 1821 under the cajolery and counsel of Asahel Nettleton.[91] By the time Nettleton captivated Farmington, revivalism had become the primary means for gathering converts. This routinization of revival was hardly expected, though not unhoped for, by New Divinity preachers thirty years before. If it can be said that Edward Dorr Griffin and other New Divinity men sowed the seeds of revival on the rocky ground of church dissension, then certainly Nettleton and subsequent revivalists reaped the benefits on the fertile soil of church consensus.

In some respects, the ecclesiastical history of First Church records an internal power struggle between the elite and the disenfranchised few, but that struggle seldom directly touched the majority of parishioners. As such, the contentions within First Church had little to do with a revival that touched so many. In other respects, however, the debacle at First Church had everything to do with the Second Great Awakening. New Divinity ministers and sympathizers, through their presence and eventual victory, reaffirmed the

90. See Louise M. Greene, *The Development of Religious Liberty in Connecticut* (1905; reprint, Freeport, N.Y., 1970), chap. 15.

91. Porter to Sprague, in Sprague, *Lectures*, 295.

conversion experience as the primary criterion for church membership. New Divinity advocates also fenced the Lord's Table, restricting participation in Communion to full members. As the New Divinity would have it, First Church became a more exclusive institution, less concerned with community inclusion and more concerned with church purity. But lest exclusivity reduce the church to a faithful few, regular outpourings of revival now provided the context for the entrance of numerous converts into the church. God's covenant with New England, though discarded, crept in the back door. A limited, voluntary church of saints now replaced an inclusive city on a hill as a beacon to the world. In the *novus ordo seclorum*, a new order of saints beheld and spread a new light.

6

"PROFESSORS AND PROFLIGATES"

The Awakened

"The work of the Lord goes on without abatement . . . and it is now extending from town to town, as rapidly as ever fire did in the green woods."[1] So wrote Edward Dorr Griffin to a fellow minister following the initial eruption of revival in northwestern Connecticut in 1798. The towns to which Griffin referred not only included the immediate area of Litchfield and Hartford counties but extended west into New York and north into Massachusetts, Vermont, and New Hampshire. In Litchfield and Hartford counties nearly thirty parishes experienced surges in church membership, ranging from 20 to over 150 new communicants and totaling nearly 1700 during the 1798–1800 revivals.[2]

The Second Great Awakening was no respecter of persons. Like the Great Awakening, it was a "great and general" revival, drawing converts from a broad social base: young and old, single and married, male and female, rich and poor. "It was not one particular class of people that was impressed," the Rev. Joshua Williams of Harwinton recalled.

> Some of the most unlikely, to human appearance, have been the subjects of this work. The high and the low, the weak and the strong,

1. Edward D. Griffin to Lynde Huntington, 14 March 1799, BL.
2. See Appendix 3.

the rich and the poor, the mere moralist and scoffer, the professor and the profligate, the profane and the inconsiderate, people of almost all occupations and ranks among us, and of almost every age and station, have been wrought upon and called out from the midst of their acquaintances and neighbors.[3]

Nor was the spiritual harvest restricted to a single type of community. Although most of the revivals occurred in villages or rural hamlets, larger, commercially oriented towns such as Litchfield, Farmington, and Hartford were affected as well. The diverse appeal of the Awakening suggests that its outbreak was not precipitated by a single set of economic or social factors restricted in its influence to a select group; rather, the revival was triggered by a broad range of ecclesiastical and social problems that the New Divinity addressed vigorously. As the traditional shapers and interpreters of New England culture, the clergy persuaded a wide variety of individuals to resolve the pressing issues of life by seeking salvation. New Divinity ministers largely created the preconditions for revival in a society steeped in the conversion experience as the accustomed way of addressing and answering both personal and social problems. As I showed in the previous chapter, the potential for revival was rooted firmly in the internal ecclesiastical life of New England. For those in the Edwardsean tradition, the conversion experience remained the paradigmatic way of being, becoming, and remaining religious. Periods of social strain merely accentuated the need to find a spiritual solution to the problem at hand. In those perilous times, the New Divinity men assured their listeners that a resolution to personal disorientation and community fragmentation came only through spiritual renewal.

Although the call to conversion was answered by all types of persons, some groups predominated. Married adult males were more likely to convert than young unattached males; females were more likely to convert than males; and of any single group (considering gender and marital status), married females were the most likely to convert. The Awakening was not a youthful phenomenon, but a rite of passage for adults, many of whom were either born or in childhood during the American Revolution. For young adults, but particularly males, economic and demographic changes in northwestern Connecticut aroused anxiety and uncertainty about the future. For females, the New Divinity language of conversion, with its paradoxical vocabulary of "sensual spirituality," appealed to and even reinforced culturally prescribed notions of femininity. Moreover, public expression and leadership roles for women were confined to the religious arena. Together, these differing conditions in the lives of males and females inclined them to heed the impassioned pleas of pastors, friends, and neighbors, and to accept God's gracious offer of salvation.

---

3. *CEM* 1 (June 1801): 465–66; see also Asahel Hooker's account in *CEM* 1 (March 1801): 344.

The next two chapters look at the ordinary people of the Awakening. This chapter compares and contrasts converts from the Great Awakening with the Second Great Awakening, considers economic and other social factors that may have created a receptivity to revival, and then briefly views lay involvement in the revival. Chapter 7 refines generalizations made in this chapter about the predisposition of some groups to revival and focuses more specifically on the nature of conversion and the spiritual life.

The Great Awakenings Compared

To whom did the Second Great Awakening appeal? A quantitative comparison with the Great Awakening in Connecticut, focusing on the age, gender, and marital status of church admittants prior to and during the two Awakenings, offers a useful measuring device for discerning the nature and extent of the second Awakening. I have relied upon data from Gerald Moran for the years through the Great Awakening (to 1750), added the statistical study of another student of revivals for the years 1750 to 1798, and then supplied my own data for the revivals from 1798 to 1800.[4] Church membership records sampled for the Second Great Awakening reveal that successive waves followed the initial outburst.[5] During the first quarter of the nineteenth century, significant ingatherings occurred from 1806 to 1808 and from 1813 to 1822—the latter wave representing the revivalistic successes of Asahel Nettleton.

For Gerald Moran, the key to understanding the nature of church admissions from the mid-1630s to 1700 lies in "the developmental crisis of generativity." "Most Puritan men and women," he contends, "underwent conversion or entered the church only after they had advanced far beyond puberty and the traditional age of adolescence and entered into adulthood."[6] Regeneration followed maturation; that is, most Puritans converted following marriage and the procreation of children. Adult conversions coincided with a parental desire to transmit the benefits of the faith to their children.

4. Gerald F. Moran, "The Puritan Saint: Religious Experience, Church Membership, and Piety in Connecticut, 1636–1776" (Ph.D. diss., Rutgers University, 1974); Jeffrey Potash, "An Inquiry into the Dynamics of the Second Great Awakening in New England (Seminar paper, History 737, University of Chicago, 1977). Potash's data from 1750 to 1798 are drawn from a sampling of 287 males and 158 females from ten churches. See Appendix 4 for an explanation of my sample.

5. Charles R. Keller, *The Second Great Awakening in Connecticut* (New Haven, Conn., 1942), charts the following years as revival peaks: 1797–1801, 1802, 1807–8, 1812, 1815–16, 1820–21, and 1825–26 (37, 41, 42). These waves of revival continued up to the Civil War. See *Contributions to the Ecclesiastical History of Connecticut* (New Haven, Conn., 1861), 199.

6. Moran, "Puritan Saint," 167, 159.

Church admissions for the four decades (1700–39) preceding the Great Awakening in Connecticut indicate trends similar to the seventeenth century, though the age of church admission begins to decline at a faster rate than during the previous century (see Table 6.1).

Table 6.1   Church Admissions, 1700–1739

Age	Percentage of males	Percentage of Females
Under 20	6.9	19.3
20–24	19.1	32.5
25–29	26.4	23.1
30–34	20.4	11.2
35–39	9.8	5.5
40–44	6.2	3.5
45–49	4.4	2.4
50 +	6.8	2.3

SOURCE: Moran, "The Puritan Saint," 280. (Reproduced with permission)

Whereas the normative range for male admissions during the seventeenth century was above age thirty, in the period 1700 to 1739 the norm fell to a range between twenty-five and thirty-four (46.8 percent). In addition, just over one-quarter (26 percent) joined the church prior to age twenty-five. Similarly, the female normative range dipped to between twenty and twenty-nine (55.6 percent). Nineteen percent were admitted below the age of twenty, while 25 percent became communicants after reaching the age of thirty. The vast majority of church members—both male (80 percent) and female (77 percent)—continued to be married.[7]

Beginning in 1740, the Great Awakening in Connecticut produced a "new saint." Youthfulness and a single marital status characterized the typical convert (see Table 6.2).

Over one-half (53.6 percent) of the male converts were under the age of twenty-five, representing a dramatic drop in the normative range from the previous four decades. In addition, over 30 percent (31.3) fell into the prior normative range between ages twenty-five and thirty-four, while 15.2 percent were admitted beyond the age of thirty-five. Among female converts nearly 90 percent were under the age of thirty: 46.7 percent under age twenty and 42.4 percent between the ages of twenty and twenty-nine. The youthfulness of the Great Awakening convert correlates with a drop in the admissions of

7. Ibid., 303–6.

Table 6.2   Church Admissions, 1740–1749

Age	Percentage of Males	Percentage of Females
Under 20	26.8	46.7
20–24	26.8	27.0
25–29	18.3	15.4
30–34	13.0	6.7
35–39	6.7	2.5
40–44	3.9	1.8
45–49	2.1	0.0
50 +	2.5	0.0

SOURCE: Moran, "The Puritan Saint," 280. (Reproduced with permission)

marrieds. During the century preceding the Awakening, over three-fourths of all admittants were married, whereas during the revival, 43 percent of the male converts and 45 percent of the female converts were married.[8] In short, the new saint of the 1740s was young, unmarried, unestablished, and dependent upon parents.

In one respect, however, these new converts revealed strong ties to their ancestors. From the beginning of colonial settlement, New England Congregationalists perpetuated church membership through familial lines.[9] Moran estimates that 80 percent of the revival converts had at least one parent within the local church.[10] The question, then, was not *who* would seek admission to the church, but *when*. The Great Awakening merely added a disproportionate number of young people to the church within a compressed time span.

The influx of youthful converts was a temporary phenomenon. In the 1750s, church admissions returned to the pre-Awakening pattern. According to Moran's findings, the percentage of male converts under the age of twenty fell to 1.7 percent by 1775.[11] Data accumulated for Litchfield and Hartford counties from 1750 to 1798 resemble the pre-Awakening trends (see Table 6.3). Male admittants during the last half of the eighteenth century were slightly older than their counterparts of the first four decades of the century.

8. Ibid.
9. Philip Greven, *The Protestant Temperament: Patterns of Child-Rearing, Religious Experience, and the Self in Early America* (New York, 1979); on Connecticut, see James P. Walsh, "The Great Awakening in the First Congregational Church of Woodbury, Connecticut," *William and Mary Quarterly*, 3d ser., 28 (October 1971): 543–62. For an exception to the general pattern of familial faith in colonial Connecticut, see Peter Onuf, "New Lights in New London: A Group Portrait of the Separatists," *William and Mary Quarterly*, 3d ser., 37 (October 1980): 627–43.
10. Moran, "Puritan Saint," 343.
11. Ibid., 284.

Fewer were admitted under the age of twenty (.7 percent), while the normative range lay between twenty-five and thirty-nine (62.9 percent)—five years above the 1700–1739 range.

New female members from 1750 to 1798 were also slightly older than the pre-Awakening members. The normative range for the latter period fell between the ages of twenty and thirty-four (59.7 percent), compared with a normative range between twenty and twenty-nine (74.9 percent) for the former period. Also, over twice as many females were admitted over the age of thirty-five (32.3 percent) as had been admitted during the earlier period (13.7 percent). Typically, nearly all were married—94.8 percent of the men and 84.5 percent of the women—again, slightly higher than the pre–Great Awakening level.[12]

Table 6.3   Church Admissions, 1750–1798

Age	Percentage of Males	Percentage of Females
Under 20	0.7	7.9
20–24	14.7	17.7
25–29	25.5	22.9
30–34	21.3	19.1
35–39	16.1	14.5
40–44	6.3	6.7
45–49	7.7	1.4
50 +	7.7	9.7

SOURCE: Potash, "An Inquiry," 9. (Reproduced with permission)

Upsurges or periodic revivals characterized the decades prior to both major awakenings.[13] The commonly cited theme of declension more often betrayed rhetoric than fact. Indeed, during the two decades prior to the Second Great Awakening—that postrevolutionary period generally portrayed by scholars as the "ebb-tide of religious life"—the Congregational churches of Barkhamsted, Bristol, Norfolk, Plainville, and Farmington admitted from fifteen to fifty new converts each.[14] Piety did not wane, nor did church

12. Potash, "An Inquiry," 10.

13. For the episodic nature of church admissions from 1630 to 1739, see Robert G. Pope, The Half-Way Covenant: Church Membership in Puritan New England (Princeton, N.J., 1969), and Moran, "Puritan Saint." For pre–Great Awakening (1700–1739), see Walsh, "Great Awakening."

14. Winthrop S. Hudson, Religion in America, 2d ed. (New York, 1973), 115–16. Hudson omits this metaphor in his subsequent editions. For other standard references to postrevolutionary declension,

admissions fall off at an absolute rate. Rather, church admission rates resembled waves that periodically whitecapped, then gathered into a tidal wave labeled an awakening.

Given the similarities in church communicants prior to the two Awakenings, how do the converts of the first and second Great Awakenings compare? In one respect, the converts of the New Divinity Second Great Awakening look strikingly like their predecessors: many continued to be drawn from the same Puritan stock. As Charles Backus recognized, "Grace is not hereditary, but the prayers of godly ancestors are often answered in the bestowment of spiritual blessings on their posterity."[15] The most likely candidates for conversion tended to be those instructed in the catechism and nurtured in a pious family. Empirical data gathered by Stephen Grossbart on church admission patterns in eastern Connecticut, as well as data compiled by others, corroborate evidence culled from accounts of the revivals in northwestern Connecticut that indicates that a significant portion of converts came from families well versed in religious matters and those in which at least one of the family members was a church member.[16]

Joseph Washburn observed that Farmington converts came from families "where religion is professed and carefully inculcated by one or both of the

---

see Leonard W. Bacon, *A History of American Christianity* (New York, 1897), 219; Robert Baird, *Religion in the United States of America* (1844; reprint, New York, 1969), 221; Frank G. Beardsley, *A History of American Revivals*, 3d ed. (New York, 1912), 81; Charles L. Thompson, *Times of Refreshing: A History of American Revivals from 1740 to 1877* (Chicago, 1877), 68; Richard J. Purcell, *Connecticut in Transition, 1775–1818* (Washington, D.C., 1918), 8; Henry K. Rowe, *The History of Religion in the United States* (New York, 1924), 62; and Keller, *Second Great Awakening*, 27.

Church records as well as ministerial accounts document the postrevolutionary revivals. For written accounts, see Records of the First Church of Christ, Farmington, vol. 6, CSL; *CEM* 1 (April 1801): 379; *CEM* 1 (September 1800): 102; and *CEM* 1 (February 1801): 311; see also Mary Hewitt Mitchell, *The Great Awakening and Other Revivals in the Religious Life of Connecticut* (New Haven, Conn., 1934). For revised correctives to the postwar spiritual-declension view, see Douglas H. Sweet, "Church Vitality and the American Revolution: Historiographical Consensus and Thoughts toward a New Perspective," *Church History* 45 (September 1976): 341–57; Richard D. Shiels, "The Second Great Awakening in Connecticut: Critique of the Traditional Interpretation" *Church History* 49 (December 1980): 401–15; Stephen A. Marini, *Radical Sects of Revolutionary New England* (Cambridge, Mass., 1982); and Terry D. Bilhartz, *Urban Religion and the Second Great Awakening: Church and Society in Early National Baltimore* (Madison, N.J., 1986).

15. Charles Backus, *The Scripture Doctrine of Regeneration Considered, in Six Discourses* (Hartford, Conn., 1800), 73.

16. Stephen R. Grossbart, "Seeking the Divine Favor: Conversion and Church Admission in Eastern Connecticut, 1711–1832," *William and Mary Quarterly*, 3d ser., 46 (October 1989): 729. Grossbart's longitudinal study of five churches supports much of my own findings. For similar conclusions, see Mary P. Ryan, "A Women's Awakening: Evangelical Religion and the Families of Utica, New York, 1800–1840," *American Quarterly* 30 (Winter 1978): 602–23, esp. 612–13; Curtis D. Johnson, *Islands of Holiness: Rural Religion in Upstate New York, 1790–1860* (Ithaca, N.Y., 1989), 61; and Michael J. Crawford, *Seasons of Grace: Colonial New England's Revival Tradition in Its British Context* (New York, 1991), 11–12.

parents, [rather] than from those of a different description."[17] Pastors describing revivals in West Hartford, Bristol, Goshen, West Britain, and Washington from 1799 to 1806 reiterated Washburn's judgment.[18] In the 1805 revival in Harwinton, Joshua Williams estimated that as many as nine out of ten converts were "the children of religious parents, or . . . lived in pious and praying families."[19] A casual survey of the names of converts reveals that every revived community had a sizable number with identical surnames. At times both parents and their children were captivated by the revival, as was the case with the Gillett family of Torrington, where Nathan Gillett and his wife were admitted to the church in May 1799, and then were followed four months later by their children. Perhaps the experience of siblings was more common than that of spouses. Brothers and sisters often appear in membership lists grouped together in twos or threes—a confirmation that indeed families, not isolated individuals, were touched by the Awakening. As in the past, the family, with its extended kinship ties, remained the primary unit from which church membership was drawn. What Gerald Moran called "the familial context of regeneration" persisted into the second Awakening.[20]

In other respects, however, the second Awakening converts differed significantly from converts of the Great Awakening. Table 6.4 lists age categories for male and female church admittants of the two major revivals. A wide divergence separates the ages of the first and second Great Awakening converts. The youthful nature of the first Awakening is not nearly as predominant in the second. Consider the differences in male converts. The mean age of the Great Awakening male converts was 26.5, whereas the mean age for the Second Great Awakening male increased to 31.5—a figure nearly identical with each of the two pre-Awakening means. Whereas over one-half (53.6 percent) of the Great Awakening converts were under the age of twenty-five, only about one-third (32.6 percent) of the Second Great Awakening converts were under this age. Nearly all (84.9 percent) of the Great Awakening converts were under the age of thirty-five, whereas just over 60 percent of the second Awakening converts fell into this cohort.

The difference in ages between female converts of the two Awakenings is more dramatic than between males. The "average" second Awakening female communicant was considerably older (nearly twenty-nine) than the Great Awakening female communicant (nearly twenty-three). Almost 90 percent of the female converts of the Great Awakening were under the age of twenty-

17. *CEM* 1 (April 1801): 382.

18. Nathan Perkins, "Two Discourses on the grounds of a Christian's hope . . ." (Hartford, Conn., 1800), 31; *CEM* 1 (July 1800): 27; *CEM* 1 (August 1800): 59; *CEM* 1 (March 1801): 343; *CEM* 7 (October 1806): 147.

19. *CEM* 7 (April 1807): 368.

20. Moran, "Puritan Saint," 187.

Table 6.4 Comparative Statistical Data on Communicants from the First and Second Great Awakenings

Age	Percentage of Males		Percentage of Females	
	First Great Awakening	Second Great Awakening	First Great Awakening	Second Great Awakening
Under 20	26.8	14.0	46.7	14.0
20–24	26.8	18.6	27.0	23.4
25–29	18.3	12.6	15.4	16.2
30–34	13.0	15.7	6.7	11.5
35–39	6.7	15.7	2.5	11.9
40–44	3.9	8.2	1.8	8.1
45–49	2.1	7.0	0.0	8.1
50 +	2.5	8.2	0.0	6.8
Mean Age	26.5	31.5	22.8	28.8

SOURCES: For the Great Awakening, Moran, "The Puritan Saint," 280; for the Second Great Awakening, see Tables A4.3 and A4.4.

nine, compared to just over 50 percent (53.6) for converts of the second Awakening. On the other hand, there were twice as many converts between the ages of thirty and thirty-nine (23.4 percent) in the second Awakening as there were in the first (9.2 percent). Finally, Great Awakening converts above the age of forty were statistically negligible (1.8 percent), whereas nearly one-quarter (23.6 percent) of the second Awakening female converts fell into the above-age-forty cohort.[21]

Correlating with the older ages of the Second Great Awakening converts was a greater percentage of married communicants than among Great Awakening communicants (see Table 6.5). Fewer than one-half of the male and female Great Awakening converts were married, whereas nearly three-quarters (73.7 percent) of the male and over one-half (55 percent) of the female second Awakening converts were married. Just over one-half (51 percent) of those married were admitted together as couples.

In addition to the age and marital differences between converts of the two Awakenings, sex ratios also diverged. During the Great Awakening, a proportionately greater percentage of males converted than in previous decades, although in general, female converts vastly outnumbered male

21. The ages of males and females in Grossbart's findings for the Second Great Awakening from 1798–1832 are slightly lower than mine. Males converted and joined churches in their mid to late twenties, females in their mid twenties (see Grossbart, "Seeking the Divine Favor," 706).

Table 6.5 Married Admittants, 1795–1800

Church, Date (Total Admissions)	Sample Number	% of Total Admissions	Males			Females			Total No. Married	% of Married to Total Sample	No. of Couples Admitted Simultaneously
			Total	No. Married	% Married	Total	No. Married	% Married			
Barkhamsted, 1799 (20)	19	95.0	7	4	57.0	12	7	58.0	11	57.8	4
Bristol, 1799–1800 (103)	95	92.0	32	22	54.0	63	38	60.0	60	63.0	15
Canton Center, 1799 (56)	42	75.0	18	18	100.0	24	18	75.0	36	85.7	13
Durham, 1803 (41)	39	95.0	7	3	43.0	32	15	47.0	18	46.0	3
Farmington, 1795–1800 (151)	149	99.0	35	23	66.0	114	62	54.0	85	57.0	18
Goshen, 1799–1800 (90)	81	90.0	20	20	100.0	61	25	41.0	45	55.5	15
Torrington, 1799–1800 (47)	42	89.0	14	7	50.0	28	18	64.0	25	59.5	6
West Avon, 1799 (36)	34	94.0	22	18	82.0	12	11	92.0	29	85.0	8
Windsor, 1799 (34)	32	94.0	5	3	60.0	27	11	41.0	14	43.7	1
Total (578)	533	92.0	160	118	73.7	373	205	55.0	323	60.6	83*

*83 × 2 = 166, or 51.0 percent of total married admissions.

Source: Church Records, CSL.

converts during the colonial period.[22] Beginning with the 1795 revival in Farmington, however, proportionately more females entered the churches. From 1795 to 1806, female communicants outnumbered males at a ratio of 5 to 2.7; from 1807 to 1822 the ratio increased slightly to just over two females for every male communicant (see Table 6.6). During the first decades of the nineteenth century the clergy not only reiterated the fact of disproportionate female numbers—an observation they had been making for over a century—but now some clergy expressed outright dismay at male disinterest in religion. When the Rev. Thomas Robbins noted that he was "considerably dejected in spirits" following an evening conference meeting where "few men attend[ed]," he was not alone. A number of his ministerial colleagues shared his sentiments.[23] The overwhelming presence of females and the conspicuous absence of males had become a startling reality. Northwestern Connecticut followed other parts of New England and New York in the trend toward the "feminization" of American Protestantism.[24]

Table 6.6   Sex Ratios, 1795–1822

Date	Males	Females	Ratio
1795–1806	311	577	5.38 : 10
1807–1822	325	683	4.75 : 10
Total	636	1260	5.0 : 10

SOURCE: Table A4.4.

22. Women admittants during the Great Awakening averaged about 56 percent (Moran, "Puritan Saint," 326).

23. Thomas Robbins, *The Diary of Thomas Robbins, D.D., 1796–1854*, ed. Increase N. Tarbox (Boston, 1886), 1:456; William A. Hallock, *Memoir of Harlan Page; or, The Power of Prayer and Personal Effort for the Souls of Individuals* (New York, 1835), 135, 142. For a similar response in Maine, see Jothan Sewall, *A Memoir of Rev. Jothan Sewall, of Chesterville, Maine* (Boston, 1853), 250.

24. See Grossbart, "Seeking the Divine Favor"; Nancy F. Cott, *The Bonds of Womanhood: "Woman's Sphere" in New England, 1780–1835* (New Haven, Conn., 1977), 126–59; Richard D. Shiels, "The Feminization of American Congregationalism, 1730–1835," *American Quarterly* 33 (Spring 1981): 46–62; idem, "The Scope of the Second Great Awakening: Andover, Massachusetts, as a Case Study," *Journal of the Early Republic* 5 (Summer 1985): 223–46; Harry S. Stout and Catherine E. Brekus, "Declension, Gender, and the 'New Religious History,'" in *Belief and Behavior: Essays in the New Religious History*, ed. Philip R. Vandermeer and Robert P. Swierenga (New Brunswick, N.J., 1991), 15–37; Ryan, "Women's Awakening"; idem, *Cradle of the Middle Class: The Family in Oneida County, New York, 1790–1865* (New York, 1981), 75; Johnson, *Islands of Holiness*, 53–66; and David G. Hackett, *The Rude Hand of Innovation: Religion and Social Order in Albany, New York, 1652–1836* (New York, 1991), 85. See also Terry D. Bilhartz, "Sex and the Second Great Awakening: The Feminization of American Religion Reconsidered," in *Belief and Behavior*, ed. Vandermeer and Swierenga, 117–35, for similar conclusions about Baltimore.

To summarize: unlike the Great Awakening, the New Divinity Second Great Awakening did not overwhelmingly appeal to a particular age group. Ministers reported that the revival touched a broad spectrum of people. In some parishes, the young and "heads of families" predominated; in others, young, single females abounded; in yet others, the diversity of ages was the only generalization that could be made. Taken together, however, most converts of the Second Great Awakening were female and most were married. Over three-quarters (76.6 percent) of the male converts were evenly distributed within the five age categories under forty, whereas a maximum of twelve percentage points separated any one age category among the three-quarters (77 percent) of female converts under age forty. Many of the revived had a religious upbringing and prior opportunities to heed the call to repent and be saved. The infusion of New Divinity evangelical preaching, leadership, and organization, as well as the general outpouring of revival, snared those who had repeatedly ignored their lost condition and who presumably would have continued to do so had not the Awakening erupted.

Economic and Demographic Trends

An examination of economic developments in Connecticut offers clues to the attraction of the Second Great Awakening among some portions of the adult population. Contrary to the conventional understanding, the Connecticut in which these converts lived was not entirely "the land of steady habits," isolated from disruptive changes in the early Republic.[25] The village revivals took place in a preindustrial, predominantly agricultural society in the midst of an "economic revolution."[26] Beginning after the War for Independence and escalating in the last decade of the eighteenth century, Connecticut's economic revolution was characterized by the emergence of commercial agriculture and a shift in the focus of economic life from the coastal to inland counties.[27] Litchfield, Farmington, and Hartford benefited greatly from this newfound prosperity, serving as marketing and transportation centers linked

25. Keller, *Second Great Awakening*, entitles chapter 1 "The Land of Steady Habits." This phrase has been employed since the eighteenth century to describe Connecticut as an enclave of political and social stability. For a revisionist overview of the "land of steady habits," see Christopher Collier, "Steady Habits Considered and Reconsidered," *Connecticut Review* 5 (April 1972): 28–37.

26. The term is from Gaspare J. Saladino, "The Economic Revolution in Late Eighteenth-Century Connecticut" (Ph.D. diss., University of Wisconsin, 1964). For a more recent summary of eighteenth-century economic developments, see Bruce C. Daniels, "Economic Developments in Colonial and Revolutionary Connecticut: An Overview," *William and Mary Quarterly*, 3d ser., 37 (July 1980): 429–50.

27. Saladino, "Economic Revolution," chap. 10.

through turnpikes to the outlying rural areas. Undoubtedly the spread of revivals was facilitated by these roads, for during the last two decades of the century, numerous turnpikes were repaired or constructed in Litchfield and Hartford counties.[28] Built to ease the outward flow of agricultural surplus and distribution of goods to the interior, the roads served both itinerant New Divinity clerical teams and inveterate revival goers. For some revival enthusiasts, neither distance nor "storm, cold, and bad roads" foiled plans to attend conference meetings.[29] Most conference goers (and New Englanders in general) traveled on foot; the more prosperous rode on horseback or, during winter months, glided over the snow in horse-drawn sleighs.[30]

Litchfield, with a sizable population of 4,285 in 1800, served as the hub of the transportation systems for western Connecticut and the Hudson River towns of New York.[31] Products for export were sent from Litchfield to either Hartford or New Haven, then by water route to their destination. The years of the Second Great Awakening in Connecticut coincided with the "golden years" in Litchfield's history.[32] According to Timothy Dwight, the area of Litchfield was "uncommonly handsome, consisting of open extensive valleys, hills gracefully ordered, . . . [and] a collection of good farmers' houses, luxuriant fields, and flourishing orchards."[33] In this cultured community, which boasted Tapping Reeve's famous law school and Sally Pierce's school for grooming proper young ladies, revivals ensued a decade after the initial outbursts of 1798. Litchfield's citizens had withstood the excitement of the Great Awakening and, according to the Rev. Dan Huntington, many were determined to thwart the second Awakening.[34] However, once convinced that the revivals in surrounding communities were neither divisive nor excessively raucous, Litchfield's inhabitants embraced the revival spirit. After 1810, when Lyman Beecher accepted a call from First Church, the town functioned as the base of operations from which Beecher launched his many benevolent and reform programs.

28. Ibid., 344–47, 401; Daniels, "Economic Developments," 444–45; Edward C. Kirkland, *Men, Cities, and Transportation: A Study in New England History, 1820–1900* (Cambridge, Mass., 1948), 37–38. Ezra Stiles noted the increasing use of the road connecting New Haven and Boston. In 1787, two stages ran between the two cities; by 1795, twenty different stages ran each week (see *The Literary Diary of Ezra Stiles*, ed. Franklin B. Dexter [New York, 1901], 3:561).

29. *CEM* 1 (October 1800): 133; see also *CEM* 1 (April 1801): 380, and *CEM* 6 (April 1806): 390.

30. Jack Larkin, *The Reshaping of Everyday Life, 1790–1840* (New York, 1988), 214.

31. Town population figures can be misleading, since most of the population lived outside the main village. For example, in 1781, the main village areas of Farmington and Litchfield had only 300 residents each, or 5 percent and 10 percent respectively of the entire populations of the towns. Hartford had a residential density of 31 percent in 1786. See Bruce C. Daniels, *The Connecticut Town: Growth and Development, 1635–1790* (Middletown, Conn., 1979), app. 10, 197.

32. Alain C. White, comp., *The History of the Town of Litchfield, Connecticut, 1720–1920* (Litchfield, Conn., 1920), 91.

33. Timothy Dwight, *Travels in New England and New York*, ed. Barbara M. Solomon (Cambridge, Mass., 1969), 2:257.

34. *CEMRI* 1 (August 1808): 313–14.

Farmington (population 2,809 in 1800) was linked to Connecticut's northwestern backcountry by newly constructed turnpikes and for a time competed with Hartford for the area's trade.[35] By 1800, the town had been transformed from a quaint, rural village into a bustling commercial center. With newly acquired wealth, Farmington residents developed lavish tastes, importing goods and luxuries from New York City, the West Indies, Europe, and as far away as China.[36] To this thriving community came divine visitations in the early 1790s. Under the stated supply preaching of the youthful Edward Dorr Griffin, a revival shook First Church in the fall of 1793, adding over sixty communicants. Nearly seventy more converted during the 1799–1800 revivals, with repeated infusions occurring in the next thirty years.[37]

Nor did the revivals bypass Connecticut's capital and foremost city of commerce and finance. During the state's economic expansion, Hartford solidified its position as the center of trade.[38] It also operated as the nucleus for the developing evangelical empire in New England. Various publishing firms such as Hudson and Goodwin, and Gleason and Lincoln served the printing needs of the evangelical community, and numerous voluntary organizations headquartered there as well.[39] Hartford was also a hotbed of the Awakening where a trio of New Divinity pastors pressed repeatedly for revival. As early as 1794, Nathan Strong reported the first of a rash of revivals at First Church that broke out again in 1798–99, 1808, and 1815.[40] Abel Flint of South Church, who Strong noted was "greatly animated in this business" of revival, conducted repeated revivals as well.[41] Their colleague in West Hartford, Nathan Perkins, experienced the same cycle of revivals and displayed his New Divinity stripes through his intimate involvement in the establishment of the Theological Institute of Connecticut.[42] All three pastors guided the institutional aspect of the Awakening by serving as contributing editors to the *Connecticut Evangelical Magazine* and as members of the Connecticut Missionary Society.

Apart from Litchfield, Farmington, and Hartford, the remaining revived

35. Saladino, "Economic Revolution," 348–49; James Hammond Trumbull, ed., *The Memorial History of Hartford County, Connecticut, 1633–1884* (Boston, 1886), 1:185.

36. On Farmington's economic boom during these years, see Christopher P. Bickford, *Farmington in Connecticut* (Canaan, N.H., 1982), 223–30.

37. See Noah Porter to William Buell Sprague, 12 March 1832, in William B. Sprague, *Lectures on Revivals of Religion*, 2d ed. (New York, 1833), 291–95.

38. Saladino, "Economic Revolution," 347.

39. See Keller, *Second Great Awakening*, and Richard D. Shiels, "The Connecticut Clergy in the Second Great Awakening" (Ph.D. diss., Boston University, 1976).

40. George Leon Walker, *History of First Church in Hartford, 1633–1883* (Hartford, Conn., 1884), 345–62.

41. Nathan Strong to Jedidiah Morse, 21 February 1799, Morse Family Papers, SML.

42. On Perkins's ministry, see Matthew Spinka, *A History of the First Church of Christ Congregational, West Hartford, Connecticut* (West Hartford, Conn., 1962), 47–84.

towns in northwestern Connecticut were economically insignificant.[43] As the map in Appendix 3 indicates (see Figure A3.1), all but one of the awakened communities were located west of the Connecticut River. Two-thirds of the revivals in the formative period took place in Litchfield County, the last area of Connecticut to be settled. Demographic pressure from other areas of the state led to the settlement of this hilly, rugged terrain of marginal land quality.[44] Between 1737 and 1761, the state legislature carved fourteen new towns out of this county. Significantly, Litchfield County was little more than a frontier when the Great Awakening shook the eastern portions of Connecticut.[45] In many cases, the process of town incorporation coincided with the Awakening; hence, few of the severe disruptions and ecclesiastical divisions that plagued Connecticut towns during the Great Awakening and its aftermath struck this sparsely settled area.

The late settlement of Litchfield County helps to explain why, on the eve of the Second Great Awakening, Litchfield was the most religiously homogeneous county in Connecticut. In 1790 Congregationalists in Connecticut continued to vastly outnumber adherents of other denominations by a five to one ratio, but in certain counties dissenting societies held significant minorities.[46] As Bruce Daniels notes, "The older, more commercial counties had more heterogeneous and pluralistic social structures that inclined them more towards a fragmented religious structure."[47] Baptists and New Divinity sympathizers competed in coastal New London County, while the Episcopalians made significant inroads in New Haven and Fairfield counties.[48] Tolland County, afflicted severely by the disruptions of the Great Awakening, was the most pluralistic in religious composition. Litchfield's religious profile diverged markedly from these other counties. Inundated with New Divinity men, less established, less commercial, and hence less pluralistic than other

43. Percy W. Bidwell, "Rural Economy in New England at the Beginning of the Nineteenth Century," Connecticut Academy of Arts and Sciences (New Haven), *Transactions* 20 (1916): 252.

44. Daniels, *Connecticut Town*, 32.

45. According to Richard Bushman, three-fourths of the ecclesiastical separations during the Great Awakening and its aftermath (1740–55) occurred east of the Connecticut River (see *From Puritan to Yankee: Character and Social Order in Connecticut, 1690–1765* [Cambridge, Mass., 1967], 191).

46. The most recent and most accurate calculations are in Daniels, *Connecticut Town*. He notes that "in 1790 there were 307 societies in the colony [i.e., state]: 203 Congregationalist, 58 Anglican, 30 Baptist, 14 Strict Congregationalist, and 2 Quaker. While dissenting societies comprised about one-third of the total number, they were only about 20 percent of the population" (104). For a general discussion of the growth and development of church societies, see ibid., chap. 4. See also Edmund B. Thomas, Jr., "Politics in the Land of Steady Habits: Connecticut's First Political Party System, 1789–1820" (Ph.D. diss., Clark University, 1972), who, by adding the actual number of ministers occupying pulpits in 1790, calculates Congregational strength at 84.3 percent, Separatist at 3.1 percent, Episcopalian at 9.9 percent, and Baptist at .4 percent (11).

47. Daniels, *Connecticut Town*, 100–101.

48. On New Divinity strength in New London County, see Stiles, *Diary* 3:464, and Allen C. Guelzo, *Edwards on the Will: A Century of American Theological Debate* (Middletown, Conn., 1989), 92–93.

counties, Litchfield County had the highest concentration of persons per Congregational society in the state, as well as the highest concentration of New Divinity churches.[49] As a result, the range of religious options for the inhabitants of Litchfield County was more constricted than for those living in other counties. Personal religious taste and choice mattered less than a single community standard, for religious energies were not diverted by competing denominations. In this homogeneous setting, the overwhelming religious influence was the local New Divinity–pastored Congregational church.

Admittedly, internal dissent could lead to internecine ecclesiastical battles, but rarely did disgruntled parishioners leave to form a church of their own. During the last decades of the eighteenth century, the New Divinity solidified its strength, drove out dissenters, and made the "Western Heresie" (as an opponent called it) the prevailing view in Litchfield County.[50] The "safety-valve" frontier thesis of Frederick Jackson Turner applies appropriately to this region, as less confining frontier settlements to the north and to the west beckoned those who rebelled against the rigid conventions of conservative Connecticut. Former Farmington resident John Mix sounded a familiar refrain of many restless Americans in the early Republic when, writing from Kaskaskia, Illinois, he informed his sister that "we are troubled with no grand juror's spies, tything-men, etc., every man following the dictates of his own conscience."[51] Another Farmington resident offered generous buyer's terms for his four-hundred-acre farm in hopes of exiting "this holy state" as quickly as possible.[52]

The timing of Litchfield's settlement and receptivity to the revival conforms to a pattern of revival activity found in both the Great Awakening and other regions that experienced the Second Great Awakening. Local and regional studies by social and religious historians reveal a correlation between demographic and economic variables and revival activity. In general, unchurched frontier areas are most receptive to revival, followed by recently settled towns (such as those in Litchfield County), and then by diverse, mobile, volatile urban areas. Stable, older villages or towns appear the least receptive.[53]

49. Daniels, *Connecticut Town*, 99–100.

50. John Devotion to Ezra Stiles, 22 December 1768, in *Extracts from the Itineraries and other Miscellanies of Ezra Stiles . . .* , ed. Franklin B. Dexter (New Haven, Conn., 1916), 475. On religious dissenters leaving the state for more congenial climes, see Francis Atwater, comp., *History of the Town of Plymouth, Connecticut* (Meriden, Conn., 1895), 429, and Arthur Goodenough, *The Clergy of Litchfield County* (Litchfield, Conn., 1909), 14. Ammi Robbins observed that Norfolk contained "very few sectaries" (*CEM* 1 [February 1808]: 313).

51. Quoted in Bickford, *Farmington in Connecticut*, 257.

52. Ibid.

53. Harry Stout makes this summary of colonial research for the Great Awakening in *The New*

The awakened communities ranged in geographical size from twenty-five to fifty square miles and in population from about one thousand to twenty-five hundred.[54] These villages were constituted in a typical New England fashion: a small cluster of houses (usually fewer than fifty) surrounded the meetinghouse and common, while the remainder of the town population resided on farms scattered in outlying areas. Each village had at least one minister, lawyer, and physician, as well as the ubiquitous local tavern keeper. A few merchants ran small industries related to an agriculture-based economy: mercantile stores, tanneries, and small-scale waterwheel-driven mills for lumber, grain, and cloth. Finally, each village had its own group of skilled laborers: blacksmiths, carpenters, joiners, and cobblers.

Livestock dominated Connecticut's agricultural economy. By 1800 the state was one of the largest commercial producers in the nation.[55] Farmers in the northwest part of the state specialized in raising horses, cattle, and sheep. Goshen, a village visited with repeated revivals, had some of the state's best grazing land (an exception to the norm in Litchfield County). In this hilly town, situated atop the Green Mountain Range and located thirty miles west of Hartford, farmers achieved fame for their enormous cheese production. Their profits prompted Timothy Dwight to remark that the inhabitants were "probably more wealthy than any other collection of farmers in New England."[56] Goshen's per capita wealth was closely tied to the exodus of Connecticut's inhabitants during the 1790s. In general, the greater the population drain in agricultural areas, the greater the potential income for

---

England Soul: Preaching and Religious Culture in Colonial New England (New York, 1986), 196 (see n. 37 for references). On similar connections for the Second Great Awakening in New England and New York, see Paul E. Johnson, A Shopkeeper's Millennium: Society and Revivals in Rochester, New York, 1815–1837 (New York, 1978); Whitney R. Cross, The Burned-Over District: The Social and Intellectual History of Enthusiastic Religion in Western New York, 1800–1850 (1950; reprint, New York, 1965); Randolph A. Roth, The Democratic Dilemma: Religion, Reform, and the Social Order in the Connecticut River Valley of Vermont, 1791–1850 (New York, 1987); and Johnson, Islands of Holiness. For the Second Great Awakening in the South and West, see John B. Boles, The Great Revival, 1787–1805: The Origins of the Southern Evangelical Mind (Lexington, Ky., 1972); Dickson D. Bruce, Jr., And They All Sang Hallelujah: Plain-Folk Camp-Meeting Religion, 1800–1845 (Knoxville, Tenn., 1974); Charles A. Johnson, The Frontier Camp Meeting: Religion's Harvest Time (Dallas, Tex., 1955); and T. Scott Miyakawa, Protestants and Pioneers: Individualism and Conformity on the American Frontier (Chicago, 1964). For a general application to revivals in America, see William G. McLoughlin, Revivals, Awakenings, and Reform: An Essay on Religion and Social Change in America, 1607–1977 (Chicago, 1978).

54. For general descriptions of these towns, see John Warner Barber, Connecticut Historical Collections: History and Antiquities of Every Town in Connecticut (New Haven, Conn., 1836), and John C. Pease and John M. Niles, A Gazetteer of the States of Connecticut and Rhode Island (Hartford, Conn., 1819). The populations for Hartford, Litchfield, and Farmington in 1800 were 5,347; 4,285; and 2,809, respectively (source: Second Census of the United States: Return of the Whole Number of Persons within . . . the United States [Washington, D.C., 1801], 18–20). In 1789, the average town size in Connecticut was 49.6 square miles (see Daniels, Connecticut Town, 41).

55. Saladino, "Economic Revolution," 340.

56. Dwight, Travels 2:259.

those who remained at home. During the very years of its commercial prosperity, Goshen experienced the heaviest population loss of any town in Litchfield County.[57]

Population pressure combined with soil depletion led an estimated 100,000 inhabitants to exit the state in the 1790s.[58] By the early nineteenth century, Litchfield County followed the pattern of older Connecticut counties whose populations had reached an economic saturation point in the previous century: it led the state in out-migration. The infertility of the soil along with overseas market demands forced many farmers to convert their land from tillage to grazing. In turn, these developments lessened the demand for farm labor and quickened the pace of emigration to cheaper, more plentiful, and more fertile lands to the west and north. While the birthrate offset an absolute loss of inhabitants, Connecticut's population increased a mere 5.5 percent from 1790 to 1800, compared with a national growth rate of 35 percent.[59] The economic result of this vast westward and northward colonization movement benefited the state's residents, for the draining of population relieved pressure upon the overused land.[60]

The social situation emerging from this brief sketch of demographic and economic trends is one of flux amid stability. That is to say, the Second Great Awakening occurred in a religiously homogeneous area, but also in a region adjusting economically both to the shift from a subsistence to a market-oriented economy and to the exigencies of soil depletion and out-migration. These economic and demographic developments were particularly critical for married, middle-aged adults with children. This group, in the prime of life, when economic stability and assurances about the future were crucial, lived in a world of change. New Divinity ministers sensed these very real concerns or, perhaps truer to fact, bemoaned the dire spiritual results from these preoccupations. Joseph Washburn feared that his middle-aged parishioners were distracted "from day to day, from week to week, even upon the Lord's day, by the cares and pursuits of the world—the thoughts of your farms, merchandise, luxuries, diversions, and pleasures."[61] And Charles Backus gave notice: "Let the middle aged . . . be warned of their danger. . . . Be not

57. Saladino, "Economic Revolution," 342.

58. Ibid. The population drain in southern New England (including the states of Rhode Island, Massachusetts, and Connecticut) actually began in the mid–eighteenth century but became particularly acute from 1790 to 1820. Bidwell estimates that 800,000 left southern New England during this period ("Rural Economy in New England," 387); Daniels estimates that 66,000 exited Connecticut from 1760 to 1790 ("Economic Developments," 447).

59. Bidwell, "Rural Economy in New England," 386 (table 2).

60. Saladino, "Economic Revolution," 380.

61. Joseph Washburn, Sermons on Practical Subjects (Hartford, Conn., 1807), 69.

swallowed up with the cares of this life, and the deceitfulness of riches."[62] But to many of these folk, uncertainty and survival, not riches, must have been the real issue. Friends, relatives, and neighbors abandoned the community for the fertile, open spaces of the Western Reserve, New Hampshire, Vermont, and upstate New York. What about those who remained behind? Should they take a chance and begin anew? For some, continued opportunities for economic profit at home were reason enough to remain. But would similar avenues be open to their own children? Clearly, the land could not sustain more population and remain profitable. An uncertain future lay ahead for the present and the rising generations.

This unstable situation may explain why the Awakening appealed to those with the most to gain—as well as the most to lose. Table 6.7 indicates that in its formative stage, the revival affected a disproportionate share of adults. While the proportion of church admissions to the general population remained nearly constant in the age-forty-five-and-above cohort, the other two cohorts reveal inverse proportional relations. In the general population under the age of twenty-six, a huge pool existed from which to draw potential converts. Indeed, nearly two-thirds of the population of Connecticut was under age twenty-six, and yet the revivals drew from roughly one-half of that population. The opposite is true for what we might call the "middle-aged" category. From this cohort the Awakening drew well over two times the proportionate population. Only one-fifth of the overall population of Hartford

Table 6.7 Comparative Statistical Data on Church Admissions and the Population of Hartford and Litchfield Counties, 1800

	Percentage of Males		Percentage of Females	
Age	Church Admissions	Overall Population	Church Admissions	Overall Population
Under 26	32.6 (under 25)	65.8	37.4 (under 25)	64.3
26–44	52.2 (age 25–44)	19.6	47.7 (age 25–44)	20.5
45+	15.2	14.6	14.9	15.2

SOURCES: Church admissions: Tables A4.3 and A4.4; population: *Second Census of the United States* (1801), 20. (Note the slight disparity in the first two age cohorts between church admissions and overall population.)

62. Charles Backus, "A Discourse on the Nature and Influence of Godly Fear . . ." (Hartford, Conn., 1802), 39; see also *CEM* 1 (February 1801): 312.

and Litchfield counties fell between the ages of twenty-six and forty-four, but the Awakening drew approximately one-half of its male and female converts from this group. In short, the Second Great Awakening in Connecticut was a middle-aged phenomenon in a region with relatively few middle-aged inhabitants.

Despite a shift in economic orientation, rural northwestern Connecticut remained a society informed and shaped primarily by family values. The incursion of a market economy—characterized more by the exportation of agricultural goods than the importation of consumer goods—did not alter the basic structure of rural life. For Connecticut's inhabitants (and for Americans in general), the town village, the country neighborhood, and a few dozen surrounding farms defined the normal boundaries of everyday movement.[63] Social historians have observed the "intimate relation between agricultural production and parental values, between economic history and family history."[64] In late eighteenth-century rural New England, the family remained the prime economic unit as well as the main social institution. The results of the Awakening support the primacy of the lineal family, for as already noted, it was not uncommon for family members to seek salvation together or for converts to be drawn from families where piety had long been practiced. In the minds of New Divinity leaders, the family, with the father as its head, formed the primary religious unit. Repeating the warnings of New England Puritans, New Divinity pastors reminded their parishioners that a decline in "family religion" led to ruin.[65]

James Henretta has noted that the family "constituted a significant and reliable guide to behavior and uncertainties of the world."[66] But to what extent did the village revivals relieve the "uncertainties of the world," especially economic uncertainties?[67] Judging from the disproportionate

---

63. Larkin, Everyday Life, 213.

64. James A. Henretta, "Families and Farms: Mentalité in Pre-Industrial America," William and Mary Quarterly, 3d ser., 35 (January 1978): 21. The extent of economic and social change (the incursion of a capitalist economy) in rural New England from the Revolution to the Civil War has been a lively debated issue. Henretta argues that most farmers were not market-oriented (i.e., they were not "Yankees": individualistic, profit-oriented, ambitious), even though a rudimentary market exchange existed; rather, most desired to preserve the integrity of the household. For a similar conclusion, as well as a summary of interpretations, see Christopher Clark, The Roots of Rural Capitalism: Western Massachusetts (Ithaca, N.Y., 1990), introd.

65. Sermons, on Various Important Doctrines and Duties of the Christian Religion (Northampton, Mass., 1799), 251.

66. Henretta, "Families and Farms," 32.

67. Many clerical references citing the connection between the revivals and economic matters (apart from typical laments about worldly concerns interfering with religious devotion) focused on the assurance that the revivals did not disturb normal economic activity. Ebenezer Porter reported that conference meetings "seemed not all to interfere with necessary, temporal employments" (CEM 7 [October 1806]: 147). Giles Cowles noted that the revival in Plymouth occurred during the harvest season, yet "it was believed by unbiased and candid observers, that worldly business did not suffer by

number of middle-aged converts, the Awakening appeared to address such uncertainties. Apart from the anxiety issue, one scholar suggests that, in a general religious sense, the practice of New Divinity theology enabled New Englanders to make the transit from a traditional to a modern economy by placing limits on acquisitive behavior.[68] Edward Dorr Griffin warned his parishioners that the thief and the murderer were not the only ones who "hold the truth in unrighteousness"; included among their degenerate ranks were "the speculator, the man of hard bargains, the wretch who, unsatisfied with the profits of a fair trade, takes advantage of your ignorance or necessities to extort from you what belongs not to him."[69] Christians imbued with gracious affections displayed love and truth in the marketplace as much as in the meetinghouse. Their selfless behavior, contends William Breitenbach, enabled them to move "from a cluster of convenanted communities to a conglomeration of converted individuals." New Divinity theology "smoothed the way for acquisitive and egocentric behavior, not through the cynical conclusion that society could survive the activities of sinful men, but through the optimistic promise that saints would respect limits."[70] Virtuous behavior had more than its own rewards, for when applied to the marketplace, it tempered inclinations toward heedless greed. In this way, the New Divinity revivals relieved not only uncertainty about the future but guilt about the newfound prosperity of farmers. Profit was acceptable as long as one checked ambition with the practice of New Divinity ethics. The ethic of disinterested benevolence enjoined its practitioners to sacrifice personal gain for the good of others. Sinners who disdained disinterested benevolence, wrote Jacob Catlin, were "eagerly employed to get riches" and to "enrich themselves on the earnings of others."[71] To the New Divinity, the man of speculative economic gain was nearly as abhorrent as the man of speculative religious knowledge: the one elevated riches to the highest end, the other elevated the mind to the highest end. Both lay bare the hubris of fallen humanity. But saints who lived by the New Divinity code sought "not the interest of friends, family, or of our whole country; but, the good of God's whole kingdom at large."[72] In fact, suggested Joseph Washburn in a sermon underscoring the need to examine motives, the regenerate should emulate the early Christian

---

means of the religious attention" (CEM [August 1801]: 67). Both comments reflect the clergy's desire to portray the Awakening as a calm, orderly event of God's doing, not man's.

68. William Breitenbach, "Unregenerate Doings: Selflessness and Selfishness in New Divinity Theology," American Quarterly 34 (Winter 1982): 479–502; see also Bilhartz, "Sex and the Second Great Awakening," in Belief and Behavior, ed. Vandermeer and Swierenga, 124–25.

69. Edward Dorr Griffin, Sermons not before published, on various practical subjects (New York, 1844), 61.

70. Breitenbach, "Unregenerate Doings," 502. For similar attitudes among the followers of revivalist Charles Grandison Finney, see Johnson, Shopkeeper's Millennium.

71. Sermons on Important Subjects (Hartford, Conn., 1797), 500.

72. Ibid., 41.

church by sharing the "goods of the world" with a brother in need.[73] In so doing—by displaying these cardinal virtues—New Divinity saints would shape the market rather than allow an emerging free-rein market mentality to shape them.

Some areas of Connecticut benefiting from the economic revolution were initially unaffected by the outpouring of divine showers. The eastern inland counties of Tolland and Windham shared in Connecticut's economic resurgence, yet few New Divinity revivals occurred in those regions until after 1812.[74] The reason for the lag appears to have been the absence of New Divinity hegemony in eastern Connecticut. Once New Divinity men established a foothold in the west, they turned Litchfield and (less so) Hartford counties into a citadel of New Divinity power. From these counties emanated New Divinity–inspired evangelistic enterprises, such as the Connecticut Home Mission Society (1798) and the American Board of Commissioners for Foreign Missions (1810). Not until Asahel Nettleton's itinerate tours in the decade following the War of 1812 did revivals in eastern Connecticut begin to approach the magnitude of those in the west.

Connecticut's economic revolution explains not only why men turned to religion but also why they turned away from or were unaffected by the revivals. A rough comparison of the sizes of Connecticut's churches per adult population on the eve of each of the major revivals indicates that two decades prior to the Great Awakening, church members composed nearly one-half of the adult population, whereas prior to the Second Great Awakening, church members composed less than 20 percent.[75] Perhaps the newly acquired wealth induced not guilt but an indifference toward things religious. The increasing complexity of economic relations, and social intercourse in general, reduced the church to one among several competitors for men's allegiance.

Even if one could correlate a particular economic condition for male converts, it still would not adequately explain why female converts outnumbered males two to one. Several historians have suggested misleadingly that

73. Washburn, Sermons, 96.

74. Saladino, "Economic Revolution," 338. A notable exception was the church in Somers, pastored by Charles Backus, an important New Divinity leader. See CEM 1 (July 1800): 19, for an account of the 1797 revival in Somers.

75. Potash, "An Inquiry," 18. Estimates vary for nationwide church membership relative to the total population in 1800. Robert T. Handy, A History of the Churches in the United States and Canada (New York, 1977), put the figure at one in ten (163); Winthrop S. Hudson, Religion in America, 3d ed. (New York, 1981), figured one in fifteen (129). These numbers can be misleading, for church membership alone is not a reliable guide to the number attending church on a regular basis. Recent scholarship indicates that about four-fifths of the colonial population attended church in 1700, whereas about three-fifths attended in 1780. See Patricia U. Bonomi and Peter R. Eisenstadt, "Church Adherence in the Eighteenth-Century British American Colonies," William and Mary Quarterly, 3d ser., 39 (April 1982): 245–76.

the Second Great Awakening was an adolescent phenomenon, particularly attractive to young, single women working in New England factories. For these uprooted farm girls, a newfound religious commitment provided psychological ballast in a sea of economic and social disruption. Religion provided comfort for young women from rural communities as they encountered the dislocating effects of industrialization.[76] However, although there is no doubt that revivals attracted factory girls, such conditions did not occur until the 1820s, with the introduction of the first factories in New England. Moreover, the formative phase of the second Awakening affected more older, married females than younger, unattached ones. In the following chapter I will suggest that the dictates of New Divinity theology, with its language of submission, augmented female cultural constraints and expectations and made women particularly susceptible to conversion.

A final argument against relying too heavily upon economic explanations for the eruption of revival is the diversity of converts themselves.[77] This heterogeneity, both in age and character type, suggests that the Awakening appealed to those from different social and economic backgrounds. Included among the converts were not only upstanding individuals with prior ties to the faith but also others of less respectable status. The "intemperate," the "profane," Universalists, infidels, illiterates, and those without a religious background—in general, those without New Divinity virtues—responded to the "still, small voice."[78]

In a provocative and oft-cited essay, Donald Mathews offered his own hypothesis about the origins of the revivals. As a nationwide phenomenon, the Second Great Awakening "was made possible by the persistent combination of social strain, ecclesiastical turmoil, and purposive leadership."[79] Applying Mathews's general thesis to the specific context of Connecticut, I have argued, first, that the New Divinity provided the "purposive leadership" to trigger, promote, and sustain the Awakening. Second, New Divinity leaders often fomented "ecclesiastical turmoil." In the case of Farmington First Church, they succeeded in securing pure church principles, but not without a decade of church upheaval. The specifics of Mathews's third point—"social strain"—have been addressed in part, but deserve further comment.

76. Nancy F. Cott, "Young Women in the Second Great Awakening in New England," *Feminist Studies* 3 (Fall 1975): 15–29.

77. Johnson, *Islands of Holiness*, chap. 6: "The Failure of Economic Explanations of Rural Revivalism," provides applicable arguments against social and economic reductionist explanations for revival.

78. For references to these less respectable types, see James Morris, "Revival of Religion in South Farms," James Morris MSS, SML; Medad Rogers to Benjamin Trumbull, 6 October 1800, Benjamin Trumbull (1735–1820) Collection, Box 5, SML; William Griswold Hooker to his father, Col. Nodiah Hooker of Farmington, 3 January 1805, Hooker Family Collection, Box 7, SML; *CEM* 1 (July 1800): 25–26; *CEM* 1 (September 1800): 110–13; *CEM* 1 (March 1801): 344, 347–52; *CEM* 2 (April 1802): 385; *CEM* 6 (July 1805): 32; and *CEM* 6 (August 1806): 388.

79. Donald G. Mathews, "The Second Great Awakening as an Organizing Process, 1780–1830: An Hypothesis," *American Quarterly* 21 (Spring 1969): 40.

Relying upon sociological theory, Mathews notes that in periods of stress, those most open to change, reorientation, or conversion fit into bipolar categories. On the one hand, there are people who have no transcendent guiding force to give meaning to both the mundane and the momentous events in their lives. On the other hand, there are those whose interpretative framework is so habitual that all events are judged from an ingrained mental outlook without thoughtful reflection. "Thus," Mathews concludes, "people oppressed by the ambiguous social strain of the 1780s and 1790s would be susceptible to evangelical preaching if they had no religious orientation but desperately needed one—or if they had one so rigid that social pressure merely strengthened it."[80] Clearly, converts of the village revivals in Connecticut fit into the latter category. New Divinity pastors articulated the sins weighing down New England: infidelity, a carelessness evidenced in the neglect of family prayer, disregard for the Sabbath, an inattention to the spiritual needs of youth, and a general preoccupation with secular concerns. Such clerical reminders of trespasses against God were common enough for New Englanders, but when delivered with passionate demands for immediate repentance, they intensified an already anxious condition. Moreover, the worldview of Connecticut's inhabitants had been shaped by a Puritan past that placed the conversion experience at the core of religious life. This legacy, rightly noted Griffin, created "a general bias in favor of revivals."[81] Viewed in this sense, the Second Great Awakening represented a patterned response or a near-instinctual reaction, reflecting a prior way of dealing with personal sins and social disorientation. A religious past that emphasized regeneration provided the context for alleviating present individual and social upheaval. The ingathering of so many adult converts suggests that for many years these people had lived careless, indifferent lives that the revivalists now exposed.

After tracing the concept of conversion "from Puritanism to revivalism," Jerald Brauer concluded that "as long as there is *homo religiosus* there will be conversion, and as long as there is conversion in America, there will be revivals."[82] The revivals of the Second Great Awakening in Connecticut were viewed by its leaders as a natural (though at the same time a supernatural) way of building up the church. The leaders of the Awakening lived off—or better yet, capitalized upon—the investment of their predecessors in the faith. A myth surrounded the Great Awakening that the New Divinity perpetuated: God's natural way of building up his Church was through revivals.

80. Ibid., 34.

81. Quoted in William B. Sprague, *Memoir of the Rev. Edward D. Griffin, D.D.* (New York, 1839), 166–67.

82. Jerald C. Brauer, "Conversion: From Puritanism to Revivalism," *Journal of Religion* 58 (July 1978): 243.

To the participants of the Connecticut revivals, the Second Great Awakening represented an intensification or a reaffirmation of faith. A revival, by definition, is just that. To some extent before, but increasingly after the Great Awakening, the colonial covenant community was supplanted by a "pure church" of saints whose numerical strength relative to the population was decreasing. Parish boundaries continued to be important only insofar as they defined a geographical unit for administrative purposes: the calling of a minister, the settling of his salary, repairs on the meetinghouse, and so forth.[83] They no longer gave definition to the spiritual community, for parish residers vastly outnumbered church members. In such a context, the Second Great Awakening reestablished the bonds of community, and yet a different kind of spiritual community was brought into being—a voluntary community of minority-status saints. The revivals not only answered the prayers of the clergy and the needs of individuals for salvation, they also answered the yearnings of individuals for a clearly defined community in an era of uncertainty.

Clerical confessions of minimal participation in some of the revivals should be understood in light of the quest for community. In order to uphold God's sovereignty, some clergy downplayed their role when in fact they strove mightily to revive their parishioners. At other times, however, clerical involvement did indeed appear secondary. During the revival in Litchfield, the Rev. Dan Huntington admitted that "ministers have had little else to do, but to look on and see the Lord display himself."[84] More telling were those occasions when spiritually energized laity approached their pastors rather than vice versa. Lay people initiated conference meetings that quickly took on a life of their own apart from clerical impetus.[85] Jeremiah Hallock reported that prior to the outbreak of revival in Canton Center, a weekly "praying conference" was organized by "a few serious people. And it was here, in this conference, that the work began, and here it has been the greatest."[86] At the close of his account of the revival, Hallock noted, "I must confess I never felt so useless since I entered on the ministry."[87] Shortly before his death, he

83. For dissenting groups, especially Baptists, parish boundaries represented not only administrative units but also the perpetuation of the oppressive measures of the Standing Order. As their presence in that region was insignificant, the grass-roots Baptist fight for disestablishment was carried on outside northwestern Connecticut. See William G. McLoughlin, *New England Dissent: Baptists and the Separation of Church and State, 1670–1830* (Cambridge, Mass., 1971), vol. 2, chaps. 48, 49.

84. *CEMRI* 1 (August 1808): 317.

85. See Chapter 2.

86. *CEM* 1 (November 1800): 182. Hallock was probably referring to the weekly concert of prayer held for over twenty years in his study and attended by the church deacons. See Cyrus Yale, *The Godly Pastor: Life of the Rev. Jeremiah Hallock, of Canton, Conn.* (New York, [1854]), 156.

87. *CEM* 1 (November 1800): 184.

reiterated that lay assistance during revivals was more valuable than the work of an evangelist.[88]

Some pious church members regularly held conference meetings in their homes. One evening, after Zeloda Barrett of New Hartford heard Hallock preach, she attended a conference meeting held at the home of Captain Joseph Cowles.[89] In another instance, a woman gathered the devout and curious for a conference at her home shortly before her death.[90] The intensity of these communal experiences impressed the Rev. Ebenezer Porter. "At conferences," he wrote, "people collected as though awake, and in earnest. Even those, whom age and infirmity might well have excused, were often seen miles from home, at an evening meeting."[91]

The creation of a new community of saints united all who shared the experience of conversion. However, these experiences and the nature of this community were rooted in both transcendent and social realities. In its fundamental sense, conversion signified a transaction initiated by a gracious God through Jesus Christ whereby sinful humans were brought to salvation. The saved now entered a new life of love and service to God; following death, they eternally enjoyed him in heaven. And yet the steps, or pathway, to conversion varied, often assuming forms related to age and gender. Furthermore, different behavioral responses accompanied these divergent patterns of conversion.

In the same way, the community of saints expressed the corporate response of worship and fellowship to the divine transaction. Yet that community not only exhibited a spiritual reality but also performed a social function—again related to age and gender. Conversion and community, though expressions of a divine reality, manifested themselves in socially related ways. The body was not one member but many.

88. Yale, *Godly Pastor*, 22.

89. Diary of Zeloda Barrett, 17 March 1804, CHS. In eastern Connecticut the use and popularity of these meetings apparently caught on a bit later. Harriet Winslow of Norwich reported that weekly evening meetings held at the homes of parishioners were initiated by her pastor in 1808 (see Miron Winslow, *Memoir of Mrs. Harriet L. Winslow, Thirteen Years a Member of the American Mission in Ceylon* [New York, 1840], 13).

90. *CEM* 1 (November 1800): 192.

91. *CEM* 7 (October 1806): 145–46. These conferences were popular throughout New England and New York. For examples, see *CEM* 6 (August 1805): 69, and *CEM* 6 (June 1806): 474.

7

"TROPHIES OF SOVEREIGN, VICTORIOUS GRACE"

Themes in Piety and Conversion

Bennet Tyler spent his career defending the New Divinity. Following study with Asahel Hooker at Goshen, he pastored in South Britain, Connecticut, and joined the brotherhood of ministers in team revivalism; as president of Dartmouth, he ignited spiritual fires at the college; during his pastorate in Portland, Maine, he challenged Nathaniel Taylor's revisions of the traditional Calvinist understanding of sin and human nature; as the first president of the Theological Institute of Connecticut, he sought to ensure that ministerial aspirants were educated the New Divinity way; as a devotee of Asahel Nettleton, he compiled the great revivalist's memoirs and sermons; finally, he left for posterity a collection of New Divinity revival narratives drawn primarily from the *Connecticut Evangelical Magazine*. For Tyler, as for all New Divinity men, the earmark of true spirituality was struggle—a cosmic struggle between Satan and the Moral Governor of the universe; an inner struggle between the sinful self and the claims of a holy, sovereign God; and an outer struggle between right New Divinity theology and others' wrong theology. By the 1820s, however, the anguished struggles so characteristic of anxious and convicted sinners in the turn-of-the-century village revivals—those very struggles that legitimized New Divinity revivals—had ceased. Tyler recalled that "the converts in these [early New Divinity] revivals, were not made that easy way, in which many professed converts in recent times have been made, without any struggle in their minds, and without feeling any sensible opposition to God and the claims of the gospel; but they endured great conflicts."[1] For converts of New Divinity revivalism, the travail of the supernatural second birth was no less difficult to endure than that of the natural first birth. To "take the kingdom by violence" (Matthew 11:12) was not easy—not that it ever had been for visible saints of the Puritan tradition. But New Divinity revivalists called for immediate and absolute submission to divine authority in a postrevolutionary age basking in the new light of human independence. For those radically transformed by God's grace, the pangs of guilt and the persistence of anxiety proved to be a greater psychic burden than the cheery confidence of human self-reliance could carry. By nearly all accounts, whether lay or clerical, the new birth was induced by preaching the "hard sayings" of New Divinity dogma: total human depravity and accountability, the curse of the law, the sovereignty of God, and the demand for immediate repentance. Ammi Robbins recounted how these doctrines "drive them from their hiding place."[2] Tried and true, they were the catalysts in the transformation of sinners into "trophies of sovereign, victorious grace."[3]

New Divinity ministers, like other ministers through the ages, considered young people the prime targets of their preaching. Unlike the fixed minds of adults, the pliable minds of youth were "attentive, and more easily impressed with the solemn and weighty things of eternity, than after they have hardened themselves more in sin. . . . The twig is easily bent; but the matured oak is inflexible."[4] "Zeno" informed the young that the longer they delayed, "the less of your finding a pardoning God," and Nathan Strong warned his listeners that "piety doth not depend on age." No, "every year, every day is adding to the difficulty of repentance and reformation."[5]

Prior to the 1798 revivals, the Litchfield South Association urged ministers to pay special attention to the spiritual needs of the young people in their parishes.[6] Later the association adopted the "Berkshire plan" for the instruc-

1. Bennet Tyler, comp., New England Revivals, As They Existed at the Close of the Eighteenth, and the Beginning of the Nineteenth Centuries (Boston, 1846), x.

2. CEM 1 (March 1801): 339.

3. CEM 2 (November 1801): 177. The very same phrase is used by Charles Backus, "Qualifications and Duties of the Christian Pastor: A Sermon delivered . . . October 29, 1795 . . ." (Boston, 1795), 18, and by Nathan Perkins, "The Doctrines Essential to Salvation," American National Preacher 7 (January 1833): 119.

4. CEM 1 (February 1800): 303; see also Joseph Washburn, Sermons on Practical Subjects . . . (Hartford, Conn., 1807), 37; Edward Dorr Griffin, Sermons, not before published, on various practical subjects (New York, 1844), 12; and Nathan Strong, "A Sermon, on the Use of Time; addressed to men in several ages of life . . ." (Hartford, Conn., 1813), 9.

5. CEM 4 (July 1803): 38; Nathan Strong, "A Funeral Sermon . . . delivered . . . January 6, 1807, at the Funeral of the Rev. James Cogswell, D.D. . . ." (Hartford, Conn., 1807), 7.

6. Litchfield South Association Records, June 1796, Original Records of Litchfield County Association and Consociation, 1752–1814, CLH.

tion of children and youth.[7] Borrowed from New Divinity brethren in Berkshire County, Massachusetts, the plan called for catechizing youth on a regular basis by the minister or deacons, teaching the shorter Westminster catechism in the schools, and promoting religious teaching at home.

At a later meeting, the association took action on an issue that had long plagued Connecticut's established churches. As a corporate body, it rejected the Half-Way Covenant, ruling that "only the children of such parents as come to the Lord's Supper ought to be baptized."[8] The association gave formal support to an issue that most churches settled by 1800, for by the turn of the century nearly all of Connecticut's Congregational churches rejected the provisions of the Half-Way Covenant.[9] In effect, the rejection of the covenant meant that the conversion experience, not moral probity, was the primary criterion for the extension of covenantal benefits to children. The overthrowing of the covenant in favor of a pure church of saints partially explains why the revivals were particularly operative on marrieds. "The heads of families," observed Charles Backus, "who were the subjects of this work expressed astonishment that they had lived so long without any just sense of duty which they owed to their offspring."[10] Unconverted parents who previously assumed that their children would own the covenant were now faced with the harsh reality that without their own conversion, the benefit of baptism would not be passed on to a future generation.

The New Divinity Way to Salvation

The insistence on a church of the pure grew out of the New Divinity doctrine of regeneration. Because regeneration was instantaneous and not gradual, no form of preparation, whether through half-way church status or attending on the means of grace, altered one's sinful condition in the sight of God. As a result of this either/or dichotomy, a sinner's anxiety was further exacerbated: she was told that God despised her efforts, and that in fact she worsened, not bettered, her condition by placing confidence in forms of preparation. What then was she to do? Throw yourself down at the Savior's feet, exhorted the New Divinity. Give up all of your efforts for loss. But then she queried, How do I get to that place of abandonment? The answer: Attend to the means of grace, not as means but as responsibilities, disavowing any necessary

7. Ibid., 2 June 1801; *CEM* 1 (February 1800): 301–4.
8. Litchfield South Association Records, 19 October 1802, CLH.
9. See James P. Walsh, "The Pure Church in Eighteenth Century Connecticut" (Ph.D. diss., Columbia University, 1967).
10. *CEM* 1 (July 1800): 20.

connection between attending and salvation. Any form of preparation was false, if by it the sinner assumed either that she contributed to her salvation or that God regenerated progressively. This tight (or tortured) Edwardsean logic underlay the crescendo of emotional response culminating in the crisis of conversion.[11]

Despite their aversion to preparationist schemes, however, the New Divinity did not repudiate wholesale the use of morphologies of conversion. As old as Puritanism itself, the practice of charting the various spiritual or psychological states that led to conversion enabled one to measure progress toward salvation. But the New Divinity put no stock in assiduously following a traditional form with the expectation that salvation would result. With Edwards they agreed that "some have gone too far towards directing the Spirit of the Lord, and marking out his footsteps for him, and limiting him to certain steps and methods."[12] Thus, to refer to a New Divinity morphology of conversion is something of a misnomer; nevertheless, the New Divinity men did recognize a pattern, or form, by which God superintended the drawing of sinners to himself. In fact, in his "Faithful Narrative" (1737), Edwards himself offered a model of conversion that nearly all New Divinity narratives of conversion followed. Because of its popularity—it was reprinted at least sixty times—the "Faithful Narrative" became the authoritative text of American revivalism for over a century.[13] Still, this work should be seen as part of larger genre of conversion narratives dating back to early English Puritanism. Although subjected to alterations in context, the basic structure of the form of conversion remained remarkably constant in the history of Puritanism and its progeny.[14] Whether found in the English setting as an affirmation of God's covenant vis-à-vis the corrupt Church of England or in New England as a primary requisite for church membership or as competition with the Half-Way Covenant or, finally, as the central feature and recruiting device in the Great Awakening, the morphology of conversion remained intact. Nearly two centuries separated William Perkins's classical formulation

---

11. Under one of the "negative signs" of true religious affections, Edwards gave considerable space to rejecting the conditional salvation implicit in morphologies of conversion. He wrote, "There is no connection in the nature of things, between anything that a natural man may experience, while in a state of nature, and the saving grace of God's spirit. . . . God has revealed no certain connection between salvation, and any qualification in men, but only grace and its fruits" (see *WJE: Religious Affections*, ed. John E. Smith [New Haven, Conn., 1959], 160).

12. Ibid., 161.

13. Michael J. Crawford, *Seasons of Grace: Colonial New England's Revival Tradition in Its British Context* (New York, 1991), 189, 239; Virginia Lieson Brereton, *From Sin to Salvation: Stories of Women's Conversions, 1800 to the Present* (Bloomington, Ind., 1991), 29.

14. Jerald C. Brauer, "Conversion: From Puritanism to Revivalism," *Journal of Religion* 58 (July 1978): 232–33.

from Nathan Perkins's paradigm in 1800, and yet the essential aspects of the stages of conversion remained.[15]

During periods of religious awakening, the time span between initial angst and actual conversion was often distilled into days or even hours. However, some converts' experiences duplicated the more protracted interval that characterized those years of less religious intensity. In that case, months, or even years, could transpire from the initial state of awareness to the actual moment of conversion. Whatever the duration, the New Divinity charted the path of conversion in the following stages:[16] First, the mind was "arrested," "awakened," or "alarmed" over its condition of "stupidity," "sleepfulness," "indifference," "ignorance," or "insensibility to moral beauty."[17] Participants in the village revivals attributed this initial stage to several factors: the preaching of Calvinism with a renewed vigor; personal illness; the death of a child, relative, or close friend; other misfortunes; the reading of devotional material; or the influence of others through their prayers, counsel, or example.

Once aroused, potential converts were "slain by the law": they recognized their "deep and awful" guilt before a holy God. Nathan Perkins observed that "convictions were different in degrees, duration, and terror," and "yet they were alike in substance."[18] To wit, the moral law convicted all who realized that they could not fulfill its obligations. The guilt-stricken were overcome with feelings of worthlessness and vileness. At this point, some retreated to "inability," claiming that the rigid doctrine of predestination obliterated human response. For others, despair ensued, eventuating in expressions of obstinacy and opposition to God's law. The New Divinity often referred to this condition as "selfishness."

The next stage was crucial, for the potential convert moved from despondency and complaints about the harshness of the law to an admission that God was both just in his condemnation and yet loving in his mercy. Once the "whole character of God" was seen, the sinner found relief. According to the New Divinity formula, this condition resulted in regeneration, when God's saving grace effected the making of a new heart. A person's selfishness was now transformed into "selflessness," or, as Edward Dorr Griffin put it, the subjects of conversion "found their hopes . . . on the persuasion that they have discovered in themselves the exercise of love to God and man,

---

15. On William Perkins, see Edmund S. Morgan, *Visible Saints: The History of a Puritan Idea* (Ithaca, N.Y., 1965), 68–69; on Nathan Perkins, see his "Two Discourses on the Grounds of the Christian's Hope . . ." (Hartford, Conn., 1800), 43–46, 50–53.

16. Nearly every clerical report on revival includes a description of the conversion experience. For examples, see *CEM* 1 (July 1800): 19–21, 28–29; *CEM* 1 (August 1800): 61–62; *CEM* 1 (October 1800): 134–35; *CEM* 1 (December 1800): 218–22; *CEM* 1 (April 1801): 384; *CEM* 6 (May 1806): 427; and *CEMRI* 1 (August 1808): 315–16.

17. Washburn, *Sermons*, 28.

18. Perkins, "Two Discourses," 43.

originating not in selfishness."[19] The saint's behavior and newfound love of God were no longer motivated by the selfish desire to avoid the torments of hell (what the Edwardseans called "legal repentance"), but by the glory and beauty of God ("evangelical repentance"). To make their point, New Divinity ministers often noted how converts had no idea that regeneration was taking place; that is, converts became so absorbed in God's glory that they lost all interest in their own personal transformation.[20] In the words of Edwards, joy came in "annihilating themselves before God; when they are nothing and God is all."[21] Here was the ultimate expression of "disinterested benevolence," the peak experience in the transition from selfishness to selflessness.

The saint's new love for God originated in the heart, not in the mind, for mere orthodoxy was insufficient to convert. As one New Divinity advocate asserted, "It is, indeed, necessary that tenets be correct. . . . But correct opinion must not be rested in, as embracing the sum and substance of vital religion. A speculative faith does not always interest and engage the religious feelings of the heart."[22] The author's views were, once again, indebted to Edwards. In *The Religious Affections*, Edwards had constructed a taxonomy of genuine piety in which unmistakable proof of the truly regenerate was catalogued under "twelve signs of gracious affections." Unlike Protestant scholastics and others who embraced a crude dualistic faculty psychology, Edwards affirmed the interconnectedness of will and understanding. As he noted in his discussion of the fourth sign of grace, "Spiritual understanding consists primarily in a sense of the heart of that spiritual beauty. I say, a sense of heart; for it is not speculation merely that is concerned in this kind of understanding; nor can there be a clear distinction made between the two faculties of understanding and will as acting distinctly and separately, in this matter."[23] And yet for purposes of clarity, and to demonstrate the priority of the heart in the true apprehension of religion, Edwards differentiated between

19. *CEM* 1 (December 1800): 221–22; see also Perkins, "Two Discourses," 50.

20. *CEM* 1 (July 1800): 19, 29; *CEM* 1 (October 1800): 134–35; *CEM* 1 (April 1801): 385–86; *CEM* 6 (May 1806): 431; see also Jonathan Edwards, "A Faithful Narrative of the Surprising Work of God," in *WJE: The Great Awakening*, ed. C. C. Goen (New Haven, Conn., 1972), 173, 177.

21. Edwards, 'Faithful Narrative,' in *WJE: The Great Awakening*, 183. For early nineteenth-century Evangelicals, as for Edwards, the 'annihilation of self' was a constant theme. This phrase meant generally the abasement of the prideful self, or the removal of selfish desires to fulfill the will of God. In this sense, annihilation of self was a precondition to the attainment of holiness. For examples of references to 'annihilation'—all from females—see Lyman Beecher, *The Autobiography of Lyman Beecher*, ed. Barbara M. Cross (Cambridge, Mass., 1966), 1:58 (Roxanna Beecher); Benjamin B. Wisner, *Memoir of the Late Mrs. Susan Huntington, of Boston, Mass.*, 3d ed. (Boston, 1829), 104, 252, 276; and Miron Winslow, *Memoir of Mrs. Harriet L. Winslow, Thirteen Years a Member of the American Mission in Ceylon* (New York, 1840), 38. For a discussion of the psychology of the self in Puritanism, Edwards, and the New Divinity, see James Hoopes, *Consciousness in New England: From Puritanism and Ideas to Psychoanalysis and Semiotics* (Baltimore, 1989).

22. *CEM* 5 (November 1804): 170–71.

23. Edwards, *WJE: Religious Affections*, 272.

the two faculties. He often referred to understanding as "mere speculative knowledge," or "mere notional knowledge." Such knowledge was an assent to "words" or "signs," not the immediate object of consciousness.[24] But the mind's faculty of the will—the sense of the heart—"don't [sic] only speculate and behold, but relishes and feels."[25] The regenerate exhibited a new heart, a new "taste." Unlike the five physical senses, the new sense was a metaphysical or, better yet, a supernatural sixth sense that enlightened the mind's understanding.

Following Edwards's religious psychology, converts exulted in the Bible as a new book. What was once a dull, dry compendium consisting of mere words and signs was now inspiring, instructive, and apprehended by a new sense. Charles Backus noted that the Bible appeared to fresh converts in a new light, "not because any new truth is revealed, but because their hearts have a new relish, and in consequence of this, they discover new beauties in the law and gospel."[26]

In describing this new sense of the heart, Edwards appealed primarily to the sensory metaphors of Scripture and, less so, to the sentiment of Puritan writers and John Calvin. What he proposed was, paradoxically, a "sensual spirituality." "Spiritual knowledge," wrote Edwards in his conclusion to the fourth sign of grace, "primarily consists in a taste or relish of the amiableness and beauty of what is true and holy."[27] These words of sentiment were fully appropriated by the New Divinity men. Thus, "true religion," wrote a contributor to the *Connecticut Evangelical Magazine*, "is a *feeling sense* of the excellence of divine truth."[28] Jeremiah Hallock recounted that conversion "did not appear to consist so much in a new doctrinal knowledge, but in different affections of the heart."[29] Other metaphors linked to the five senses reinforced the "sensual" nature of the conversion experience. For example, the new Christian was endowed with new sight, "a kind of spiritual discernment, much as we distinguish colors by our eyes."[30]

Despite the heightened sensations of touch, taste, and sight, the assurance of salvation was imperfect. An awareness of doubt was the last step in the conversion process. Those who expressed unblinking confidence of their

---

24. For a discussion of the philosophical background to Edwards's distinction between speculative knowledge and a sense of the heart, see James Hoopes, "Jonathan Edwards's Religious Psychology," *Journal of American History* 69 (March 1983): 849–65.

25. Edwards, *WJE: Religious Affections*, 272.

26. Charles Backus, *The Scripture Doctrine of Regeneration Considered, in Six Discourses* (Hartford, Conn., 1800), 22; see also Perkins, "Two Discourses," 52–53; CEM 2 (August 1801): 63; CEM 3 (December 1802): 236; CEM 6 (July 1805): 33; CEM 6 (November 1805): 188; CEM 7 (April 1807): 393; and Edwards, "Faithful Narrative," in *WJE: The Great Awakening*, 181.

27. Edwards, *WJE: Religious Affections*, 281.

28. CEM 4 (November 1804): 171.

29. CEM 6 (May 1806): 427.

30. CEM 4 (June 1804): 447.

salvation assumed a godlike prescience—a sure sign of damnation. But those who recognized the uncertainty of their experience admitted human fragility and misperception—as sure a sign as humanly possible of salvation.[31] Sally Lee confided to her brother Jonathan at Yale that "we are told [in Scripture] that the heart is deceitful above all things and desperately wicked *who can know it* and I am much afraid of deceiving myself and resting in the false presumptive hope of the hypocrite." She then begged Jonathan—a new convert of six months—to "pray that I may not be left to deceive myself."[32] Such tentativeness led many new converts to delay immediate application for church membership. According to Ebenezer Porter, the "most common" length of time between the Awakening's "hopeful conversions" and a public profession of faith was six months.[33]

The recognition of doubt was part of the general process of self-examination, a spiritual discipline enjoined upon all converts.[34] Because Satan delighted in deceiving the regenerate of their newfound faith, joy, and love, the surest way to counter deceit—a form of self-ignorance—was through continual introspection. The dual purpose of this exercise was to detect the inward working of the Holy Spirit as well as "to acquire the true knowledge of ourselves, of our natural turn of mind, of our passions, and of our various prejudices." Like the conversionist paradigm, the process of self-examination followed a certain form. A saint began with the recognition that he was *simul justus et peccator*. Regeneration, with its attendant justification (and that is the order in which the New Divinity viewed it), did not remove sinful inclinations. "BEHOLD I AM VILE," asserted Edward Griffin, "is the language of self-examination."[35] Conversion and self-examination began with the same premise—an admission of human sinfulness and divine holiness. Typically, converts examined themselves by reviewing their personal diaries at regular intervals (birthdays and New Year's Day were common) or, in a more public forum, by meditating on specific hymns of self-examination at conference meetings.[36]

At times, exercises of self-scrutiny, particularly among young females,

31. Backus, *Scripture Doctrine of Regeneration*, 170n.

32. Sally Lee to Jonathan Lee, 7 December 1808, Jonathan Lee Papers, MSS Group 958, Box 1, SML; see also Mary Treadwell Hooker Diary, CSL, 3; and Julia Churchill Diary, 31 May 1818, MS. 65733, CHS.

33. Ebenezer Porter, *Letters on the Religious Revivals* . . . (Boston, 1858), 84. Porter was comparing the "legitimate" converts at the turn of the century to the dubious converts who were immediately admitted into churches during the Finney revivals of the 1830s.

34. For examples, see *CEM* 1 (July 1800): 32–34; *CEM* 5 (May 1805): 414–18; *CEMRI* 2 (April 1809): 146–48; *CEMRI* 2 (May 1809): 78–91; *CEMRI* 4 (July 1811): 148–52; and *CEMRI* 7 (January 1814): 9–18.

35. *CEM* 1 (December 1800): 226.

36. For example, see "Self-Examination," in *The Hartford Selection of Hymns*, comp. Nathan Strong, Abel Flint, and Joseph Steward (Hartford, Conn., 1799), no. 145, pp. 120–21.

reduced converts to a state of despondency and even depression. To the experienced practitioner, however, prolonged anxiety was a sure sign of the Enemy at work. "I would recommend daily practice," advised Griffin to a young lady, "in order to prevent this intrusion of gloom."[37] For Griffin, converts reaffirmed their new adoption in Christ by continual submission to God. They could also fend off the wiles of the Devil by recourse to hymns of encouragement. The last stanza of "A young convert falling into darkness" in the popular *Hartford Selection of Hymns* reminded the new Christian of Christ's ultimate triumph:

> When Satan comes to tempt your minds,
>   Then meet him with these blessed lines,
> Jesus our Lord has swept the field,
>   And we're determined not to yield.[38]

Both the morphology of conversion and the practice of self-examination were defined and tightly controlled by the clergy. By channeling conversion and piety into prescribed forms, the New Divinity steered clear of the emotional excesses and dubious conversions of the Great Awakening.[39] Edwards, the great teacher, had warned of unbridled enthusiasm, calling it a "bastard religion."[40] At bottom, Satan himself was the culprit. Transforming himself into an angel of light, the deceiver destroyed "hopeful and happy revivals of religion." Without fail, ministers' reports of revival stressed the "remarkable regularity" or the "orderly and solemn" nature of the revivals.[41] Though couched in clerical rhetoric, Giles Cowles captured the prevailing mood in his description of the 1799 revival in Bristol:

> There hath not been discovered any appearance of a spirit of enthusiasm or delusion, or of spiritual pride and ostentation; nor of censoriousness and rash judging of others; but on the contrary, a spirit of humility and meekness, of fear and a sound mind; arising from a rational conviction of sin, and principle of gospel benevolence; each one appearing to esteem others better than himself, and to work out his own salvation with fear and trembling; and at the same time to express an ardent desire that others might taste and see the goodness of the Lord.[42]

---

37. "Letter written by Dr. Edward Dorr Griffin to a young Lady," n.d., CHS.
38. *Hartford Selection of Hymns*, no. 137, pp. 112–13.
39. See Tyler, *New England Revivals*, viii.
40. Edwards, *WJE: Religious Affections*, 287.
41. For examples, see the following descriptions of revival in the *CEM*: 1 (July 1800): 19, 23, 28; 1 (August 1800): 59; 1 (September 1800): 101, 104; 1 (April 1801): 381.
42. *CEM* 2 (July 1801): 27.

As guardians of the faith, the New Divinity men asserted their right to discern the signs of grace. Again, they followed Edwards's advice: "Great and strict therefore should be the watch and guard that ministers maintain against such things, especially at a time of great awakenings: for men, especially the common people, are easily bewitched with such things."[43] Contra Jefferson, for whom the voice of the people was the voice of God (*vox populi, vox Dei*), neither Edwards nor the New Divinity expressed confidence in the spiritually uninformed masses. All efforts were made to control "animal passions"—those paroxysms of "bodily distortions and outcries."[44] Thus Joseph Washburn at Farmington preached "the most essential and important truth in a simple manner, before the mind, without making any violent assault upon the passions."[45] More important, the clerically controlled conference meeting— the primary vehicle of revival—"became indispensibly necessary to prevent enthusiasm and disorder."[46] In those cases where a minister could not be present, the New Divinity recommended that "there should be some person or persons, of mature age and of sound experience in religion, to take the lead."[47] Clearly, both Edwards and the New Divinity encouraged lay leadership, but it had to accord with established standards of propriety.

The New Divinity ministers' continual reiteration of the restrained nature of the revival, as well as their persistent emphasis upon a certain form of the conversion experience, indicated a desire to assure critics that the revival was a legitimate outpouring of God's spirit, not a counterfeit of Satan's doing. Armed with Edwards's treatise *The Religious Affections*, they verified the genuine or spurious nature of religious excitement. Their attempt to guide the Awakening was motivated neither by a fear of status decline nor a concomitant need for social control (though the latter was undoubtedly a result); rather, their justification for *spiritual* control had a history that stretched back half a century. Edwards's interpretation of the past Great Awakening taught the New Divinity men to shepherd their flocks with great care, to return any strays from the fold with great haste, and to silence the bleatings of the excited or wayward with strict supervision. "When the passions become boisterous," stated Charles Backus bluntly, "the mind is in a very unfit state for serious reflection."[48] If the revivals exhibited too much "animal passion" or enthusiasm, if they did not conform to clerically approved patterns, then they could not be deemed genuine.[49] At first blush, the revivals appeared

---

43. Edwards, *WJE: Religious Affections*, 287–88.

44. Backus, *Scripture Doctrine of Regeneration*, 169n.

45. *CEM* 1 (April 1801): 383; see also Edward Dorr Griffin's report on revival in *CEM* 1 (December 1800): 218; Backus, *Scripture Doctrine of Regeneration*, 169n; and Perkins, "Two Discourses," 42.

46. Perkins, "Two Discourses," 41.

47. *CEMRI* 4 (May 1811): 182.

48. Backus, *Scripture Doctrine of Regeneration*, 169n.

49. Edwards differentiated between the affections and the passions as follows:

remarkably homogeneous: all converts experienced conversion according to an accepted paradigm; all revivals manifested similar characteristics. And yet within these patterns, the conversion experience varied in intensity and meaning. In some respects, the clergy shaped and approved these divergent experiences. In others, however, they were casualties to the conventions of popular culture.

Gender, Piety, and Conversion Narratives

By the end of the eighteenth century, different notions of male and female religiosity evolved to where they bore specifically upon the nature of piety, the conversion experience, and Christian community.[50] These notions were rooted in an ideology that characterized females as subordinate to males. By divine decree, men were the heads of the households and women were helpmeets to their husbands. By nature, males were intellectually superior and less given to emotional extremes than were females. While men exceeded women in intelligence, women surpassed men in the display of cardinal Christian virtues: humility, meekness, patience, purity, and, above all, submission. Christian virtues became synonymous with female virtues; Christian piety became essentially female piety. The affectionate heart, expressed toward God, spouse, and children, carried feminine connotations, while the rational head, necessary to understand Christian doctrine and to conduct oneself in public, conveyed masculine traits.

Such differences had important implications for the experience of conversion. The Anglo-American evangelical tradition provided converts with a rich and wide-ranging vocabulary to describe the conversion experience. That vocabulary was drawn from a variety of sources, including Scripture (the King James Version), other conversion narratives (e.g., Edwards's "Faithful Narra-

---

"Affection . . . seems to be something more extensive than passion; being used for all vigorous lively actings of the will or inclination; but passion for those that are more sudden, and whose effects on the animal spirits are more violent, and the mind more overpowered, and less in its own command" (*WJE: Religious Affections*, 98).

50. For a more thorough discussion of these developments, see Martha Tomhave Blauvelt, "Women and Revivalism," in *Women and Religion in America: The Nineteenth Century*, ed. Rosemary R. Reuther and Rosemary Skinner Keller (New York, 1981), 1–9; Ruth H. Bloch, "American Feminine Ideals in Transition: The Rise of the Moral Mother, 1785–1815," *Feminist Studies* 4 (June 1978): 101–26; Nancy F. Cott, *The Bonds of Womanhood: "Woman's Sphere" in New England, 1780–1835* (New Haven, Conn., 1977), esp. chap. 4; Barbara Welter, "The Feminization of Religion in Nineteenth-Century America," in *Clio's Consciousness Raised*, ed. Lois Banner and Mary Hartman (New York, 1973), 135–57; and Amanda Porterfield, *Female Piety in Puritan New England: The Emergence of Religious Humanism* (New York, 1992), esp. 153–56.

tive"), and a common lexicon (e.g., the use of terms such as "careless lives," "rebels against God," "hopeful conversions"). Thus, ministers and potential converts had at their disposal both a paradigm of conversion (a general morphology of conversion) as well as a common vocabulary to describe the workings of that paradigm. Despite this shared frame of reference, new saints constructed conversion narratives in a self-selecting manner congruent with the emerging distinctions of gender. On the one hand, females utilized more freely than males the language of personal intimacy, of sensual spirituality, of Edwards's religious affections. Males, on the other hand, employed the language of formal theological discourse, of law, reason, and restraint. While the New Divinity clergy utilized both forms of discourse—and in this respect upheld the ideal of an androgynous religious experience—and while exceptions can always be found, in general men and women told or wrote the stories of their conversions using gender specific rhetoric. Moreover, even after becoming "members of one body," new converts failed to break down or abandon these gender distinctions. Though equal in God's eyes, men and women continued to inhabit unequal social worlds.[51]

In this context, the New Divinity view of the conversion experience as a matter of the heart had a greater attraction to women. The sensual images employed to describe the experience, as well as the heavy emphasis upon submission to divine authority, appealed more to female than to male sensibilities. This emphasis upon a feminized Christianity acknowledged a long-known fact: New England women outnumbered men in church membership. Earlier, Puritan divines had attributed the female majority to the consequences of God's curse on Eve.[52] Although Eve's sin brought suffering to women in childbirth and consigned them to a subordinate status, God afforded merciful compensation by giving them tender hearts, hearts more receptive to divine things than those of males. By the eighteenth century, the negative association with Eve had been dropped and was replaced with more compelling biblical

51. For similar conclusions, see Brereton, *Sin to Salvation*, 3–40. In "'In a Different Voice': Male and Female Narratives of Religious Conversion in Post-Revolutionary America," *American Quarterly* 41 (March 1989): 34–62, Susan Juster affirms that males and females took different paths to conversion according to gender, although she concludes that at the moment of conversion, "gender distinctions were mitigated, even eradicated. Converted men and women stood before God in the same position: as moral agents, integrated into the Christian community" (57). Her conclusion does not go far enough. Indeed, converts may have stood before God as equals, but whether they stood before *each other* as equals is another matter. Becoming members of a new community of saints did not necessarily imply a breaking down of gender distinctions. Membership in the community empowered women, but within a well-defined subcommunity. For a broader discussion of male and female roles within the evangelical community, see James Davison Hunter, *Evangelicalism: The Coming Generation* (Chicago, 1987), chap. 4.

52. Cott, *Bonds of Womanhood*, 127–28.

models. "The seductress Eve," writes Jan Lewis, "now became the Eve to carry man into virtue."[53]

Economic and political developments in the infant nation reinforced these views.[54] While the complexity of economic relations accelerated the differentiation of gender roles in urban areas, even within traditional rural New England families, where tasks were interdependent, men and women assumed distinct roles and occupied different space.[55] A man's life moved in a centrifugal direction; it was outward or public, whether he engaged in political or economic life. A woman's life moved in a centripetal direction; it was inward or private, limited to the domestic sphere but nevertheless invested with moral authority. To the mother was assigned the responsibility for inculcating piety into her children. Feminine piety, domesticity, and maternity went hand in hand; "the peculiar delicacy and tenderness of the female mind," wrote Charles Backus, "give to mothers great influence in forming the manners of their offspring."[56] The preponderance of female converts in the Second Great Awakening, then, was not hard to explain. After interviewing eighty converts, James Morris concluded:

> It is . . . noticeable that by far the great number are females.—God means to require in a peculiar manner the agency of women to cooperate with him, in his providence in bringing on the millennial peace—Under the pious culture of the mother, he means that children shall be born into his spiritual kingdom in infancy, so that they may devote their whole lives to his fear and service—he means that his praise shall literally be perfected out of the Mouths of Babes & Sucklings.[57]

Differences in expressions of piety were not limited to gender distinctions but were further refined by age discrepancies. The experiences of young males and females were congruent with their adult counterparts, but clerical attitudes and young people's perceptions of and involvement in the Awakening are sufficiently different to merit separate analysis.

53. Jan Lewis, "The Republican Wife: Virtue and Seduction in the Early Republic," *William and Mary Quarterly*, 3d ser., 44 (October 1987): 705.

54. See Bloch, "American Feminine Ideals," 114–15; Cott, *Bonds of Womanhood*, chap. 1; and Linda K. Kerber, *Women of the Republic: Intellect and Ideology in Revolutionary America* (Chapel Hill, N.C., 1980), chaps. 3, 9.

55. Jack Larkin, *The Reshaping of Everyday Life, 1790–1840* (New York, 1988), 17.

56. Backus, *Scripture Doctrine of Regeneration*, 72.

57. James Morris, "Revival of Religion in South Farms," James Morris MSS, SML.

Young Converts

The clergy portrayed the influence of youth in the village revivals far in excess of the actual numbers converted. Some scholarly observers have taken the clergy at their word and so portrayed the Awakening as an adolescent phenomenon, but statistical data for the formative phase of the revival indicate otherwise.[58] According to clerical reports of revival, the category of youth included the ages twelve through twenty-three and normally signified an unattached marital status. Only about one-third (35.7 percent) of the sampled converts were under age twenty-five—a figure that includes marrieds and unmarrieds; thus, the actual percentage of those classified as youth was less than one-third.[59]

There are several reasons for the disproportionate attention given to the young. First, in a number of parishes the revival began among a handful of youth.[60] They in turn triggered religious excitement and anticipation among the general populace. Youth, then, were given a high profile because they appeared to be the catalysts for revival. Second, the behavioral response of converted youths was the most tangible of any group. Whereas conversion for most adults occasioned more of an internal transformation in attitude than a radical outward change in behavior, conversion for youth prompted "the putting away of childish things." "Youthful" or "carnal" amusements were abandoned; solemnity supplanted levity. The new converts traded the dissipations of the ballroom, card tables, and trashy novels for the inspiration of the conference meetings and the Bible.[61] On one occasion, following a divine outpouring in New Hartford, the youth diverted money collected for a dance to the coffers of the church.[62] More typically, large numbers of inquisitive or converted youths gathered together for prayers, testimonies,

---

58. See Nancy F. Cott, "Young Women in the Second Great Awakening in New England," *Feminist Studies* 3 (Fall 1975): 16, and Joseph F. Kett, *Rites of Passage: Adolescence in America, 1790 to the Present* (New York, 1977), 64.

59. See Tables A4.2 and A4.3.

60. *CEM* 1 (July 1800): 19; *CEM* 1 (September 1800): 102; *CEM* 1 (October 1800): 137; Nathan Strong to Jedidiah Morse, 21 February 1799, Morse Family Papers, SML. In Bennet Tyler's compiled descriptions of revivals in New England from 1797 to 1814, fifteen of twenty-four revivals originated with youth (*New England Revivals*).

61. *CEM* 1 (July 1800): 23; *CEM* 1 (August 1800): 58; *CEM* 1 (September 1800): 102; *CEM* 5 (November 1805): 188; *CEM* 7 (April 1807): 393; Cyrus Yale, *The Godly Pastor: Life of the Rev. Jeremiah Hallock, of Canton, Conn.* (New York [1854]), 246. By 1796, the Farmington Village Library had over four hundred volumes, mostly secular in nature, including novels, poetry, travel books, and history (see Christopher P. Bickford, *Farmington in Connecticut* [Canaan, N.H., 1982], 278). Cf. Quincy Blake, "The Story of Farmington," 1936 (Typewritten), CSL, who noted that there were more books on religion and theology than any other single topic. For an example of the popularity of dance in the early Republic, see Candace Roberts Diary, April 1801–October 1806, Main Vault, CSL. She mentions attending balls two or three times a week.

62. Yale, *Godly Pastor*, 246.

song, and instruction. On a social level, the conference meeting for youth functioned as an alternative to "worldly" frivolity, as well as a rite of passage from youthful indiscretions to adult sobriety.

A final reason for the excessive attention given to youth reflected clerical hopes for the future. To youth was entrusted the future prospects of the church and nation, and given the degenerate state of affairs, their conversion was imperative. Early conversion not only secured salvation but also ensured the perpetuation of the church and the social stability of the Republic. In particular, young males were reminded that one of the fruits of salvation was "usefulness." "Deacon Goodyear" reasoned that "early piety secures salvation to the subjects of it, should they die in youth. If they live to old age it lays a foundation for long and happy improvement in the divine life, for great experience and comfort in walking with God, for great usefulness in the church, and in the world."[63] The parents of Horace Cowles implored him to find salvation so that he "might fill up your future days with duty to God, usefulness to your Country, yourself & Friends."[64] In his sermon "On the Use of Time, addressed to men in the several ages of life," Nathan Strong advised young males not only to prepare for the next world but also to acquire industrious habits in the present world for "some useful employment."[65] Such admonitions had an unmistakable male bias, for "usefulness" implied some kind of public presence, whether in the realm of politics or the marketplace, areas off limits to females.

Not surprisingly, to young males, religious leaders emphasized the practical benefits of conversion. The new birth would enable a young man to find a decent job, to pursue an honest, "lawful calling." "The religion of Jesus Christ," advised a writer in the *Connecticut Evangelical Magazine*, "when embraced and practiced, will prepare you . . . to grace the stage of life. . . . This will qualify you to train up families for God; it will prepare you for a peaceful and comfortable life."[66] Attendant upon male conversion, then, was the inculcation of Christian (and emerging middle-class) virtues: sobriety, thrift, a decent job, and a comfortable life.

For young females, conversion centered on the development of feminine virtues. The fact that young, single females outnumbered their male counterparts by a ratio of over two to one suggests that female conversion signaled a preparedness for marriage and future maternal responsibilities.[67] As such, female expressions of piety focused on conquering personal vices and cultivating virtues appropriate to a life of domesticity. One of the most besetting sins for young females was "idleness," "vanity," or "trifling amuse-

63. *CEM* 5 (December 1804): 228.
64. Isaac and Lucinda Cowles to Horace Cowles at Yale, 13 April 1800, Julius Gay Misc. MSS, FVL.
65. Strong, "Sermon on the Use of Time," 8.
66. *CEM* 1 (November 1800): 197.
67. On male-female ratios, see Chapter 6 and table A4.4.

ment." Prior to her conversion, Julia Cowles used her seventeenth birthday to reflect on lost opportunities and squandered time. "The command is, 'Redeem the time, because the days are evil,' but instead of redeeming the precious time I have wasted it in idleness and folly."[68] A certain "Emelia" wanted others to admire her fine dress in "the *gay circle, the ball room,* and *the pew"*—that is, before she came to her spiritual senses and converted.[69] The chief sin prompting these laments about time wasted in worldly delights was self-centeredness and pride—the very opposite of God-centeredness and humility. How could a young female assume the selfless task of domesticity if absorbed in her own pleasure?[70]

The theme of submission pervades female expressions of piety. Males recognized the importance of humiliation—for conversion necessitated it—but they appeared less preoccupied with it and much less effusive in their language on the subject. Females were prone to subjectivize, or personalize, the act of submission by relating it to Jesus, whereas males expressed a more objective language of submitting to God's divine government. At a conference meeting, one female found her "heart glowing with the most ardent love toward the Savior. . . . Tears flowed without control. The language of my heart was, O my dear Savior, come, and take an everlasting possession of my soul; I bid thee a hearty welcome, to my heart, and would now lie low, at thy feet for ever."[71] A young diarist from Newington reiterated this theme of abject humiliation before her Lord. One of the stanzas from a poem entitled, "O for a revival in this Place," reveals the popular female sentimentality:

> Into this place Dear jesus come,
> May sinners see themselves undone,
> And trembling bow at the Dear feet
> Pleading for grace before it's too late.[72]

The conversion of the young was induced by a variety of means. For some, peer pressure bestirred the conscience. Although a fifteen-year-old girl "hated her best friends who were affording her spiritual instruction during her convictions and opposition of heart to God," she eventually succumbed,

68. *The Diaries of Julia Cowles, 1797–1803*, ed. Laura Hadley Moseley (New Haven, Conn., 1931), 70; see also [anonymous], Religious Diary, 1813–1817, MS. 72914, CHS.

69. *CEM* 2 (May 1802): 422.

70. There was a direct correlation between the female emphasis upon "time management" and her household work as domestic "business" (see Kerber, *Women of the Republic,* 253; see also Wisner, *Memoir of Huntington,* 93).

71. *CEM* 6 (May 1806): 430–31.

72. "O for a revival in this place" (1813), inserted in Julia Churchill (1792–1822) Diary, 9 May to 12 October 1818–1821, Newington, CHS.

following two months of increased conviction and anxiety.[73] For others, exposure to popular British devotional authors proved critical. One girl attributed her conversion to Richard Baxter's *Saints of the Everlasting Rest*; another felt that Philip Doddridge's *Rise and Progress of Religion* "spoke directly to her."[74] Another young female experienced "serious impressions" after she encountered the following lines in the "Young Child's Resolutions":

> 'Tis time to seek to God and pray,
> For what I want for every day,
> I have a precious soul to save,
> And I a mortal body have.[75]

In addition to the influence of devotional readings and popular doggerel, hymns provided another source of spiritual arousal. Aurally engaging as well as morally compelling, hymns added an extra dimension to religious experience. In 1799, Nathan Strong, Abel Flint, and Joseph Steward published *The Hartford Selection of Hymns*, a work that supplemented and in some cases replaced selections in Isaac Watts's *Hymns and Spiritual Songs* (1707). Watts's popular hymnal, used during the Great Awakening as a dynamic vehicle through which the Holy Spirit aroused the affections, was universally accepted by New England Congregationalists following the Revolution. According to Stephen Marini, by 1800, Watts's "psalms, hymns, and spiritual songs had become the canon of Evangelical praise."[76] *The Hartford Selection*, then, drew from a familiar body of hymns while supplying other hymns appropriate to the mood of the Second Great Awakening. In this latter respect it was a "landmark of New England Hymnody," the first of its kind in America born of the revival spirit.[77] Strong noted in his preface that the recent "happy revivals of religion" in New England created the demand for a new hymnal. In selecting hymns for inclusion, he continued, "the Editors have endeavored to adapt it to the use of Christians in their closets, families, and private religious meetings, and also the feelings of persons in every state of religious impression."

What Strong had in mind was a hymnal appropriate for private use in the home, as well as for conference meetings and other evangelical gatherings. *The Hartford Selection* included a large number of selections from the *Olney Hymns* (1779), a work by the English Evangelicals John Newton and William Cowper;

73. Morris, "Revival of Religion in South Farms," SML.

74. Ibid.; *CEM* 5 (November 1805): 188.

75. *CEM* 3 (September 1802): 106.

76. Stephen A. Marini, "Rehearsal for Revival: Sacred Singing and the Great Awakening in America," in *Sacred Sound: Music in Religious Thought and Practice*, ed. Joyce Irwin (Chico, Calif., 1983), 80.

77. Louis F. Benson, *The English Hymn: Its Development and Use in Worship* (1915; reprint, Richmond, Va., 1962), 374.

to this, Strong added six of his own compositions and a number of originals from pious and poetic New Englanders. In 1821, the hymnal went to press for an eighth edition—an indication of its constant demand and popularity.[78]

The Hartford Selection reveals a balance between the head and the heart, between Calvinist dogma (little is uniquely "New Divinity" about the hymnal) and popular devotion. Although the hymns seldom mention a specific age group, those that do are directed primarily toward youth. The hymnal contains only two selections expressly written for the aged, but includes six hymns specifically targeting youth.[79] In addition, the lyrics of several others make direct references to youth.[80] Such emphases confirm the clerical preoccupation with young people as the group most in need of and most receptive to salvation. The prevailing mind-set is summarized in the title of the hymn "Youth the most accepted hour" and conveyed in its fourth stanza:

> When conscience speaks, its voice regard;
> And seize the tender hour;
> Humbly implore the promis'd grace,
> And God will give the power.[81]

Typically, youth-oriented hymns contrasted the temptations and delusory happiness of wordly things with the "true bliss" and surety of things eternal.[82] In some cases (perhaps many?), young people sought comfort, not condemnation, and so latched onto those hymns that proffered confidence and assurance. One youth followed the New Divinity morphology of conversion after a funeral triggered "first impressions."[83] The terrors of hell frightened the youth, who then realized the "selfish" motivation of seeking salvation in order

---

78. On the use of Watts and the popularity of *The Hartford Selection*, see Benson, *English Hymn*, 161–68, 372–74, and Henry Wilder Foote, *Three Centuries of American Hymnody* (Hamden, Conn., 1961), 160–64.

In 1824, Asahel Nettleton compiled his own hymnal, *Village Hymns*, a work of 600 selections, 109 of which were revival hymns. Like *The Hartford Selection*, the distinctives of New Divinity theology are not apparent, as Nettleton included selections from British authors (Watts, John Newton, William Cowper, Anne Steel, Charles Wesley, and James Montgomery), American authors (Lydia Huntley Sigourney, William B. Tappan, Abbie B. Hyde, Phoebe Brown, Samuel Davies, and John Leland), and the Canadian, Henry Alline—a group running the gamut from English Nonconformists to Arminians to Calvinist Baptists. Soon after its publication, the *Village Hymns* exceeded *The Hartford Selection* in popularity, as seven editions appeared in three years. See George Hugh Birney, Jr., "The Life and Letters of Asahel Nettleton, 1783–1844" (Ph.D. diss., Hartford Theological Seminary, 1943), 102–6; Benson, *English Hymn*, 375–76, who called *Village Hymns* "the brightest evangelical hymn book yet made in America" (376); and Foote, *Three Centuries of American Hymnody*, 189–90.

79. On hymns for the aged, see *Hartford Selection*, nos. 267, 268; for youth, see nos. 262–66, 309.

80. For example, stanza 5 of hymn no. 202, p. 156, "Rejoicing in a revival of religion": "God's chariot rolls, it frights the soul, / Of those who hate the truth; / And saints in pray'r, cry, Lord draw near, / Have mercy on the youth!"

81. *Hartford Selection of Hymns*, no. 264, p. 213.

82. See esp. "The encouragement young persons have to see and love Christ," no. 263, p. 212.

83. *CEM* 6 (May 1806): 429.

to escape everlasting punishment. At this point the soothing lyrics of "The Humble sinner Trusting in Christ" from *The Hartford Selection* brought relief:

> Cheer up, my soul, there is a mercy seat,
> Sprinkled with blood, where Jesus answers prayer;
> Humbly cast thyself beneath his feet,
> For never needy sinner perish'd there.[84]

Now the young person was in a state where "my heart was ready to thank God, that I was in his hands." With this ultimate act of submission, the youth exhibited the vital sign of true religious affection—an expression of disinterested benevolence, a willingness to be damned for the greater glory of God.

Perhaps the most common—and by far, the most intimidating—device for bringing youth to salvation was the constant reminder of death. If they survived infancy (in 1800 one white infant in seven did not live to age four), the young repeatedly encountered other threats to life. Farm accidents, natural catastrophes, and illnesses (especially malaria and tuberculosis epidemics) took their toll on youth in the early Republic, as an estimated 8 to 10 percent died between the ages of one and twenty-one.[85] Evangelical ministers used lectures, conference meetings, and funeral orations to remind the young of life's uncertainty and the necessity of immediate repentance. In contrast to the rather bland appellations chosen for adult funeral sermons, the clergy sensationalized the titles of sermons for deceased youth. In "The Living Warned to be Prepared for Death," Charles Backus exploited the fears of his young listeners:

> Dear youth of this whole audience, hearken to the warning voice which is now sounding in your ears. Look on these coffins, filled with bodies. . . . You behold the remains of *five* young persons who began the present week with you. They went on in health and vigor until near the close of the second day, when, in an instant, they were cut off from the land of the living. Their once active limbs can move no more, the bloom hath fled from their countenances, and all that was mortal of them must be buried under the clods of the valley. . . . The period will come, my young friends, when, if you be found among the impenitent, you will wish that you had never been born.[86]

Abel Flint merely foreshortened the title of Backus's sermon in his "Prepare for Death!" He importuned the youth at the funeral of nineteen-year-old John

---

84. Ibid.
85. Larkin, *Everyday Life*, 75; on disease, see 77–84.
86. Charles Backus, "The Living Warned to be Prepared for Death . . ." (Springfield, Mass., 1799), 13, 14; see also Backus, "Afflictions Improved: The substance of a discourse delivered . . . February 28, 1790 . . ." (Springfield, Mass., 1793), 15.

Strong, a recent Yale graduate and the son of his Hartford colleague Nathan Strong, "to delay not a moment to commence a life of religion." John was accidently drowned when his skittish mount jumped into the water from a ferry boat crossing the Connecticut River. "Are you ready," queried Flint of John's living classmates, "are you prepared to die?"[87] In nearby Farmington, following the recent death of a fifteen-year-old, the Rev. Joseph Washburn cautioned the youth of his parish to "remember, your life is a vapor, and will soon vanish."[88] Pious parents reiterated pastoral concerns, though at times in less graphic terms. "We live in a dying world," wrote a worried father to his spiritually apathetic son at Yale.[89] Not surprisingly, these imprecations issuing from ministers and parents had their desired effect in triggering revival. Alvan Hyde reported that divine showers fell on his parish in 1806 following his sermon at the funeral of a local lad. His text: "He being dead, yet speaketh" (Hebrews 11:4).[90]

The continual presence of death, combined with adult reminders of its consequences, filled youth with an anxiety bordering on morbidity. One youth put the matter plainly: "To prepare for death, ought to be the great business of living."[91] Another young female diarist confessed, "By the death of friends, acquaintances, and relatives, I have been brought to think of my danger. Sermons, also, and funerals, and letters have affected me. Last of all, the death of my dear L—— has showed me in a striking manner my own danger, and the necessity of a preparation for death, in youth as well as in old age."[92] Many young people were familiar with the writings of Philip Doddridge, who in his *Sermons to Young People* interrogated his young readers about their eternal destiny:

> How many of you have attended funerals of youth like yourselves, of children much younger than yourselves! They have given up the ghost, and where are they? What a change hath death made!—where are they? . . . Could your eye penetrate a few feet of earth, you would see them; but oh!, what spectacles of horror would you discover! Yet perhaps a year ago they were in the number of the most amiable objects of your sight.[93]

87. Abel Flint, "Prepare for Death! A Sermon, delivered . . . Sept. 17, 1806, at the funeral of John McCurdy Strong . . ." (Hartford, Conn., 1806), 15.

88. Washburn, *Sermons on Practical Subjects*, 188; see also Samuel-John Mills, "The Nature and Importance of the Duty of Singing Praise to God . . ." (Hartford, Conn., 1775), 19, and Philip Doddridge, "Sermons on the Religious Education of Children . . ." (Boston, 1794), 86.

89. Isaac Cowles to Horace Cowles, 3 August 1798, Julius Gay Misc. MSS, FVL; see also Doddridge, "Religious Education of Children," 34.

90. Alvan Hyde, *Memoir of Rev. Alvan Hyde, D.D. of Lee, Mass.* (Boston, 1835), 51. Another example of a graphic sermon title for deceased youth is Isaiah Potter's, "The Young Men are dead! . . . A Sermon, preached on account of the Death of Erastus Chamberlain and Reuben Currier, who were drowned on 16 of April, 1798" (Hanover, N.H., 1798).

91. *CEM* 4 (April 1804): 399.

92. *CEM* 4 (October 1803): 149; see also Julia Churchill Diary, CHS.

93. Quoted in Kett, *Rites of Passage*, 66.

Is it any wonder that some young people contemplated suicide as a relief from the psychological trauma induced by such death threats?[94]

For other youth, the specter of death and the ingrained conviction of their utter worthlessness haunted them even after their conversion. Relief came, but only momentarily, for feelings of uncertainty and guilt overshadowed the delights of reordered affections. Fears of deception produced an unresolved anxiety shouldered for life. These alternations of despair and joy indicate the ambiguous effects of the New Divinity teaching on human nature, nurture, and the morphology of conversion. Youth were continually reminded that all humans were sinful by nature; they were told that the path to conversion was filled with despair over the prospect of spending eternity in torment. According to the New Divinity, once regeneration took place, the convert's attitude and behavior were motivated by the recognition of God's glory and beauty, and not by selfish desires to avoid eternal punishment. Like their Puritan predecessors, the New Divinity men tried to maintain the balance between human sinfulness and divine holiness, between the condemnations of the law and the mercies of God's grace. The intended result was a "disinterested benevolence"—a new love for God, self, and others. And indeed, for many, this theological concept acted like a detonator, which set off the explosion of mission and reform activities in the Second Great Awakening.

For other converts, however, the contemplation of God's glory and beauty was diminished by a continual uncertainty and consciousness of guilt. By allowing the ends (youthful conversions) to justify the means (an unrelenting emphasis upon guilt and death), the clergy failed to instill in their converts the enjoyment of God's beauty. They undid the very thing they were trying to accomplish, for overwhelming guilt undermined the young saints' full appreciation of God's grace and love. Some converts lived out their lives in this quandary, while others, like Harriet Beecher Stowe and Horace Bushnell, resolved the issue once and for all by rejecting their Calvinist upbringing. Whatever the response, these differing reactions to conversion and expressions of piety among youth exhibited on a lesser scale the striking divergence between the adult male and female religious experiences.

Adult Converts

One of the more revealing aspects about the male conversion experience is the paucity of accounts relative to those of females. Men appeared reluctant

94. See CEM 1 (May 1801): 422, 424; Sally Lee to Jonathan Lee, 7 December 1808, Lee Papers, SML.

to express their inmost thoughts and emotions, while women, in keeping with cultural prescriptions, detailed their emotional highs and lows with relish. Men could indeed experience despondency and joy, but as supposed creatures of intellect and reason, they were expected to be more reasonable and objective. Perhaps if men had felt free to articulate their feelings, they would not have met the fate of one Elijah North of Farmington. Although he was "a pious, devoted man," North's suicide was "attributed to his considering himself an outcast from God and despairing over being recd by him & thinking the quicker he left this world the better."[95]

Published narratives of male conversions tended to be two-dimensional, whether reconstructed by a minister or taken verbatim from the convert himself. Private expressions allowed for a greater range of emotion, as the exchange between Jonathan Lee and his father, Myls, suggests. While Asahel Nettleton's roommate at Yale, Jonathan agonized over his frustration and guilt without the relief of conversion:

> O, my father, were I to tell you that my heart is harder than adamant, yea tenfold harder than the nether millstone, the comparison would fall infinitely short, of any adequate representation of my deplorable condition. With greater ease may the flinty rock be broken & ground to powder, than can my heart be made to yield. Wretched creature that I am! Why am I not in eternal woe! The reason lies beyond the reach of my comprehension. I am often led to think of the barren fig tree, which was spared till all possible means were used to render it fruitful.[96]

Myls responded by advising his son "to take your hand & unyielding heart in the arms of prayer and carry it to God, lay it at the foot of the cross; and make an unreserved surrender of your all for time and eternity into the hands of a *holy* and *sovereign* yet at the same time a *sin-pardoning* God in Christ Jesus."[97] It was clear from Myls's next letter that Jonathan had taken his father's advice to heart: "O! my son, you know not the pleasing sensations, the tears of joy, & the tender anxieties that have occasioned, have you then, *indeed found & seen Jesus?*"[98] He closed his letter by warning Jonathan of the possibility of deceit and the false comforts of salvation. Jonathan Lee's expressions and experience were those of a young man, however, not an adult male. Contemporaries of Lee, such as Nettleton and Samuel Mills, Jr., expressed the full range of

---

95. Julius Gay, *A Record of the Descendents of John Clark, of Farmington, Connecticut* (Hartford, Conn., 1882), 15; John Case to John M. Case, 1 June 1800, Business Letters, Box 2, FVL.
96. Jonathan Lee to Deacon Myls Lee, 7 March 1808, Lee Papers, SML.
97. Deacon Myls Lee to Jonathan Lee, 31 March 1808, Lee Papers, SML.
98. Deacon Myls Lee to Jonathan Lee, 10 July 1808, Lee Papers, SML.

emotions in their private accounts of conversion and, in so doing, offer exceptions to the rule of gender stereotyping. Like Jonathan Lee's father, both wept profusely (although over their lost condition) and described their conversions in the same self-abasing terms as typified female narratives.[99] What these accounts suggest is that those males who possessed a "feminine" outlook were likely candidates for conversion—and then for the ministry.

What kind of experience did the "typical" male convert relate—that is, a married man with children, who himself grew up in a pious family? His morphology of conversion followed the prescribed pattern. Initially awakened at a lecture or a conference meeting, he was convicted of guilt, realizing that his heart's affections were not set on God. He might experience a period of calm, only to rise up against God and then sink into despair. This period of anxiety lasted anywhere from a few weeks to a year and in some cases was accompanied by insomnia, loss of appetite, and even thoughts of suicide. Finally, a breakthrough came when he "entertained a hope" of reconciliation with God. At that time, God's ways appeared "right and all his requirements reasonable." Now the new convert served God with happiness by attending to family prayer and regular Sabbath observance.[100]

The turning point in the male experience came when he conceded the "reasonableness of God," a phrase seldom used in female conversion accounts.[101] The large percentage of married men converted and then admitted to church membership, either simultaneously with their wives or following their wives' conversions, suggests that for many males, conversion came at the behest of their spouses. And perhaps the lack of depth to some of the accounts indicates that males succumbed to conversion not so much from a desire for new affections as from wifely pressure. The account of a forty-five-year-old man who was convicted while hearing private instruction given by the pastor to his wife was not uncommon.[102]

In particular, converts from "infidelity" were quick to credit the influence of

99. Gardiner Spring, *Memoir of Samuel John Mills*, 2d ed. (New York, 1842), 15–16, 24; Bennet Tyler, *Memoir of the Life and Character of Rev. Asahel Nettleton, D.D.*, 2d ed. (Hartford, Conn., 1845), 12–13.

100. *CEM* 1 (February 1801): 308; *CEM* 1 (May 1801): 420–23; *CEM* 3 (September 1802): 106; *CEM* 3 (December 1802): 236; *CEM* 4 (November 1803): 182; *CEM* 6 (April 1806): 388–89.

101. For example, see *CEM* 1 (May 1801): 423.

102. *CEM* 1 (February 1801): 308. In her survey of conversion narratives, Brereton concludes that "there are relatively few instances in the literature of nineteenth-century conversion in which a husband was converted before his wife and exhorted her to follow suit" (*Sin to Salvation*, 30–31). For supporting assessments, see Harry S. Stout and Catherine E. Brekus, "Declension, Gender, and the 'New Religious History,'" in *Belief and Behavior: Essays in the New Religious History*, ed. Philip R. Vandermeer and Robert P. Swierenga (New Brunswick, N.J., 1991), 15–37; Richard D. Shiels, "The Scope of the Second Great Awakening: Andover, Massachusetts, as a Case Study," *Journal of the Early Republic* 5 (Summer 1985): 223–46; Mary P. Ryan, "A Women's Awakening: Evangelical Religion and the Families of Utica, New York, 1800–1840," *American Quarterly* 30 (Winter 1978): 602–23; and Curtis D. Johnson, *Islands of Holiness: Rural Religion in Upstate New York, 1790–1860* (Ithaca, N.Y., 1989), 61.

a pious spouse.[103] The charge of infidelity—a catchword for deism or Universalism or any departure from New Divinity Calvinism—applied nearly exclusively to males. Presumably the female temperament was not so inclined. Although converts from infidelity represented a mere handful of total conversions, the clergy seized upon their spectacular turnabouts as undeniable evidence of God at work.[104] The infidel symbolized man gone his own way in stubborn defiance to God's laws. Conversely, his conversion displayed the power of God at work in reducing an autonomous, resistant man to submission. "I got no relief," testified a forty-year-old convert from Universalism, "until feeling my absolute dependence, on the sovereign will of God, to dispose of me as he should see fit."[105] Although once fond of reading "Voltaire, Paine, and Allen," the former infidel now savored the Bible. Although once an opponent of divine decrees, he now derived comfort from them.[106]

As I have shown in earlier chapters, advocates of evangelical Christianity emphasized the behavioral implications of infidelity. Wrong belief, they reasoned, especially the belief that rejected the doctrine of future punishments, inevitably led to wrong conduct. "The liberal doctrine of modern times," announced Asahel Hooker, "takes for granted what is palpably false, that there is no connection between men's sentiments and their hearts, and between their hearts, and their practice."[107] Whether one espoused Universalism (all would be saved) or materialism (death is the end), the results were the same. Those who embraced these false philosophies, said Charles Backus, give "full indulgence to their sensual appetites." These infidels have "progressed in their brutishness, until many of them have confessed themselves to be wretched; and have either fallen victims to their debauchery, or have laid violent hands upon themselves, and put an end to their lives."[108] Without the light of the gospel, the operations of "depraved reason" culminated in suicide.[109]

Contributors to the *Connecticut Evangelical Magazine* noted the reformative nature of Christianity in juxtaposition to the moral degradation of deism. Christianity was touted as promoting social stability, whereas deism removed

103. *CEM* 1 (March 1801): 348; *CEM* 2 (April 1802): 385; *CEM* 6 (July 1805): 32.

104. *CEM* 1 (September 1800): 110–13; *CEM* 1 (November 1800): 179–81; *CEM* 1 (March 1801): 347–52; *CEM* 2 (April 1802): 383–88; *CEM* 6 (July 1805): 31–34.

105. *CEM* 1 (July 1800): 25.

106. *CEM* 1 (March 1801): 348; *CEM* 6 (July 1805): 33.

107. Asahel Hooker, "The Immoral and Pernicious Tendency of Error. Illustrated in a Sermon, delivered . . . Jan. 1st, 1806 . . ." (Hartford, Conn., 1806), 17–18.

108. Charles Backus, "A Discourse on the Nature and Influence of Godly Fear . . ." (Hartford, Conn., 1802), 17.

109. Ephraim Judson, "On the first promise of the Saviour in the Scriptures," in *Sermons on Important Subjects* (Hartford, Conn., 1797), 232.

restraints and openly catered to wickedness.[110] Gerald Cragg has noted how eighteenth-century religion in England and on the Continent "was convinced that the relation between belief and conduct was close," and that to deists, "right conduct" was "more important than correct belief."[111] The same was true across the Atlantic—but with a twist. The New Divinity men turned the argument of the deists on its head in order to prove that without correct belief, right conduct would never result. Their virulent opposition to the French Revolution (the "goddess of reason"), as well as their fear of the deist Jefferson's election to the presidency, were grounded in this logic. Without a moral God to ensure a moral government, all hell would break loose. Just look at the behavior of those who "tell God to depart from them," wrote Jacob Catlin, for they are a "vicious company" who drink to excess, blaspheme, swear, play cards and "chance games," and attend balls with music and dancing where "lascivious affections" are aroused. In short, infidels and wicked types spend their time "in high and jovial mirth, and in wanton gesticulations."[112]

The natural inclination of females toward fidelity offset the male proclivity toward infidelity. The contrast between these two temperaments of gender accentuated the divergence between male and female religious experiences in the Second Great Awakening. Infidelity was often associated with autonomous reason, a dominant male trait, while fidelity was identified with virtue, a trait of female provenance.[113] Historians of gender have demonstrated that during the Great Awakening, both men and woman expressed their religious experiences in consonant ways—the desire to be "tender-hearted."[114] But by the Second Great Awakening, the differentiation of gender roles carried different religious experiences as well as separate vocabularies to describe those experiences. The New Divinity sensual vocabulary of the affections conformed to the late eighteenth-century ideal of femininity. Hence, if men were to become "affectionate" Christians, in some way they would have to embrace culturally defined feminine traits. Their resistance to the revival (relative to women in numbers converted) was undoubtedly rooted in social conventions of gender.[115]

To religious men and women alike, Scripture best expressed the ideal of

110. *CEM* 4 (December 1803): 235–36.

111. Gerald R. Cragg, *Reason and Authority in the Eighteenth Century* (Cambridge, 1964), 87, 88.

112. Jacob Catlin, "The wicked, on account of worldly prosperity, and unbelief of a future State, openly reject and despise the Almighty," in *Sermons on Important Subjects*, 500–505.

113. Infidels placed "unwarrantable dependence upon reason as a guide" (*CEM* 6 [July 1805]: 32).

114. Cott, *Bonds of Womanhood*, 172; see also Margaret W. Masson, "The Typology of the Female as a Model for the Regenerate: Puritan Preaching, 1690–1730," *Signs: Journal for Women in Culture and Society* 2 (Winter 1976): 304–15.

115. For a full discussion of evangelical Protestantism and sexual identity in early America, see Philip Greven, *The Protestant Temperament: Patterns of Child-Rearing, Religious Experience, and the Self in Early America* (New York, 1979), 124–40.

feminine piety. Proverbs 31:10–31 described the "virtuous woman" of the early Republic. Contemporary commentators, of course, adorned her with late eighteenth-century cultural garb. Her main purpose in life was to raise a family, for "the domestic relations are the field of female exertion." Due to her natural religious affections, she "is distinguished by the wisdom and piety with which she educates her children." The virtuous woman does good to the poor, not in a public or ostentatious way, but privately. In recognizing her place, "she rises in loveliness in the eyes of her husband, who is occupied in doing good on a larger scale, in advancing the great interests of society and concerns of state." Finally, the virtuous woman is adept at conversation but "principally, in her own family at home and with her own sex."[116] Within the sheltering confines of the home, "her prudent and just sentiments" are formed "away from the passionate bustle of the world."[117] Thus Scripture, bolstered by contemporary cultural expectations (or vice versa), provided the rationale for women's "sphere"—a life of domesticity invested with moral authority in the raising of children and engaged in private charitable work. This ideology pervaded the memoirs of pious women published in the *Connecticut Evangelical Magazine*.[118]

Women were highly conscious of both the limitations and responsibilities within their domain. Unlike pious men, women were not called "to go forth and preach the gospel," but they could (and should) "pray to God to send forth gospel preachers."[119] Women were not to speak publicly, but they were charged with engaging in private prayer. "In this way," wrote twenty-two-year-old Harriet Winslow, "they may be eminently useful."[120] "Sisters in Christ," exhorted a contributor to the *Connecticut Evangelical Magazine*, "here is a way by which you may do much, and *not go out of your own sphere*"[121] (emphasis added). The writer urged her readers to emulate the life of Susanna Anthony, "who eminently lived a *life of prayer*." Anthony and her friend Sarah Osborn, converts of the Great Awakening in Newport, Rhode Island, were enshrined by their pastor, Samuel Hopkins, as paragons of female piety.[122]

116. *CEM* 4 (September 1803): 95–96.

117. Nathan Strong, "The Character of a Virtuous and Good Woman: A discourse, delivered . . . Oct. 4, 1809" (Hartford, Conn., 1809), 8.

118. For examples, see "Memoirs of Mrs. Sally Morton," *CEM* 5 (December 1804): 229; "Memoirs of Mrs. Lucy Jerome," *CEM* 5 (May 1805): 425–26; "Memoirs of Mrs. Clarinda Prentice," *CEM* 6 (November 1805): 185–96, and *CEM* 6 (December 1805): 222–26; "Memoirs of Mrs. Jerusha Catlin," *CEM* 7 (August 1806): 59–63; "Memoirs of Mrs. C. Welch," *CEM* 7 (November 1806): 170–75; "Memoirs of Mrs. Abigail Wells," *CEM* 7 (March 1807): 340–46; and "Memoirs of Mrs. Amelia Flint," *CEMRI* 3 (April 1810): 108–13.

119. *CEM* 3 (February 1803): 298.

120. Winslow, *Memoir of Harriet Winslow*, 123.

121. *CEM* 3 (February 1803): 298.

122. Hopkins revealed only one side of Osborn's piety. In a single week during a revival in 1766–67, Osborn attracted over five hundred people, including adult males, to her home. Some

Anthony was a prayer warrior "who probably did more toward advancing the good cause than many of the other sex, who have been piously devoted to the work of preaching the gospel, all their days."[123] The message was clear: women, though relegated to a private, domestic life, had enhanced moral authority. Though their role was constricted, their spiritual powers expanded. A man retained the titular "prerogative of government" within the home, while in fact the woman assumed the role of the "head of a family, and guide and instructress of youth"—responsibilities once shared with her spouse.[124] Now, when a young woman married, she moved into a "new sphere of action."[125] Susan Huntington, the daughter of a New Divinity minister and wife of an evangelical pastor, clearly delineated these expectations: "Legislators and governors have to enact laws, and compel men to observe them; mothers have to implant the principles, and cultivate the dispositions, which alone can make good citizens and subjects. The former have to exert authority over characters already formed; the latter, to mould the character of future man."[126] Whether these pronouncements are viewed as a compensatory response to women's limited participation in society or as an expression of a nascent feminism, pious women embraced their role with enthusiasm.[127]

Some husbands resented, and even resisted, attempts by their wives to attend conference meetings. No doubt such meetings were a conduit for the transmission of wifely and motherly virtues, but their lure by no means reinforced female passivity. The revivals, then, at once reinforced the "cult of domesticity" as well as challenged it. Women were instructed by women to "redeem a little more time from your domestic business for the devotion of the closet," but many preferred to step out and attend a more socially desirable conference meeting.[128] Such behavior rankled husbands, who

---

criticized her for transgressing her culturally prescribed role, but Osborn stoutly defended her actions. See Mary Beth Norton, "'My Resting Reaping Times': Sarah Osborn's Defense of Her 'Unfeminine Activities,'" *Signs: Journal for Women in Culture and Society* 2 (Winter 1976): 515–29.

123. *CEM* 3 (February 1803): 298–99.

124. *Sermons, on Various Important Doctrines and Duties of the Christian Religion* (Northampton, Mass., 1799), 222; *CEM* 7 (August 1806): 63; see also Strong, "Virtuous Woman," 9.

125. *CEM* 7 (November 1806): 171.

126. Wisner, *Memoir of Huntington*, 68.

127. On the ambiguous results of the influence of Evangelicalism on the new women's role, see Bloch, "American Feminist Ideals," 120, and Cott, *Bonds of Womanhood*, 203. For the past twenty-five years historians have debated the nature of the influence of Evangelicalism on women in the early nineteenth century. On the one hand, Barbara Welter, "The Cult of True Womanhood, 1820–1860," *American Quarterly* 18 (Summer 1966): 151–74, viewed Evangelicalism as a deterrent to, if not a conspiracy against, women's freedom. On the other hand, I am more inclined to agree with Joanna Bowen Gillespie, "'The Clear Leadings of Providence': Pious Memoirs and the Problems of Self-realization for Women in the Early Nineteenth Century," *Journal of the Early Republic* 5 (Summer 1985): 197–221, who argues that Evangelicalism opened up opportunities for women, albeit within a limited sphere of influence.

128. *CEM* 3 (February 1803): 299.

sensed that their spouses' newfound community deprived them of wifely affection and disrupted the traditional relation between male dominance and female submission. The husband of Sally Brown allowed her to attend church on Sunday but refused to let her frequent conference meetings in the evenings.[129] Edward Dorr Griffin related the story of a man who swore never to attend a religious service. The profligate made his house "a hell" to his pious wife; and when Griffin made a pastoral visit, the man "gnashed upon me with his teeth."[130] Another husband confessed that after his wife "became the subject of the work" of revival, he "used every indirect method to prevent her attendance at religious meetings."[131]

Apparently, these attempts by husbands to prevent their wives from attending religious gatherings were not new. Over a decade before the outbreak of the 1798 revivals, the Hartford *Courant* ran a short piece entitled "The Ladies New Catechism." The author formulated a revised catechism modeled after the Westminster shorter catechism:

> Q. For what end did you come into the world?
> A. To get a husband.
> Q. What is the way to get a husband?
> A. To dress, dance, chat, play, and go to all manner of public places, except church, for fear of being called a fanatic.[132]

The resentment men expressed toward women whose commitment to the life of the church challenged male values was returned not by a direct challenge to male authority but by the biting sting of satire.

It is clear that women desired to attend conference meetings for more than spiritual edification. These gatherings also filled a social vacuum, for the religious meetings provided the context for solidifying friendship bonds among women. Here women, many of whom lived in social isolation, discovered a community of peers outside the home with whom to share heartfelt affections. For the male, the determinant force in shaping his identity and community was his vocation.[133] Females, however, flocked to conference meetings in order to affirm their identity and find community. Shunted from public involvement and relegated to second-class citizenship, women gained a measure of independence at these meetings. The conference meeting was to females what the tavern was to males—the center of

---

129. Morris, "Revival of Religion in South Farms," SML.

130. Edward Dorr Griffin to Lynde Huntington, 14 March 1799, BL.

131. *CEMRI* 2 (March 1809): 106; see also *CEM* 1 (August 1800): 62. In some cases fathers refused to allow their children to attend conference meetings (see Morris, "Revival of Religion in South Farms," SML).

132. *Connecticut Courant and Weekly Intelligencer*, 5 June 1786.

133. Cott, *Bonds of Womanhood*, 138.

sociability.[134] The religious conference became that embryo out of which was born the numerous local female religious associations and missionary societies of the early nineteenth century. In short, the conferences offered women the only socially approved outlet for female religious involvement.[135] Men channeled their religious energies into a variety of institutional organizations: the ministry, home and foreign mission work, teaching posts, college presidencies, and a host of other voluntary associations. In the formative years of the revival, no such avenues existed for women. Thus, from the perspective of gender, the Second Great Awakening represented not so much a unified quest for community as the search for communal forms within subcommunities of saints defined by gender.

Women's conversion narratives reveal most clearly the nature and depth of the female religious experience. Many accounts were written by ministers and, as such, reveal clerical perceptions about female conversion.[136] Yet accounts penned privately by women display little variation from clerically constructed ones. Whether written by ministers or women, the female conversion experience conformed to the prescribed morphology of conversion. These formulaic accounts, however, did little to conceal the ever-present fear among the clergy that things might get out of control. There was indeed a fine line between acceptable emotional responses ("true religious affections") and unacceptable enthusiasm ("animal passions"). For the clergy, that line was crossed when new converts went about relating their experiences without the guiding presence of mature Christians or the pastor. At every turn, the New Divinity checked belief and behavior. For Asahel Nettleton, the Holy Spirit revealed New Divinity truths when the convicted retreated privately to the closet. Charles Backus, who knew only too well the effects of unchecked enthusiasm from the toll the Great Awakening had taken on his Somers congregation, believed that new converts should only talk about their conversion experiences to "their teachers, and other Christian friends."[137] He invoked the name of Edwards, who in his "Humble Inquiry"

134. On the central role of taverns in the early republic, see Larkin, *Everyday Life*, 28.

135. On female religious associations, see Cott, *Bonds of Womanhood*, 142–59.

136. The clergy differed in evaluating the accuracy of their own reports on revivals. Griffin claimed that he took "special care . . . not to paint an ideal image of what ought to be, but scrupulously to delineate the views and exercises which they [converts] have really expressed" (*CEM* 1 [December 1800]: 223). Asahel Hooker expressed less objectivity in admitting that "I may, in some measure, have mistaken my own feelings, for facts, so as thence to have represented the work, rather as what I wish to have it, than as what it would appear, to an impartial observer." He claimed, however, to have "no consciousness" of doing so (*CEM* 1 [March 1801]: 346). For the mean between these accounts, see the anonymous clerical report in *CEM* 2 (August 1801): 66.

137. Backus, *Scripture Doctrine of Regeneration*, 170n; see also Nathanael Emmons, "Autobiography," in *The Works of Nathanael Emmons, D.D.*, ed. Jacob Ide (Boston, 1842), 1:liv, and Luther Hart, "A Sermon, delivered . . . Jan. 22, 1826, at the Funeral of Reverend Alexander Gillett . . ." (New Haven, Conn., 1826), 38. Apparently older New Divinity men like Backus and Gillett, who had had their fill

counseled new converts to speak privately "to proper persons and on proper occasion, with modesty and discretion."[138]

Fearing that his own private life might be held under the scrutiny of a tactless public, Ebenezer Porter destroyed his diary in the early years of his ministry.[139] And yet to Porter, a potentially more damaging matter than the exposure of his own life was the proliferation of the private writings of females in the religious periodicals of the 1820s. Porter judged that "a false taste prevails . . . to a tedious excess."[140] Too much was told, and too much could be easily misconstrued without the proper interpretive authorities. This fear that the female imagination might run wild applied not only to narratives of religious experience but generally to anything that carried the passions out of the realm of "real" life. At the funeral of the pious "Mrs. Storrs," Backus assured his audience that she "did not spend her time reading books, which copy from the imagination rather than real life. . . . She read the Holy Scriptures."[141] By "books" Backus meant novels—the *bête noire* of the clergy. According to Evangelicals, the reading of novels not only wasted time (there was nothing "useful" about it) but, worse, degenerated the mind by playing on the imagination. In novels, chance and free will challenged the verities of Calvinism—God's sovereignty and moral determinism. Moreover, novel-reading was a private exercise removed from the purview of the clergy. The "vain imaginings" contained in novels—that is, sentiment, adventure, horror, and the like—undermined the normal structures of clerical authority by playing directly on the imagination. Novels, then, threatened clerically construed religious life in two ways: first, they challenged New Divinity dogma; and second, the very medium encouraged private interpretation. In a broad sense novels contributed to the much clerically feared "democratization of mind" in the early Republic.[142]

In all conversion experiences, whether male or female, the central issue was the submission of an obdurate heart to the claims of a holy God. Females, however, were engrossed with it. One historian observes that "the typical nineteenth-century woman convert was much more concerned with rebellious

---

of unbridled enthusiasm from the Great Awakening, expressed greater fear of new converts spreading word of their conversion experiences than did their younger colleagues. However, the issue was revisited in the 1820s when Finney permitted converts to share openly their conversion experiences.

138. Quoted in Backus, *Scripture Doctrine of Regeneration*, 169n.

139. Lyman Matthews, *Memoir of the Life and Character of Ebenezer Porter, D.D.* (Boston, 1837), 157.

140. Ibid., 159.

141. Charles Backus, "The True Christian Living and Dying unto the Lord: A sermon, delivered . . . January 31, 1798, at the funeral of Mrs. Sarah Storrs . . ." (Springfield, Mass., 1798), 13.

142. Cathy N. Davidson, *Revolution and Word: The Rise of the Novel in America* (New York, 1986), 43. My comments on the novel are indebted to Davidson, pp. 14, 42–43, 73, 114, and to William J. Gilmore, *Reading Becomes a Necessity of Life: Material and Cultural Life in Rural New England, 1780–1835* (Knoxville, Tenn., 1989), 39–40.

desires than her ancestors, for whom this had been only one among many sinful impulses."[143] The vocabulary in women's conversion accounts was filled with such terms as "subdue," "bow," "resignation," "throw down weapons," "yield," "lay down," "unconditional submission," and "rebellion."[144] "Rosetta's" conversion account typified female descriptions, as she progressed from an attitude of indifference to a conviction of guilt, and then to a posture of submission as the culmination of her religious experience:

> How blind I have been to all that is beautiful and glorious! How deaf to the voice of the charmer, who so affectionately proclaimed love and good will to the souls of perishing sinners! . . . I shall never forget the memorable time, when God impressed upon my heart such a deep sense of the greatness of my sins, and of his dreadful wrath, as revealed from heaven against all ungodliness. How like a criminal I then felt. Guilty, self-condemned, my mouth was stopped, and I had nothing to say for myself. Language can but feebly describe the anguish of my soul, till, at length, my mind was in the most surprising manner brought to submit to God; and suddenly impressed with a delightful view of his great goodness and forgiving mercy, through the Lord Jesus. . . . O! How vile I felt before God, as a sinner dreadfully guilty, and unworthy of notice! And yet, I felt unspeakably happy in praising him, as an holy and righteous God. The sorrows of repentance were sweetly mingled in the cup of the most refreshing joys.[145]

A corollary to submissiveness was purity, for through the act of submission the soul was cleansed. Both males and females expressed this desire, but like the act of submission, becoming pure had female connotations. Paradoxically, men portrayed women as naturally pure, whereas women were more apt to portray themselves as naturally polluted. Because the standard of purity was so high, women recognized how far they fell below it. Once attained, purity signaled both salvation and the appeasement of a wrathful, holy God. During and after conversion, females were struck with their "pollution of . . . heart," "awful sense of sin," "black ingratitude," and "wicked" and "dreadful" hearts.[146] Following regeneration, "the divine law appeared in all its purity" and

143. Barbara L. Epstein, The Politics of Domesticity: Women, Evangelism, and Temperance in Nineteenth-Century America (Middletown, Conn., 1981), 47; see also Brereton, Sin to Salvation, 38.

144. CEM 2 (March 1802): 338–40; CEM 3 (September 1802): 102–4; CEM 7 (March 1807): 341–42; Wisner, Memoir of Huntington, 40, 63.

145. CEM 3 (August 1802): 70–71.

146. CEM 7 (August 1806): 61; Morris, "Revival of Religion in South Farms," SML; CEM 1 (February 1801): 308; CEM 1 (November 1800): 187; [Zephaniah Moore Humphrey], Memorial Sketches: Heman Humphrey, Sophia Porter Humphrey (Philadelphia, 1869), 190–91.

magnified the distance between a righteous God and sin-prone humans.[147] The converted now realized that God "had a right to do what he would with his own."[148] There was no rest for the fainthearted, for repeated self-scrutiny was necessary to cleanse and recleanse the impure heart.

The intensity of women's conversion narratives reveals an ontological component that men's lacked. The depth of a woman's being was transformed in a way that a man's was not—or could not be—transformed because of cultural prescriptions. A rhetoric of intimacy enabled women to articulate their experiences in ways that men would find objectionable. One woman professed to Jesus that "upon the bended knees of my soul . . . I do hereby join myself to thee. . . . I do solemnly engage myself to thee."[149] Another wrote that in the midst of her conversion, "Tears flowed without control. The language of my heart was, O my dear Saviour, come, and take everlasting possession of my soul. . . . My emotions were so great, that I found it difficult to keep myself from immediately kneeling upon the floor and extending my arms where I then was in the meetinghouse."[150]

The power of their conversion experiences enabled women to apprehend God according to the New Divinity scheme. The heart delighted in God's glory, goodness, mercy, law, and love.[151] Though plagued with recurring doubts and guilt, women overcame anxiety through mutual encouragement at conference meetings and private sessions with a "spiritual guide"—frequently their pastor.[152]

Of the four groups of converts in Connecticut's Second Great Awakening, women were the most profoundly affected. They were the most numerous. And in their numerical strength, they reinforced an emerging cultural consensus that "the female breast is the natural soil of Christianity."[153] In terms of advancing their social status, the revivals accelerated the evangelical conception of women's moral authority and provided independence within the woman's domain.[154] But what the revivals gave they took away. In terms of impeding women's social status, the revivals lent support to the cult of domesticity—the confinement of women's authority to the home. And yet within these shifting and ambiguous conditions, women made the most significant contribution to the proliferation of revival. Their conversion had

147. *CEM* 7 (May 1807): 342.
148. *CEM* 6 (May 1806): 431; see also *CEM* 1 (July 1800): 34, and *CEM* 2 (August 1801): 61.
149. *CEM* 6 (November 1805): 185–87.
150. *CEM* 6 (May 1806): 431. The psychosexual allusions in both male and female vocabularies are unmistakable. For an extended discussion of this language and its behavioral implications, see Greven, *Protestant Temperament*, 124–48.
151. *CEM* 1 (February 1801): 308; *CEM* 3 (September 1802): 107; *CEM* 7 (March 1807): 342.
152. *CEM* 6 (November 1805): 188.
153. Benjamin Rush quoted by Ann D. Gordon, "The Young Ladies Academy of Philadelphia," in *Women of America: A History*, ed. Mary Beth Norton and Carol Ruth Berkin (Boston, 1979), 74.
154. Bloch, "American Feminist Ideals," 120.

a multiplier effect: as the maternal trustees for the spiritual nurture and conversion of their children, they assured the transmission of revival to succeeding generations.

In narrating the divine workings of God in the soul, the New Divinity reflected Edwards's formulations—just as their theology featured the main contours of his thought. "The Faithful Narrative" was to New Divinity piety what the *Freedom of the Will* was to New Divinity theology: a fundamental text. Moreover, other works of Edwards comprised the New Divinity canon of devotionalism: *The Religious Affections*, "Distinguishing Marks," and "A Humble Inquiry." At every turn, the long shadow of Edwards cast itself over New Divinity revivalism. From Edwards's corpus the New Divinity appropriated (although not exclusively) a vocabulary to describe the phenomena of general revival and individual conversion. Edwards's writings so seeped into the New Divinity consciousness that in recounting the events leading up to the Second Great Awakening, in describing the type of preaching most likely to trigger revival, and in delineating the qualifications of laypersons fit to lead revival, the New Divinity men manifested their debt. There was a remarkable continuity—and the New Divinity would happily own up to the accusation of plagiarism—between Edwards's descriptions of the morphology of conversion and New Divinity narratives.

Another emphasis in Edwards seized upon by the New Divinity was the distance separating God from humanity. This distance is what Bennet Tyler alluded to in noting that converts of the New Divinity revivals were "not made the easy way." To truly recognize the vast metaphysical void separating God from man involved becoming overcome with guilt, acknowledging that God could do with one as he wished, expressing an eternal indebtedness to God, but also rising up in resentment against him—all of these involved following the Edwardsean path to conversion. It hadn't been easy for Edwards, it wasn't easy for New Divinity men, and it wasn't meant to be easy for converts of New Divinity revivalism.

At the same time, however, New Divinity piety diverged from Edwards's scheme. In its attention to "usefulness," which implied an emphasis on ends, practical benefits, and time; in its differentiation of conversion narratives by gender; in its preoccupation with decorum, control, and silence; in its lack of an aesthetic (a dimension not completely missing, but not as prominent as in Edwards)—in these ways the New Divinity leaders charted a different path.

It was also a restricted path, guided generally, but not entirely, by New Divinity dogma. Conversion narratives, devotional practices, and expressions of piety were all intended to express New Divinity theological convictions. The perception of "selflessness" or "disinterested benevolence," for example, reflected a certain doctrinal understanding of God and the will. At the same time, those theological boundaries were not entirely static or uniquely New Divinity. There was a certain elasticity in expressions of piety and activity, articulated and evidenced within the broad Anglo-American evangelical tradition. As crabbed and contentious as the New Divinity men appeared at times, they never withdrew into their own exclusive sect; rather, they envisioned themselves as part of a transatlantic evangelical movement. How else to explain the proliferation of British authors and articles about British missionary movements in the *Connecticut Evangelical Magazine*? Or, how else to explain the New Divinity compilation *Hartford Selection of Hymns* (1799) and Asahel Nettleton's *Village Hymns* (1824)—two works that drew extensively from the British evangelical tradition? As dismayed as Nettleton was with the theology of Nathaniel Taylor, a fellow Calvinist, he selected some of the hymns of Charles Wesley, an Arminian, for inclusion in his hymnal. Of course, there were limits: explicit Arminianism would never appear in these hymnals; nevertheless, there was an acknowledged kinship between the New Divinity and the broader evangelical tradition. Thus, by the mid-1820s, when the New Divinity declined in the face of competing evangelical theologies, its devotional practices merged comfortably with a generic evangelical piety.

CONCLUSION

"TO WAIT GOD'S TIME IS NOT TO WAIT AT ALL"

The Passing of New Divinity Revivalism

In the first pages of this study, Edward Dorr Griffin proclaimed the year 1792 the *annus mirabilis*. In that year, several earth-shattering events coalesced to mark a turning point in the history of Christianity: the French Revolution turned into an ugly, bloody affair engulfing Europe; the modern foreign missionary movement was launched in England; and a new era of revivalism—a "second" Great Awakening—was inaugurated in New England. That Awakening was initiated by the energetic efforts of New Divinity clergy who united to stem the tide of infidelity, to revive their slumbering congregations, and to purify their churches through heartfelt evangelical preaching. They initiated, guided, sustained, and interpreted the spiritual reawakening in northwestern Connecticut. The revival, as I have argued throughout this work, was primarily a clerical event. But it was clearly more than that, for hundreds of people were saved as a result of New Divinity preaching.

Some of the results from the Awakening were obvious. New converts testified to changed lives—even dramatically changed lives. Church membership rolls bulged; by all accounts, the revivals stimulated a heightened concern for Sabbath observance, for moral probity, and for Christian zeal and charity. Beginning in the church, the home, or the school, the revival engulfed families and then whole communities, so that the revival was not merely the sum total of its converts but a communal event.[1] From the local revival, supporters of the Awakening soon extrapolated the possibility of a national revival and even the dawn of the millennium. For some young men, the revival offered the opportunity to participate fully in that national revival. Seeking to follow the "still, small voice" wherever it might lead—which typically led away from toil on the family farm—they enlisted as ministers, missionaries, or reformers in the grand goal of Christianizing not only the nation but the world.

Other results from the revival, however, were less obvious. Behind the momentous events of 1792, a Griffin-led revival claimed three women as converts: his mother, his sister, and his sister-in-law. A decade later, the first fruits of the New Divinity revival displayed this female inclination toward revivalist religion. There is a certain irony in the fact that in a man's world, eye-catching events in the public arena ushered in a new era, whereas events of a private, less stupendous nature—the predominant conversion of females in the revivals—were mentioned but went unheralded.

Other incongruities emerge. The New Divinity ministers of Litchfield and Hartford counties formed a "united brotherhood" for the promotion of revival, the legacy of which contributed to a growing consciousness of "sisterhood" among females. Again, the New Divinity men constructed a theology for their times built upon the Edwardsean balance between the head and the heart, between the faculties of the mind and the affections of the heart. Yet the balance tipped—no, plunged—toward the heart. By the early decades of the nineteenth century, the affections had become so laden with feminine connotations that the seeds of a sentimentalized Protestantism were firmly planted and then grew and blossomed throughout the century.[2]

From these unintended consequences how does one explain the intended result of New Divinity revivals: an era of crusading Protestantism, of "righteous empire" building, of millennial expectations?[3] Is there not an incongruity between female sentiment and affections and displays of male righteousness? Did these two expressions of evangelical Protestantism go their separate ways of gender, each untouched by the other? Yes and no. Yes, American religion became, in a sense, both more feminine and more

1. On the New England revival as a community event, see Michael J. Crawford, *Seasons of Grace: Colonial New England's Revival Tradition in Its British Context* (New York, 1991), 242–47, and Richard Carwardine, *Transatlantic Revivalism: Popular Evangelicalism in Britain and America, 1790–1865* (Westport, Conn., 1978), 25–26.

2. See Ann Douglas, *The Feminization of American Culture* (New York, 1977). From my statements that follow, it should be clear that I do not concur with Douglas's thesis that American religion became one-sidedly feminized in the nineteenth century. For a critical review of Douglas, see David Schuyler, "Inventing a Feminist Past," *New England Quarterly* 51 (September 1978): 291–308.

3. The term is from Martin E. Marty, *Righteous Empire: The Protestant Experience in America* (New York, 1970).

masculine; within nineteenth-century American Protestantism neither a feminine nor a masculine sexual stereotype predominated. Evangelical men came to embrace a "muscular" Christianity, while evangelical women adopted nurturing, supportive roles.[4] And no, the two gendered ways of being Christian did not necessarily go their separate ways; they complemented each other. The masculine religious image required the female image. The supposedly innate female virtues of dependence and submission were psychologically and spiritually necessary for males bent on ushering in the millennium. Herein lay the paradox of the Christian faith, though stretched to its limits: in weakness there is strength. Without the female image of frailty, submission, and dependence, there could not be the male image of strength, dominance, and independence. In the realm of politics, Linda Kerber observed "the direct relationship between the developing egalitarian democracy among men and the expectations of continued deferential behavior among women."[5] So too, in the realm of religion, an analogous relationship existed between evangelical men and women: a developing righteous empire among men rested upon the exemplary moral mother. The republican mother and the evangelical mother, then, were twin images supported by the same ideology, whether expressed in political or religious rhetoric. Some evangelical women chafed under such constraints and were unwilling to accept what men offered them: limited participation in the benevolent empire. They desired more of the supposed male image for themselves, convinced that such an image was not innate but culturally dictated. Out of these discontented few arose the feminist movement of the antebellum period.[6] Most pious women, however, accepted and even embraced their culturally restricted role, and they gained a measure of satisfaction in knowing that they were contributing to the extension of the faith. From these emerged an "apostolate of women"—teachers and missionaries—who, far more than political feminists, captured the hearts and minds of evangelical women.[7] During the early decades of the nineteenth century, an evolving role hardened into a static one: it was assumed that the cultural differences between males and females were "inherent." It only remained for the economic and political changes associated with the emergence of industrial capitalism, and in

4. See David S. Reynolds, "The Feminization Controversy: Sexual Stereotypes and the Paradoxes of Piety in Nineteenth Century America," *New England Quarterly* 53 (March 1980): 96–106.

5. Linda K. Kerber, *Women of the Republic: Intellect and Ideology in Revolutionary America* (Chapel Hill, N.C., 1980), 285. In a similar vein, Edmund S. Morgan has demonstrated the direct connection between a society dependent upon the economics of slavery and its formulation of an ideology of independence from Great Britain. See *American Slavery, American Freedom: The Ordeal of Colonial Virginia* (New York, 1975), 376, 380–87.

6. See Nancy A. Hardesty, *Women Called to Witness: Evangelical Feminism in the Nineteenth Century* (Nashville, Tenn., 1984).

7. Joan Jacobs Brumberg, *Mission for Life: The Story of the Family of Adoniram Judson* (New York, 1980), 82.

particular the separation of the home from the marketplace, to fill in the details of the Victorian social construction of reality.[8]

The decade of the 1820s marked the end of New Divinity popularity and theological hegemony in New England. By the mid-1820s, in northwestern Connecticut—the area with the highest New Divinity concentration—nearly all of the New Divinity men who had been on the scene in 1800 had either died, retired, or relocated. Charles Backus died in 1803, Ammi Robbins a decade later, and Nathan Strong in 1816. Three New Divinity stalwarts— Abel Flint, Alexander Gillett, and Jeremiah Hallock—died in 1826, and Peter Starr followed a few years later. Both Samuel Mills and Nathan Perkins lived through the 1820s, but as feeble octogenarians. Asahel Nettleton retired from the itinerant circuit in 1822. Moreover, during the same decade, four of the best and brightest third-generation New Divinity men had moved on and up to assume college or seminary presidencies: Griffin at Williams (1822–36), Humphrey at Amherst (1823–55), Porter at Andover (1828–32), and Tyler at Dartmouth (1822–28).

In the past, a full stable of young New Divinity men more than exceeded the rate of attrition. Reflecting upon the death of Joseph Bellamy in 1790 and the declining health of Samuel Hopkins and Stephen West, Ezra Stiles observed that a "younger class," who all "want to be Luthers," was vying among themselves to assume the New Divinity mantle of leadership.[9] By the 1820s, however, few stood ready to carry on the New Divinity theological tradition. At root was the inability of the third-generation New Divinity men to capture the imagination of the rising generation. As Allen Guelzo has emphasized, the third-generation New Divinity men were generally derivative thinkers who restated but could not reimagine Edwards's thought.[10] Bennet Tyler, Edward Dorr Griffin, Asahel Nettleton, and Leonard Woods (a student of Charles Backus's parlor seminary and a professor at Andover Theological Seminary) remained staunch defenders of the New Divinity, but they added little to the constructive efforts of Hopkins or Bellamy. What had once been the grist for young clerical aspirants had now become passé. What was once a movement of a significant number of disaffected young men was now the rearguard action of a few older stalwart defenders. In short, the New Divinity no longer appeared new and compelling. The climate of opinion, buoyed with increasing optimism about human capability and an enlightened (or Arminian) view of God as a loving father, judged that New Divinity explanations for human nature, human agency, and divine sovereignty no

8. See James Davison Hunter, *Evangelicalism: The Coming Generation* (Chicago, 1987), chap. 4.
9. Ezra Stiles, *The Literary Diary of Ezra Stiles*, ed. Franklin B. Dexter (New York, 1901), 3:274.
10. Allen C. Guelzo, *Edwards on the Will: A Century of American Theological Debate* (Middletown, Conn., 1989), 217–18.

longer comported with more plausible "common sense" interpretations. In this context, some New Divinity men—or at least earlier adherents of New Divinity theology—caved in under the avalanche of the philosophy of Common Sense Realism. Both Lyman Beecher and Timothy Dwight gave lip service to New Divinity views early in their careers, but both later abandoned Edwards's view of the will for the verities of Common-Sense philosophy.[11] All people intuitively knew, they and an increasing number of Evangelicals contended, that people were endowed with and indeed exercised a free will.

Beyond the crisis in leadership and the evanescence of New Divinity theology, other forces were at work in American society that undermined the vitality of the New Divinity movement. The professionalization of the ministry virtually halted the traditional New Divinity clerical education in schools of the prophets. Asahel Hooker, the last of the New Divinity "prophets" to open a home seminary, left Goshen in 1810. Institutional seminaries (Andover in 1808, Yale in 1822) replaced the informal, decentralized, and highly effective New Divinity mentoring process. With the advent of the seminary and the concomitant rise in theological scholarship, theological knowledge was now concentrated in the hands of a few, and a clerical aspirant's choices for a theological education were now greatly reduced. While seminaries provided a sense of professional legitimation, they also reorganized the dissemination of knowledge. Of course, had New Divinity men captured theological posts at Yale Divinity School, or had they maintained a strong presence at Andover Seminary, the results might have been different—but probably not much different. The appointment of Nathaniel W. Taylor to the influential position of professor of theology at Yale was more a symptom of than a cause for the passing of the New Divinity theology. Just as generic Calvinism in America was subjected to intense scrutiny and eventual rejection, so too and even more so was its New Divinity species.[12] By the end of the 1820s, the New Divinity as a popular theology was moribund.

Thus, the primary reason for the waning of New Divinity revivalism was its loss of popular appeal. Although this study has been restricted to Congregationalists in northwestern Connecticut, and although this region remained the most homogeneously religious in Connecticut, by the 1820s other Protestant groups, especially Methodists and Baptists, were making their presence felt, and indeed, their rapid growth marked the beginning of another chapter in Connecticut's Second Great Awakening.

11. Conrad Cherry, "Nature and the Republic: The New Haven Theology," *New England Quarterly* 51 (December 1978): 509–26; Guelzo, *Edwards on the Will*, 221–39; Richard Rabinowitz, *The Spiritual Self in Everyday Life: The Transformation of Personal Religious Experience in Nineteenth-Century New England* (Boston, 1989), 87–89.

12. For the demise of Calvinism in America, see Daniel Walker Howe, "The Decline of Calvinism: An Approach to Its Study," *Comparative Studies in Society and History* 14 (June 1972): 306–27.

As early as 1789, Jesse Lee began itinerating in New England. Although there were no Methodist churches in Connecticut in 1790, from that decade on, Methodist itinerants such as Lee, Francis Asbury, Richard Whatcoat, Freeborn Garrettson, Lorenzo Dow, Heman Bangs, Billy Hibbard, and others crisscrossed the state, stirred up revival, and encountered hostility and even violence from Congregationalists and Baptists. Methodist itinerants dreaded the Litchfield circuit—a form of exile that tested the most devoted elder. Not until 1827—after a generation of itinerating—did Methodists build their first church west of the Connecticut River.[13] While on tour in Litchfield County, Hibbard reported having stones hurled at him and dogs loosed upon him.[14] He also noted that the Methodists triggered much of the revival activity in Connecticut, sounding a typical Methodist refrain: "The Methodists shake the bush, and the Presbyterians [Congregationalists] and Baptists catch the birds."[15]

The initial centers of Methodist strength were located in the southern portion of the state, adjacent to the Long Island Sound, and in the eastern counties of Windham, Tolland, and New London.[16] Samuel Goodrich, the author of the popular *Peter Parley's Tales* and son of the Congregational minister in Ridgefield (Fairfield County), recalled that his father, after losing several parishioners to the Methodists, imitated their tactics. In the early nineteenth century, the Rev. Goodrich "adopted evening meetings, first at the church, and afterward at private homes. No doubt also, he put more fervor into his Sabbath discourses." Moreover, "deacons and laymen . . . were called upon to pray and exhort, and tell experiences in the private meetings, which are now called *conferences*." "Thus," concluded Goodrich, "orthodoxy was in considerable degree methodized, and Methodism in due time became orthodoxed."[17] In retrospect, the Methodists were "destined to sweep over the State," for they captured the popular imagination with their camp meetings, love feasts, singing, spirit of fellowship, and religious enthusiasm.[18] To survive the competition, Congregationalists followed their lead. As Goodrich would have it, lay involvement, prayer meetings, and religious conferences were little more than mirror reactions to the menacing Methodists. Perhaps he was right—at least for Ridgefield and other areas where Methodists made

13. Heman Bangs, *The Autobiography and Journal of Rev. Heman Bangs, with an Introduction by Rev. Bishop Janes, D.D.* (New York, 1872), 302.

14. Billy Hibbard, *Memoirs of the Life and travels of B. Hibbard*, 2d ed. (New York, 1843), 175; see also Bangs, *Autobiography*, 135.

15. Hibbard, *Memoirs*, 183; see also Bangs, *Autobiography*, 68.

16. On the general progress of the Methodists, see Francis Asbury, *The Journal and Letters of Francis Asbury*, ed. Elmer T. Clark (Nashville, Tenn., 1958), 2: passim; Richard J. Purcell, *Connecticut in Transition, 1775–1818* (Washington, D.C., 1918), 54–59; and Charles R. Keller, *The Second Great Awakening in Connecticut* (New Haven, Conn., 1942), 197–201.

17. Samuel G. Goodrich, *Recollections of a Lifetime* (New York, 1857), 1:217.

18. Goodrich, *Recollections* 1:189.

inroads beginning in the late 1790s. But as I have shown, Congregationalism had a long tradition of lay activity, expressed in visitations, prayer meetings, and conferences. Beginning with dissenting English Puritanism in the sixteenth century and extending through the Great Awakening in America, these religious forms were as much a part of the English Reformed tradition in America as they were of the newer Methodist movement. Thus, New Divinity ministers in northwestern Connecticut borrowed not from Methodists but from their own long-standing forms of piety and renewal.[19] Where they failed and where Methodists succeeded was in a style of religiosity that appealed to the masses, for Methodists offered their auditors a homespun, simple, evocative, reassuring message having less to do with the sovereign plans of God and more to do with the free decisions of humans.

Methodists also enlarged the place of the emotions. The paradigmatic biblical text for Methodists was Acts 2, where hundreds were added to the newly created church by the outpouring of the Holy Spirit. The spirit-filled Christians spoke in different tongues; they prophesied, had visions, dreamed dreams, shared meals, and went about praising God. How removed New Divinity revivals were from this scene of Holy Spirit ecstasy—a scene contemporary Methodists duplicated time after time. For the New Divinity, God's revelation was made "full" and "clear" by the end of the apostolic age. Dreams were either "extremely unimportant" or were the medium by which "evil spirits practice the arts of seduction, impressing the imagination."[20] God encountered humans in their solitude with his rational sovereign designs. "Be still and know that I am God" (Psalms 46:10) epitomized the consummate New Divinity proof-text. The New Divinity way to salvation required that the solitary individual, in abasement, acknowledge a great and sovereign God. Hymn singing, communal sharing and prayer—these were a prelude, not the centerpiece, to the work of the "still, small voice" of the Spirit. God was known (or made himself known) in silence, in the closet at home, in sober and subdued Sunday worship, in the quiet of the field, in the hush of the schoolhouse. In Farmington, the 1795 revival under Joseph Washburn was "noiseless"; in New Hartford, the 1798 outpouring was "as still almost as a burying ground"; over twenty years later, during an 1821 revival under Asahel Nettleton, "there was no commotion; but a stillness."[21]

The culminating expressions of conversion voiced by two young men of Litchfield County, both of whom acquired fame as indefatigable leaders of missions, illustrate the accent in New Divinity conversion. In the 1798

19. On eastern Calvinists adopting Methodist revival tactics, see Carwardine, *Transatlantic Revivalism*, 14–17, who names the 1820s a critical decade for this occurrence, especially in urban areas.
20. *CEM* 2 (September 1801): 97, 98; *CEM* (April 1801): 397.
21. William B. Sprague, *Lectures on Revivals of Religion*, 2d ed. (New York, 1833), 290, 293 (appendix); Edward Dorr Griffin, "Letter on religious revival in about forty adjacent parishes" (copy), 1 August 1799, Main Vault, CSL.

revivals, Samuel J. Mills, Jr., the son of Torrington's beloved pastor, and who became the recognized "father of the foreign missionary movement in the United States," found relief when God's sovereignty appeared so "holy and amiable" that he exclaimed, "O glorious sovereignty!"[22] A decade later, eighteen-year-old John Mason Peck, who became the famous Baptist home missionary in the Midwest, expressed his newfound hope in similar terms: "The character of God, his law, his providences, and the plan of grace as far as I understood it, appeared glorious and excellent."[23]

Methodists shifted this emphasis from the sovereign electing decrees of God to Jesus' free offer of salvation to all, from a distant God encountered in singular stillness to a personal Jesus encountered in communal ecstasy and emotion. The phenomenal growth of Methodism confirms Henry May's judgment that at the center of political and religious change in the first years of the nineteenth century, "the real movement was taking place in the realm of feeling."[24] Not only did the Methodists offer a more emotionally satisfying religion, but they eventually won the race for converts. The only New Divinity man who could match the tireless energy of the dozens of Methodist itinerants in Connecticut was, of course, Asahel Nettleton, whose health failed him after a decade of evangelism. While the fortunes of the Congregationalists declined, those of the Methodists rose. From 1790 to 1818, when the Congregational Standing Order was disestablished, the number of Methodist churches in Litchfield and Hartford counties had grown from zero to fifteen.[25] In 1831, Methodists founded Wesleyan University in Middletown—a hint that Methodism was well established, that it had become "orthodoxed." From 1800 to 1850, the Methodists in New England increased eighteenfold. By midcentury they were the second largest denomination in New England, the fastest growing religious group in New England, and the largest Protestant denomination in the United States.[26]

Baptist gains were less stupendous than Methodist, but nonetheless significant. Statewide, the fifty-nine churches and 4,600 members in 1800 increased to eighty-three churches and 9,200 members by 1830. By 1818, sixteen Baptist churches competed with other religious groups in Hartford and Litchfield counties.[27] Baptists, of course, had an established presence in eastern Connecticut dating back to Separatists of the Great Awakening who joined the Baptist camp. Their democratic polity, itinerating practices, demands for a regenerate membership, and lack of a learned ministry

22. Quoted in Thomas C. Richards, *Samuel J. Mills: Missionary Pathfinder, Pioneer and Promoter* (Boston, 1906), 14, 15.
23. John Mason Peck, *Forty Years of Pioneer Life: Memoir of John Mason Peck, D.D.*, ed. Rufus Babcock; introd. Paul M. Harrison (Carbondale, Ill., 1965), 17.
24. Henry F. May, *The Enlightenment in America* (New York, 1976), 308.
25. Purcell, *Connecticut in Transition*, 65 (map).
26. Abel Stevens, *A Compendious History of American Methodism* (New York, n.d.), 468.
27. Purcell, *Connecticut in Transition*, 46–54, 65 (map); Keller, *Second Great Awakening*, 194–97.

enhanced their popular appeal. There is some evidence that Baptists, like Methodists, not only shared in the early revivals of the Awakening but even triggered them. According to one Baptist source, Nathan Strong attributed the outbreak of the 1798 revival in his Hartford First Church to the initial stirrings among Hartford Baptists.[28] Moreover, Strong and the Calvinist Baptist pastor, Stephen Nelson, cooperated in the revival, held a united prayer meeting, and agreed to divide the spoils of the revival according to the congregation in which the people were awakened.[29] This incident not only testifies to the Baptists' appeal, but it also indicates Strong's willingness to recognize a common evangelical tradition. He also welcomed Francis Asbury into his pulpit—probably more to demonstrate to Asbury that Methodists would have little success than to extend an evangelical olive branch.[30]

In Litchfield County—the very den of New Divinity strength— Congregational growth was threatened by Baptists. In the throes of the 1798–99 New Divinity revivals, Burlington Baptists experienced "many additions,"[31] while only a few miles to the north in New Hartford, Edward Dorr Griffin's preaching was not enough to dissuade twelve members of his church from joining the Baptists in the years between 1797 and 1801.[32] In Bristol, Giles Cowles felt so threatened when a Baptist society was organized in December 1798 that he immediately delivered two sermons (subsequently published) defending the practice of infant baptism.[33]

Indicative of the Baptist appeal as well as of the general drift toward the democratization of American Christianity in the late eighteenth and early nineteenth centuries is the story of John Mason Peck. Born into a poor farming family in Litchfield South Farms in 1789, Peck converted to the New Divinity way in 1807 after attending a conference meeting out of curiosity. Sarah Paine converted during the same revivals and shortly thereafter, in 1808, joined Dan Huntington's Congregational church. John Peck and Sarah Paine married that same year, and soon they had a child—and a problem. Whereas Sarah had doubts about the scriptural evidence for infant baptism,

28. See Robert Turnbull, *Memorials of the First Baptist Church, Hartford, Conn., with sketches of its deceased pastors* (Hartford, Conn., 1857), 12–13. Strong makes no mention of Baptist influence in his account of the revival; see Nathan Strong to Jedidiah Morse, 21 February 1799, Morse Family Papers, SML.

29. Turnbull, *Memorials of the First Baptist Church*, 13.

30. Parsons Cooke, *A Century of Puritanism and a Century of its Opposites* (Boston, 1855), 228–29. While Methodists claimed that Congregationalists exploited their own revivalist successes by claiming their converts for themselves, Cooke claimed that Methodists made their biggest gains by stealing Christians from other denominations (280). And so went the acrimony between the upstarts and the establishment.

31. Connecticut Congregational Churches (Burlington), CLH.

32. "Those lost to Baptists," New Hartford Churches Records, CSL.

33. *History of Ashtabula County, Ohio, with Illustrations and Biographical Sketches of its Pioneers and Most Prominent Men* (Philadelphia, 1878), 94; see also Farmington Seventh Day Baptist Church Connecticut. Formerly Bristol, Burlington. Church Book, 1780–1820, Seventh Day Baptist Materials (microfilm-reel 1, no. 9), HC, SBC.

John believed there was enough evidence in Scripture to infer its validity. In 1809–10, the new parents conferred with the Rev. Lyman Beecher, Huntington's recent replacement. According to John, Beecher's attempts to offer clear-cut scriptural evidence for pedobaptism were unsatisfying. While leaning in a Baptist direction, in the spring of 1811 the Pecks moved 125 miles northwest to Windham (Green County), New York. There they encountered Baptists and Presbyterians competing for adherents. Prior to their arrival, in a scene repeated hundreds of times on the frontier, parties from both sides met and debated the merits of their respective positions on baptism. The final arbiter of the truth for the Pecks: sola scriptura. After "a year's careful investigation" of the matter, the Pecks affirmed the Baptist position, submitted to rebaptism (or, to them, their first legitimate baptism) in September of 1811, and joined the fellowship of a small Baptist church. Without a college education, John was ordained into Baptist ministry in 1813 and devoted his life to missionary service in the Midwest. Throughout his career Peck maintained the Calvinism of his youth—he saw the providence of God behind every event—but not of the distinct New Divinity variety.[34]

These examples and statistics demonstrating Methodist and Baptist gains over against Congregational losses reveal that the Awakening in northwestern Connecticut was not strictly a New Divinity affair but involved the stirrings and strivings of other religious bodies. Still, for a generation, by virtue of their overwhelming influence, the New Divinity men shaped a particular kind of religious response to the preached gospel. As New Englanders tested the meaning of freedom, and amid destabilizing threats from within and without, the New Divinity message of order, rationality, and coherence found an audience.

As early as the second decade of the nineteenth century, however, that unique way of being, becoming, and remaining religious lost its defining character and blended into a more generic form of Protestantism—a broad Evangelicalism. The formation of interdenominational tract, missionary, and benevolent societies attests to the Protestant cooperative endeavors made possible by a disregard for specific theological distinctions. To return to Mills and Peck: these two sons of Litchfield County did not necessarily repudiate their New Divinity roots, but in founding and championing inter- and nondenominational missionary, Bible, and tract societies, they certainly ignored them.

A final reason for the waning of the New Divinity movement was that like other effective protest movements, its very success proved to be its undoing. However much New Divinity men such as Griffin or Nettleton protested the

---

34. Peck, *Memoir of Peck*, 13–23, xvii–xviii.

modern temper of revivalism, they ultimately contributed to its rise.[35] Writing to a British audience in 1832, Calvin Colton noted that there were two kinds of revivals, one where "the instruments are not apparent. . . . They have seemed to come directly from the presence of the Lord, unasked for, unexpected," and another where "the instruments are obvious." The first characterized the revivals of the Great Awakening, whereas the second prevailed since the Second Great Awakening. "It is now getting to be more generally understood," continued Colton, "that to wait God's time in this matter is not to wait at all."[36]

In the Great Awakening, Jonathan Edwards preached in graphic terms what he had experienced. He called the conversions that followed "surprising," and produced a detailed account of the morphology of these conversions.[37] Those he singled out as exemplars of the profound crisis of conversion were females—Phoebe Bartlett, Abigail Hutchinson, and the woman who became his wife, Sarah Pierrepont. Is it any wonder that Edwards's followers assumed that females were more likely to be saved than males? And is it any wonder that in the very act of writing about the conversion experience Edwards tamed it, and in ways he never anticipated, quite literally domesticated it—that is, targeted the sphere of women? As C. C. Goen has so perceptively written, "when [Edwards] gave his narrative to the world, the simple fact is that no revival could ever be a surprise again. His account showed plainly what kind of preaching would awaken sleepy sinners and what sort of responses could be expected."[38] Thus, Griffin and other New Divinity men consciously set out to promote revivals—and, in Colton's phrase, their "instruments were obvious." Despite their aversion to preparationist schemes, New Divinity ministers either explained away or thoroughly obfuscated their objections to the use of means. What their audience heard was a message that exhorted them to exert themselves, and yet to acknowledge that their exertions in no way saved them; to turn immediately from sin, but with no assurances that God's regenerating Spirit would at that moment change their hearts from stone to flesh. The upshot was that the leaders of the revival grew increasingly confident that conversion would follow if only the proper means (but of course not "means" as means of grace!) were employed. As was said of Heman Humphrey, "He would sacrifice nothing to effect; he would make use of effect so

35. On Griffin's opposition to Finney's new measures, see "A Letter to a Friend on the Connexion Between the New Doctrines and the New Measures" (Albany, N.Y., 1833).

36. Calvin Colton, History and Character of American Revivals of Religion (1832, reprint, New York, 1973), 2, 5–6.

37. See "A Faithful Narrative of the Surprising Work of God," in WJE: The Great Awakening, ed. C. C. Goen (New Haven, Conn., 1972), 160–76.

38. Editor's introduction in ibid., 27.

far as it might aid him in promoting the triumph of the Gospel."[39] An emphasis upon means, then, implied technique—a device, perhaps even a gimmick, to induce conversions. Techniques are humanly contrived; they involve human decisions and calculations. In the context of the New Divinity revivals, the use of means ultimately enlarged the role of the human will and diminished the sovereignty of God. No one claimed to be saved progressively, but many claimed that they "found salvation" (which was increasingly heard more often than "God found them") by following along a clerically prescribed path. Such human predictability mitigated divine inscrutability, and so the antecedents to modern revivalism are found in the formative period of the Second Great Awakening in Connecticut.

The perpetuation of revival (both in its form and literature) was not the only legacy of the New Divinity movement. It is no small irony that Edward Dorr Griffin's death in 1837 coincided with the crowning of Queen Victoria in Britain, for many of the values identified with Victorian culture in America were anticipated by the New Divinity men. There is little to dispute in Daniel Howe's statement that "the Victorian era was ushered in during the 1830s by what was probably the greatest evangelical revival in American history," but I would suggest that much of what came to be called "Victorian" can be found in the revivals at the turn of the century.[40] In his illuminating essay, Howe delineates the values that lay at the core of Victorian culture: sobriety, moral seriousness, sexual repressiveness, conscientiousness, compulsiveness, an attention to "duty," rational order, the cult of domesticity, competition, didacticism, and a preoccupation with time.[41] As I have shown, except for lauding the blessings of unchecked competition, the New Divinity promoted all of these "Victorian" values. In addition, "Victorians appealed to the 'heart' as well as the 'head' in their literature, their pedagogy, their preaching, and their politics. In authentic Victorianism . . . however, the emotions always remained complementary and subordinate to rational order."[42] How New Divinity! According to Howe, this emphasis on the heart had its origins in eighteenth-century rhetoricians. True enough, but perhaps a more direct link to Victorian sentiment was the eighteenth-century voluntarist mode of preaching mediated to the nineteenth century through the New Divinity rhetoric of the heart and its accompanying language of sensual spirituality. Indeed, the reference to Griffin as the "prince of preachers" portended the later nineteenth-century phenomenon of pulpit orators.

The life and private writings of Susan Mansfield Huntington disclose the

---

39. [Zephaniah Moore Humphrey], *Memorial Sketches: Heman Humphrey, Sophia Porter Humphrey* (Philadelphia, 1869), 143.

40. Daniel Walker Howe, "Victorian Culture in America," in *Victorian America*, ed. Daniel W. Howe (Philadelphia, 1976), 9.

41. Ibid., 3–28.

42. Ibid., 25.

transit from a narrow New Divinity perspective to a broad evangelical view. Born in 1791, Susan was the daughter of Achilles Mansfield, New Divinity pastor of the Killingworth First Congregational Church. Following her conversion in 1807, she made a public profession of faith and joined her father's church. Catechized by her parents, Susan thoroughly learned the rudiments of New Divinity theology. In one lengthy letter written at age seventeen, she reiterated New Divinity views on the means of grace (there is not "an immediate and inseparable" connection between reading Scriptures, attending worship, and conversion, and yet "those who do not use them will, probably, never be converted") and the will, invoking the authoritative views of Edwards and Andrew Fuller, who "make a distinction between, what they call natural and moral inability to obey the commands of God." She was not merely acquainted with these views but read and commented upon the works of Edwards ("Religious Affections" and "Sermons") and Fuller ("Essays").[43]

Susan's explicit references to New Divinity dogma receded into the background after she married Joshua Huntington in 1809 and moved to Boston, where her husband was junior pastor at Old South Church. She retained her evangelical temperament, but in her posthumous *Memoir*, which consists of letters and journal entries, she never returned to the subject of New Divinity theology. Like Samuel Mills and John Mason Peck, when Susan left her home environs for another part of the country, she also left behind her distinct New Divinity views. One could argue, of course, that New Divinity theology meant little more to her than catechetical instruction means to the disinterested youngster whose parents insist upon it: the theology never takes root and withers as soon as the forced feeding stops. In such cases, what one learns and knows about theology merely reflects clerical and parental indoctrination.

To think that Susan Huntington was disinterested, however, is as inaccurate as it is cynical. Religion consumed her life; in Boston she continued to rhapsodize in Edwardsean language about the beauty and mercy of God and to bemoan her sinful condition.[44] But she was less concerned with a rational apprehension of the faith or the niceties of New Divinity theology—which was, after all, primarily a male enterprise—than with cultivating piety. Huntington's New Divinity 'sensual spirituality' fit comfortably under the rubric of what might be called 'evangelical feeling' or 'evangelical sentiment.' She praised Hannah More's novel, *A Wife for Coelebs*, for its expression of 'religious sentiments'; she chided herself for 'inconstancy of religious feeling'; and she rejoiced for "some feelings of satisfaction at being in the hands of God' during prayer. She had spiritual mood swings where at times she reveled in 'the transcendent excellence

43. Benjamin B. Wisner, *Memoir of the Late Mrs. Susan Huntington, of Boston, Mass.*, 3d ed. (Boston, 1829), 15, 38.
44. For examples, see ibid., 59, 61, 63, 105.

and beauty of holiness,' while at others she groveled in her unworthiness.[45] She feared self-deception, engaged in constant self-examination, and viewed "afflictions' as the chastening hand of God.[46]

When she became a mother, her recorded thoughts centered around her children—their spiritual welfare, education, and her methods of discipline. She embraced fully the cult of domesticity and argued that "woman's sphere" was God ordained. "The moment a woman steps out of her proper sphere," wrote Huntington, "she ceases to be, in proportion to her deviation from the path prescribed her, either amiable or respectable." At the same time she believed women should neither kowtow to men nor shirk from educational opportunities. If women were "taught to view the subject of female subordination in a philosophical and scriptural way," Huntington contended, "they would, not only be much greater helpers and blessings to their husbands and children, but in much less danger of usurping that authority which God and nature have delegated to the other sex."[47] Huntington was, in short, an "enlightened" evangelical woman of the young Republic who retained much of the piety, but little of the New Divinity theology, of her youth.

One sees in Huntington—as well as in Mills and Peck—a pattern: strict New Divinity theology perpetuated itself only in its original environment. In a broad context, this was the environment in which a Calvinism had waxed and sometimes waned for generations, and it was also an environment where people of English stock strenuously cultivated both the soil and their souls. The two are not unrelated. First, Puritanism and then New Divinity Calvinism flourished in a rural environment where the forces of nature remained as inscrutable, as unpredictable, as mysterious, and as beautiful as the God of Calvin, Edwards, Hopkins, and a host of other New Divinity men. Historically, at least since the seventeenth century in America, small farmers and artisans—the very people who resided in Litchfield and Hartford counties— were those most attracted to and most persistent in Calvinism.[48] Once New Divinity Calvinism was removed from its rural home environment and subjected to stiff competition on the frontier (say, from Baptists, Methodists, or Presbyterians) or in the city (say, from Unitarians in Boston or Methodists in Hartford)— its hard edges softened. Or once the environment in which the New Divinity flourished was altered by commercial conditions or the standard of living, New Divinity Calvinism declined. Once the soil no longer exacted a human toll, so New Divinity theology and piety—so characterized by struggle—no longer exacted its toll on the soul. What I am suggesting is neither the complete

45. Ibid., 33, 31, 65, 37.
46. For examples, see ibid., 36–39, 49, 59, 85–88.
47. Ibid., 134.
48. Howe, "Decline of Calvinism," 321. In *Berkshire County: A Cultural History* (New Haven, Conn., 1959), Richard Birdsall makes a similar claim for the New Divinity in western Massachusetts (42).

dissolution of New Divinity theology nor a deterministic theory to explain that dissolution. Rather, I am suggesting that certain changing social, economic, and theological conditions in a postrevolutionary political climate contributed to the decline of the New Divinity—just as a certain set of conditions led to its rise.[49]

After 1825, what then remained of the New Divinity? Apart from scholarly intrigue and the efforts of Andover Seminary's Edwards Amasa Park to resurrect theological interest, little remained of the specific New Divinity theological agenda. The concept of "disinterested benevolence," expressed first by Edwards as a metaphysical concept and then reworked into an ethical one by Samuel Hopkins, was embraced as a motive for "selfless" antebellum reform and perhaps even contributed to the creation of an antebellum black theology.[50] But above all, what persisted in a Susan Huntington, a John Mason Peck, and a Samuel Mills, and what was exported to the city, the frontier, and the lands abroad—and what remains to this day as a central feature of American Evangelicalism—was a religion of the heart. Jonathan Edwards, of course, must be largely credited for inventing the rhetoric of the religious affections, and his New Divinity sons and their sons transmitted the language of the heart to succeeding generations. But there was no birthright to the language, no designated heir to the affections. The daughters of the New Divinity staked out their own interest, and indeed, they eventually claimed—and continue to claim—a larger share.

49. For a comparative analysis of the social and environmental factors that led to the decline of Calvinism, see Howe, "Decline of Calvinism," 306–27.

50. On reform, see Ronald G. Walters, *American Reformers, 1815–1860* (New York, 1978), 27, and William G. McLoughlin, *Revivals, Awakenings, and Reform: An Essay on Religion and Social Change in America, 1607–1977* (Chicago, 1978), 77–80, 128–29; on black theology, see John Saillant, "Lemuel Haynes and the Revolutionary Origins of Black Theology, 1776–1801," *Religion and American Culture: A Journal of Interpretation* 2 (Winter 1992): 79–102.

APPENDIXES

Appendix 1 New Divinity Revivalist Clergy in Litchfield and Hartford Counties,* 1798–1808

I have employed at least one of the following criteria in identifying New Divinity clergy involved in revivals: (1) their accounts of revival (nearly all of which appear in the *Connecticut Evangelical Magazine*) comport with New Divinity theology; (2) their theological works and/or sermons express New Divinity themes; (3) they were educated by New Divinity men in "schools of the prophets"; (4) they advocated "pure church" principles; (5) they identified themselves or others identified them as "New Divinity men," "Edwardseans," "followers of Bellamy," "Hopkinsians," "strict Calvinists," etc. Biographical data were gathered primarily from Franklin B. Dexter, ed., *Biographical Sketches of the Graduates of Yale College with Annals of the College History*, 6 vols. (New York, 1885–1912), and William Buell Sprague, ed., *Annals of the American Pulpit*, 9 vols. (New York, 1857–69).

*Note: Heman Humphrey ministered in Fairfield County, David Smith in Middlesex County, and Charles Backus in Tolland County.

ANDREWS, JOSIAH (1775–1853): b. Southington, Connecticut; father's occupation, farmer; Yale, 1797; theological teacher, Abel Flint; m. sister of wife of Abel Flint; missionary tour in Pennsylvania and western New York, 1800; settled in Killingworth, 1802; dismissed in 1811; encountered opposition to his New Divinity preaching; missionary to western settlements, 1812–18; settled in Perth Amboy, New Jersey, 1819; dismissed in 1822; deposed from ministry in 1827; preaching: "animated," "popular"; a "high Calvinist." (Dexter, 5:239–43; account of revival: *CEM* 4 [May 1804]: 419–21; *CEM* 5 [July 1804]: 31–37)

BACKUS, CHARLES (1749–1803): b. Norwich, Connecticut; father's occupation, parents died in childhood; Yale, 1769; theological teacher, Levi Hart; settled in Somers, 1774–1803; educated approximately fifty men for the ministry; preaching: changed during ministry from metaphysical speculation to practical sermons. (Dexter, 3:310–16; Sprague, 2:61–68; account of revival: *CEM* 1 [July 1800]: 19–21)

COWLES, GILES HOOKER (1766–1835): b. Farmington, Connecticut; father's occupation, unknown; Yale, 1789; theological teacher, Jonathan Edwards, Jr.; settled in Bristol, 1792; dismissed in 1810; missionary in the Western Reserve, 1810–35; preaching: "neither striking nor animated," "not great facility of extemporizing." (Dexter, 4:634–35; Sprague, 2:330–31; account of revival: *CEM* 1 [August 1800]: 55–64; *CEMRI* 2 [April 1809]: 143–45)

FLINT, ABEL (1765–1825): b. Windham, Connecticut; father's occupation, unknown; Yale, 1785; settled at Hartford Second Church (South), 1791–1824; served as an officer in numerous evangelical societies, including secretary of the Board of Trustees, Connecticut Missionary Society, and editor of the *CEM*; preaching: "popular . . . impressive." (Dexter, 4:404–7; Sprague, 2:273–75)

GILLETT, ALEXANDER (1749–1826): b. Granby, Connecticut; father's occupation, unknown; Yale, 1770; theological teacher, Timothy Pitkin; settled in Farmingbury, 1773; dismissed in 1791 (conflict over New Divinity principles); settled in Torrington, 1792–1826; made numerous missionary tours; preaching: unpopular, speech impediment, loved to study. (Dexter, 3:379–81; Sprague, 2:68–71; account of revival: *CEM* 1 [October 1800]: 131–36)

GRIFFIN, EDWARD DORR (1770–1837): b. East Haddam, Connecticut; father's occupation, wealthy farmer; Yale, 1790; theological teacher, Jonathan Edwards, Jr.; settled in New Hartford, 1795–1801; settled in Newark, 1801–9; professor of pulpit eloquence, Andover Theological Seminary, 1809–11; settled at Park Street Church, Boston, 1811–15; settled at Newark Second

Presbyterian, 1815–21; president, Williams College, 1821–36; preaching: see Chapter 5. (Dexter, 4: 666–76; Sprague 4:26–43; account of revival: *CEM* 1 [December 1800]: 217–23; *CEM* 1 [January 1801]: 265–68)

HALLOCK, JEREMIAH (1758–1826): b. Brookhaven (Long Island), New York; father's occupation, farmer; no college education; theological teachers, Timothy Dwight, Joseph Strong, Abraham Fowler, Samuel J. Mills, Stephen West; m. Mercy Humphrey, sister of the wife of Abraham Fowler, New Divinity minister; Yale, 1788 (honorary M.A.); settled in West Simsbury, 1785–1826; preaching: neither eloquent nor intellectual, but had a "graphic power." (Sprague, 2:229–34; account of revival: *CEM* 1 [October 1800]: 137–42; *CEM* 1 [November 1800]: 177–84; *CEM* 6 [May 1806]: 425–32)

HART, IRA (1771–1829): b. Bristol, Connecticut; father's occupation, unknown (farmer); parents moved to Paris, New York, at the beginning of Ira's college education, causing him "pecuniary embarrassment"; Yale, 1797; theological teacher, Timothy Dwight; settled in Middlebury, 1798; dismissed in 1809 (conflict with church over strict discipline); settled in North Stonington, 1809–29; preaching: "earnest, popular." (Dexter, 5:287–89; account of revival: *CEM* 3 [August 1802]: 64–69; *CEM* 3 [September 1802]: 102–9)

HART, LUTHER (1783–1834): b. Goshen, Connecticut; father's occupation, house carpenter; converted in 1799 revival in Torrington; prepared for college under Alexander Gillett; Yale, 1807 (strained the family's finances); instructor, Morris's Academy in Litchfield South Farms, 1808; theological teacher, Ebenezer Porter; settled in Plymouth, 1810–34; preaching: "simple, clear, and sententious." (Dexter 6:119–21; Sprague, 2:523–26)

HAWLEY, RUFUS (1740–1826): b. Granby, Connecticut; father's occupation, farmer; Yale, 1767; theological teacher, Justus Forward (probable); settled in Northington Parish, West Avon, 1769–1820; preaching: plain, conversational, doctrinal. (Dexter, 3:230–32; account of revival: *CEM* 1 [September 1800]: 102–5)

HOOKER, ASAHEL (1762–1813): b. Bethlehem, Connecticut; father's occupation, farmer (lacked means to send him to college); Yale, 1789; theological teacher, William Robinson; m. Phoebe Edwards, granddaughter of Jonathan Edwards; settled in Goshen, 1791; educated approximately thirty men for the ministry; dismissed in 1810; settled in Norwich, 1812–13; "Edwardean theologically"; preaching: "edifying . . . searching." (Dexter, 4:640–43; Sprague, 2:316–21; account of revival: *CEM* 1 [March 1800]: 341–47)

HUMPHREY, HEMAN (1779–1861): b. West Simsbury, Connecticut; father's occupation, "substantial farmer"; Yale, 1805; theological teachers,

Timothy Dwight, Asahel Hooker; settled in Fairfield (Fairfield County), 1807; dismissed in 1817; settled in Pittsfield, Massachusetts, 1817; dismissed in 1823; president, Amherst College, 1823–55. (Dexter, 5:761–70)

HUNTINGTON, DAN (1774–1864): b. Lebanon, Connecticut; father's occupation, farmer; theological teacher, Timothy Dwight; Yale, 1794; tutor, Williams College, 1794–95; tutor, Yale College, 1795–98; settled in Litchfield, 1798; dismissed in 1809; settled in Middletown, 1809; dismissed in 1816; declared himself a Unitarian after retiring from the ministry, then returned to orthodoxy. (Dexter, 5:109–12; account of revival: *CEMRI* 1 [August 1808]: 313–18)

MILLER, JONATHAN (1761–1831): b. Torringford, Connecticut; father's occupation, unknown; Yale, 1781; theological teacher, unknown; settled in Burlington (West Britain), 1783–1831; furnished the *CEM* with about forty sermons; preaching: a "lack of refinement." (Dexter, 4:195–97; account of revival: *CEM* 1 [July 1800]: 21–27)

MILLER, WILLIAM F. (1768–1818): b. Avon, Connecticut; father's occupation, farmer; Yale, 1786; theological teacher, unknown; settled in Bloomfield, 1791; dismissed in 1811; decided opponent of Half-Way Covenant; preaching: prophetic interest. (Dexter, 4:495–98; account of revival: *CEM* 1 [January 1801]: 268–72; *CEM* 1 [February 1801]: 305–10)

MILLS, SAMUEL J. (1743–1833): b. Kent, Connecticut; father's occupation, farmer; Yale, 1764; theological teachers, Joel Bordwell, Joseph Bellamy; settled in Torringford, 1769–1822; preaching: practical, argumentative, extemporaneous, eloquent. (Dexter, 3:75–77; Sprague, 1:672–77; account of revival: *CEM* 1 [July 1800]: 27–30)

PERKINS, NATHAN (1748–1838): b. Norwich, Connecticut; father's occupation, "extensive landholder," "respectable"; College of New Jersey (Princeton), 1770; theological teacher, Benjamin Lord; m. Catherine, daughter of the Rev. Timothy Pitkin; settled in West Hartford, 1772–1838; a founder of the Connecticut Missionary Society; editor, *CEM*; preaching: doctrinal, practical. (Sprague, 2:1–4; account of revival: *CEMRI* 2 [February 1808]: 69–73)

PORTER, EBENEZER (1772–1834): b. Cornwall, Connecticut; father's occupation, a man of means—magistrate, state legislator; Dartmouth, 1792; theological teachers, Joseph Bellamy, John Smalley; m. Lucy Merwin, daughter of the Rev. Noah Merwin; settled in Washington, 1796; dismissed in 1811; professor of pulpit eloquence at Andover Theological Seminary, 1812–26; president, Andover, 1828–32; preaching: doctrinal, practical, emotional, simple, evangelical. (Sprague, 2:351–61; account of revival: *CEM* 7 [October 1806]: 143–48)

ROBBINS, AMMI (1740–1813): b. Branford, Connecticut; father's occupation, clergyman (Philemon); Yale, 1760; theological teachers, Levi Hart, Joseph Bellamy; brother-in-law to Peter Starr; settled in Norfolk, 1761–1813; preaching: extemporaneous. (Dexter, 2:670–73; Sprague, 1:369–70; account of revival: *CEM* 1 [February 1801]: 311–14; *CEM* 1 [March 1801]: 338–41)

SMITH, DAVID (1767–1862): b. Norwich, Connecticut; father's occupation, unknown; Yale, 1795; theological teachers, Ephraim Judson, Jacob Catlin; settled in Durham (Middlesex County), 1799–1832; m. daughter of the Rev. Elizur Goodrich, Jr.; stated supply, 1832–61; preaching: "thoroughly Calvinistic." (Dexter, 5:163–67; account of revival: *CEM* 7 [April 1807]: 391–96; *CEMRI* 2 [March 1809]: 104–7)

STARR, PETER (1744–1829): b. Danbury, Connecticut; father's occupation, unknown; Yale, 1764; theological teachers, David Brinsmade, Joseph Bellamy; settled in Warren, 1772–1829; m. Ammi Robbins's sister; preaching: "methodical, lucid, and instructive . . . not brilliant or specially interesting." (Dexter, 3:82–83; account of revival: *CEM* 1 [September 1800]: 100–101)

STRONG, NATHAN, JR. (1748–1816): b. Coventry, Connecticut; father's occupation, clergyman (Nathan Strong, Sr.); Yale, 1769; theological teacher, unknown; settled in Hartford, 1773–1816; editor, *CEM* and *CEMRI*, 1800–1815; a founder of the Missionary Society of Connecticut; preaching: "short, but clear, strong and pithy . . . great facility at extemporizing." (Dexter, 3:357–63; Sprague, 2:34–41)

TYLER, BENNET (1783–1858): b. Middlebury, Connecticut; father's occupation, unknown; Yale, 1804; theological teacher: Asahel Hooker; settled in South Britain, 1808; dismissed in 1822; president, Dartmouth College, 1822–28; settled in Portland, Maine, 1828; dismissed in 1834; president, Theological Institute of Connecticut, 1834–57. (Dexter, 5:716–24)

WASHBURN, JOSEPH (1766–1805): b. Middletown, Connecticut; father's occupation, unknown; Yale, 1793; theological teacher, Enoch Huntington; settled in Farmington, 1795–1805; preaching: doctrinal, practical, simple. (Dexter, 5:92–94; account of revival: *CEM* 1 [April 1801]: 378–86; *CEM* 1 [May 1801]: 420–31)

WATERMAN, SIMON (1736–1813): b. Norwich, Connecticut; father's occupation, unknown; Yale, 1759; theological teacher, unknown; settled in Wallingford, 1761; dismissed in 1787; settled in Plymouth, 1787; dismissed in 1809 (due to his "enthusiastic Federalist" views); theologically, "followed Bellamy"; preaching: "good . . . devoted to the spiritual interests of his people." (Dexter, 2:629–31; account of revival: *CEM* 2 [July 1801]: 23–27; *CEM* 2 [August 1801]: 60–67)

WILLIAMS, JOSHUA (1761–1836): b. Rocky Hill, Connecticut; father's occupation, unknown; Yale, 1780; theological teacher, unknown; settled in Southington (Long Island), New York, 1784; dismissed in 1789; settled in Harwinton, 1790; dismissed in 1822; preaching: "more effective as a pastor than as a preacher." (Dexter, 4:167–69; account of revival: *CEM* 1 [June 1801]: 462–73; *CEM* 7 [April 1807]: 365–70)

Appendix 2 The New England Ministry in Transition: Comparative Data on Pastors Reporting Revival to the *Connecticut Evangelical Magazine*, 1798–1808

Name of Minister	Year Graduated from Yale	Number of Pastorates	Years in Each Pastorate
Stephen West	1755	1	60
Simon Waterman	1759	2	26,22
Ammi Robbins	1760	1	50+
Peter Starr	1764	1	57
Samuel J. Mills, Sr.	1764	1	50
Rufus Hawley	1767	1	50
Charles Backus	1769	1	30
Nathan Strong, Jr.	1769	1	40+
Alexander Gillett	1770	2	18,34
Nathan Perkins[a]	1770	1	66
Gershom Lyman	1773	1	35
Jeremiah Hallock[b]	—	1	40
Joshua Williams	1780	2	5,32
Jonathan Miller	1781	1	38
Jacob Catlin	1784	1	40
Aaron Woolworth	1784	1	34
Gordon Dorrance[a]	1786	1	40
Silas Churchill	1787	1	42
Alvan Hyde	1788	1	40
Giles H. Cowles	1789	1	18
Asahel Hooker	1789	2	19,2
Edward Dorr Griffin	1790	4	5,8,4,6
Jesse Townsend	1790	3	12,5,3
Timothy M. Cooley	1792	1	60
Ebenezer Porter[c]	1792	1	18
Samuel Shepherd	1793	1	50

Joseph Washburn	1793	1	10
Dan Huntington	1794	2	11,7
David Smith	1795	1	30
Jonathan Belden	1796	2	5,8
Bancroft Fowler	1796	4	14,5,3,6
William F. Miller	1796	1	20
Josiah Andrews	1797	2	9,3
Jedidiah Bushnell[d]	1797	1	33
Ira Hart	1797	2	11,20
Aaron Dutton	1803	1	36
Luther Hart	1807	1	25

SOURCES: *Connecticut Evangelical Magazine* (Hartford, Conn., 1800–1807); *Connecticut Evangelical Magazine and Religious Intelligencer* (Hartford, Conn., 1808); Franklin B. Dexter, ed., *Biographical Sketches of the Graduates of Yale College with Annals of the College History*, 6 vols. (New York, 1885–1912); William Buell Sprague, ed., *Annals of the American Pulpit*, 9 vols. (New York, 1857–69).

NOTE: For a comprehensive analysis of the New England ministry in transition from 1750 to 1850, see Donald M. Scott, *From Office to Profession: The New England Ministry, 1750–1850* (Philadelphia, 1978), and John A. Andrew III, *Rebuilding the Christian Commonwealth: New England Congregationalists and Foreign Ministers, 1800–1830* (Lexington, Ky., 1984). Scott uses 1795 as a break point in the transition (p. 74), whereas Andrews favors 1800 as the break point (p. 47).

[a]College of New Jersey.

[b]Not a college graduate; for purposes of analysis, the approximate date is given had Hallock graduated.

[c]Dartmouth College.

[d]Williams College.

Appendix 3   Connecticut Revivals, 1798–1800

Key

Number	Town	Pastor	Converts (Admittants)
1	Norfolk	Ammi Robbins	156
2	Colebrook	Jonathan Edwards, Jr.	26
3	Hartland	Nathaniel Gaylord	27
4	Winchester	Publius Bogue	29
5	Barkhamsted	Ozias Eells	26
6	Goshen	Asahel Hooker	90
7	Torrington	Alexander Gillett	47
8	Torringford	Samuel Mills	–
9	New Hartford	Edward Dorr Griffin	100
10	Canton Center	Jeremiah Hallock	65
11	Bloomfield	William Miller	53
12	Windsor	Henry A. Rowland	34
13	Warren	Peter Starr	90
14	Morris	Amos Chase	27
15	Harwinton	Joshua Williams	100
16	Burlington	Jonathan Miller	40
17	Bristol	Giles Cowles	103
18	Avon (West)	Rufus Hawley	43
19	Farmington	Joseph Washburn	68
20	West Hartford	Nathan Perkins	125
21	Hartford	Nathan Strong (First Church)	150
		Abel Flint (South Church)	
22	Kent	Joel Bordwell	25
23	Bethlehem	Azel Backus	24
24	Watertown	Uriel Gridley	27
25	Plymouth	Simon Waterman	51
26	Southington	William Robinson	21
27	New Britain	John Smalley	17
28	Middlebury	Ira Hart	56
29	Washington	Ebenezer Porter	54
30	Somers	Charles Backus	52
			1,699

SOURCES: *Connecticut Evangelical Magazine* (Hartford, Conn., 1800–1807); *Contributions to the Ecclesiastical History of Connecticut* (New Haven, Conn., 1861); Church Records, CSL.

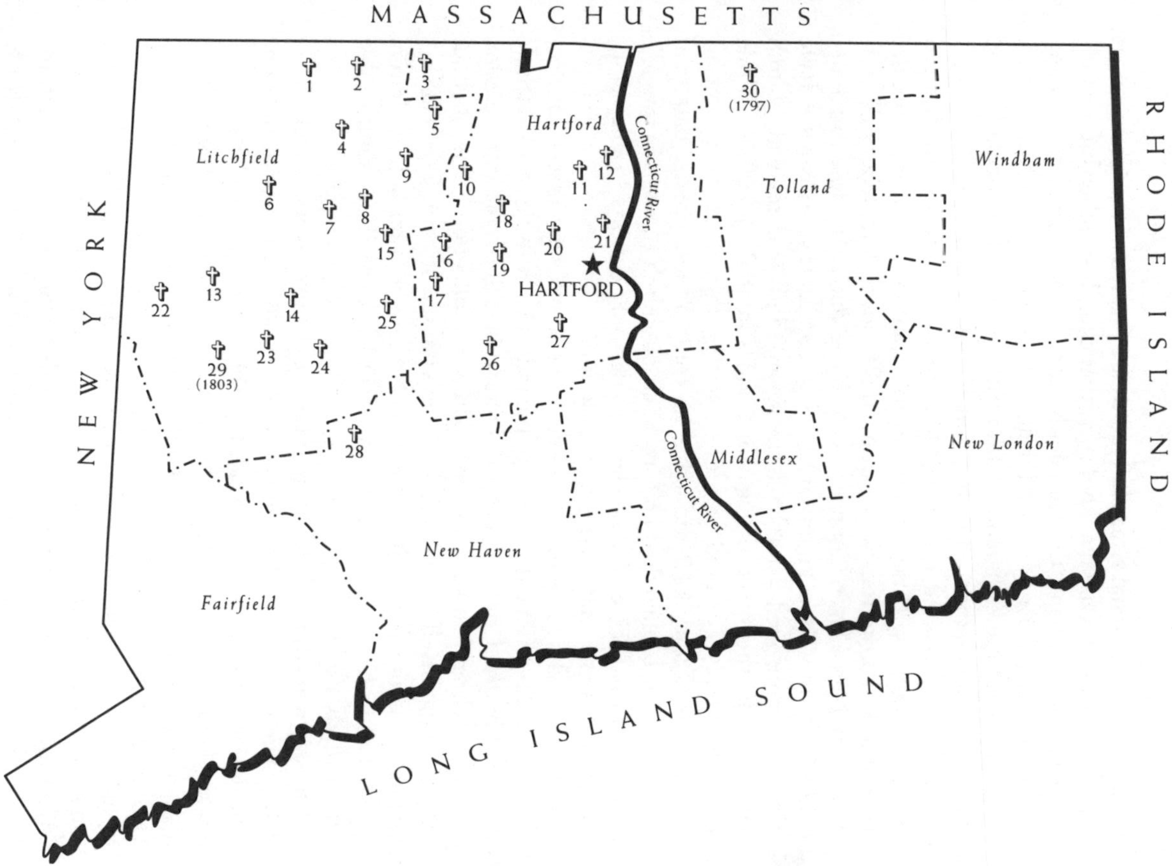

FIG. A3.1. Connecticut Revivals, 1798–1800 (see key, page 252)

Appendix 4   Statistical Sample of Church Admissions

Connecticut Congregational Church Records are located at the Connecticut State Library, Hartford. One quickly learns that church membership records were not kept for historians: they are neither precise nor complete, and any statistics-based study must be viewed in light of inevitable inaccuracies and omissions. However, New England Congregationalists were particularly good record keepers—better than other religious bodies.

My sample in Table A4.1 includes nine revived churches in Hartford and Litchfield counties: Barkhamsted, Bristol, Canton Center, Farmington, Goshen, Norfolk, Torrington, West Avon, and Windsor. Middlebury (Waterbury Township, New Haven County) was included due to its close proximity to Litchfield County (see Figure A3.1). For comparative reasons I have included one nonrevived church (Kensington) and one revived church (Durham) outside the orbit of Hartford and Litchfield counties. While revivals were initially centered in these counties, they were by no means confined to them. Tables A4.2 through A4.5 contain more precise data than Table A4.1 as I have broken down raw numbers of church admissions into age and gender cohorts (Tables A4.2, A4.3), gender-only cohorts (Table A4.4), and nonmarried, single-status cohorts (Table A4.5).

The criteria for choosing the churches listed above were threefold: first, completeness of church records; second, the indexing of these records (State Library Index) by the Connecticut State Library; and third, the interpolation of the State Library Index into the Barbour Collection. The Barbour Collection, though itself incomplete, contains vital statistics on Connecticut's inhabitants. To complement the records sources above, I consulted church, town, and family histories (genealogical records), as well as Family Bible Records at the State Library.

Despite a great deal of labor intensive detective work, errors were inevitable. The presence in the same town of so many people with the same given name and surname quickly reveals the web of kinship ties characteristic of New England settlement, but for the historian trying to track down dates of births, marriages, and church admissions, such homogeneous name-giving can cause nightmares.

The most thorough data were gathered for Farmington First Church, where I accumulated vital information on over 80 percent of the 151 admittants from 1795 to 1800. Membership patterns in other churches, where both the size of the church and the dimension of the sample were smaller, tended to mirror First Church. The agreement of the comprehensive data from Farmington with the more selective data from other churches supports the overall accuracy of the total sample.

Table A4.1 Church Admissions, 1790–1805

Church	1790	1791	1792	1793	1794	1795	1796	1797	1798	1799	1800	1801	1802	1803	1804	1805
Barkhamsted	2	2	3	1	10	6	9	3	3	20	6	6	7	0	2	0
Bristol				10	2	12	9	7	1	67	36	1	1	1	0	1
Canton Center	4	2	0	3	2	2	2	3	0	56	9	13	0	0	0	19
Durham											8	0	5	41	9	13
Farmington						42	20	13	8	42	26	2	3	3	0	4
Goshen			4	9	7	3	3	3	1	72	18	2	0	8	2	7
Kensington	2	7	2	2	3	3	4	2	2	0	5	2	3	1	1	1
Middlebury								1	0	15	41	5	3	7	0	3
Norfolk	6	6	1	9	2	8	2	11	3	111	45	18	4	2	1	2
Torrington										38	9	0	2	3	0	0
West Avon	1	5	2	14	8	0	2	1	3	36	7	2	2	1	1	4
Windsor	1	5	5	3	3	18	3	1	2	34	2	2	1	0	0	0

Table A4.2 Ages of Male and Female Admittants, 1795–1803

Church, Date (Total Admissions)	Sample No.	%	Under 20 M	F	20–24 M	F	25–29 M	F	30–34 M	F	35–39 M	F	40–44 M	F	45–49 M	F	Over 50 M	F
Barkhamsted, 1799 (20)	8	40	3						1	1		1	1	1				
Bristol, 1799–1800 (103)	76	74	4	8	8	10	4	9	3	5	3	4	2	2	2	2	5	5
Canton Center, 1799 (56)	16	30			1	2	2	2	3	1	2		1			1		1
Durham, 1803 (41)	26	63	3	1		5	2	4	1	2		4				3	3	
Farmington, 1795–1800 (151)	122	81	4	10	8	20	1	17	5	9	6	7	2	8	4	10	3	8
Goshen, 1799–1800 (90)	43	48		2	1	7	3	1	2	6	5	6	3	3	2	1		1
Torrington, 1799–1800 (47)	32	68	2	7	3	4	2	3	1	1	2	2	1	3		1		
West Avon, 1799 (36)	27	75	2	1	4	2	3	1	4	1	2	2	1	1	1	1		
Windsor, 1799 (34)	19	56	1	4		5		1	1	1	1	2		1				2
Totals (578)	369	64	19	33	25	55	17	38	21	27	21	28	11	19	9	19	11	16
Percentage of sample			5.1	8.9	6.8	14.9	4.6	10.2	5.7	7.3	5.7	7.6	3.0	5.1	2.4	5.1	3.0	4.3
(combined)			14.0		21.7		14.9		13.0		13.3		8.1		7.5		7.3	
Percentage of total males			14.0		18.6		12.6		15.7		15.7		8.2		7.0		8.2	
Percentage of total females			14.0		23.4		16.2		11.0		11.9		8.1		8.1		6.8	

Males: 134 (36%)
Females: 235 (63%)

Table A4.3 Ages of Male and Female Admittants, 1795–1800
(Dimension of Sample above 67%)

Church (Total Admissions)	Sample No.	Sample %	Under 20 M	Under 20 F	20–24 M	20–24 F	25–29 M	25–29 F	30–34 M	30–34 F	35–39 M	35–39 F	40–44 M	40–44 F	45–49 M	45–49 F	Over 50 M	Over 50 F
Bristol (103)	76	74	4	8	8	10	4	9	3	5	3	4	2	2	2	2	5	5
Farmington (151)	122	81	4	10	8	20	1	17	5	9	6	7	2	8	4	10	3	8
Torrington (47)	32	68	2	7	3	4	2	3	1	1	2	2	1	3		1		
West Avon (36)	27	75	2	1	4	2	3	1	4	1	2	2	1	1	1	1	1	
Totals (337)	257	76	12	26	23	36	10	30	13	16	13	15	6	14	7	14	9	13
			38		59		40		29		28		20		21		22	
Percentage of sample			4.7	10.0	8.9	10.0	3.9	11.7	5.0	6.2	5.0	5.8	2.3	5.4	2.7	5.4	3.5	5.0
			14.7		22.9		15.5		11.3		10.8		7.8		7.8		8.6	
Percentage of total males			12.9		24.7		10.7		14.0		14.0		6.5		7.5		9.7	
Percentage of total females				15.9		22.0		18.3		9.8		9.1		8.5		8.5		7.9

Males: 93 (36.2%)
Females: 164 (63.8%)

Table A4.4 Male and Female Admittants during Revivals, 1795–1822

Church (Total Male/Female)	1795–1800		1801–1802		1803–1804		1805–1806		1807–1808		1809–1812		1813–1817		1818–1819		1820–1821		1822	
	M	F	M	F	M	F	M	F	M	F	M	F	M	F	M	F	M	F	M	F
Barkhamsted (15/32)	7	13					8 19 [1806]													
Bristol (74/108)	40	63									23	17			11	28				
Canton Center (81/140)	31	25							23 38 [1808–1809]				46	88						
Durham (41/91)					10 31 [1803]		4	27					8 22 [1814–1816]							
Farmington (155/350)	36	115							4	21	8	28	13	38			84	136		
Goshen (65/151)	29	61							19	33			17 57 [1812–1820]							
Kensington (13/34)													13 34 [1816]							
Middlebury (54/108)	19	37											24 45 [1814–1817]						11	26
Norfolk (78/118)	64	92					14 26 [1806–1811]													
Torrington (33/61)	18	29											15 32 [1816–1817]							
West Avon (24/12)	24	12															10 28 [1821]			
Windsor (17/55)	7	27																		

Table A4.5 Single Admittants, 1795–1800

Church Date	Est. Total	Sample No.	Sample %	Under 20		20–24		25–29		30–34		35–39		40–44		45–49		Over 50	
				M	F	M	F	M	F	M	F	M	F	M	F	M	F	M	F
Bristol 1799–1800	39	26	67.0	3	6	4	8	1	1	1	1	1							
Durham 1803	22	12	55.0	3	1		4	1	1		2								
Farmington 1795–1800	53	44	83.0	3	8	6	14		8	1	2				1		1		
Goshen 1799–1800	29	7	24.0		2		3		1				1						
Torrington 1799–1800	18	15	83.0	2	7	3	3												
West Avon 1799–1800	6	5	83.0	2	1	2													
Windsor 1799	16	8	50.0	1	4		3												
Total	183	117	64.0	14	29	15	35	2	11	2	5	1	1		1		1		

NOTE ON PRIMARY SOURCES

Manuscript

I have drawn from the manuscript sources in a number of depositories, but those collected at the Connecticut State Library have proved indispensable. Here I have consulted local church records (see Appendix 4), diaries, and papers of persons living in Hartford and Litchfield counties during the Second Great Awakening.

The associational and consociational meeting records of the Congregational churches are kept at the Congregational Library (Connecticut Conference of the United Church of Christ), Hartford. While the General Association meetings records have been published, the records for the district associations remain in manuscript volumes in the basement of the Congregational Library. Some useful information regarding clerical concerns and organization for revival was gleaned from the Original Records of Litchfield County Association and Consociations, 1725–1814 (the county association was divided into North and South Associations in 1791), and the Hartford North Association (in Consociation Records, 1790–1820). In addition, the library has a large collection of manuscript sermons by Connecticut ministers, of which those by Asahel Hooker and Alexander Gillett were pertinent.

Other manuscript sermons by the New Divinity men who figure in the present study are located at the Connecticut Historical Society, Hartford; the Congregational Library, Boston; the American Antiquarian Society, Worcester, Massachusetts; and Williams College Library, Williamstown, Massachusetts.

The private correspondence of ministers offers an inside view into the world of the clergy. Collections of particular value are the Edward Hooker Letter Collection and Lavius Hyde Letter Collection at the Congregational Library, Boston; the Gratz Collection at the Historical Society of Pennsylvania; and the Benjamin Trumbull Collection at Sterling Memorial Library, Yale University. About ten letters to and from Edward Dorr Griffin are located in an assortment of collections at Sterling Memorial Library, though only a few contained information of any value to this study. The Connecticut State Library and the Beinecke Library, Yale University, each have a letter by Griffin describing the 1798–99 revivals.

The story of Farmington First Church was pieced together by consulting several archives. The state library has, of course, the church's records. In addition, the Jonathan Treadwell Papers offer revealing commentary on the train of clerical candidates following Allen Olcott. Distinctly different opinions from Treadwell's are found in the Julius Gay Collection at the Connecticut Historical Society. Finally, Joseph Washburn's "Regester," illustrating the clerical exchange system, is at Sterling Memorial Library.

Manuscript sources for popular piety during the Awakening are somewhat scarce, yet those uncovered were quite helpful. James Morris's account of the revival in South Farms (Litchfield), found at Sterling Memorial Library, was especially valuable, as were diaries (nearly all by females) at the Connecticut Historical Society and the state library. The Cowles family correspondence in the Julius Gay Miscellaneous Manuscript Collection at the Farmington Village Library, as well as the Lee Papers at Sterling Memorial Library, offer glimpses into the nature of familial piety.

Printed Materials

The *Connecticut Evangelical Magazine* (1800–1807), suspended and then renamed the *Connecticut Evangelical Magazine and Religious Intelligencer* (1808–15), is a veritable treasure trove of source material on the Second Great Awakening. Its contents include articles on doctrine, prophecy, home and foreign missions (many of the latter reprinted from British religious publications), selections of hymns, narratives of revivals, and the biographies and memoirs of pious Christians. The story of the Second Great Awakening throughout

New England is told primarily from a clerical perspective in the revival narratives. Although there is a formulaic style to all of these reports, they are nonetheless the most important source for documenting the indigenous roots of the revival.

Ministers' printed sermons and memoirs are another indispensable source for revealing the nature and message of the Awakening. The "Half-Century" sermons of Ammi Robbins, Nathan Perkins, Peter Starr, and Noah Porter offer descriptions of the 1798–1800 revivals, as do Nathan Perkins's "Two Discourses" and Jeremiah Hallock's sermon at the dedication of Canton's new meeting house in 1815. The memoirs of Jeremiah Hallock, Heman Humphrey, Edward Dorr Griffin, Asahel Nettleton, and Ebenezer Porter provide valuable information on clerical piety and involvement in the Awakening.

The theology of revival is explained and defended in the *Connecticut Evangelical Magazine, Sermons on Important Subjects,* Charles Backus's *Scripture Doctrine of Regeneration,* Joseph Washburn's *Sermons on Practical Subjects,* and the collected works and occasional sermons of Backus, Griffin, Nathan Perkins, and Nathan Strong. Williams College has a comprehensive collection of printed works by and about Griffin. In his memoirs Griffin mentions his diary, but neither the librarian at Williams nor other archivists at major depositories know of its whereabouts.

BIBLIOGRAPHY

Primary Sources

Manuscripts

American Antiquarian Society, Worcester, Massachusetts
    Sermon Collection, 1640–1875
Beinecke Rare Book and Manuscript Library, Yale University, New Haven, Connecticut
    Edward Dorr Griffin MSS
Boston Public Library, Boston, Massachusetts
    Mellen Chamberlain Collection
Congregational Library, Boston, Massachusetts
    Edward Hooker Letter Collection
    Lavius Hyde Letter Collection
    MS Sermons
Congregational Library, Hartford, Connecticut
    Connecticut Congregational Churches
    Consociation Records, 1790–1820 (includes Hartford North Association Minutes, 1714–1800)
    Extracts from the Minutes of the General Association of Connecticut, 1800–1811
    Original Records of Litchfield County Association and Consociation, 1752–1814 (includes Litchfield South Association Records)
    Sermons by Connecticut Ministers

Connecticut Historical Society, Hartford, Connecticut
    Zeloda Barrett Diary
    Julia Churchill Diary
    Farmington, First Congregational Church Documents concerning the controversy
        over the Rev. Allen Olcott, 1786–91
    Julius Gay Collection of Farmington MSS
    Edward Hooker Letter Book
    Jonathan Miller Sermons, Conference Books
    Religious Diary (1813–17) (anonymous)
    Jonathan Trumbull, Jr., Collection
Connecticut State Library, Hartford, Connecticut
    Quincy Blake, "The Story of Farmington," 1936 (Typewritten)
    Church Records:
        Barkhamsted Congregational, 1781–1914
        Bristol First Congregational, 1742–1897
        Burlington Congregational
        Canton Center Congregational
        Durham First Church of Christ (Congregational)
        Farmington First Congregational
        Goshen First Congregational
        Kensington (Berlin) Congregational, 1709–1889
        Middlebury Congregational, 1790–1915
        New Hartford First Congregational, 1739–1853
        Norfolk Church of Christ (Congregational), 1760–1948
        Torrington First Congregational and Ecclesiastical Society, 1741–1901
        West Avon Congregational, 1717–1941
        Windsor First Congregational, 1636–1932
    Family Bible Records
    Jonathan Fitch Diary
    Edward Dorr Griffin MSS
    Mary Treadwell Hooker Diary
    Candace Roberts Diary
    Jonathan Treadwell Papers, 1706–1870
Farmington Village Library (Farmington Room), Farmington, Connecticut
    Business Letters
    Mary Ann Cowles Diary (1819–24)
    Julius Gay Miscellaneous MSS
    David Gleason Diary
Historical Commission, Southern Baptist Convention, Nashville, Tennessee
    Seventh Day Baptist Materials (Microfilm)
Historical Society of Pennsylvania, Philadelphia, Pennsylvania
    Gratz Collection
Sterling Memorial Library, Yale University, New Haven, Connecticut
    Historical MSS
    Hooker Family Collection
    Jonathan Lee Papers
    James Morris MSS
    Morse Family Papers
    Park Family Papers
    Erastus Scranton Diary
    Benjamin Trumbull (1735–1820) Collection
    Joseph Washburn Family Papers

Williams College Library, Williamstown, Massachusetts
    Williamsiana, Misc. MSS
Yale Divinity School Library, Yale University, New Haven, Connecticut
    Jonathan Marsh Collection

Published Sources

Newspapers and Religious Periodicals

Connecticut Courant and Weekly Intelligencer (Hartford), 1783, 1786
Connecticut Evangelical Magazine, 1800–1807.
Connecticut Evangelical Magazine and Religious Intelligencer, 1808–15
Monthly Anthology and Boston Review, 1805–6, 1809–10

Biographies, Diaries, and Memoirs

Asbury, Francis. The Journal and Letters of Francis Asbury. 3 vols. Edited by Elmer T. Clark.
    Nashville, Tenn.: Abingdon Press, 1958.
Bangs, Heman. The Autobiography and Journal of Rev. Heman Bangs; with an Introduction by Rev.
    Bishop Janes, D. D. New York: W. Tibbals & Son, 1872.
Beecher, Lyman. The Autobiography of Lyman Beecher. 2 vols. Edited by Barbara M. Cross.
    Cambridge, Mass.: Harvard University Press, 1966.
Bentley, William. The Diary of William Bentley, D.D., Pastor of the East Church, Salem,
    Massachusetts. 4 vols. 1905–14. Reprint. Gloucester, Mass.: Peter Smith, 1963.
Clark, Sereno D. The New England Ministry Sixty Years Ago: The Memoir of John Woodbridge, D.D.
    Boston: Lee & Shepard, 1877.
Cooke, Parsons. Recollections of Rev. E. D. Griffin; or, Incidents Illustrating his Character. Boston:
    Sabbath School Society, 1855.
Cowles, Julia. The Diaries of Julia Cowles, 1797–1803. Edited by Laura Hadley Moseley. New
    Haven, Conn.: Yale University Press, 1931.
Cummings, Asa, comp. Memoir and Select Thoughts of the late Rev. Edward Payson, D.D.
    Philadelphia: J. & J. L. Gibon, 1851.
Dexter, Franklin B., ed. Biographical Sketches of the Graduates of Yale College with Annals of the
    College History. 6 vols. New York: H. Holt & Co., 1885–1912.
Dwight, Timothy. Travels in New England and New York. 4 vols. Edited by Barbara Miller
    Solomon. Cambridge, Mass.: Harvard University Press, 1969.
Emmons, Nathanael. "Autobiography." In The Works of Nathanael Emmons, D.D. 6 vols. Edited
    by Jacob Ide, 1:ix–xxxvii. Boston: Crocker & Brewster, 1842.
Goodrich, Samuel Griswold. Recollections of a Lifetime. 2 vols. New York: Miller, Orton & Co.,
    1857.
Hallock, William A. Memoir of Harlan Page; or, The Power of Prayer and Personal Effort for the Souls
    of Individuals. New York: American Tract Society, 1835.
Hibbard, Billy. Memoirs of the Life and travels of B. Hibbard. 2d ed. New York: Pierce & Reed,
    1843.
Hopkins, Samuel. Sketches of the Life of the Late, Rev. Samuel Hopkins, D.D. Edited by Stephen
    West. Hartford, Conn.: Hudson & Goodwin, 1805.
[Humphrey, Zephaniah Moore]. Memorial Sketches: Heman Humphrey, Sophia Porter Humphrey.
    Philadelphia: J. B. Lippincott & Co., 1869.

Huntington, Dan. *Memories, Counsels, and Reflections, by an Octogenary.* Cambridge, Mass.: Metcalf & Co., 1857.

Hyde, Alvan. *Memoir of Rev. Alvan Hyde, D.D. of Lee, Mass.* Boston: Perkins, Marvin & Co., 1835.

Hyde, Nancy Maria. *The Writings of Nancy Maria Hyde, of Norwich, Conn., connected with a Sketch of Her Life.* Norwich, Conn.: Russell Hubbard, 1816.

Matthews, Lyman. *Memoir of the Life and Character of Ebenezer Porter, D.D.* Boston: Perkins & Marvin, 1837.

Nash, Ansel. "Memoir of Edward Dorr Griffin." *American Quarterly Register* 13 (May 1841): 365–85.

Park, Edwards A. *Memoir of Nathanael Emmons; with sketches of his friends and pupils.* Boston: Congregational Board of Publication, 1861.

Peck, John Mason. *Forty Years of Pioneer Life: Memoir of John Mason Peck, D.D.* Edited from his journals and correspondence by Rufus Babcock. Introduction by Paul M. Harrison. Carbondale: Southern Illinois University Press, 1965.

Riddel, Samuel H. "Memoir of the Rev. Nathan Strong, D.D." *American Quarterly Register* 13 (November 1840): 129–43.

Robbins, Thomas. *The Diary of Thomas Robbins, D.D., 1796–1854.* 2 vols. Edited by Increase N. Tarbox. Boston: Beacon Press, 1886.

Sewall, Jothan. *A Memoir of Rev. Jothan Sewall, of Chesterville, Maine.* Boston: Tappan & Whittemore, 1853.

Sprague, William Buell. *Memoir of the Rev. Edward D. Griffin, D.D.* New York: Taylor & Dodd, 1839.

————, ed. *Annals of the American Pulpit.* 9 vols. New York: R. Carter & Bros., 1857–69.

Spring, Gardiner. *Memoir of Samuel John Mills.* 2d ed. New York: Saxton & Miles, 1842.

Stiles, Ezra. *Extracts from the Itineraries and Other Miscellanies of Ezra Stiles . . . With a Selection from His Correspondence.* Edited by Franklin B. Dexter. New Haven, Conn.: Yale University Press, 1916.

————. *The Literary Diary of Ezra Stiles.* 3 vols. Edited by Franklin B. Dexter. New York: Charles Scribner's Sons, 1901.

Tyler, Bennet. *The Life and Labours of Asahel Nettleton.* Edited by Andrew Bonar. 1859. Reprint. London: Banner of Truth Trust, 1975.

————. *Memoir of the Life and Character of Rev. Asahel Nettleton, D.D.* 2d ed. Hartford: Robins & Smith, 1845.

Winslow, Miron. *Memoir of Mrs. Harriet L. Winslow, Thirteen Years a Member of the American Mission in Ceylon.* New York: American Tract Society, 1840.

Wisner, Benjamin B. *Memoir of the Late Mrs. Susan Huntington, of Boston, Mass.* 3d ed. Boston: Crocker & Brewster, 1829.

Worcester, Samuel M. *The Life and Labors of Rev. Samuel Worcester, D.D.* 2 vols. Boston: Crocker & Brewster, 1852.

Yale, Cyrus. *The Godly Pastor: Life of the Rev. Jeremiah Hallock, of Canton, Conn.* New York: American Tract Society, [1854].

Church Records, Sermons, and Theological Works

Backus, Charles. "Afflictions Improved: The substance of a discourse delivered at Somers, Lord's Day, February 28, 1790. Occasioned by the late death of Miss Bethiah Kingsbury of Franklin, in Connecticut, who, with three brothers and a sister, all in their youth, together with her parents, were removed from the world in a few years." Springfield, Mass.: James R. Hutchins, 1793.

————. "The Benevolent Spirit of Christianity Illustrated; in a sermon delivered at the ordination of the Reverend Thomas Snell, to the pastoral care of the Second Church in Brookfield, Massachusetts, June 27th, 1798." Worcester, Mass.: Leonard Worcester, 1798.

————. "A Discourse on the Nature and Influence of Godly Fear; containing also a minister's address to his church and congregation, together with a few interesting events in their history." Hartford, Conn.: Hudson & Goodwin, 1802.

————. "The Faithful Ministers of Jesus Christ Rewarded: A sermon, delivered at the ordination of the Rev. Azel Backus, to the pastoral care of the church in Bethlem, April 6, 1791." Litchfield, Conn.: Collier & Buel, [1791].

————. "The High Importance of Love to Jesus Christ in the Minister of the Gospel: A sermon, delivered at the ordination of the Reverend John Hubbard Church, to the pastoral charge of the Church in Pelham, New-Hampshire. October 31, 1799." Amherst, N.H.: Preston, 1799.

————. "The Living Warned to be Prepared for Death: A sermon, occasioned by the death of six young persons who were drowned in a pond in Wilbraham, Massachusetts, April 29, 1799: and delivered May 2, when the funeral of five of them was attended." Springfield, Mass.: Timothy Ashley, 1799.

————. "Ministers Serving God in the Gospel of His Son: A sermon delivered at the ordination of the Rev. Timothy Mather Cooley, to the pastoral care of the First Church in Granville, February 3, 1796." West Springfield, Mass.: Davidson, 1796.

————. "The Principal Causes of the Opposition to Christianity Considered; in a sermon, delivered at the ordination of the Rev. Zephaniah Swift Moore, to the pastoral care of the Congregational church in Leicester, Massachusetts, January 10, 1798." Worcester, Mass.: Leonard Worcester, 1798.

————. "Qualifications and Duties of the Christian Pastor: A sermon, delivered at Wilmington, in Massachusetts, October 29, 1795, at the ordination of the Reverend Freegrace Reynolds, A.M., to the work of the ministry in that place." Boston: Hall, 1795.

————. *The Scripture Doctrine of Regeneration Considered, in Six Discourses.* Hartford, Conn.: Hudson & Goodwin, 1800.

————. "A Sermon Delivered at Tolland December 29, 1795, before the Uriel Lodge of Free Masons." Hartford, Conn.: Hudson & Goodwin, 1796.

————. "A Sermon Delivered Jan. 1, 1801; containing a brief review of some of the distinguishing events of the Eighteenth Century." Hartford, Conn.: Hudson & Goodwin, 1801.

————. "A Sermon, preached at Enfield, February 16, 1799; at the funeral of Mrs. Agnes Prudden, consort of the Rev. Nehemiah Prudden." Hartford, Conn.: Hudson & Goodwin, 1799.

————. "A Sermon, preached before His Excellency Samuel Huntington, esq. L.L.D. governor, and the Honorable the General Assembly of the state of Connecticut, convened at Hartford, on the Day of the Anniversary Election. May 9, 1793." Hartford, Conn.: Hudson & Goodwin, 1793.

————. "The True Christian Living and Dying unto the Lord: A sermon, delivered at Long Meadow, Massachusetts, January 31, 1798, at the funeral of Mrs. Sarah Storrs, consort of the Rev. Richard Salter Storrs." Springfield, Mass.: Francis Stebbins, 1798.

Brace, Joab. "Half-Century Discourse. History of the Church in Newington; its doctrine, its ministers, its experience: presented in the discourse delivered on Tuesday the 16th of January, 1855, on the relinquishment of his active service, at the close of half a century from his ordination in that place." Hartford, Conn.: Case, Tiffany, 1855.

Catlin, Jacob. *A Compendium of the System of Divine Truth, contained in a series of essays, in which the principal subjects contained in the Holy Scriptures, are carefully arranged, briefly discussed, and improved.* Middletown, Conn.: E. & E. Clark, 1824.

Colton, Calvin. *History and Character of American Revivals of Religion.* 1832. Reprint. New York: AMS Press, 1973.

Doddridge, Philip. "Sermons on the Religious Education of Children; preached at Northampton." Boston: Samuel Hall, 1794.

Dwight, Timothy. "A Discourse, in Two Parts, delivered July 23, 1812, on the National Fast, in the chapel of Yale College." New Haven, Conn.: Howe & DeForest, 1812.

————. "A Discourse on Some Events of the Last Century, delivered in the Brick Church in New Haven, on Wednesday, January 7, 1801." New Haven, Conn.: Ezra Read, 1801.

Edwards, Jonathan. *The Works of Jonathan Edwards: Freedom of the Will.* Edited by Paul Ramsey. New Haven, Conn.: Yale University Press, 1957.

————. *The Works of Jonathan Edwards: The Great Awakening.* Edited by C. C. Goen. New Haven, Conn.: Yale University Press, 1972.

————. *The Works of Jonathan Edwards: Original Sin.* Edited by Clyde A. Holbrook. New Haven, Conn.: Yale University Press, 1970.

————. *The Works of Jonathan Edwards: Religious Affections.* Edited by John E. Smith. New Haven, Conn.: Yale University Press, 1959.

————. *The Works of President Edwards.* 4 vols. New York: Leavitt, Trow & Co., 1844.

Edwards, Jonathan, Jr. "The Duty of Ministers of the Gospel to Preach the Truth; illustrated in a sermon: delivered at the ordination of the Rev. Edward Dorr Griffin, A.M., to the pastoral charge of the Church of Christ in New-Hartford. June 4th, A.D. 1795." Hartford: Hudson & Goodwin, 1795.

Flint, Abel. "Prepare for Death! A sermon, delivered at Hartford, Sept. 17, 1806, at the funeral of John McCurdy Strong, son of the Rev. Nathan Strong, D.D., who was drowned in Connecticut River, on the evening of September 16." Hartford, Conn.: Lincoln & Gleason, 1806.

Gillett, Alexander. "On the Proper Mode of Preaching the Gospel: A sermon delivered . . . at the ordination of the Rev. Timothy P. Gillett." New Haven, Conn.: Oliver Steele, 1808.

Griffin, Edward Dorr. "An Address delivered to the Class of Graduates of Williams College, at the Commencement, Sept. 4, 1822." Pittsfield, Mass.: Phineas Allen, 1822.

————. "An Address to the Public, on the subject of the African School, lately established under the care of the Synod of New-York and New-Jersey. By the directors of the institution." New York: J. Seymour, 1816.

————. "The Causal Power in Regeneration Proper Direct Upon the Mind, and not exerted through the medium of motives. Argued upon the principles of the exercise system, though the author believes in a temper or nature anterior to exercise." North Adams, Mass.: A. H. Wells, 1834.

————. "The Claims of Seamen: A sermon, preached November 7, 1819, in the Brick Church, New-York, for the benefit of the Marine Missionary Society of that city." New York: J. Seymour, 1819.

————. "Dr. Griffin's Letter to Deacon Hurlbut, on the subject of Open Communion." Williamstown, Mass.: R. Bannister, n.d. [1829?].

————. *The Doctrine of Divine Efficiency, defended against certain Modern Speculations.* New York: Jonathan Leavitt, 1833.

————. "Foreign Missions: A sermon, preached May 9, 1819, at the anniversary of the

United Foreign Missionary Society, in the Garden-Street Church, New-York."
   New York: J. Seymour, 1819.

———. "God Exalted and Creatures Humbled by the Gospel: A sermon preached on
   Sabbath evening, May 30, 1830, in Murray Street Church, New York; being one
   of a course of lectures on the evidences of divine revelation, by different preachers
   appointed for that purpose." New York: Sleight & Robinson, 1830.

———. "A Humble Attempt to Reconcile the Differences of Christians Respecting the
   Extent of the Atonement, by showing that the controversy which exists on the
   subject is chiefly verbal. To which is added an appendix, exhibiting the influence
   of Christ's obedience." New York: Dodge, 1819.

———. "The Kingdom of Christ: A missionary sermon preached before the General
   Assembly of the Presbyterian Church, in Philadelphia, May 23, 1805." Andover,
   Mass.: Flagg & Gould, 1821.

———. "A Letter to a Friend on the Connexion Between the New Doctrines and the New
   Measures." Albany, N.Y.: Hosford & Wait, 1833.

———. "Living to God: A sermon, preached June 16, 1816, at the Brick Presbyterian
   Church in the City of New-York." New York: Dodge & Sayre, 1816.

———. "An Oration delivered June 21, 1809, on the day of the author's induction into the
   office of Bartlett Professor of Pulpit Eloquence, in the Divinity College at
   Andover." Boston: Farrand, Mallory & Co., [1809].

———. "A Plea for Africa: A sermon preached October 26, 1817, in the First Presbyterian
   Church in the City of New-York, before the Synod of New-York and New-Jersey,
   at the request of the Board of Directors of the African School established by the
   Synod." New York: Gould, 1817.

———. "Regeneration Not Wrought by Light." The National Preacher 6 (February 1832):
   321–36.

———. A Series of Lectures, delivered in Park Street Church, Boston, on Sabbath Evening. Boston:
   Nathaniel Willis, 1813.

———. "A Sermon on the Art of Preaching, delivered before the Pastoral Association of
   Massachusetts, in Boston, May 25, 1825." Boston: T. R. Marvin, 1825.

———. "A Sermon preached before the Annual Convention of the Congregational
   Ministers of Massachusetts, in Boston, May 29, 1828." Boston: T. R. Marvin, 1828.

———. "A Sermon, preached October 20, 1813, at Sandwich, Massachusetts, at the
   Dedication of the Meeting House, recently erected for the use of the Calvinistic
   Congregational Society in that town." Boston: Nathaniel Willis, 1813.

———. "A Sermon preached September 2, 1828, at the Dedication of the New Chapel
   connected with Williams College, Massachusetts." Williamstown, Mass.: Ridley
   Bannister, 1828.

———. "A Sermon preached September 14, 1826, before the American Board of Missions,
   at Middletown, Connecticut." Middletown, Conn.: E. & H. Clark, 1826.

———. "A Sermon, preached September 2, 1827, before the candidates for the bachelor's
   degree in Williams College." Ridley Bannister, 1827.

———. Sermons by the Late Rev. E. D. Griffin, to which is prefixed a Memoir of his life, by W. B.
   Sprague, D.D. 2 vols. New York: John S. Taylor, 1839.

———. Sermons, not before published, on various practical subjects. New York: M. W. Dodd, 1844.

———. "A Speech Delivered before the American Bible Society, in the City of New-York,
   May 11, 1820." N.p., [1820?].

Hallock, Jeremiah. "A Sermon, delivered at the Dedication of the Meeting House in
   Canton, January 5, 1815." Hartford, Conn.: Peter Gleason, 1815.

Hart, Levi. "Liberty Described and Recommended; in a sermon, preached to the corporation of Freemen in Farmington, at their meeting on Tuesday, September 20, 1774, and published at their desire." Hartford, Conn.: Ebenezer Watson, 1775.

———. "Religious Improvement of the Death of Great Men. A discourse, addressed to the congregation of the North Society in Preston, on Lord's Day, Dec. 29, 1799, occasioned by the death of Gen. George Washington." Norwich, Conn.: Thomas Hubbard, 1800.

Hart, Luther. "The Gospel Ministry a Display of Divine Benevolence: A sermon, delivered at Watertown, Conn. at the installation of the Rev. Darius O. Griswold, January 19, 1825." Hartford, Conn.: Peter Gleason, 1825.

———. "A Sermon, Delivered at Torrington, Lord's Day, Jan. 22, 1826, at the Funeral of Reverend Alexander Gillett: together with a memoir of his life and character." New Haven, Conn.: T. G. Woodward, 1826.

———. "A View of the Religious Declension in New England, and of its Causes, during the latter half of the Eighteenth Century." *Quarterly Christian Spectator*, 3d ser., 5 (June 1833): 207–37.

Hooker, Asahel. "The Immoral and Pernicious Tendency of Error. Illustrated in a Sermon, delivered at the Ordination of the Rev. James Beach . . . in Winsted, Jan. 1st, 1806. . . ." Hartford, Conn.: Lincoln & Gleason, 1806.

———. "The Moral Tendency of Man's Accountableness to God; and of its influence on the happiness of society: A sermon, preached on the day of the general election, at Hartford, in the state of Connecticut, May 9, 1805." Hartford, Conn.: Hudson & Goodwin, 1805.

———. "The Use and Importance of Preaching the Distinguishing Doctrines of the Gospel. Illustrated in a sermon, at the Ordination of the Rev. John Keep; to the pastoral charge of the Congregational church, in Blandford, Oct. 30, 1805." Northampton, Mass.: William Butler, 1806.

Hopkins, Mark. "A Discourse Occasioned by the death of the Rev. Edward Dorr Griffin, delivered November 26, 1837, in the Chapel." Troy, N.Y.: Tuttle, Belcher & Burton, 1837.

Huntington, Dan. "The Love of Jerusalem, the Prosperity of a People: A sermon, preached at the anniversary election, Hartford, May 12, 1814." Hartford, Conn.: Hudson & Goodwin, 1814.

Hyde, Alvan. "A Sermon Delivered at Lee, December 15, 1796, being the day appointed by authority for a public thanksgiving." Stockbridge, Mass.: Rosseter & Willard, 1797.

Leith, John H., ed. *Creeds of the Churches*. Rev. ed. Atlanta: John Knox Press, 1973.

Miller, Jonathan. "The Importance of the Church: A sermon, delivered at the Ordination of the Rev. Heman Humphrey, at Fairfield, Apr. 16, 1807." Bridgeport, Conn.: Hezekiah Ripley, 1807.

Miller, William F. "A Dissertation on the Harvest of Mystical Babylon. Book III." Hartford, Conn.: Hudson & Goodwin, 1808.

———. "Signs of the Times, or the Sure Word of Prophecy: A Dissertation on the Prophecies of the Sixth and Seventh Vials, and on the subsequent great day of battle, immediately preceding the millennium." Hartford, Conn.: Hudson & Goodwin, 1803.

Mills, Samuel-John. "The Nature and Importance of the Duty of Singing Praise to God, considered, in a sermon, delivered at Litchfield, March 22, 1775." Hartford, Conn.: Ebenezer Watson, 1775.

[Ogden, John]. "A Short History of late Ecclesiastical Oppressions in New England and Vermont." Richmond, Va.: James Lyon, 1799.

Park, Edwards A., ed. *The Atonement: Discourses and Treatises by Edwards, Smalley, Maxcy,*

Emmons, Griffin, Burge, and Weeks, With an Introductory Essay by Edwards A. Park. Boston: Congregational Board of Publications, 1859.

Perkins, Nathan. "The Benign Influence of Religion on Civil Government and National Happiness. Illustrated in a Sermon, preached before His Excellency Jonathan Trumbull, esq., governor: His Honor John Treadwell, esq., lieutenant governor: the honorable the Council: and House of representatives of the state of Connecticut, on the Anniversary Election, May 12th, 1808." Hartford, Conn.: Hudson & Goodwin, 1808.

————. "The Doctrines Essential to Salvation." *American National Preacher* 7 (January 1833): 113–19.

————. "The Gospel Glad Tidings of Good Things; illustrated in a discourse, preached at Herkimer-union-church and society, at the ordination of the Rev. Elihu Mason, to the gospel ministry." Herkimer, N.Y.: J. H. & H. Prentiss, 1810.

————. "A Half-Century Sermon, delivered at West-Hartford, on the 13th day of October, 1822; in which a church and congregation are commended to God and the word of His grace." Hartford, Conn.: George Goodwin, 1822.

————. "A Minister of the Gospel Taking Heed to Himself and Doctrine; illustrated in a discourse delivered at the ordination of Rev. John Langdon . . . 15th of May, 1816. . . ." New Haven, Conn.: T. G. Woodward, 1816.

————. "The National Sins, and National Punishment in the Recently Declared War, considered in a sermon, delivered July 23, 1812, on the day of the public fast appointed by the Governor and Council of the state of Connecticut, in conse-quence of the declaration of war against Great-Britain." Hartford, Conn.: Hudson & Goodwin, 1812.

————. "A Preached Gospel, the Great Instituted Means of Salvation; illustrated in a discourse . . . at the ordination of the Rev. Elijah G. Welles." Hartford, Conn.: Lincoln & Gleason, 1808.

————. "A Sermon Delivered at the Interment of the Rev. Timothy Pitkin. . . ." Hartford, Conn.: Hudson & Goodwin, 1812.

————. "A Sermon delivered at the Ordination of Rev. Hezekiah N. Woodruff, to the pastoral office over the First church of Christ, in Stonington, July 2, 1789." New London, Conn.: T. Green & Son, 1790.

————. "A Sermon, preached at the Installation of the Rev. Mr. Solomon Wolcott, in the pastoral office over the church of Christ in Wintonbury, May 24th, 1786." Hartford, Conn.: Hudson & Goodwin, [1786].

————. *Twenty-four Discourses on Some of the Important and Interesting Truths, Duties and Institutions of the Gospel, and the general excellency of the Christian religion.* . . . Hartford, Conn.: Hudson & Goodwin, 1795.

————. "Two Discourses on the Grounds of the Christian's Hope; containing a brief account of the work of God's Holy Spirit in a remarkable revival of religion in West Hartford, in the year 1799. Delivered on the first Sabbath of the year 1800." Hartford, Conn.: Hudson & Goodwin, 1800.

Porter, Ebenezer. *Letters on the Religious Revivals which prevailed about the beginning of the present century.* Boston: Congregational Board of Publication, 1858.

————. "A Sermon, Delivered at the New Brick Meeting House, in Hartford, on the evening of May 15, 1810. . . ." Hartford, Conn.: Peter B. Gleason, 1810.

Porter, Noah. "Half-century discourse; on occasion of the fiftieth anniversary of his ordination as pastor of the First church, in Farmington, Conn., delivered Novem-ber 12th, 1856." Farmington, Conn.: Samuel S. Cowles, 1857.

————. "Memorial of a Revival: A sermon, delivered in Farmington, at the anniversary thanksgiving, Dec. 6, 1821. With an Appendix." Hartford, Conn.: G. Goodwin & Sons, 1822.

———. "Perjury Prevalent and Dangerous: A sermon, delivered in Farmington, at the Freeman's meeting, September, 1813." Hartford, Conn.: Peter B. Gleason, 1813.

Potter, Isaiah. "The Young Men are dead!—Sudden untimely death a serious lesson of instruction to the living. A Sermon, preached on account of the Death of Erastus Chamberlain and Reuben Currier, who were drowned on 16 of April, 1798." Hanover, N.H.: Benjamin True, 1798.

Records of the General Association of Connecticut, 1738–1799. Hartford, Conn.: Case, Lockwood & Brainard Co., 1888.

Records of the General Association of Connecticut, 1800. Hartford, Conn.: N.p., [1890].

Robbins, Ammi. "The Empires and Dominions of this World, made Subservient to the Kingdom of Christ, who ruleth over all: A sermon, delivered in presence of His Excellency Samuel Huntington, esq., L.L.D. governor, and the honorable the General assembly, of the state of Connecticut, convened at Hartford, on the day of the anniversary election. May 14, 1789." Hartford, Conn.: Hudson & Goodwin, 1789.

———. "A Half-Century Sermon, delivered at Norfolk, October 28, 1811, fifty years from the ordination of the author to the work of the ministry in that place." Hartford, Conn.: Peter B. Gleason, 1811.

Sermons on Important Subjects; Collected from a number of ministers, in some of the Northern States of America. Hartford, Conn.: Hudson & Goodwin, 1797.

Sermons, on Various Important Doctrines and Duties of the Christian Religion. Northampton, Mass.: William Butler, 1799.

Smalley, John. "The Inability of the Sinner to Comply with the Gospel, his inexcusable guilt in not complying with it, and the consistency of these with each other, illustrated, in two Discourses, on John VIth. 44th." Boston: John Kneeland, 1772.

———. "The Law in all Respects Satisfied by Our Saviour, in regard to those only who belong to him; or, None but believers saved, through the all-sufficient satisfaction of Christ. A second sermon, preached at Wallingford, with a view to the Universalists." Hartford, Conn.: Hudson & Goodwin, 1786.

———. "On the Evils of a Weak Government: A sermon, preached on the general election at Hartford, in Connecticut, May 8, 1800." Hartford, Conn.: Hudson & Goodwin, 1800.

Smith, David. "The Disposition and Duty of a Faithful Minister, illustrated in a sermon, delivered at the ordination of Timothy Tuttle." New London, Conn.: Samuel Green, 1811.

Sprague, William Buell. *Lectures on Revivals of Religion.* 2d ed. New York: D. Appleton & Co., 1833.

Spring, Gardiner. "Death and Heaven: A Sermon preached at Newark at the interment of the Rev. Edward D. Griffin, D.D." New York: J. S. Taylor, 1838.

Starr, Peter. "A Half-Century Sermon, delivered at Warren, March 8, 1822, fifty years from the ordination of the author to the work of the ministry in that place." Norwalk, Conn.: S. W. Benedict, 1823.

Strong, Nathan. "The Character of a Virtuous and Good Woman. A discourse, delivered by the desire and in the presence of The Female Beneficent Society, in Hartford, Oct. 4, 1809." Hartford, Conn.: Hudson & Goodwin, 1809.

———. "A Fast Sermon, delivered in the North Presbyterian meeting house, in Hartford, July 23, 1812." Hartford, Conn.: Peter B. Gleason, 1812.

———. "A Funeral Sermon: A sermon delivered at Hartford, January 6, 1807, at the Funeral of the Rev. James Cogswell, D. D., late pastor of the church in Scotland, in the town of Windham." Hartford, Conn.: Hudson & Goodwin, 1807.

————. "The Mutability of Human Life: A sermon preached March 10, 1811." Hartford, Conn.: Hudson & Goodwin, 1811.

————. "On the Universal Spread of the Gospel: A sermon, delivered January 4th, the first sabbath in the 19th century of the Christian era." Hartford, Conn.: Hudson & Goodwin, 1801.

————. "Political Instruction from the Prophecies of God's Word: A sermon, preached on the state Thanksgiving, Nov. 29, 1798." Hartford, Conn.: Hudson & Goodwin, 1798.

————. "A Sermon at the Ordination of Thomas Robbins, at Norfolk, June 19, 1803, with charge." Hartford, Conn.: Hudson & Goodwin, 1803.

————. "A Sermon, delivered at the Consecration of the New Brick Church in Hartford, December 3, 1807." Hartford, Conn.: Hudson & Goodwin, 1808.

————. "A Sermon, delivered in the North Presbyterian church in Hartford, August 20th, at the funeral of the Honourable Chauncey Goodrich, lieutenant governor of the state of Connecticut. . . . " Hartford, Conn.: Peter B. Gleason, 1815.

————. "A Sermon, on the Use of the Time; addressed to men in the several ages of life. Delivered at Hartford, Jan. 10th, 1813." Hartford, Conn.: Peter B. Gleason, 1813.

————. Sermons, on Various Subjects, Doctrinal, Experimental, and Practical. Vol. 1. Hartford, Conn.: Hudson & Goodwin, 1798.

————. Sermons, on Various Subjects, Doctrinal, Experimental, and Practical. Vol. 2. Hartford, Conn.: John Babcock, 1800.

————. "A Thanksgiving Sermon, delivered November 27th, 1800." Hartford, Conn.: Hudson & Goodwin, 1800.

Strong, Nathan, Abel Flint, and Joseph Steward, comps. The Hartford Selection of Hymns. From the most approved authors. To which are added a number never before published. Hartford, Conn.: John Babcock, 1799.

Tennent, Gilbert. "The Danger of an Unconverted Ministry." In The Great Awakening: Documents Illustrating the Crisis and Its Consequences, edited by Alan Heimert and Perry Miller, 71–99. Indianapolis, Ind.: Bobbs-Merrill, 1967.

"The Theological Questions of President Edwards, Senior, and Dr. Edwards, His Son." Providence, R.I.: Miller & Hutchens, 1822.

Trumbull, Benjamin. "A Century Sermon; or, Sketches of the history of the eighteenth century, interspersed and closed with serious practical remarks. Delivered at North-Haven, Jan. 1, 1801." New Haven, Conn.: Read & Morse, 1801.

Tyler, Bennett, comp. New England Revivals, As They Existed at the Close of the Eighteenth, and the Beginning of the Nineteenth Centuries. Boston: Massachusetts Sabbath School Society, 1846.

————, comp. Remains of the late Rev. Asahel Nettleton, D.D. Hartford, Conn.: Robins & Smith, 1845.

Walker, Williston, ed. The Creeds and Platforms of Congregationalism. 1893. Reprint. Philadelphia: Pilgrim Press, 1969.

Washburn, Joseph. Sermons on Practical Subjects; by the late Reverend Joseph Washburn, A.M., pastor of a church of Christ in Farmington. To which is added, a sermon of the Rev. Asahel Hooker, delivered at Farmington, on the occasion of Mr. Washburn's death. Hartford, Conn.: Lincoln & Gleason, 1807.

Waterman, Simon. "Death Chosen Rather than Life; or, the upright happy in death. A sermon, preached in Watertown, December 14, 1787. At the Funeral of the Rev. John Trumbull, senior pastor of the church in Westbury, who departed this life December 13th, 1787, in the 73d year of his age, and 48th of his ministry." Hartford, Conn.: Hudson & Goodwin, 1788.

West, Stephen. "A Sermon, delivered on the Public Fast, April 9th, 1801." Stockbridge, Mass.: Heman Willard, 1801.

Whitman, Samuel. "Practical Godliness the Way to Prosperity: A sermon preached before the General Assembly of the colony of Connecticut, at Hartford in New England, May 13, 1714. The day for the election of the Honourable the governour, the deputy governour, and the worshipful the assistants there." New London, Conn.: Timothy Green, 1714.

Woods, Leonard. *History of the Andover Theological Seminary*. Boston: J. R. Osgood & Co., 1885.

Secondary Sources

Abbott, Susan Emma. *Woodruff Genealogy; Descendents of Mathew Woodruff of Farmington, Connecticut*. Milford, Conn.: N.p., 1963

Ahlstrom, Sydney E. *A Religious History of the American People*. New Haven, Conn.: Yale University Press, 1972.

Allmendinger, David F., Jr. *Paupers and Scholars: The Transformation of Student Life in Nineteenth-Century New England*. New York: St. Martin's Press, 1975.

Alvord, Frederick, and Ira R. Gridley, comps. *Historical Sketch of the Congregational Church and Parish of Canton Center, Conn., formerly West Simsbury*. Hartford, Conn.: Case, Lockwood & Brainard, 1886.

Andrew, John A., III. *Rebuilding the Christian Commonwealth: New England Congregationalists and Foreign Missions, 1800–1830*. Lexington: University Press of Kentucky, 1976.

Andrews, Alfred. *Memorial, Genealogy, and Ecclesiastical History of First Church, New Britain, Connecticut*. Chicago: A. H. Andrews, 1867.

Appleby, Joyce. *Capitalism and the New Social Order: The Republican Vision of the 1790s*. New York: New York University Press, 1984.

Atwater, Francis, comp. *History of the Town of Plymouth, Connecticut*. Meriden, Conn.: Journal Publishing Co., 1895.

Bacon, Leonard W. *A History of American Christianity*. New York: Christian Literature Co., 1897.

Baird, Robert. *Religion in the United States of America*. 1844. Reprint. New York: Ayer Co., 1969.

Banner, James M., Jr. *To the Hartford Convention: The Federalists and the Origins of Party Politics in Massachusetts, 1789–1815*. New York: Alfred A. Knopf, 1970.

Barber, John Warner. *Connecticut Historical Collections: History and Antiquities of Every Town in Connecticut*. New Haven, Conn.: John W. Barber, 1836.

Beardsley, Frank G. *A History of American Revivals*. 3d ed. New York: American Tract Society, 1912.

Beasley, James R. "Emerging Republicans and the Standing Order: The Appropriations Act Controversy in Connecticut, 1793 to 1795." *William and Mary Quarterly*, 3d ser., 29 (October 1972): 587–610.

Benedict, David. *A General History of the Baptist Denomination in America, and other parts of the world*. 2 vols. New York: Lewis Colby & Co., 1848.

Benson, Louis F. *The English Hymn: Its Development and Use in Worship*. 1915. Reprint. Richmond, Va.: John Knox Press, 1962.

Berk, Stephen E. *Calvinism versus Democracy: Timothy Dwight and the Origins of American Evangelical Orthodoxy*. Hamden, Conn.: Archon Press, 1974.

Bickford, Christopher P. *Farmington in Connecticut*. Canaan, N. H.: Phoenix Publishers, 1982.

Bidwell, Percy W. "Rural Economy in New England at the Beginning of the Nineteenth Century." Connecticut Academy of Arts and Sciences (New Haven). *Transactions* 20 (1916): 241–399.

Bilhartz, Terry D. *Urban Religion and the Second Great Awakening: Church and Society in Early National Baltimore.* Madison, N.J.: Fairleigh Dickinson University Press, 1986.

Birdsall, Richard D. *Berkshire County: A Cultural History.* New Haven, Conn.: Yale University Press, 1959.

———. "Ezra Stiles versus the New Divinity Men." *American Quarterly* 17 (Summer 1965): 248–58.

———. "The Second Great Awakening and the New England Social Order." *Church History* 39 (September 1970): 345–64.

Birney, George Hugh, Jr. "The Life and Letters of Asahel Nettleton, 1783–1844." Ph.D. diss., Hartford Theological Seminary, 1943.

Blauvelt, Martha Tomhave. "Society, Religion, and Revivalism: The Second Great Awakening in New Jersey, 1780–1830." Ph.D. diss., Princeton University, 1974.

———. "Women and Revivalism." In *Women and Religion in America: The Nineteenth Century,* edited by Rosemary R. Reuther and Rosemary Skinner Keller, 1–9. San Francisco: Harper & Row, 1981.

Bloch, Ruth H. "American Feminine Ideals in Transition: The Rise of the Moral Mother, 1785–1815." *Feminist Studies* 4 (June 1978): 101–26.

———. *Visionary Republic: Millennial Themes in American Thought, 1756–1800.* New York: Cambridge University Press, 1985.

Boardman, George N. *A History of New England Theology.* Chicago: N.p., 1899.

Boles, John B. *The Great Revival, 1787–1805: The Origins of the Southern Evangelical Mind.* Lexington: University Press of Kentucky, 1972.

Bonomi, Patricia U., and Peter R. Eisenstadt. "Church Adherence in the Eighteenth-Century British American Colonies." *William and Mary Quarterly,* 3d ser., 39 (April 1982): 245–76.

Brauer, Jerald C. "Conversion: From Puritanism to Revivalism." *Journal of Religion* 58 (July 1978): 227–43.

———. *Protestantism in America: A Narrative History.* Rev. ed. Philadelphia: Westminster Press, 1965.

Breitenbach, William. "The Consistent Calvinism of the New Divinity Movement." *William and Mary Quarterly,* 3d ser., 41 (April 1984): 241–64.

———. "Unregenerate Doings: Selflessness and Selfishness in New Divinity Theology." *American Quarterly* 34 (Winter 1982): 479–502.

Brereton, Virginia Lieson. *From Sin to Salvation: Stories of Women's Conversions, 1800 to the Present.* Bloomington: Indiana University Press, 1991.

Bristol, Connecticut. Hartford, Conn.: N.p., 1907.

Brown, Abiel J. *Genealogical history, with short sketches and Family Records of the Early Settlers of West Simsbury, now Canton, Connecticut.* Hartford, Conn.: Case, Tiffany & Co., 1856.

Brown, Richard D. "Spreading the Word: Rural Clergymen and the Communications Network of Eighteenth Century New England." *Proceedings of the Massachusetts Historical Society* 94 (1982): 10–22.

Bruce, Dickson D., Jr. *And They All Sang Hallelujah: Plain-Folk Camp-Meeting Religion, 1800–1845.* Knoxville: University of Tennessee Press, 1974.

Brumberg, Joan Jacobs. *Mission for Life: The Story of the Family of Adoniram Judson, the Dramatic Events of the First American Foreign Mission, and the Course of Evangelical Religion in the Nineteenth Century.* New York: Free Press, Macmillan Co., 1980.

Bushman, Richard. *From Puritan to Yankee: Character and Social Order in Connecticut, 1690–1765.*

Cambridge, Mass.: Harvard University Press, 1967; New York: Norton Library, 1970.

———. "Jonathan Edwards as Great Man: Identity, Conversion, and Leadership in the Great Awakening." In *Religion in American History*, edited by John M. Mulder and John F. Wilson, 105–26. Englewood Cliffs, N.J.: Prentice-Hall, 1978.

Butler, Jon. *Awash in a Sea of Faith: Christianizing the American People*. Cambridge, Mass.: Harvard University Press, 1990.

———. "Enthusiasm Described and Decried: The Great Awakening as Interpretive Fiction." *Journal of American History* 69 (September 1982): 305–25.

Calhoun, Daniel H. *Professional Lives in America, 1750–1850*. Cambridge, Mass.: Harvard University Press, 1965.

Carwardine, Richard. *Transatlantic Revivalism: Popular Evangelicalism in Britain and America, 1790–1865*. Westport, Conn.: Greenwood Press, 1978.

Chaney, Charles L. "God's Glorious Work: The Theological Foundations of the Early Missionary Societies in America, 1787–1817." Ph.D. diss., University of Chicago, 1973.

Cherry, Conrad. "Nature and the Republic: The New Haven Theology." *New England Quarterly* 51 (December 1978): 509–26.

Chipman, Richard Manning. *The History of Harwinton, Connecticut*. Hartford, Conn.: Williams, Wiley & Turner, 1860.

Clark, Christopher. *The Roots of Rural Capitalism: Western Massachusetts, 1780–1860*. Ithaca, N.Y.: Cornell University Press, 1990.

Collier, Christopher. "Steady Habits Considered and Reconsidered." *Connecticut Review* 5 (April 1972): 28–37.

Conforti, Joseph A. *Samuel Hopkins and the New Divinity Movement: Calvinism, the Congregational Ministry, and Reform in New England between the Great Awakenings*. Grand Rapids, Mich.: Eerdmans Publishing Co., 1981.

———. "The Invention of the Great Awakening, 1795–1842." *Early American Literature* 26 (1991): 99–118.

Conkin, Paul K. *Cane Ridge: America's Pentecost*. Madison: University of Wisconsin Press, 1990.

Constantin, Charles Joseph, Jr. "The New Divinity Men." Ph.D. diss., University of California, Berkeley, 1972.

Contributions to the Ecclesiastical History of Connecticut. New Haven, Conn.: William L. Kingsley, 1861.

Cooke, Parsons. *A Century of Puritanism and a Century of its Opposites*. Boston: S. K. Whipple & Co., 1855.

Corrigan, John. *The Prism of Piety: Catholick Congregational Clergy at the Beginning of the Enlightenment*. New York: Oxford University Press, 1991.

Cott, Nancy F. *The Bonds of Womanhood: "Woman's Sphere" in New England, 1780–1835*. New Haven, Conn.: Yale University Press, 1977.

———. "Young Women in the Second Great Awakening in New England." *Feminist Studies* 3 (Fall 1975): 15–29.

Cowing, Cedric B. *The Great Awakening and the American Revolution: Colonial Thought in the Eighteenth Century*. Chicago: Rand McNally, 1971.

Cowles, Calvin Duvall, comp. *Genealogy of the Cowles Family in America*. 2 vols. New Haven, Conn.: N. p., 1929.

Cragg, Gerald R. *Reason and Authority in the Eighteenth Century*. Cambridge: Cambridge University Press, 1964.

Crawford, Michael J. *Seasons of Grace: Colonial New England's Revival Tradition in Its British Context*. New York: Oxford University Press, 1991.

Crissey, Theron Wilmot, comp. *History of Norfolk, Litchfield County, Connecticut*. Everett: Massachusetts Publishing Co., 1900.

Cross, Whitney R. *The Burned-Over District: The Social and Intellectual History of Enthusiastic Religion in Western New York, 1800–1850*. 1950. Reprint. New York: Harper & Row, Torchbooks, 1965.

Daniels, Bruce C. *The Connecticut Town: Growth and Development, 1635–1790*. Middletown, Conn.: Wesleyan University Press, 1979.

———. "Economic Developments in Colonial and Revolutionary Connecticut: An Overview." *William and Mary Quarterly*, 3d ser., 37 (July 1980): 429–50.

Davidson, Cathy N. *Revolution and Word: The Rise of the Novel in America*. New York: Oxford University Press, 1986.

Davidson, James West. *The Logic of Millennial Thought: Eighteenth-Century New England*. New Haven, Conn.: Yale University Press, 1977.

———. "Searching for the Millennium: Problems for the 1790s and the 1970s." *New England Quarterly* 45 (June 1972): 241–61.

Davis, Emerson. *The Half Century; or, A History of the Changes that have taken place, and events that have transpired, chiefly in the United States, between 1800 and 1850*. Boston: Tappan & Whittemore, 1851.

Dolan, Jay P. *Catholic Revivalism: The American Experience, 1830–1900*. Notre Dame, Ind.: University of Notre Dame Press, 1978.

Douglas, Ann. *The Feminization of American Culture*. New York: Alfred A. Knopf, 1977; Avon Books, 1978.

Downey, James. *The Eighteenth Century Pulpit*. Oxford: Clarendon Press, 1969.

Durfee, Calvin. *A History of Williams College*. Boston: A. Williams & Co., 1860.

Eliade, Mircea. *Myth and Reality*. Translated by Willard R. Trask. New York: Harper & Row, 1963.

Elsbree, Oliver W. *The Rise of the Missionary Spirit in America, 1790–1815*. Williamsport, Pa.: Williamsport Printing Co., 1928.

Englizian, H. Crosby. *Brimstone Corner: Park Street Church, Boston*. Chicago: Moody Press, 1968.

Epstein, Barbara L. *The Politics of Domesticity: Women, Evangelism, and Temperance in Nineteenth-Century America*. Middletown, Conn.: Wesleyan University Press, 1981.

Ferm, Robert L. *Jonathan Edwards the Younger: 1745–1801*. Grand Rapids, Mich.: Eerdmans Publishing Co., 1976.

Fischer, David H. *The Revolution of American Conservatism: The Federalist Party in the Era of Jeffersonian Democracy*. New York: Harper & Row, 1965.

Foote, Henry Wilder. *Three Centuries of American Hymnody*. Hamden, Conn.: Shoe String Press, 1961.

Foster, Charles I. *An Errand of Mercy: The Evangelical United Front, 1790–1837*. Chapel Hill: University of North Carolina Press, 1960.

Foster, Frank H. *A Genetic History of the New England Theology*. Chicago: University of Chicago Press, 1907.

Foster, Stephen. "A Connecticut Separate Church: Strict Congregationalism in Cornwall, 1780–1809." *New England Quarterly* 39 (September 1966): 309–33.

Fowler, William Chauncey. *History of Durham, Connecticut; From the First Grant of Land in 1622 to 1866*. Hartford, Conn.: Wiley, Waterman & Eaton, 1866.

Gambrell, Mary L. *Ministerial Training in Eighteenth-Century New England*. New York: Columbia University Press, 1937.

Gaustad, Edwin S. *The Great Awakening in New England*. New York: Harper & Row, 1957.

Gay, Julius. *A Record of the Descendents of John Clark, of Farmington, Connecticut*. Hartford, Conn.: Case, Lockwood & Brainard Co., 1882.

Gillespie, Joanna Bowen. "'The Clear Leadings of Providence': Pious Memoirs and the Problems of Self-realization for Women in the Early Nineteenth Century." *Journal of the Early Republic* 5 (Summer 1985): 197–222.

Gilmore, William J. *Reading Becomes a Necessity of Life: Material and Cultural Life in Rural New England, 1780–1835.* Knoxville: University of Tennessee Press, 1989.

Goen, Clarence C. *Revivalism and Separatism in New England: Strict Congregationalists and Separate Baptists in the Great Awakening.* New Haven, Conn.: Yale University Press, 1962.

Goodenough, Arthur. *The Clergy of Litchfield County.* Litchfield, Conn.: N.p., 1909.

Goodman, Paul. *The Democratic-Republicans of Massachusetts.* Cambridge, Mass.: Harvard University Press, 1964.

Greene, M. Louise. *The Development of Religious Liberty in Connecticut.* 1905. Reprint. Freeport, N.Y.: Books for Libraries Press, 1970.

Greven, Philip. *The Protestant Temperament: Patterns of Child-Rearing, Religious Experience, and the Self in Early America.* 1977. Reprint. New York: Meridian Books, 1979.

Griffin, Clifford S. *Their Brothers' Keepers: Moral Stewardship in the United States, 1800–1865.* New Brunswick, N.J.: Rutgers University Press, 1960.

Grossbart, Stephen R. "Seeking the Divine Favor: Conversion and Church Admission in Eastern Connecticut, 1711–1832." *William and Mary Quarterly*, 3d ser., 46 (October 1989): 696–740.

Guelzo, Allen C. *Edwards on the Will: A Century of American Theological Debate.* Middletown, Conn.: Wesleyan University Press, 1989.

Hackett, David G. *The Rude Hand of Innovation: Religion and Social Order in Albany, New York, 1652–1836.* New York: Oxford University Press, 1991.

Hall, David D. *The Faithful Shepherd: A History of the New England Ministry in the Seventeenth Century.* New York: W. W. Norton & Co., 1974.

———. *Worlds of Wonder, Days of Judgment: Popular Religious Belief in Early New England.* New York: Alfred A. Knopf, 1989.

Hall, Eileen Greevey. *The Town of New Hartford, Litchfield County, Connecticut, in 1775 to 1852.* New Hartford, Conn.: Esperanza Press, 1976.

Hall, Peter Dobkin. *The Organization of American Culture, 1700–1900: Private Institutions, Elites, and the Origins of American Nationality.* New York: New York University Press, 1982.

Hambrick-Stowe, Charles E. *The Practice of Piety: Puritan Devotional Disciplines in Seventeenth-Century New England.* Published for the Institute of Early American History and Culture. Chapel Hill: University of North Carolina Press, 1982.

Handy, Robert T. *A History of the Churches in the United States and Canada.* New York: Oxford University Press, 1976.

Hardesty, Nancy A. *Women Called to Witness: Evangelical Feminism in the Nineteenth Century.* Nashville, Tenn.: Abingdon Press, 1984.

Haroutunian, Joseph. *Piety versus Moralism: The Passing of the New England Theology.* 1932. Reprint. Introduction by Sydney E. Ahlstrom. New York: Harper & Row, Torchbooks, 1970.

Harrison, Richard A., ed. *Princetonians, 1769–1775: A Biographical Dictionary.* Princeton, N.J.: Princeton University Press, 1980.

Hatch, Nathan O. "The Christian Movement and the Demand for a Theology of the People." *Journal of American History* 67 (December 1980): 545–67.

———. *The Democratization of American Christianity.* New Haven, Conn.: Yale University Press, 1989.

———. "Evangelicalism as a Democratic Movement." In *Evangelicalism and Modern America,* edited by George Marsden, 71–82. Grand Rapids, Mich.: Eerdmans Publishing Co., 1984.

Hatch, Nathan O., and Harry S. Stout, eds. *Jonathan Edwards and the American Experience*. New York: Oxford University Press, 1988.

Heimert, Alan E. *Religion and the American Mind, from the Great Awakening to the Revolution*. Cambridge, Mass.: Harvard University Press, 1966.

Henretta, James A. *The Evolution of American Society, 1700–1815*. Lexington, Mass.: D. C. Heath & Co., 1973.

———. "Families and Farms: *Mentalité* in Pre-Industrial America." *William and Mary Quarterly*, 3d ser., 35 (January 1978): 3–32.

Henry, Stuart C. *George Whitefield: Wayfaring Witness*. Nashville, Tenn.: Abingdon Press, 1957.

Hibbard, Augustine George. *History of the Town of Goshen, Connecticut*. Hartford, Conn.: Case, Lockwood & Brainard Co., 1897.

Historical Sketch of the Congregational Society and Church in Bristol, Connecticut. Hartford, Conn.: D. B. Moseley, 1852.

History of Ashtabula County, Ohio, with Illustrations and Biographical Sketches of its Pioneers and Most Prominent Men. Philadelphia: J. B. Lippincott & Co., 1878.

Hofstadter, Richard. *The Paranoid Style in American Politics and Other Essays*. 1952. Reprint. New York: Random House, Vintage Books, 1967.

Hooker, Edward. *The Descendents of Rev. Thomas Hooker, Hartford, Connecticut, 1586–1908*. Rochester, N.Y.: E. R. Andrews, 1909.

Hoopes, James. *Consciousness in New England: From Puritanism and Ideas to Psychoanalysis and Semiotics*. Baltimore: Johns Hopkins University Press, 1989.

———. "Jonathan Edwards's Religious Psychology." *Journal of American History* 69 (March 1983): 849–65.

Howe, Daniel Walker. "The Decline of Calvinism: An Approach to Its Study." *Comparative Studies in Society and History* 14 (June 1972): 306–27.

———. "Victorian Culture in America." In *Victorian America*, edited, with an introductory essay, by Daniel Walker Howe, 3–28. Philadelphia: University of Pennsylvania Press, 1976.

Hudson, Winthrop S. *Religion in America*. 2d and 3d eds. New York: Charles Scribner's Sons, 1973, 1981.

Hunter, James Davison. *Evangelicalism: The Coming Generation*. Chicago: University of Chicago Press, 1987.

Jedrey, Christopher M. *The World of John Cleaveland: Family and Community in Eighteenth-Century New England*. New York: W. W. Norton & Co., 1979.

Johnson, Charles A. *The Frontier Camp Meeting: Religion's Harvest Time*. Dallas, Tex.: Southern Methodist University Press, 1955.

Johnson, Curtis D. *Islands of Holiness: Rural Religion in Upstate New York, 1790–1860*. Ithaca, N.Y.: Cornell University Press, 1989.

Johnson, Paul E. *A Shopkeeper's Millennium: Society and Revivals in Rochester, New York, 1815–1837*. New York: Hill & Wang, 1978.

Juster, Susan. "'In a Different Voice': Male and Female Narratives of Religious Conversion in Post-Revolutionary America." *American Quarterly* 41 (March 1989): 34–62.

Keller, Charles Roy. *The Second Great Awakening in Connecticut*. New Haven, Conn.: Yale University Press, 1942.

Kerber, Linda K. *Women of the Republic: Intellect and Ideology in Revolutionary America*. Published for the Institute of Early American History and Culture. Chapel Hill: University of North Carolina Press, 1980.

Kett, Joseph F. *Rites of Passage: Adolescence in America, 1790 to the Present*. New York: Basic Books, 1977.

Kilbourne, Payne Kenyon. *Sketches and Chronicles of the Town of Litchfield, Connecticut*. Hartford, Conn.: Case, Lockwood & Co., 1859.

Kirkland, Edward C. *Men, Cities, and Transportation: A Study in New England History, 1820–1900*. Cambridge, Mass.: Harvard University Press, 1948.

Kuklick, Bruce. *Churchmen and Philosophers: From Jonathan Edwards to John Dewey*. New Haven, Conn.: Yale University Press, 1985.

Larkin, Jack. *The Reshaping of Everyday Life, 1790–1840*. New York: Harper & Row, 1988.

Larned, Ellen D. *History of Windham County, Connecticut*. 2 vols. Worcester, Mass.: By the author, 1874–80.

Lewis, David W. "The Reformer as Conservative: Protestant Counter-subversives in the Early Republic." In *The Development of American Culture*, edited by Stanley Coben and Lorman Ratner, 64–91. Englewood Cliffs, N.J.: Prentice-Hall, 1970.

Lewis, Jan. "The Republican Wife: Virtue and Seduction in the Early Republic." *William and Mary Quarterly*, 3d ser., 44 (October 1987): 689–721.

Lucas, Paul R. *Valley of Discord: Church and Society along the Connecticut River, 1636–1725*. Hanover, N.H.: University Press of New England, 1976.

McLoughlin, William G. *Modern Revivalism: Charles Grandison Finney to Billy Graham*. New York: Ronald Press Co., 1959.

———. *New England Dissent: Baptists and the Separation of Church and State, 1670–1830*. 2 vols. Cambridge, Mass.: Harvard University Press, 1971.

———. *Revivals, Awakenings, and Reform: An Essay on Religion and Social Change in America, 1607–1977*. Chicago: University of Chicago Press, 1978.

———, ed. *The American Evangelicals, 1800–1900*. New York: Harper Torchbooks, 1968.

McWilliams, William Carey. *The Idea of Fraternity in America*. Berkeley and Los Angeles: University of California Press, 1973.

Main, Jackson Turner. *The Antifederalists: Critics of the Constitution, 1781–1788*. Published for the Institute of Early American History and Culture. Chapel Hill: University of North Carolina Press, 1961.

———. *Society and Economy in Colonial Connecticut*. Princeton, N.J.: Princeton University Press, 1985.

Marini, Stephen A. *Radical Sects of Revolutionary New England*. Cambridge, Mass.: Harvard University Press, 1982.

———. "Rehearsal for Revival: Sacred Singing and the Great Awakening in America." In *Sacred Sound: Music in Religious Thought and Practice*, edited by Joyce Irwin, 71–91. Chico, Calif.: Scholars Press, 1983.

Marty, Martin E. *The Infidel: Freethought and American Religion*. Cleveland, Ohio: Meridian Books, 1961.

———. *Righteous Empire: The Protestant Experience in America*. New York: Dial Press, 1970.

Masson, Margaret W. "The Typology of the Female as a Model for the Regenerate: Puritan Preaching, 1690–1730." *Signs: Journal for Women in Culture and Society* 2 (Winter 1976): 304–15.

Mathews, Donald G. "The Second Great Awakening as an Organizing Process, 1780–1830: An Hypothesis." *American Quarterly* 21 (Spring 1969): 23–43.

May, Henry F. *The Enlightenment in America*. New York: Oxford University Press, 1976.

May, Sherry Pierpont. "Asahel Nettleton: Nineteenth-Century American Revivalist." Ph.D. diss., Drew University, 1969.

Mead, Sidney E. *Nathaniel William Taylor, 1786–1858: A Connecticut Liberal*. Chicago: University of Chicago Press, 1942.

Meyer, Donald H. *The Democratic Enlightenment*. New York: Putnam, 1976.

Miller, Perry. *Errand into the Wilderness*. 1956. Reprint. New York: Harper Torchbooks, 1964.

———. "From the Covenant to the Revival." In *The Shaping of American Religion*, edited by

James W. Smith and A. Leland Jamison, 322–68. Princeton, N.J.: Princeton University Press, 1961.

————. *The Life of the Mind in America: From the Revolution to the Civil War*. New York: Harcourt, Brace & World, 1965.

Mitchell, Mary Hewitt. *The Great Awakening and Other Revivals in the Religious Life of Connecticut*. Published for the Tercentenary Commission. New Haven, Conn.: Yale University Press, 1934.

Miyakawa, T. Scott. *Protestants and Pioneers: Individualism and Conformity on the American Frontier*. Chicago: University of Chicago Press, 1964.

Moran, Gerald Francis. "The Puritan Saint: Religious Experience, Church Membership, and Piety in Connecticut, 1636–1776." Ph.D. diss., Rutgers University, 1974.

Morgan, Edmund S. "The American Revolution Considered as an Intellectual Movement." In *Paths of American Thought*, edited by Arthur M. Schlesinger, Jr., and Morton White, 11–33. Boston: Houghton Mifflin Co., 1963.

————. *American Slavery, American Freedom: The Ordeal of Colonial Virginia*. New York: W. W. Norton & Co., 1975.

————. *The Gentle Puritan: A Life of Ezra Stiles, 1727–1795*. New Haven, Conn.: Yale University Press, 1962.

————. *The Puritan Family: Religion and Domestic Relations in Seventeenth-Century New England*. New York: Harper Torchbooks, 1966.

————. *Visible Saints: The History of a Puritan Idea*. 1963. Reprint. Ithaca, N.Y.: Cornell University Press, Cornell Paperbacks, 1965.

Murray, Iain H. *Jonathan Edwards: A New Biography*. London: Banner of Truth Trust, 1987.

Nash, Gary B. "The American Clergy and the French Revolution." *William and Mary Quarterly*, 3d ser., 22 (July 1965): 392–412.

Noll, Mark A. "Moses Mather (Old Calvinist) and the Evolution of Edwardsianism." *Church History* 49 (September 1980): 473–85.

————. *One Nation under God? Christian Faith and Political Action in America*. New York: Harper & Row, 1989.

————. "Revival, Enlightenment, Civic Humanism, and the Development of Dogma: Scotland and America, 1735–1843." *Tyndale Bulletin* 40 (1989): 49–76.

Noricks, Ronald Harold. "To Turn Them from Darkness': The Missionary Society of Connecticut on the Early Frontier." Ph.D. diss., University of California, Riverside, 1975.

North, Catherine M. *History of Berlin, Connecticut*. Rearranged and edited, with foreword, by Adolph Burnett Bensen. New Haven, Conn.: Tuttle, Morehouse & Taylor Co., 1916.

North, Dexter. *John North of Farmington, Connecticut, and His Descendents: With a Short Account of Other Early North Families*. Washington, D.C.: N. p., 1921.

Norton, Mary Beth. "'My Resting Reaping Times': Sarah Osborn's Defense of Her 'Unfeminine Activities.'" *Signs: Journal of Women in Culture and Society* 2 (Winter 1976): 515–29.

Norton, Mary Beth, and Carol Ruth Berkin, eds. *Women of America: A History*. Boston: Houghton Mifflin Co., 1979.

Onuf, Peter. "New Lights in New London: A Group Portrait of the Separatists." *William and Mary Quarterly*, 3d ser., 37 (October 1980): 627–43.

Opie, John. "Conversion and Revivalism: An Internal History from Jonathan Edwards to Charles Grandison Finney." Ph.D. diss., University of Chicago, 1953.

Orcutt, Samuel. *History of Torrington, Connecticut*. Albany, N.Y.: J. Munsell, 1878.

Pease, John C., and John M. Niles. *A Gazetteer of the States of Connecticut and Rhode Island*. Hartford, Conn.: William S. Marsh, 1819.

Peck, Epaphroditus. *A History of Bristol, Connecticut*. Hartford, Conn.: Lewis St. Bookshop, 1932.

Pettit, Norman. *The Heart Prepared: Grace and Conversion in Puritan Spiritual Life*. New Haven, Conn.: Yale University Press, 1966.

Phillips, Joseph W. *Jedidiah Morse and New England Congregationalism*. New Brunswick, N.J.: Rutgers University Press, 1983.

Pope, Robert G. *The Half-Way Covenant: Church Membership in Puritan New England*. Princeton, N.J.: Princeton University Press, 1969.

Porterfield, Amanda. *Female Piety in Puritan New England: The Emergence of Religious Humanism*. New York: Oxford University Press, 1992.

Potash, Jeffrey. "An Inquiry into the Dynamics of the Second Great Awakening in New England." Seminar paper, History 737, University of Chicago, 1977.

Purcell, Richard J. *Connecticut in Transition, 1775–1818*. Washington, D.C.: American Historical Association, 1918.

Rabinowitz, Richard. *The Spiritual Self in Everyday Life: The Transformation of Personal Religious Experience in Nineteenth-Century New England*. Boston: Northeastern University Press, 1989.

Reynolds, David S. "The Feminization Controversy: Sexual Stereotypes and the Paradoxes of Piety in Nineteenth Century America." *New England Quarterly* 53 (March 1980): 96–106.

Root, James Pierce. *Root Genealogical Records, 1600–1870*. New York: D. C. Root, Anthony & Co., 1870.

Roth, Randolph A. *The Democratic Dilemma: Religion, Reform, and the Social Order in the Connecticut River Valley of Vermont, 1791–1850*. New York: Cambridge University Press, 1987.

Rowe, Henry K. *The History of Religion in the United States*. New York: Macmillan Co., 1924.

Rudisill, Dorus Paul. *The Doctrine of the Atonement in Jonathan Edwards and His Successors*. New York: Poseidon Books, 1971.

Rudolph, Frederick. *Mark Hopkins and the Log: Williams College, 1836–1872*. New Haven, Conn.: Yale University Press, 1956.

Ryan, Mary P. *Cradle of the Middle Class: The Family in Oneida County, New York, 1790–1865*. New York: Cambridge University Press, 1981.

———. "A Women's Awakening: Evangelical Religion and the Families of Utica, New York, 1800–1840." *American Quarterly* 30 (Winter 1978): 602–23.

Saillant, John. "Lemuel Haynes and the Revolutionary Origins of Black Theology, 1776–1801." *Religion and American Culture: A Journal of Interpretation* 2 (Winter 1992): 79–102.

Saladino, Gaspare J. "The Economic Revolution in Late Eighteenth-Century Connecticut." Ph.D. diss., University of Wisconsin, 1964.

Sandeen, Ernest R. *The Roots of Fundamentalism: British and American Millenarianism, 1800–1930*. 1970. Reprint. Grand Rapids, Mich.: Baker Book House, 1978.

Schaff, Philip. *America: A Sketch of Its Political, Social, and Religious Character*. 1854. Reprint. Introduction by Perry Miller. Cambridge, Mass.: Harvard University Press, 1961.

Schmotter, James W. "Ministerial Careers in Eighteenth-Century New England: The Social Context, 1700-1760." *Journal of Social History* 9 (Winter 1975): 249–67.

Schneider, Herbert W. *The Puritan Mind*. 1930. Reprint. Ann Arbor: University of Michigan Press, 1958.

Schuyler, David. "Inventing a Feminist Past." *New England Quarterly* 51 (September 1978): 291–308.

Scott, Donald M. *From Office to Profession: The New England Ministry, 1750–1850*. Philadelphia: University of Pennsylvania Press, 1978.

Shiels, Richard D. "The Connecticut Clergy in the Second Great Awakening." Ph.D. diss., Boston University, 1976.

————. "The Feminization of American Congregationalism, 1730–1835." *American Quarterly* 33 (Spring 1981): 46–62.

————. "The Scope of the Second Great Awakening: Andover, Massachusetts, as a Case Study." *Journal of the Early Republic* 5 (Summer 1985): 223–46.

————. "The Second Great Awakening in Connecticut: Critique of the Traditional Interpretation." *Church History* 49 (December 1980): 401–15.

Shuffelton, Frank. *Thomas Hooker, 1586–1647.* Princeton, N.J.: Princeton University Press, 1977.

Silverman, Kenneth. *Timothy Dwight.* New York: Twayne Publishers, 1969.

Smelser, Neil J. *Theory of Collective Behavior.* New York: Free Press of Glencoe, 1963.

Snyder, K. Alan. "Foundations of Liberty: The Christian Republicanism of Timothy Dwight and Jedidiah Morse." *New England Quarterly* 56 (September 1983): 382–97.

Spener, Philip Jacob. *Pia Desideria.* Translated, edited, and introduced by Theodore G. Tappert. Philadelphia: Fortress Press, 1964.

Spinka, Matthew. *A History of the First Church of Christ Congregational, West Hartford, Connecticut.* West Hartford, Conn.: N. p., 1962.

Stauffer, Vernon. *New England and the Bavarian Illuminati.* New York: Columbia University Press, 1918.

Stephens, Abel. *A Compendious History of American Methodism.* New York: Eaton & Mains, [1870].

Stewart, Donald H. *The Opposition Press of the Federalist Period.* Albany: State University Press of New York, 1969.

Stewart, George C., Jr. *A History of Religious Education in Connecticut to the Middle of the Nineteenth Century.* New Haven, Conn.: Yale University Press, 1924.

Stout, Harry S. *The Divine Dramatist: George Whitefield and the Rise of Modern Evangelicalism.* Grand Rapids, Mich.: Eerdmans Publishing Co., 1991.

————. *The New England Soul: Preaching and Religious Culture in Colonial New England.* New York: Oxford University Press, 1986.

Stowe, Harriet Beecher. *Oldtown Folks.* 40th ed. Boston: Houghton Mifflin & Co., 1869.

Sutton, William R. "Benevolent Calvinism and the Moral Government of God: The Influence of Nathaniel W. Taylor in the Second Great Awakening." *Religion and American Culture: A Journal of Interpretation* 2 (Winter 1992): 23–47.

Sweet, Douglas H. "Church Vitality and the American Revolution: Historiographical Consensus and Thoughts toward a New Perspective." *Church History* 45 (September 1976): 341–57.

Sweet, Leonard I. "Views of Man Inherent in New Measures Revivalism." *Church History* 45 (June 1976): 206–21.

Thomas, C. Richards. *Samuel J. Mills: Missionary Pathfinder, Pioneer, and Promoter.* Boston: Pilgrim Press, 1906.

Thomas, Edmund B., Jr. "Politics in the Land of Steady Habits: Connecticut's First Political Party System, 1789–1820." Ph.D. diss., Clark University, 1972.

Thompson, Charles L. *Times of Refreshing: A History of American Revivals from 1740 to 1877.* Chicago: T. Palmer, 1877.

Thornbury, John F. *God Sent Revival: The Story of Asahel Nettleton and the Second Great Awakening.* Grand Rapids, Mich.: Evangelical Press, 1977.

Tracy, Patricia J. *Jonathan Edwards, Pastor: Religion and Society in Eighteenth-Century Northampton.* New York: Hill & Wang, 1979.

Trumbull, James Hammond, ed. *The Memorial History of Hartford County, Connecticut, 1633–1884.* 2 vols. Boston: E. L. Osgood, 1886.

Tucker, Louis Leonard. *Puritan Protagonist: President Thomas Clap of Yale College.* Published for the Institute of Early American History and Culture. Chapel Hill: University of North Carolina Press, 1962.

Turnbull, Robert. *Memorials of the First Baptist Church, Hartford, Conn., with sketches of its deceased pastors.* Hartford, Conn.: Case, Tiffany & Co., 1857.

Valeri, Mark. "The New Divinity and the American Revolution." *William and Mary Quarterly,* 3d ser., 46 (October 1989): 741–69.

Vandermeer, Philip R., and Robert P. Swierenga, eds. *Belief and Behavior: Essays in the New Religious History.* New Brunswick, N.J.: Rutgers University Press, 1991.

Wadsworth, Mary Jane. "The Wadsworth Family in America, 1632–1977." Typed manuscript copy at Connecticut State Library, 1978.

Walker, George Leon. *History of the First Church in Hartford, 1633–1883.* Hartford, Conn.: Brown & Gross, 1884.

Walsh, James P. "The Great Awakening in the First Congregational Church of Woodbury, Connecticut." *William and Mary Quarterly,* 3d ser., 38 (October 1971): 543–62.

———. "The Pure Church in Eighteenth Century Connecticut." Ph.D. diss., Columbia University, 1967.

Walters, Ronald G. *American Reformers, 1815–1860.* New York: Hill & Wang, 1978.

Weber, Donald. *Rhetoric and History in Revolutionary New England.* New York: Oxford University Press, 1988.

Weisberger, Bernard. *They Gathered at the River: The Story of the Great Revivalists and Their Impact upon Religion in America.* Boston: Beacon Books, 1958.

Welter, Barbara. "The Cult of True Womanhood, 1820–1860." *American Quarterly* 18 (Summer 1976): 151–74.

———. "The Feminization of Religion in Nineteenth-Century America." In *Clio's Consciousness Raised,* edited by Lois Banner and Mary Hartman, 137–57. New York: Harper & Row, 1973.

White, Alain C., comp. *The History of the Town of Litchfield, Connecticut, 1720–1920.* Litchfield, Conn.: Enquirer Printing, 1920.

White, Eugene E. *Puritan Rhetoric: The Issue of Emotion in Religion.* Carbondale: Southern Illinois University Press, 1972.

Whittemore, Robert C. *The Transformation of the New England Theology.* American University Studies, Series VII: Theology and Religion, vol. 23. New York: Peter Lang, 1987.

Wiebe, Robert H. *The Opening of American Society: From the Adoption of the Constitution to the Eve of Disunion.* New York: Hill & Wang, 1984.

Wood, Gordon S. *The Creation of the American Republic, 1776–1787.* Published for the Institute of Early American History and Culture. Chapel Hill: University of North Carolina, 1969.

———. "The Democratization of Mind in the American Revolution." In *The Moral Foundations of the American Republic,* edited by Robert H. Horowitz, 103–28. Charlottesville: University of Virginia Press, 1979.

Wright, Conrad. *The Beginnings of Unitarianism in America.* Boston: Beacon Press, 1955.

Youngs, J. William T. *God's Messengers: Religious Leadership in Colonial New England, 1700–1750.* Baltimore: Johns Hopkins University Press, 1976.

INDEX